"Black music history has shaped the fabric of our world and has brought such rich textures to it. I am elated that Jay Warner has embarked on such a worthwhile endeavor."

— Gladys Knight

"Many blessings on your fabulous book. Peace."

— Whitney Houston

"Wow, this is very informative and great for the younger generation to know where the true music and artists came from. This is what you call good research."

— Carl Gardner, The Coasters

"Jay Warner is as much an artist as the people he talks about in this book. This is a wonderful journey through musical history."

— Nick Caldwell, The Whispers

"This great book documents the past and tells the story of black music today, while leading us to the future."

— Maurice White, Earth, Wind & Fire

"What an innovative way to commemorate history by remembering my most favorite and influential music makers of all times. They are the artists I patterned my vocals after: Aretha Franklin, Jackie Wilson, and others."

— Wanda Vaughn, The Emotions

Published by Hal Leonard Corporation
7777 Bluemound Road
P.O. Box 13819
Milwaukee, WI 53213

Trade Book Division Editorial Offices
19 West 21st Street
Suite 201
New York, New York 10010

Library of Congress Cataloging-in-Publication Data
Warner, Jay.
  On this day in black music history / Jay Warner.-- 1st ed.
     p. cm.
  ISBN 0-634-09926-4
  1. African Americans--Music--Chronology. 2. Music--United States--Chronology. I. Title.
ML3479.W39 2006
780.89'96073--dc22

                              2005034096

Cover photos, courtesy of Retna
Interior photos, courtesy of Photofest unless otherwise noted

Printed in the United States of America
First Edition

Visit Hal Leonard online at **www.halleonard.com**

7777 W. BLUEMOUND RD. P.O. BOX 13819 MILWAUKEE, WI 53213

On This Day In Black Music History

Hal Leonard books are available at your local bookstore, or you may order through Music Dispatch at 1-800-637-2852 or **www.musicdispatch.com**.

Foreword

I recently heard an old proverb: Those who ignore the past are doomed to repeat its mistakes. It led me to theorize that those who don't know music history are blind to its future.

Black music in particular has such a rich and varied past; not recognizing its landmarks, struggles, and events is to ignore its history, heritage, and potential.

Long before the rapidly paced 21st century, the world lived by calendars and clocks. Both world and personal history has been measured in anniversaries and target dates.

By putting things in a timeframe of days, months, and years, it gains a measurable perspective in a world of overwhelming information. I, for example, was born March 14; produced Lesley Gore's "It's My Party," my first hit, on March 30, 1963; received my first Grammy on May 15 that same year; and produced "We Are the World" on January 28, 1985. Obviously, I'll always remember these dates among others, like the births and deaths of loved ones.

History is basically about people, what they've done, and what's befallen them. Calendars have become universal yardsticks, timelines tying the lives of people together while separating the mundane from the magical moments of our lives, and so it leads to the logical conclusion that important dates in history should also be chronicled in music.

Jay Warner has taken on the monumental task of encapsulating more than 100 years of black music's wide-ranging culture, values, trends, successes, and foibles with a unique twist that allows us to see events from different years, eras, and generations on a daily basis in order to make the information digestible for an "on the go" generation as well as a reminder for past generations of our achievements and importance in the grand scheme of things.

Like much of African-American history, the agony and ecstasy of black music were slow to be recognized on the whole and long overdue. Not to dwell on the negative however, thank God someone had the imagination to do it now.

It has elevated black people like no other cultural achievement. Today, black music from gospel, spiritual, blues, folk, R&B, and jazz to rock 'n' roll, reggae, soul, hip-hop, and rap stands equally alongside all forms of past and contemporary music as a testament to African-American success and potential.

The past is a roadmap of the future. All races can only benefit from that knowledge, one day at a time.

Quincy Jones, July 2005

Introduction

When I wrote *On This Day in Music History* in 2003, I'd intended to do an overview of some fifty years of music history in a day-by-day format. I soon realized it was a starting point to music's glorious past, but by no means an ending point.

Acknowledging everything from space limitations and writers cramp to newly emerging facts that I could now couple with dates, I sensed that in trying to paint the vast canvas of a musical mosaic, I had barely wetted my brush. Hence, the idea to expand the base more specifically to a music subject that could be fleshed out to a greater degree. And what more worthy a continuation than black music. Its story is older than rock 'n' roll—which was predominant in my previous work—and in fact contributed mightily to rock 'n' roll's birth and development.

From W.C. Handy, the Soul Stirrers, Billie Holiday, Robert Johnson, and Duke Ellington to Boyz II Men, Queen Latifah, Usher, and Snoop Doggy Dog, the music of black America is more than a musical history. It is the reflection of a race, culture, and heritage that had been gaining slow but steady momentum ever since Africans were brought to these shores as slaves.

For more than a hundred years, black music has been an ongoing force that influenced world cultures and music of a wide variety. American rock 'n' roll pioneers from Elvis Presley and Jerry Lee Lewis to the '50s pop and rock 'n' roll stars like Danny & the Juniors, Paul Anka, Pat Boone, and hundreds more were taking their cues from gospel, R&B, and African-American rock 'n' roll vocal groups. Ask any of the pioneering British bands and artists of the '60s and '70s—from the Beatles and the Rolling Stones to Elton John and Rod Stewart—and they'll tell you their musical roots were in American blues, R&B, and rock 'n' roll.

Black music of every generation begat new generations of stars that built on its core of driving rhythms, passionate and relatable lyrics and exciting vocal and instrumental performances. One example of a vocal group family tree illustrates the timeline from hip-hop of the '90s to black pop of the '30s.

Boyz II Men were influenced by the New Edition of the '80s, who were subsequently influenced by the '70s Jackson Five. They, in turn, were fans of the '60s Delphonics, who were inspired by Little Anthony & the Imperials, who took their cue from the '50s Flamingos, who were huge fans of the '40s Ravens, who, in turn, were influenced by the Mills Brothers of the '30s.

Delving deeper into a specific music category created new and unique challenges such as pairing little documented events with reliable dates of their occurrence and going back sixty to a hundred years was certainly more difficult then dealing with ten- to fifty-year spreads but the final work is, I hope worthy of the effort and the frustrations.

Bringing a day-by-day format to black music history opened up a whole new prospective as to the comparison of often ironic and thought-provoking quotes and events on the same and subsequent days. The eventual picture of how these days and months turned into encapsulated sound bytes of song stories, stars lives, and activities culminated in ongoing views of their history and, therefore, black music history.

After all, in January, eighteen-year-old Aretha Franklin began her pursuit of a secular music career, and in December, she was recognized with a Kennedy Center honor for her lifetime achievements. In between are the crib notes of black music history.

—Jay Warner, October 2005

On This
Day In
Black
Music
History

January

#1 R&B Song 1944: "Ration Blues," Louis Jordan

Born: Milt Jackson, 1923; Rapper Grandmaster Flash (Joseph Sadler), 1958

1923 Legendary jazz vibraphonist Milt Jackson was born. He went on to become a pioneer in the genre known as bebop after being discovered by Dizzy Gillespie in 1945.

1949 Trombonist, trumpeter and vocalist supreme Billy Eckstine entered the R&B hit list with "Blue Moon," reaching #12 and #21 pop. It would be Billy's version that the Marcels would wildly revamp for their 1961 hit.

1955 The Five Keys jumped on the R&B charts with their wacky rock 'n' roll novelty, "Ling Ting Tong," reaching #5 and #28 pop. It was their first hit since "The Glory of Love" four years earlier.

1966 The Three Degrees barely scrapped the bottom of the Top 100 with "Look in My Eyes" (#97), a song originally recorded by the Chantels in 1961. Both records were produced by Richard Barrett, who was also manager of the girl groups. Meanwhile, the Supremes reached #11 on the pop charts with their *Supremes at the Copa* album, recorded live the previous year.

1966 Sam & Dave's "You Don't Know Like I Know" charted, reaching #37 R&B and becoming the soul legends' first chart record in a recording career spanning nineteen years.

1988 Prince and Miles Davis performed at a benefit for the homeless in Minneapolis, MN.

1990 B.B. King enjoyed the famous Rose Bowl Parade from atop the Mississippi Tournament of Roses Association float.

January

#1 R&B Song 1987: "The Way You Make Me Feel," Michael Jackson

Born: Arthur Prysock, 1929; Earl Grant, 1931

1955 Johnny Ace, who died on Christmas Day of the evils of "Russian Roulette," was buried today at the Clayborn Temple AME Church in Memphis. More than 5,000 mourners attended, including pallbearers Little Junior Parker, Willie Mae Thornton, Roscoe Gordon, and B.B. King. Ace was formerly in King's band before joining the Beale Streeters.

1957 Jackie Wilson recorded his last sides with the Dominoes (including "To Each His Own") for Decca before embarking on his tremendous solo career.

1960 Little Anthony & the Imperials performed "Tears on My Pillow" and "Shimmy, Shimmy, Ko-Ko-Bop" on Dick Clark's *American Bandstand* Saturday-night show.

1961 Eighteen-year-old Aretha Franklin began her pursuit of a secular-music career, heavily emphasizing the blues in her performance in Philadelphia at the Showboat.

1963 Dionne Warwick sang her debut single, "Don't Make Me Over," on *American Bandstand*.

1971 The Stylistics charted with "You're a Big Girl Now," reaching #7 R&B and #73 pop. It was the first of a career thirty-two R&B hits and seventeen Top 100 singles through 1992. The Philadelphia quintet formed out of two local groups, the Monarchs and the Percussions.

1999 Gospel artist Kirk Franklin, with the help of Mary J. Blige, R. Kelly, Bono, and Crystal Lewis & the Family charted with "Lean on Me" reaching #26 R&B. At the same time, Faith Evans featuring Puff Daddy entered the R&B hit list "All Night Long" peaking at #3 and #9 pop.

January

3

#1 R&B Song 1976: "Walk Away from Love," David Ruffin

Born: Willie Mitchell, 1928; Zulema (Zulema Cusseaux), 1947

1957 Fats Domino recorded "I'm Walkin'," which eventually reached #1 R&B and #4 pop.

1967 Joe Tex performed at the Saville Theater in London with opening act Gladys Knight & the Pips.

1970 The Fifth Dimension reached the Top 100 with "Blowing Away" (#21), their fourth hit from the *Age of Aquarius* album.

1977 The Spinners performed at the Circle Star Theater in California. Lead singer Philip Wynne then abruptly left the group for what turned out to be an unsuccessful solo career.

1989 *The Arsenio Hall Show* debuted on Fox TV with Luther Vandross singing the 1975 Major Harris hit, "Love Won't Let Me Wait."

1992 Queen Latifah, Naughty by Nature, MC Lyte, Public Enemy, and the Geto Boys performed at Madison Square Garden in New York for what was billed as the World's Greatest Rap Show Ever.

1998 Stevie Wonder, SWV, Kirk Franklin, Puff Daddy, Wyclef Jean, and Redman performed on ABC-TV's *Savion Glover's Nu York* show.

1998 B.B. King's latest album, featuring thirteen duets with artists such as the Rolling Stones, Eric Clapton, Heavy D, Bonnie Raitt, Willie Nelson, and Van Morrison, reached #73 pop today.

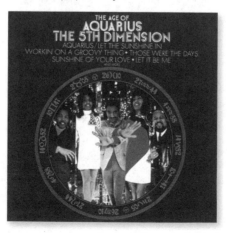

January

#1 Song 1969: "I Heard It Through the Grapevine," Marvin Gaye

Born: Arthur Conley, 1946

1959 Clyde Otis (the first black A&R director for a major label) signed Brook Benton to Mercury Records. The former gospel singer would go on to have thirty-seven R&B charters through 1978.

1964 Betty Harris's second of three Top 100 singles, "His Kiss," charted today. Betty was originally a maid for blues singer Big Maybelle. Her career started when Maybelle brought her onstage for duets.

1968 Jimi Hendrix was arrested in Gothenberg, Sweden, while on tour and jailed for the night for destroying a hotel room during a fight. He was once quoted as saying: "I'm the one who's got to die when it's time for me to die, so let me live my life the way I want to."

1969 The Temptations' approach to soul with psychedelic overtones, "Cloud Nine," reached #2 R&B and #6 pop with new lead Dennis Edwards replacing David Ruffin. Edwards originally sang with another Motown act, the Contours.

1974 Marvin Gaye performed at the Oakland Alameda County Coliseum in Oakland, CA. It was his first concert in five years.

1975 LaBelle's "Lady Marmalade" charted today on its way to #1—the only chart topper they would ever achieve.

1997 The Isley Brothers charted with "Tears," reaching #12 R&B. It was their last of an amazing seventy-four R&B hit singles during the century dating back to 1962. Forty-four of those had gone into the Top 20.

January

#1 Jukebox Song 1957: "Since I Met You Baby," Ivory Joe Hunter

Born: Wilbert Harrison, 1929; Johnny Adams, 1932

1929 The man who made the Leiber-Stoller song "Kansas City" a rock 'n' roll classic, Wilbert Harrison, was born in Charlotte, NC. Harrison was one of twenty-three children.

1952 Wynonie Harris became the only artist ever to have his hit list debut and last hit both chart on the same date (in different years) when he charted with "Lovin' Machine," reaching #5 R&B. On this day in 1946 his first charter, "Wynonie's Blues," charted, en route to #3 R&B.

1963 Jan Bradley had her biggest hit when "Mama Didn't Lie" charted, eventually reaching #14. When other hits failed to follow, Bradley went on to be a social worker.

1974 Diana Ross's "Last Time I Saw Him" hit the Top 100 today, peaking at #14.

1975 Phoebe Snow's "Poetry Man" rhymed its way onto the hit list, up to #5 pop. It was the first (and biggest) of five Top 100 singles for Snow.

1994 Earth, Wind & Fire and Curtis Mayfield were inducted into the Image Hall of Fame in Pasadena, CA, at the twenty-sixth annual NAACP Image Awards.

Curtis Mayfield

January

#1 R&B Song 1962: "Unchain My Heart,"
Ray Charles

Born: Paul Wilson (the Flamingos), 1935;
Doris Troy, 1937; Van McCoy, 1944; Shirley
Brown, 1947; Kathy Sledge (Sister Sledge),
1959

1951 Lucky Millinder and His Orchestra charted with "I'll Never Be Free" (#8 R&B) with famed Annisteen Allen and Big John Greer doing the vocals. Millinder's first four chart 78s all reached #1, including "Who Threw the Whiskey in the Well," which spent eight weeks at the top.

1951 Jazz diva Dinah Washington charted with "Harbor Lights," reaching #10 R&B. The Platters would take it to #15 (#8 pop) in 1960, having carefully studied Washington's version.

1958 The Silhouettes' one and only hit, "Get a Job," (#1) was released.

1967 The Supremes recorded an album of Disney songs, although the collection was never released. Only the song "When You Wish Upon a Star" ever saw the light of day, when it was issued on their thirty-fifth and last chart album (#112 pop), *Diana Ross & the Supremes 25th Anniversary*, in 1986.

1990 Stevie Wonder performed at a fund-raiser for the Inner-City Foundation for Excellence in Education at the Great Western Forum in Inglewood, CA.

1996 In a bizarre incident of unneeded publicity for a record, O.J. Simpson called a Los Angeles radio station and requested that Mariah Carey and Boyz II Men's megahit, "One Sweet Day," be played in dedication to his deceased wife, Nicole (whom he allegedly murdered).

January

7

#1 R&B Song 1956: "The Great Pretender," the Platters

Born: Jazz trumpeter Henry "Red" Allen, 1908

1955 Marion Anderson debuted at the Metropolitan Opera House in New York City. She was the first black singer to become a member of the Met.

1956 The Cadillacs charted with their rock 'n' roll classic, "Speedoo," reaching #3 R&B and #17 pop. The song title was lead singer Earl Carroll's nickname.

1963 Chubby Checker's fifteenth hit, "Dancin' Party," (#12), earned him a plagiarism suit by Gary "U.S." Bonds, who felt the "Chubster's" single was too similar to Bonds's 1961 hit, "Quarter to Three."

1967 Kim Weston, dueting with Marvin Gaye, charted with "It Takes Two" (#14). It was her biggest of six Top 100 singles starting in 1963.

1967 Aaron Neville's "Tell It Like It Is" reached #2 pop and #1 R&B (for five weeks). The song would later become an anthem used by the Black Power movement. Neville, who was influenced by the Spaniels' lead singer, Pookie Hudson, sang with a vocal group, the Avalons, and played with the R&B band the Hawketts before joining his brothers in the Neville Brothers.

1997 Prince performed at the Tower Theater in Philadelphia with the receipts going to his Love 4 One Another charity.

Marion Anderson

January

#1 Song 1977: "You Don't Have to Be a Star," Marilyn McCoo & Billy Davis Jr.

Born: Shirley Bassey, 1937; Little Anthony (Gourdine), 1940; R. Kelly (Steven Williams), 1967

1940 The legendary lead singer of the Imperials, Little Anthony, was born in Brooklyn, New York.

1944 Duke Ellington & His Orchestra charted with "Do Nothing Till You Hear From Me." It became his biggest R&B hit, spending eight weeks at #1.

1949 John Lee Hooker's debut record, "Boogie Chillen'," charted on its way to #1 R&B. When the record hit, Hooker was still employed as a janitor at Chrysler Motors in Detroit. The former member of the Fairfield Four gospel group would go on to legendary status as a pioneering blues man

1960 The Count Basie Orchestra headlined at the Apollo Theater.

1965 Chuck Berry, backed by an English group known as the Five Dimensions, started a British tour with the Moody Blues and Long John Baldry at the Odeon Theater, Lewisham, London. The grueling twelve nights included twice-nightly performances.

1983 Michael Jackson and Paul McCartney's duet, "The Girl Is Mine," reached #2 pop and #1 R&B.

2001 Laura Webb Childress, tenor vocalist for the Bobbettes, died. She and her four schoolmates were barely in their teens when they formed the Harlem Queens but soon became the rage with their classic, "Mr. Lee," a song they wrote about their fifth-grade teacher, which went to #1 R&B and #6 pop in 1957. It made them the first all-girl rock 'n' roll group to have a Top 10 hit.

January

9

#1 Song 1988: "So Emotional," Whitney Houston

Born: Kenny Clarke, 1914; Bulee "Slim" Gaillard, 1911; Big Al Downing, 1940

1914 One of the founders of bebop and the original drummer with the famed Modern Jazz Quartet, Kenny Clarke was born today in Pittsburgh, PA. Clarke played with jazz greats from Louis Armstrong and Ella Fitzgerald to Dizzy Gillespie and Miles Davis and was known for his unique cymbal work and accenting rim shots.

1956 The Coasters recorded "Down in Mexico" and "Brazil," among four sides, with Leiber and Stoller producing at Hollywood Recorders in Los Angeles.

1961 Sam Cooke started his record label, SAR Records, becoming one of the first black artists to have his own imprint. His partners were J. W. Alexander and manager Roy Crain. He used an initial from each to come up with SAR. The label would later have hits with the Valentinos, which included the Womack Brothers. One of the Womack siblings, Cecil, would later marry Sam's daughter Linda and become the duo Womack & Womack.

1971 The Supremes and the Four Tops (thanks to the incredible Motown Marketing Machine) reached #14 pop and #7 R&B with a competent (though lesser by comparison) remake of the Ike & Tina Turner classic, "River Deep, Mountain High."

1979 Earth, Wind & Fire performed at the Music for UNICEF concert at the United Nations General Assembly Hall in New York.

1998 Janet Jackson received her eighteenth gold RIAA certification, this time for "Together Again." It put her in first place among female artists with the most gold singles.

Sam Cooke

January

#1 R&B Song 1970: "I Want You Back," the Jackson 5

Born: Bandleader Buddy Johnson, 1915; jazz drummer Max Roach, 1925; bluesman Eddy Clearwater, 1935

1948 The legendary Ravens had their R&B chart debut with "Write Me a Letter" (#5). Today that highly collectible blues ballad 78 is worth $100.

1956 Rock 'n' roll took an exciting turn with the release of Frankie Lymon & the Teenagers' "Why Do Fools Fall in Love" (#6 pop, #1 R&B). The success of Frankie and the group heralded the "kiddie" lead sound in rock 'n' roll, which brought more than one hundred similarly styled acts to the recording scene over the next five years.

1958 New York's Saint Nick's Sports Center hosted a rock 'n' roll show and dance featuring the girl groups, the Chantels and the Deltairs, along with the Five Satins and the Dubs.

1963 Sam Cooke appeared at Miami's Harlem Square Club. The performance was recorded by RCA, but executives felt his sensual performance was too much for the times. The album didn't come out until 1985.

1970 The Fight for Sight Organization awarded Stevie Wonder the 1969 Show Business Inspiration Award.

1976 Blues legend Howlin' Wolf (Chester Arthur Burnett, named after the twenty-first President, Chester A. Arthur) died of kidney disease in Hines, Illinois. His band at various times included Ike Turner, Little Junior Parker and James Cotton. Wolf was likely the most seminal blues influence on '60s rock 'n' roll, particularly among British groups like the Rolling Stones, Led Zeppelin, Cream and even the Beatles.

1995 Chaka Khan, Dionne Warwick, and Patti LaBelle, among others, performed at the Universal Amphitheater in Universal City, CA, at a tribute concert honoring Ella Fitzgerald.

1997 James Brown received a star on Hollywood's Walk of Fame.

January

11

 # 1 R&B Song 1947: "Ain't Nobody Here but Us Chickens," Louis Jordan

Born: Bluesman Clarence "Pinetop" Smith, 1904; bluesman Slim Harpo (James Moore), 1924; Janice Pought (the Bobbettes), 1944; Mary J. Blige, 1971

?1956 The Robins first session as the Coasters included "Down in Mexico" (#8 R&B) and "Brazil."

1964 The Sapphires, a Philadelphia-based R&B trio led by Carol Jackson, charted en route to their biggest hit, "Who Do You Love" (#25).

1966 Patti LaBelle & the Bluebelles began a tour of England, starting at the Cromwellian Club in London.

1986 The R&B/funk band Zapp entered the R&B hit list with "Computer Love Part 1," reaching #8. The four Troutman brothers (Roger, Tony, Larry, and Lester) would do it all over again eight years later when, with the added vocals of Charlie Wilson (Gap Band) and Shirley Murdock, they did a new version of "Computer Love," which reached #65. In a bizarre circumstance, Roger died in 1999 when he was shot by brother Larry, who in turn killed himself in a murder-suicide. Larry was fifty-four, while Roger was forty-seven.

1992 Boyz II Men won the Best New Artist category at the NAACP twenty-fourth annual Image Awards at the Wiltern Theater in Los Angeles, while Patti LaBelle was named Entertainer of the Year and the O'Jays won the trophy for Outstanding Vocal Group. Also inducted into the Image Hall of Fame were the Temptations.

1996 Michael Jackson's album *HIStory: Past, Present and Future Book I* was certified by the Recording Industry Association of America (RIAA) to be six times platinum.

January

#1 R&B Song 1974: "Until You Come Back to Me," Aretha Franklin

Born: Bandleader Jay McShann, 1909; Maggie Bell, 1945; George Duke, 1946

1939 Songwriter Jack Lawrence brought a tune he'd written to an Ink Spots recording session. The song was the standard-to-be, "If I Didn't Care."

1968 In an instance of hysterical casting, an episode of TV's *Tarzan* featured the Supremes…as nuns.

1979 Donna Summer became the Queen of Disco at the sixth annual American Music Awards when she won Favorite Single Disco, Favorite Album Disco and Favorite Female Artist Disco trophies.

1985 Persistence paid off when Qwest Records released James Ingram's "Yah Mo B There" in England for the third time in eleven months. It charted today reaching #12. Guess they weren't satisfied, as it charted the two previous times as well (#44, #69).

1990 Bobby Brown was to receive the Martin Luther King Jr. Musical Achievement Award at Boston's Symphony Hall during a Tony Bennett/Count Basie Orchestra concert. But there was one small glitch in the proceedings: He never showed up.

1991 When you're hot, you're hot. Whitney Houston received an award from the American Cinema Foundation for Distinguished Achievement even though she had not yet starred in a film.

1993 Frankie Lymon & the Teenagers were inducted into the Rock and Roll Hall of Fame by Stevie Wonder at its eighth annual awards ceremony in Los Angeles. Also inducted were Sly & the Family Stone by George Clinton.

1995 Al Green was inducted into the Rock and Roll Hall of Fame at its tenth annual awards ceremony. Green's presenter was Natalie Cole, while the B-52's inducted Martha & the Vandellas. Also inducted were the '40s and '50s pioneers, Sonny Til & the Orioles.

1996 Janet Jackson signed a recording extension worth more than $80 million with Virgin Records. It was a four-album deal that included a $35 million advance and a reported twenty-four percent royalty—more than twice what most artists get.

1998 Lloyd Price was inducted into the Rock and Roll Hall of Fame at its thirteenth annual awards ceremony in New York.

January

13

#1 R&B Song 1951: "Teardrops From Your Eyes," Roy Brown

Born: Bobby Lester (the Moonglows), 1932

1951 Almost two and a half years after his first hit, Muddy Waters charted again, this time with "Louisiana Blues," reaching #10 R&B. Waters's hard-edged sound was enhanced by his band, which included such stalwarts as Little Walter (harmonica), Willie Dixon (bass), Otis Spann (piano), Elgin Evans (drums), and Jimmy Rogers (guitar).

1958 The original version of "Dedicated to the One I Love" by the "5" Royales was released. Three years later it became a hit (#3) for the Shirelles and again in 1967 for the Mamas & the Papas (#2).

1961 The Shells made their performance debut on the strength of their current hit, "Baby Oh Baby" (#21 pop), at the Apollo in New York as opening act for Sam Cooke. The record was originally released in 1957 and went nowhere.

1962 In one of the great travesties of R&B history, a record would assure the successful career of one member of a group while ignoring the others to the point of obscurity. Gene Chandler's "Duke of Earl" charted today on its way to immortality (#1 R&B for five weeks and #1 pop for three weeks). The travesty: It was not Chandler and some backing vocalists, but a group called the Dukays (a quintet that had previously charted with "The Girl's a Devil"), which Chandler had been a member of since 1959. The label decided to ignore the group, crediting only Chandler. The Dukays were soon a footnote in history while Gene (real name Gene Dixon, who took his stage name from movie idol Jeff Chandler) went on to have thirty-six R&B hits through 1986.

1962 Chubby Checker & the Dreamlovers' recording of "The Twist" charted for the second time in two years and went on to reach #1 pop, the first and only time in rock 'n' roll history (other than a Bing Crosby Christmas record) that a record returned to #1 after a chart absence of more than a year.

1962 One of the Miracles best of their early releases, "What's So Good About Goodbye," charted, reaching #16 R&B and #35 pop.

1979 Singer/songwriter Donny Hathaway committed suicide. Best known for his duet hits with Roberta Flack, including "Where Is the Love?," and "The Closer I Get to You," he jumped from the fifteenth floor of the Essex Hotel in New York. He was only thirty-three.

January

#1 Jukebox Song 1956: "At My Front Door," the El Dorados

Born: Songwriter Allen Toussaint, 1938; singer Linda Jones, 1944; LL Cool J (James Todd Smith), 1968

1956 Little Richard's debut single for Specialty Records, "Tutti Frutti," charted, reaching #17 pop and #2 R&B for six weeks. Little Richard (Richard Wayne Penniman, one of eleven brothers and sisters), who ran off at twelve to join Dr. Hudson's Traveling Medicine Show and sell snake oil at carnivals, began singing with Sugar Foot Sam's Minstrel Show in the late '40s and Buster Brown & his Band in 1950.

1966 Patti LaBelle & the Bluebelles performed on Britain's TV show *Ready, Steady, Go!* while promoting their new single, "Over the Rainbow."

1967 The Fifth Dimension hit the Top 100 with "Go Where You Wanna Go" (#16), their first of thirty charters through 1976.

1970 Diana Ross performed in her last show as a Supreme at Las Vegas's Frontier Hotel.

Little Richard

While onstage she introduced her replacement, Jean Terrell, who was the sister of famed boxer Ernie Terrell.

1978 Natalie Cole charted, reaching #10 pop with "Our Love" but, more importantly hitting #1 R&B. In doing so she had her fifth chart topper in a little more than two years.

1995 Babyface had his thirty-second Top 10 hit as a songwriter when Madonna's "Take a Bow" reached #8 today. Babyface also dueted with Madonna on the hit recording. His first Top 10 as a songsmith was the 1987 Whispers hit, "Rock Steady."

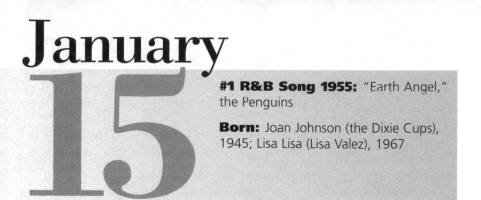

January 15

#1 R&B Song 1955: "Earth Angel," the Penguins

Born: Joan Johnson (the Dixie Cups), 1945; Lisa Lisa (Lisa Valez), 1967

1928 Blues great-to-be Howlin' Wolf played his first gig in the south before eventually moving to Chicago.

1955 LaVern Baker charted with "Tweedle Dee" (#14), her first of twenty pop Top 100 45s between 1955 and 1966. She also had twenty-one R&B hits and was inducted into the Rock and Roll Hall of Fame in 1991.

1960 Little Junior Parker, Bo Diddley, Bobby Bland, Etta James, Bill Doggett, and the Isley Brothers performed at the Regal Theater in Chicago.

1972 Isaac Hayes began a European tour with a performance in West Germany.

1990 Patti LaBelle received a Lifetime Achievement Award at the annual Congress of Racial Equality (CORE) awards dinner in New York.

1991 LL Cool J's "Around the Way Girl" which sampled Rick James's "All Night Long," was certified platinum in sales.

1992 On TV's *Entertainment Tonight* Brenda Lee, the diminutive dynamite damsel, suggested that the all-male line-up of inductees into that night's Rock and Roll Hall of Fame should include the likes of the Shirelles, Mary Wells, Dionne Warwick, and herself. "The women who pioneered rock 'n' roll…were just as important as the males," she stated.

1992 The Rock and Roll Hall of Fame inducted Bobby "Blue" Bland, Jimi Hendrix, Sam & Dave, Elmore James, and Booker T. & the M.G.'s for the seventh Annual awards ceremony at the Waldorf-Astoria Hotel, New York. Little Richard inducted the Isley Brothers and brought down the house when he sang "Shout" with them at the post-awards party. Also inducted was pioneer New Orleans bluesman, Professor Longhair, whom presenter Aaron Neville called "The Grandfather of rock 'n' roll. Where did rock 'n' roll come from? It's the baby of R&B."

1994 The Old School Reunion Tour began, with rappers the Sugar Hill Gang, Kurtis Blow, Kool Moe Dee, and Houdini, among others.

January

16

#1 R&B Song 1943: "See See Rider," Bea Booze

Born: Barbara Lynn, 1942; Sade (Helen Folasade Adu), 1959; Debbie Allen, 1950; Maxine Jones (En Vogue), 1966; Aaliyah (Aaliyah Haughton), 1979

1975 Sly & the Family Stone performed at Radio City Music Hall in New York at the beginning of an eight-day stay. The West Coast group apparently didn't stir much East Coast excitement, as the attendance was off by two thirds of the hall's capacity.

1984 Michael Jackson received an astonishing seven awards at the American Music Awards eleventh annual event, including Favorite Male Artist, Pop/Rock; Favorite Male Artist, Soul R&B; Favorite Album, Pop/Rock; Special Award of Merit, Favorite Video, Pop/Rock; Favorite Single, Pop/Rock; and Favorite Video, Soul/R&B

1988 Tina Turner performed before more than 180,000 fans at Rio de Janeiro's American Stadium, which would put her in the Guinness Book of Records for the attendance feat set by a solo performer.

1991 Tina Turner and ex-husband Ike Turner were inducted into the Rock and Roll Hall of Fame at its sixth annual induction ceremonies. Producer Phil Spector accepted the award in their absence. Ike was in prison at the time for driving under the influence of cocaine. The same night, Bobby Brown inducted soul legend Wilson Pickett into the Hall. Howlin' Wolf, the legendary blues great, was also inducted posthumously by Robert Cray (sixty-three years and a day after his first performance), and blues pioneer John Lee Hooker was inducted. Tracy Chapman inducted the Impressions. LaVern Baker and Jimmy Reed were also inducted. In all, seven of the eight acts inducted were black artists.

1993 Boyz II Men reached #3 pop and #4 R&B with the Five Satins classic, "In the Still of the Nite," bringing the immortal song and song styling of the Five Satins to a whole new generation of music buyers. The Boyz version was from the TV miniseries, *The Jacksons*. The Satins' standard originally made it only to #24 in 1956. The same night, Boyz II Men won the Best Vocal Group category at the NAACP twenty-fifth annual Image Awards, at the Civic Auditorium, Pasadena, California.

1999 Prince's "1999" was reissued and charted today, reaching #45 R&B. The record had originally been issued in 1982; the label must have been curious to see how it would do in the actual year of its title.

January

17

#1 R&B Song 1976: "Wake Up Everybody (Part 1)," Harold Melvin & the Blue Notes

Born: Elsberry Hobbs (the Drifters), 1936; William Hart (the Delfonics), 1945; Sheila Hutchinson (the Emotions), 1953

1970 Billy Stewart, known for hits like "Sitting in the Park," "I Do Love You," and creative soul reworkings of standards like "Summertime" and "Secret Love," died when his car plunged into the Neuse River, just south of Smithfield, NC, while he was on tour. He was only thirty-two.

1971 Marvin Gaye sang "The National Anthem" at Super Bowl V in Miami before the game between the Miami Dolphins and the Baltimore Colts.

1990 Hank Ballard was inducted into the Rock and Roll Hall of Fame at their fifth annual induction ceremonies at the Waldorf-Astoria Hotel in New York. Ballard broke down in tears during the ceremony while dedicating the award to his wife, Theresa, who had been killed by a hit-and-run driver three months prior in New York City. Also inducted were the Platters, Louis Armstrong, Ma Rainey, and the Four Tops by presenter Stevie Wonder.

1992 Michael Jackson's TV show on CBS, *Michael Jackson…The Legend Continues*, aired with guests Smokey Robinson, Dick Clark, and Quincy Jones.

1993 Dionne Warwick and Luther Vandross performed at the Lincoln Memorial in Washington, DC at "An American Reunion: The People's Inaugural Celebration." Vandross sang "Stand by Me" with the song's original hitmaker, Ben E. King.

1996 Gladys Knight & the Pips were inducted into the Rock and Roll Hall of Fame by Mariah Carey. Also inducted were the Shirelles.

1997 The Isley Brothers performed at New York's famous rock venue, the Beacon Theater.

#1 R&B Song 1975: "You're the First, the Last, My Everything," Barry White

Born: Berman Patterson (the Cleftones), 1938; Martha Reeves (the Vandellas), 1941; David Ruffin (the Temptations), 1941

1962 Ike & Tina Turner performed their current chart 45, "Poor Fool," on American Bandstand.

1975 Minnie Riperton, former member of the rock R&B sextet, Rotary Connection, charted on the way to #1 with "Lovin' You."

1986 Dionne Warwick and her friends (Gladys Knight, Elton John, and Stevie Wonder) began a four-week stay at #1 with "That's What Friends Are For." It became a million-seller and the biggest selling single of the year. For Knight, it became her tenth of eleven R&B #1s.

1989 Tina Turner inducted legendary record producer Phil Spector into the Rock and Roll Hall of Fame at its fourth annual ceremony. Spector produced and co-wrote Tina's epic single, "River Deep, Mountain High." Little Richard also inducted the late Otis Redding while he and Mick Jagger sang "I Can't Turn You Loose" at the post-awards party. Also inducted were the legendary Temptations and Stevie Wonder, who at thirty-eight was the youngest inductee to date.

1991 Prince played the Rock in Rio II Festival's opening evening at Rio de Janeiro's Maracana Soccer Stadium in front of more than 60,000 people.

1996 Citing irreconcilable differences, Michael Jackson's bride of eighteen months, Lisa Marie Presley, filed for divorce in Los Angeles.

Minnie Riperton

January

#1 R&B Song 1974: "I've Got to Use My Imagination," Gladys Knight & the Pips

1956 The Platters' second album, *The Platters Volume Two*, charted, reaching #12 on the pop charts. All five of their albums through 1960 made the pop Top 20, an amazing achievement for a black vocal group at that time. They would go on to sell more than 50 million records.

1962 The Drifters, the Impressions, Gladys Knight & the Pips, B.B. King, Gene McDaniels, and a new comedian named Flip Wilson performed at the Apollo Theater in New York City.

1977 Aretha Franklin sang "God Bless America" a cappella at Jimmy Carter's Inaugural Eve Gala in Washington, DC.

1985 The Commodores charted with "Nightshift," which was a tribute to Jackie Wilson and Marvin Gaye. The song reached #1 R&B and #3 pop while becoming their last of seven R&B #1s. It was also their only #1 without former lead, Lionel Richie.

1991 Janet Jackson's "Love Will Never Do (Without You)" reached #1 pop, giving her the historic distinction of becoming the first artist to have seven Top Five pop hits from the same album.

1993 Chuck Berry sang "Good Golly Miss Molly" and "Reelin' and Rockin'" with an all-star band, comprised of his daughter Ingrid, Little Richard, Greg Phillinganes, Stephen Stills, David Pack, Max Weinberg, and Nathan East at *An American Reunion: The 52nd Presidential Gala* at the Capital Center, in Landover, MD.

1993 Michael Jackson performed at President-elect Bill Clinton's *An American Reunion: The 52nd Presidential Gala* at the Capital Center in Landover, MD. The show was broadcast on ABC-TV.

1994 Willie Dixon was inducted into the Rock and Roll Hall of Fame at the ninth annual awards ceremony at New York's Waldorf-Astoria Hotel. He was given the award by presenter Chuck Berry, who also performed "Roll Over Beethoven" at the after-show bash. Also inducted was Bob Marley, by presenter Bono of U2.

1997 Stevie Wonder performed in Washington, DC, at the 53rd Inaugural Gala for President Clinton.

1997 The Shirelles were honored in their hometown of Passaic, NJ, when Passaic High School renamed their assembly Shirelle Auditorium.

January

#1 R&B Song 1951: "Bad, Bad Whiskey," Amos Milburn and His Aladdin Chickenshackers

Born: Leadbelly (Huddie William Ledbetter), 1889; Luther Tucker, 1936; Ron Townson (the Fifth Dimension), 1933; Billy Powell (the O'Jays), 1942

1889 Known as "the King of the twelve-string," blues legend Leadbelly was born in Mooringsport, LA. One explanation for his name was that he had a load of buckshot in his stomach from one of his numerous fights.

1958 The Chantels' classic, "Maybe," charted, eventually reaching #15.

1963 Ray Charles performed "You Don't Know Me" and "What'd I Say" on Dinah Shore's NBC-TV show.

1968 Folk musician/vocalist Richie Havens performed with the elite of the '60s folk scene including Bob Dylan, Pete Seeger, Arlo Guthrie, and Judy Collins at a Carnegie Hall tribute to Woody Guthrie.

1979 In what would at first glance appear to be a "clash" of cultures, Bo Diddley performed as the opening act for the eclectic punk rock band the Clash on their debut U.S. tour.

1986 Stevie Wonder, the Pointer Sisters, Eddie Murphy, and Bill Cosby performed in concerts to honor the first annual observance of Martin Luther King Jr.'s birthday as a national holiday.

1988 The Drifters and the Supremes were inducted into the Rock and Roll Hall of Fame during its third annual ceremony.

1991 Anita Baker, who had won at least one Grammy in each of the past five seasons, was given the Best R&B Vocal Performance, Female award at the thirty-third annual awards ceremony at Radio City Music Hall in New York.

1993 En Vogue performed at MTV's *Rock and Roll Inaugural Ball* in Washington, DC, singing "The Star-Spangled Banner."

1994 The Pointer Sisters received a star on the Hollywood Walk of Fame and became only the second female group to receive one. The first was the Supremes.

January

21

#1 R&B Song 1967: "Tell It Like It Is," Aaron Neville

Born: Richie Havens, 1941; Edwin Starr (Charles Hatcher), 1942; Billy Ocean (Leslie Sebastian Charles), 1950

1962 Jackie Wilson performed on Ed Sullivan's Sunday-night TV show. He sang "My Heart Belongs to Only You."

1982 B.B. King donated his record collection, including more than 7,000 rare blues discs, to the University of Mississippi Center for the Study of Southern Culture.

1984 Legendary vocalist Jackie Wilson died in Mount Holly, NJ after an eight-year coma brought on by a heart attack while onstage (September 25, 1975). He was singing "Lonely Teardrops" at the time. Attending the funeral were numerous stars, including the Spinners, Berry Gordy Jr., and the Four Tops. "Mr. Excitement" was only forty-nine.

1987 Aretha Franklin was inducted into the Rock and Roll Hall of Fame by Rolling Stones member Keith Richards during the second annual awards presentation in New York City. Also enshrined were Bo Diddley, the Coasters, B.B. King, Smokey Robinson, Jackie Wilson, Marvin Gaye, and Clyde McPhatter of the Drifters. The latter three were posthumously inducted, and McPhatter was enshrined by another Drifters lead singing great, Ben E. King. Wilson was inducted exactly three years after he died.

1989 Bobby Brown reached the top of the pop-album charts with *Don't Be Cruel*, a collection that would hang around the Top 200 for ninety-seven weeks. The album became an international hit, going on to #3 in England.

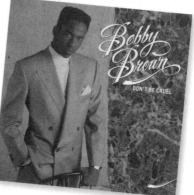

1989 Willie Dixon and Bo Diddley, among others, performed at a Celebration for Young Americans at President Bush's inauguration in Washington, DC. Diddley stated humbly, "I thank you in advance for the great round of applause I am about to get."

1997 Jimi Hendrix was honored in his hometown of Seattle—twenty-seven years after he died—with a statue on the corner of Pine and Broadway.

January 22

#1 R&B Song 1972: "Let's Stay Together," Al Green

Born: Reverend Clarence LeVaughn "C.L." Franklin, 1915; Sam Cooke, 1931; Nolan Strong (the Diablos), 1934; Addie "Micki" Harris (the Shirelles), 1940

1955 Ray Charles entered the R&B charts with "I've Got a Woman," his first of eleven #1 singles through 1993.

1958 The Chantels recorded five sides, including their hit follow-up to "Maybe," "Every Night" (#16 R&B, #39 pop).

1962 Gene Chandler performed "Duke of Earl" on *American Bandstand*. The single only charted two days earlier on the R&B lists and Chandler's appearance lip-synching the group record (actually the Dukays) kicked the sales into overdrive, eventually reaching #1 pop and R&B.

1968 The Supremes sang at the Talk of the Town club in London. Taking in the performance were Paul McCartney and actor Michael Caine.

1970 The Soul Together tour began at the Royal Albert Hall in London and included Clarence Carter, Arthur Conley, Sam & Dave, and Joe Tex. Soon after the tour, Sam & Dave split up.

1977 Cameo made the R&B chart for the first time with "Rigor Mortis," reaching #33. They originally formed in 1974 as the New York City Players. At one time the group, headed by Larry Blackmon, had as many as thirteen members.

1983 Michael Jackson charted with the immortal "Billie Jean," reaching #1 pop for seven weeks and #1 R&B for nine weeks. It would become Michael's biggest solo hit of a career forty-six pop charters through 2001. Only when it reached #1 would MTV (who had an anti-black video policy at the time) air the video—and then only under enormous pressure from CBS Records.

1990 MC Hammer won awards at the seventeenth annual American Music Awards for Favorite Artist Rap Music, and Favorite Album, Rap Music, largely on the strength of the megahit "U Can't Touch This." Hammer was originally a bat boy for the Oakland As and began his recording career with a $40,000 investment from two As players, Dwayne Murphy and Mike Davis. As a batboy, he was nicknamed Little Hammer due to his physical similarity to Hammerin' Hank Aaron.

January

23

#1 R&B Song 1943: "What's the Use of Getting Sober (When You Gonna Get Drunk Again)," Louis Jordan

Born: Eugene Church, 1938; Jerry Lawson (the Persuasions), 1944; Anita Pointer (the Pointer Sisters), 1948

1956 James Brown and his vocal group and band the Famous Flames were signed to Federal Records. Their signing bonus was $200.

1961 Actor/singer Paul Robeson died in Philadelphia. He was the strong-voiced star of numerous films, including *Showboat* and *King Solomon's Mines*.

1961 Ben E. King charted with his first solo single, "Spanish Harlem," reaching #15 R&B and #10 pop. Ben (born Benjamin Earl Nelson) spent several months working with the Moonglows while still in high school before joining the Crowns, formerly the Five Crowns.

Paul Robeson

1974 The Staples Singers performed at the eighth annual MIDEM Festival in Cannes, France. The gathering is the music publishing business's equivalent of the Cannes Film Festival, which is held in the same place and which attracts more than 7,000 music publishers and related businesspeople from around the world.

1986 Chuck Berry was inducted into the Rock and Roll Hall of Fame at its inaugural induction ceremonies by the Rolling Stones' Keith Richards at the Waldorf-Astoria in New York. Along with Chuck, Fats Domino, Little Richard, Sam Cooke, and Ray Charles were inducted, with the presentation to Charles coming from Quincy Jones. Blues great Robert Johnson also was honored and had the unique distinction of being the artist with the smallest catalog of recorded work by far (only twenty-nine recordings) to be inducted. James Brown, too was inducted—thirty years to the day after his first record contract was signed.

1988 Michael Jackson's "The Way You Make Me Feel" reached #1, giving its producer, Quincy Jones, the distinction of having the longest time span between #1 singles. He started twenty-five years earlier with Lesley Gore's "It's My Party" in 1963.

January

#1 R&B Song 1987: "Stop to Love," Luther Vandross

Born: Sax player Jimmy Forrest, 1920; Zeke Carey (the Flamingos), 1933; Ann Cole, 1934; Aaron Neville, 1941

1953 The "5" Royales debuted on the R&B hit list with "Baby, Don't Do It," which hit the top spot for three weeks, making it their biggest of seven hits through 1957. Every one of their charters made the Top 10. Lowman Pauling of the group wrote the Shirelles hit "Dedicated to the One I Love." It was the "5" Royales' failed 45 that first turned the girl group on to the song.

1970 Jamaican Reggae artist Jimmy Cliff had his chart debut with "Wonderful World, Beautiful People," which reached #25 pop. It would take Cliff thirteen more years to hit the R&B charts with his single "Special."

1970 The Chairmen of the Board charted with their first and biggest hit, "Give Me Just a Little More Time," reaching #3 pop and #8 R&B.

1976 The O'Jays reached #5 pop and #1 R&B with "I Love Music (Part I)." It was their fourth million-selling single in three and a half years.

1982 Diana Ross sang the National Anthem at Superbowl XVI in Pontiac, MI's Pontiac Silverdome.

1987 Exposé charted with "Come Go with Me" (#5 pop). It was the first of their twelve hits through 1989.

1993 Chaka Khan sang "Ain't That Peculiar" and "How Sweet It Is" at a tribute to Marvin Gaye in France during the twenty-seventh annual MIDEM music convention. Also performing were the Pointer Sisters.

2004 Janet Jackson and Justin Timberlake performed at the halftime ceremonies for Superbowl XXXVIII in Jacksonville, FL. Unfortunately for Jackson, the event would become more well known for her "wardrobe malfunction," when Timberlake ripped off the front of her costume, exposing her breast on worldwide TV.

January

#1 Song 1985: "That's What Friends Are For," Dionne Warwick & Friends

Born: Jazz saxophonist Benny Golson, 1929; Etta James (Jamesetta Hawkins), 1938; Stacy Lattisaw, 1966; Alicia Keyes (Alicia Augello Cook), 1981

1953 The Flamingos signed with Chicago's Chance Records.

1964 One of the first black artists to pursue the business side, Lloyd Price (who began his own Kent label in 1953 and Double L in 1963) began a fund to help black students obtain scholarships for college.

1976 Stevie Wonder and Isaac Hayes performed with Bob Dylan on his Rolling Thunder Revue in the Houston Astrodome.

1982 Rick James won Favorite Album, Soul/R&B honors at the American Music Awards' ninth annual event in Los Angeles.

1993 Mariah Carey received the Favorite Female Artist, Pop/Rock and Favorite Album, Adult Contemporary trophies at the twentieth annual American Music Awards.

1994 Michael Jackson, who was accused of child molestation in August 1993, settled out of court for reportedly $20 million while his attorney, Johnny Cochran, went to great pains to establish that it was "in no way an admission of guilt."

1998 Queen Latifah, Martha & the Vandellas, the Temptations, Smokey Robinson, and Boyz II Men sang during halftime at Superbowl XXXII at Qualcomm Stadium in San Diego, CA.

January

#1 R&B Song 1957: "Blue Monday," Fats Domino

Born: Eartha Kitt, 1928; Huey "Piano" Smith, 1934; Jean Knight, 1943; Anita Baker, 1957; Kirk Franklin, 1970

1951 Little Esther Phillips recorded "Heart to Heart," singing lead for the Dominoes and in duet with Clyde McPhatter.

1957 Little Richard's single "The Girl Can't Help It" from the Jayne Mansfield film of the same name charted on its way to #49 pop and #7 R&B. At the same time, Richard's "Long Tall Sally" peaked at #3 in England. By now Richard had already starred in three rock 'n' roll films, *Don't Knock the Rock* with Bill Haley, *The Girl Can't Help It*, and Alan Freed's *Mr. Rock & Roll*.

1974 Bobby Womack charted with "Looking for a Love," reaching #1 R&B for three weeks and #10 pop. It was his biggest hit of forty five charters between 1962 and 1994. The song was a remake of his first chart 45, twelve years earlier.

1987 Diana Ross hosted the fourteenth annual American Music Awards at the Shrine Auditorium in Los Angeles. Meanwhile, Janet Jackson, who was nominated in nine categories, walked away with two awards, Best Female R&B Video Artist and Best R&B Single for "Nasty."

1993 R. Kelly's debut album, *Born Into the 90's*, was certified platinum by the RIAA even though it only reached #42 pop, mainly on the strength of its #3 position on the R&B hit list.

1999 Michael Jackson wound up at Cedars Medical Center in Miami with a broken wrist while working on an album, but the cause of the injury was not disclosed.

January

27

1955 Lillian Leach & the Mellows' third and fourth singles, "I Still Care" and "Yesterday's Memories," were recorded. The Jay-Dee singles cost sixty-nine cents each. Today the former is worth $200 and the latter $150.

1958 Little Richard, in his quest to become a Seventh Day Adventist minister, joined the Oakwood Theological College in Huntsville, AL. He would later state: "If God can save an old homosexual like me, he can save anybody." Of course he's also quoted as saying: "If there was anything I loved better than a big penis, it was a bigger penis."

1967 Aretha Franklin recorded her first sides for Atlantic Records at Rick Hall's Florence Alabama Music Emporium (FAME) studios in Muscle Shoals. The day's work produced the classic, "I Never Loved a Man (the Way I Love You)."

1984 Michael Jackson received second-degree burns to his head while on the set of a Pepsi commercial from an accidental explosion. He was taken to Cedars-Sinai Medical Center in Los Angeles for treatment. Pepsi would later pay Michael $1.5 million in restitution, which the singer promptly donated to the Brotman Memorial Hospital of Los Angeles.

1990 Michael Jackson received the Entertainer of the Decade award from the American Cinema Awards Foundation, as presented to him by movie queen Sophia Loren.

1991 Whitney Houston performed "The Star-Spangled Banner" at Superbowl XXV in Miami. The response was so great that a single and video were rush released.

1993 Eleven days after reaching its peak at #3 on the pop charts, "In the Still of the Night (I Remember)," by Boyz II Men was certified platinum by the RIAA.

1996 Mary J. Blige charted both pop and R&B today with what would become her biggest hit, "Not Gonna Cry" from the movie *Waiting to Exhale*. It attained the #1 spot pop for two weeks and #1 R&B for five weeks.

1994 Janet Jackson was touted as Best Female Sex Symbol and Best Female Singer while the rap trio Cypress Hill came out on top in *Rolling Stone*'s Music Awards and Readers poll as Best Rap Group of the Year.

January 28

1950 Larry Darnell, an early pioneer of the New Orleans sound, hit #1 on the R&B charts with "For You My Love."

1950 The Robins charted with "If It's So Baby" which was their second release, reaching #10 R&B. The group formed in Los Angeles in 1947 and would go on to issue thirty-seven singles through 1961, most of which were produced by Leiber & Stoller.

1955 Fats Domino, the Moonglows, Joe Turner, the Clovers, and Faye Adams began a forty-two-performance tour in New York called the Top Ten R&B Show.

1970 Richie Havens, Jimi Hendrix, Harry Belafonte, and a cross section of stars from the Rascals to the cast of *Hair* performed in a seven-hour anti–Vietnam War benefit concert at New York's Madison Square Garden. When Hendrix's drummer Buddy Miles stated to the audience, "I'm sorry, we just can't get it together," a furious Hendrix retorted: "That's what happens when Earth fucks with space. Never forget that," and walked to the wings in the middle of the second song, "Earth Blues."

1985 The sign on the wall said "Check Your Egos at the Door," and with that realization from Quincy Jones, forty-five major stars entered A&M Studios in Hollywood to record the song Michael Jackson and Lionel Ritchie had written (in only two hours) called "We Are the World." The recording was to act as a fund-raiser for the USA for Africa fund. Among the icons at the mike were Ray Charles, Stevie Wonder, Michael Jackson, Tina Turner, Diana Ross, Lionel Richie, James Ingram, Dionne Warwick, Bruce Springsteen, Paul Simon, Bob Dylan, Steve Perry, and Willie Nelson. It took more than ten hours to do the single recording. Prince was invited but didn't come.

1990 Aaron Neville sang the National Anthem at the Superdome in New Orleans at Superbowl XXIV, between the San Francisco 49ers and the Denver Broncos.

1991 MC Hammer received the Soul R&B Single for "U Can't Touch This," Soul R&B Album and Rap Album for *Please Hammer Don't Hurt 'Em*, Soul R&B Artist, and Rap Male Artist awards at the American Music Awards eighteenth annual ceremonies.

January

29

1952 One of the best-known artist/writers of his day, bluesman Willie Dixon ("Spoonful," "Little Red Rooster") died of a heart attack in Burbank, CA.

1960 Brook Benton was the headliner at the Apollo Theater.

1967 The Jimi Hendrix Experience performed at London's famed Saville Theatre with the Who.

1977 Natalie Cole charted with "I've Got Love on My Mind," reaching #5 pop and #1 R&B for five weeks. It would be her biggest hit of a career eighteen pop hits and thirty-one R&B winners through 1997. The record was also her fourth #1 of her first five chart singles.

1994 James Ingram began a tour of Asia starting in Kuala Lumpur, Malaysia.

1994 Mary Wilson of the Supremes was seriously injured (though she recovered) in a car accident on a California highway.

1998 Bad boy Bobby Brown was convicted on drunk driving charges in a Fort Lauderdale court. The judge sentenced Brown to five days in jail along with having to attend DUI school. He also had to submit to random drug and alcohol testing and spend thirty days in an alcohol and drug rehab facility. Along with that, he had to pay $500 in fines and was ordered to serve one hundred hours of community service along with a one-year suspension of his driver's license.

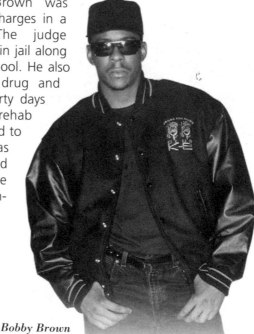

Bobby Brown

January

#1 R&B Song 1961: "Shop Around," the Miracles

Born: Jazz trumpeter Roy Eldridge, 1911; Ruth Brown, 1928; Luther Ingram, 1944; Jackie Ross, 1946; Jody Watley, 1959

1958 The Silhouettes' standard rocker, "Get a Job," charted en route to #1. The '70s group Sha Na Na named themselves after a line in the song.

1960 Dee Clark and Chuck Berry were the performing guests on Dick Clark's nighttime *American Bandstand*.

1961 The Shirelles' "Will You Love Me Tomorrow" reached the top of the pop charts (with Carole King playing drums). It was the first single by a rock 'n' roll girl group to reach #1.

1965 Shirley Bassey charted on her way to #8 with "Goldfinger," from the James Bond movie. It was her first of four Top 100 singles. Meanwhile, the best of the blue-eyed soul duos, the Righteous Brothers, entered the R&B hit list with the powerful evergreen "You've Lost That Lovin' Feelin'" peaking at #3 while rising to #1 pop.

1965 The Manhattans had their first chart single, "I Wanna Be (Your Everything)," which went to #12 R&B, on their way to a career full of hits including sixteen pop and forty-six R&B entries through 1990.

1965 Sam Cooke's "A Change Is Gonna Come" charted on its way to #9 R&B. It would be Sam's last of nineteen Top 10 hits from 1957 through 1965. The song was Sam's answer to Bob Dylan's "Blowin' in the Wind." Cooke influenced a diverse group of future stars including Michael Jackson, Otis Redding, and Al Green.

1985 USA for Africa's "We Are the World" was played on the radio for the first time. Over the next ten years the recording would sell in excess of 7.2 million singles and albums and help raise more than $588 million for the charity.

1995 Babyface received the Best Male Artist, Soul/R&B prize at the American Music Awards twenty-second annual show in Los Angeles. He also performed his duet hit with Madonna, "Take a Bow."

January

31

#1 R&B Song 1981: "Fantastic Voyage," Lakeside

Born: Roosevelt Sykes, 1906; Harold "Chuck" Willis, 1928; Marvin Junior (the Dells), 1936

1958 Little Richard officially announced that he had retired at the peak of his career to become an Evangelist. His conversion lasted all of four years.

1970 The Jackson 5's "I Want You Back" debut Motown single reached #1 pop and would reach #1 R&B for four weeks. The song was originally conceived for Gladys Knight & the Pips.

1973 Bobby Womack performed at the Sports Arena in San Diego, CA, as the opening act for Santana. Womack, who by now had already charted R&B seventeen times, was a prolific guitarist, having recorded with the likes of Aretha Franklin, Janis Joplin, Ray Charles, King Curtis, Joe Tex, and Wilson Pickett. In fact, Pickett recorded seventeen of Bobby's songs in just three years.

1979 With one chart record to his credit, Prince appeared as the opening act on a Rick James tour and promptly instigated a fight with the King of Punk Funk.

1987 New Edition charted with "Tears on My Pillow," reaching #41 R&B and featuring Little Anthony, who with the Imperials sang the original legendary hit almost thirty years earlier in 1958.

1993 Michael Jackson performed at Superbowl XXVII's halftime show at the Rose Bowl in Pasadena, CA. The performance and the game between the Buffalo Bills and the Dallas Cowboys had an estimated record-breaking audience of more than 133 million people.

1999 Stevie Wonder performed at Superbowl XXVII's halftime show in Miami, FL.

New Edition

February

#1 R&B Song 1960: "Smokie Part 2," Bill Black's Combo

Born: James Johnson, 1894; Joe Sample (the Crusaders), 1939; Rick James (James Johnson Jr.), 1948

1894 James Johnson (not the king of punk funk), known as the father of stride piano, was born in New Brunswick, NJ. The '20s piano style was a combination of blues, boogie-woogie, ragtime, and classical, requiring big hands that could pound a piano with a barrelhouse technique. None were better than Johnson, who taught the king of stride and ragtime, Fats Waller, how to play. In 1923, Johnson wrote a theatrical musical, *Runnin' Wild*, which was responsible for the '20s dance craze, the Charleston.

1947 Legendary blues artist and harmonica player Sonny Boy Williamson charted with "Shake the Boogie," reaching #4 R&B. By the time he was done, the Tennessee native had influenced generations of blues musicians including Howlin' Wolf, Muddy Waters, John Lee Hooker, Little Walter, the Yardbirds, and Junior Wells.

1948 James Johnson, known as Rick James (and the king of punk funk), was born in Buffalo, NY. Starting with a Canadian group called the Minah Birds (including a youthful Neil Young), James went on to have twelve pop and twenty-seven R&B hits as an artist while writing and producing Top 5 smashes for Eddie Murphy ("Party All the Time") and the Mary Jane Girls ("In My House").

1963 The Dreamlovers, who backed up Chubby Checker on most of his hits and who scored their own Top 10 single with "When We Get Married," performed on Dick Clark's *American Bandstand*.

1968 In the '50s, a two-sided hit was a common occurrence though it had all but vanished in the highly competitive '60s until Dionne Warwick pulled it off with "I Say a Little Prayer," which peaked at #4 pop and #8 R&B. Its flip, "(Theme From) The Valley of the Dolls" reached #2 pop and #13 R&B. Warwick recorded the film song at the request of the movie's female lead, Barbara Parkins.

1972 Aretha Franklin sang "Take My Hand, Precious Lord" at the funeral of her mentor and old friend Mahalia Jackson in Chicago.

1992 Vanessa Williams soared onto the Top 100 with "Save the Best for Last." It was her biggest hit, reaching #1 both pop and R&B. Nine years earlier, Vanessa became the first black woman to win the Miss America pageant.

February

2

#1 Song 1959: "Smoke Gets in Your Eyes," the Platters

Born: Edward "Sonny" Stitt, 1924; Wilbert "Red" Prysock, 1926; Clarence Quick (the Dell-Vikings), 1937

1951 B.B. King reached #1 R&B with his 78, "3 O'Clock Blues." It was his eighth single release and first charter. Born Riley King, he got his nickname when he was a deejay on WDIA in Memphis: When the stations' publicist called him the Beale Street Blues Boy, which later became just Blues Boy and later still, B.B. Playing piano on the record was the man who discovered him, Ike Turner.

1956 The Coasters signed to Atco Records and went on to have nineteen hits in fifteen years.

1956 The Soul Stirrers featuring Sam Cooke (formerly of the Highway Q.C.'s) recorded what would become their biggest gospel single, "Touch the Hem of His Garment."

1963 Bobby "Blue" Bland hit the R&B chart with both sides of his newest release. "Call on Me," would eventually reach #6 (#22 pop) while the B-side, "That's the Way Love Is" made it to #1 for two weeks (#33 pop). Over the previous five years, Bland and his band played more than three hundred shows a year.

1994 "To think, I've been doing this for thirty fucking years," Diana Ross reflected while performing at MIDEM '94 in Cannes, France where she received the Commander in the Order of Arts and Letters award from the French Minister of Culture.

Bobby "Blue" Bland

February

#1 R&B Song 1958: "Get a Job," the Silhouettes

Born: Lil Harding Armstrong, 1898; Mabel Mercer, 1900; Varetta Dillard, 1933; Johnny "Guitar" Watson, 1935; David Lershey (the Dell-Vikings), 1937; Johnny Bristol, 1939; Charlie James (the Cleftones), 1940; Dennis Edwards (the Temptations), 1943

1928 Chicago's legendary Regal Theater opened. A showcase for the top black acts in blues, gospel, jazz, and R&B, the Regal often had seven shows a day including a feature film. The venue seated 3,500 and cost adults fifty cents and kids fifteen cents admission.

1937 The Mills Brothers recorded the hit "Pennies From Heaven."

1958 The Blossoms, a girl group of professional backup singers who had worked with literally hundreds of artists—including Elvis Presley, Paul Anka, Dionne Warwick, Bobby Darin, the Beach Boys, the Mamas & the Papas—finally released their own single, "Have Faith in Me." When it didn't chart, they went back to the lucrative world of session singing.

1958 Known as "the day the music died," the Big Bopper, Buddy Holly, and Ritchie Valens crashed in a light plane while leaving Mason City, IA, for a performance. The Big Bopper (J. P. Richardson), known for his hit "Chantilly Lace," convinced musician Waylon Jennings to give up his seat on the aircraft, since he wanted to quickly see a doctor about his bad cold rather then remain on the drafty tour bus that kept breaking down.

1968 Otis Redding's "(Sitting on) The Dock of the Bay" charted, rising to #1 R&B (three weeks) and #1 pop (four weeks). The posthumously-issued 45 would sell more than a million copies and even reach #3 in England.

1968 Sam & Dave charted with "I Thank You," reaching #4 R&B and #9 pop. It was their seventh Top 10 R&B hit in two years.

1968 The Supremes were so big in England that a performance they made in a London club the month before was recorded and aired tonight as a British TV special called *The Supremes Live at the Talk of the Town*.

February

#1 R&B Song 1989: "Can You Stand the Rain," New Edition

Born: Bernie West (the Five Keys), 1930; Florence LaRue (the Fifth Dimension), 1944

1950 The Robins' "Double Crossing Blues" charted, reaching #1 R&B with Little Esther (Phillips) singing lead. The record topped the charts for nine weeks. The group originally called themselves the Four Bluebirds and went on to become the nucleus of the Coasters.

1954 The Drifters recorded "Honey Love" (#1 R&B, #21 pop), their first single at Fulton Recording Studio in New York City along with their legendary versions of "White Christmas," "Bells of St. Mary's," and the forerunner of "The Twist," "Whatcha Gonna Do" (#2 R&B).

1956 James Brown and the Famous Flames recorded their now legendary first single, "Please, Please, Please" at King/Federal Studios in Cincinnati, OH, launching Brown's career.

1966 The Jimi Hendrix Experience debut single peaked at #6 on the British charts. The recording never made the American hit lists and it would be more than a year before Hendrix made the charts again.

1977 The Pointer Sisters performed on Dick Clark's twenty-fifth anniversary edition of *American Bandstand*.

1998 Dionne Warwick performed at New York's Apollo Theater.

Jimi Hendrix

February

#1 R&B Song 1983: "Outstanding," the Gap Band

Born: Barrett Strong, 1941; Ann Sexton, 1950; Bobby Brown, 1969

1941 Barrett Strong was born in Mississippi. Introduced to Berry Gordy by Jackie Wilson, Strong had Motown's first hit with "Money" (#2 R&B). Strong later paired with Norman Whitfield to write a slew of hits for the Temptations, including "Papa Was a Rolling Stone," "Just My Imagination," and "Cloud Nine."

1957 The Platters played Ben Maksik's Town & Country Club over a thirteen-day period after returning from a tour of Australia and the Far East. Despite eleven huge hits, this was the first time they were performing in the New York area.

1960 Jesse Belvin, Jackie Wilson, Little Willie John, and Arthur Prysock performed at the Robinson Auditorium in Little Rock, AK. As was the "custom" at the time, there were two shows, the early for blacks and the second for whites. After the white band didn't show, Jackie Wilson refused to perform and stories circulated that the acts had to quickly retreat from Little Rock.

1960 The Cadillacs, Bobby Day, Big Maybelle, Bo Diddley, and others performed at Alan Freed's revue at the Apollo Theater.

1964 Twelve-year-old Stevie Wonder performed on *The Ed Sullivan Show*. "Little Stevie" (Steveland Judkins) was inspired by the music of Ray Charles as a child and was proficient on harmonica, piano, and drums by the age of seven and writing songs at the age of eight. He was signed to Motown Records' Tamla affiliate when he was only ten.

1977 The Bar-Kays charted R&B with "Too Hot to Stop (Part 1)" reaching #8. The funk band out of Memphis amassed thirty-two hits through 1995, starting with "Soul Finger" in 1967.

1983 The newly-formed New Edition made their New York performance debut at the world famous Copacabana. The group was put together by manager/producer Maurice Starr to be an '80s version of the Jackson 5.

1998 Thirty-four years after his first appearance on *The Ed Sullivan Show* launched his national recognition, Stevie Wonder performed for President Bill Clinton and Britain's Prime Minister Tony Blair at the White House.

February

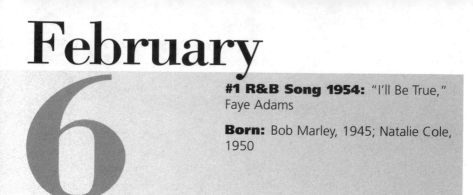

#1 R&B Song 1954: "I'll Be True," Faye Adams

Born: Bob Marley, 1945; Natalie Cole, 1950

1954 The Drifters' "Such a Night" (#2 R&B) and the Ravens' "September Song" were released.

1960 One day after performing in Little Rock, AK, with Jackie Wilson, Arthur Prysock, and Little Willie John, Jesse Belvin was killed in a car crash along with his wife and driver on the way to their next performance.

1961 Chubby Checker & the Dreamlovers charted R&B on their way to #1 and their second million-seller with "Pony Time." The song was a revision of Clarence "Pinetop" Smith's "Boogie Woogie" in 1928, and Checker's version beat out a competing recording by Don Covay & the Goodtimers that reached only #60 pop. The Dreamlovers were never credited on the label and since Checker was considered a solo act (even though the prominent harmonies of the group were evident on all his hits), they are relegated to a footnote in history rather than full participants in the hit's success.

1965 Little Anthony & the Imperials' classic "Hurt So Bad" charted, en route to #10 pop.

1971 Marvin Gaye's critically acclaimed "What's Goin' On" was released. It reached #2 pop and #1 R&B.

1971 The Jackson 5's "Mama's Pearl" charted, reaching #2 pop and R&B. It was kept from the top spot by the Osmonds' "One Bad Apple," which was offered to Motown for the Jacksons but rejected as sounding too adolescent.

1988 Public Enemy, one of rap music's most contentious acts, made their chart debut with "Bring the Noise." The group, in keeping with their image, would soon perform at New York's Rikers Island Prison. One of their managers referred to them as "the black panthers of rap."

1990 A national holiday was proclaimed in Jamaica to commemorate the birth of Bob Marley.

February

7

#1 R&B Song 1976: "Turning Point," Tyrone Davis

Born: Eubie Blake, 1883; Wilma Lee, 1921; King Curtis (Curtis Ousley), 1934; Earl King, 1934

1883 Ragtime piano legend Eubie Blake was born in Baltimore. In 1915, while playing with Joe Porter's Serenaders, he met Noble Sissle and by 1921 the twosome had written the play *Shuffle Along*, the first all-black Broadway musical. Blake died on February 12, 1983, five days after his 100th birthday.

1953 Lloyd Price charted with "Ain't It a Shame" reaching #4 R&B, his fourth Top 5 hit in a row. Two years later, Fats Domino would take the tune to the Top 10 on the pop charts.

1953 The Buccaneers' "Dear Ruth" was issued by two students working out of a storefront in Philadelphia. The 69-cent single is an $800 collectible today.

1964 Ben E. King performed on *Ready, Steady, Go!*, the British TV equivalent of *American Bandstand*.

1984 Michael Jackson was entered into the *Guinness Book of World Records* as the album *Thriller* passed 25 million copies sold.

1987 The Robert Cray Band charted on their way to #22 pop with their blues/rock-styled single, "Smoking Gun." Cray and company would chart pop three times but surprisingly would never reach the R&B hit list.

1989 A Georgia State legislative representative introduced a bill to make Little Richard's "Tutti Frutti" the state's official rock song.

1994 Gangsta rapper Dr. Dre won the Best Artist, Rap/Hip Hop award at the American Music Awards twenty-first annual ceremonies in Los Angeles.

Eubie Blake

February

8

#1 R&B Song 1975: "Happy People," the Temptations

Born: Blues guitarist Alonzo "Lonnie" Johnson, 1889; Floyd Dixon, 1929

1960 The Biggest Show of Stars 1960 package tour landed in the Memorial Coliseum in Greenville, SC, starring Clyde McPhatter, the Crests, the Isley Brothers, and the Clovers, among others.

1975 Earth, Wind & Fire charted on their way to #1 with "Shinning Star." It would become their only chart topper, both pop and R&B. The group would go on to have eight #1s R&B in a career spanning four decades. Maurice White, leader of the band, was originally in the Ramsey Lewis Trio.

1986 Billy Ocean's "When the Going Gets Tough, the Tough Get Going" reached #1 in Britain and eventually #2 pop and #6 R&B stateside. The song was from the film *The Jewel of the Nile* starring Michael Douglas and Kathleen Turner.

1997 Erykah Badu topped the R&B charts today with her single, "On and On." She would go on to have six more charters through 2002. The Dallas vocalist was influenced by such artists as Rick James, Teena Marie, Marvin Gaye, and Chaka Khan.

Erykah Badu

February

#1 R&B Song 1952: "3 O'Clock Blues,"
B.B. King

Born: Barbara Lewis, 1943; Major Harris
(the Delfonics), 1947

1957 The Dell-Vikings classic "Come Go with Me" was released today, reaching #4 pop and #2 R&B.

1959 Lloyd Price's "Where Were You (On Our Wedding Day)" was issued, eventually reaching #4 R&B and #23 pop. At the same time, Price was on tour with Little Anthony & the Imperials, the Coasters, and Clyde McPhatter in the Biggest Show of Stars 1959 tour.

1962 The Vibrations, Bobby Lewis, the Ronettes, the Capris, and Tommy Hunt (the headliner) and his old group the Flamingos performed at the Apollo Theater in New York.

1963 Ruby (Nash) and the Romantics' day came when "Our Day Will Come" charted, storming to #1. It was their first of eight hits through 1965.

1979 Still a fledgling act, Prince performed at a showcase in Minneapolis. Reaction to his openly sexual stage routine was decidedly mixed.

1985 Patti LaBelle charted R&B with "New Attitude" from the movie *Beverly Hills Cop*, reaching #3 R&B and #17 pop.

1990 Diana Ross performed at Detroit's Fox Theater, grossing more than $700,000 for three shows in three days.

1991 Flavor Flav of Public Enemy was arrested, charged, and eventually convicted of assault on his girlfriend and mother of their three children. He would get only a thirty-day sentence.

February

10

#1 R&B Song 1951: "Somebody's Gotta Go," Cootie Williams & His Orchestra

Born: Roberta Flack, 1939; Jimmy Merchant (Frankie Lymon & the Teenagers), 1940

1951 Ray Charles had his first chart 45 under his own name when "Baby Let Me Hold Your Hand" entered the R&B hit list, rising to #5.

1958 The Chesters' debut, "The Fires Burn No More," was released. The group went on to become Little Anthony & the Imperials.

1958 The Shirelles (originally called the Poquellos) had their first single issued today. The song, "I Met Him on a Sunday," reached #49 and was also their first of twenty-six hits over the next nine years.

1968 The Four Tops became the first black artists to reach #1 on the British album charts when their compilation of greatest hits took the top spot today. The historic event didn't last long. A week later, the Supremes would do the same thing.

1979 Stevie Wonder, Smokey Robinson, Diana Ross, and Marvin Gaye's tribute to Berry Gordy's father, "Pops, We Love You," peaked at #59 pop.

1994 Snoop Doggy Dog performed at Leicester Square's Equinox in London. His British touring debut was spoiled when he was kicked out of his hotel when management learned of his murder charge. Things got worse when *The Daily Star* newspaper announced in bold front-page type, "Kick This Evil Bastard Out."

1996 The pop charts were ruled by Babyface as four of the Top 20 singles on the Top 100 were written and produced by him, including Whitney Houston's "Exhale (Shoop Shoop)" (#2), Mary J. Blige's "Not Gon' Cry" (#6), Brandy's "Sittin' Up in My Room" (#13), and TLC's "Diggin' on You" (#19).

February

#1 R&B Song 1966: "Are You Lonely for Me," Freddie Scott

Born: John Mills (the Mills Brothers), 1889; Raoul Cita (the Harptones), 1928; Brandy (Brandy Norwood), 1979

1956 The first rock 'n' roll stage show in the Bronx, NY, was held at the Opera House Movie Theater featuring the Cadillacs, the Heartbeats and the Valentines.

1964 The Chiffons were the opening act on the Beatles' historic first American concert at Washington Coliseum, Washington, DC.

1985 Sade's *Diamond Life* won the Best British Album, Prince won Best International Solo Artist, and *Purple Rain* won Best Film Soundtrack at the fourth annual Brit Awards at London's Grosvenor House Hotel

1989 Paula Abdul's debut album *Straight Up* topped the national charts today. Not bad for a woman who began as a choreographer for the Los Angeles Lakers (for $50 per game) while still a freshman at Cal-State Northridge College.

1997 Erykah Badu's debut album, *Baduizm*, was released, bringing her Billie Holiday/Dinah Washington–styled vocals to the masses. Within three weeks the album would chart on its way to becoming #1 R&B.

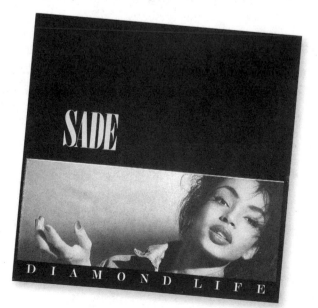

February

#1 R&B Song 1955: "Pledging My Love," Johnny Ace

Born: Gene McDaniels, 1935

1955 Fats Domino charted with "Thinking of You," eventually reaching #14 R&B which would have been pretty good for most acts but it was the first Fats Domino single to not make the Top 10 in twelve tries. To make up for it, Domino went on another streak of fourteen straight Top 10 R&B hits starting with "Don't You Know" and ending with "Blue Monday," which gave him twenty-five of his first twenty-six singles in the Top 10.

1957 The Coasters recorded their two-sided hits "Searchin' " (#3 pop, #1 R&B) and "Youngblood" (#8 pop, #1 R&B), at Hollywood Recorders in Los Angeles.

1960 Little Anthony & the Imperials, Chuck Berry, Baby Washington, and the Mello-Kings performed at New York's Apollo Theater. The Mello-Kings were white, but they were being booked at black venues because their recordings, like the rock 'n' roll standard "Tonite, Tonite," sounded like the work of a black group.

1966 Stevie Wonder reached # 1 for five weeks and #3 pop with "Uptight (Everything Is Alright)" and #14 in his British chart debut where he would become one of the most popular American artists of all time, charting fifty-four times through 1991. Wonder once said: "People at school told me I couldn't make it, that I'd end up making potholders."

1993 Maxi Priest, Cutty Ranks, and the Wailers performed at the Bob Marley Day Festival tribute at Long Beach, CA's Long Beach Arena.

1997 Michael Jackson's wife Debbie gave birth to a son named Prince Michael Jackson. The *National Enquirer* paid $2 million for rights to photos of "Prince Michael"—and that was just for North America.

2000 The tenor saxophonist who gained fame singing the blues in his coffin, Screamin' Jay Hawkins, died in Paris, France. Known for his hit, "I Put a Spell on You," he passed away at age seventy.

2001 Leroy Sanders, bass singer for the '50s groups the Upfronts, the Pelicans, and the Cubans, died. When Sanders and other members of the Cubans were chosen to sing backup for Carl Burnett on the hit "Those Oldies But Goodies," the group became Little Caesar & the Romans. Sanders also performed with various members of the Drifters, Platters, and Coasters.

February

#1 R&B Song 1960: "Shop Around,"
the Miracles

Born: King Floyd, 1945

1943 Charlie Barnet and His Orchestra charted with the often-covered "That Old Black Magic," reaching #2 R&B and #15 pop, and making it one of music history's most popular versions.

1954 The Vocaleers' collectors' classic "Will You Be True" ($300) and the Charmers' "The Beating of My Heart" ($800) were issued today.

1965 LaVern Baker charted with "Fly Me to the Moon," reaching #31 R&B. It was the last solo hit for Little Miss Sharecropper, as she was known, though she did have one more chart single in a duet with Jackie Wilson on "Think Twice" (#37 R&B). In all, she had twenty-one hits starting in 1955 and was considered one of the finest female R&B singers of the '50s.

1965 Junior Walker & the All-Stars charted with "Shotgun," eventually reaching #1 R&B for four weeks and #4 pop. The song came about when the band, playing a benefit in Benton Harbor, MI, noticed a few teens doing a new dance called "the Shotgun." That night in his motel room, Walker wrote the song to match the dance.

1978 Al Green Day was announced by the city of Los Angeles as he performed at the Dorothy Chandler Pavilion. Most artists given a day in their honor usually have that honor bestowed by their hometown. Green was from Forest City, AK, but apparently, Los Angeles decided to adopt him.

1984 Donna Summer's remake of the Drifters' 1960 hit "There Goes My Baby" peaked at #21 pop and #20 R&B.

1993 Dr. Dre's (formerly of N.W.A.) debut solo album *The Chronic* reached #3 pop with new rapper Snoop Doggy Dog performing several raps on the record. The twenty-two-year-old Snoop (Calvin Broadus) had already had a career's worth of destructive lifestyle anchored by his teen membership in the Long Beach Insane Crips gang, along with jail time for selling cocaine and gun possession. Still, Snoop could really rap.

February

#1 R&B Song 1976: "Inseparable," Natalie Cole

Born: Gregory Hines, 1946

1953 Legendary R&B entrepreneur and producer George Goldner formed the RAMA label. Its first release was the 5 Budds' "I Was Such a Fool" ($500).

1961 The Platters sued their label, Mercury Records, after amassing thirty-two hits because the label refused to issue singles not sung by lead Tony Williams, who left the group in 1960. As the debate raged, Mercury released twelve more 45s through 1964, all old previously-recorded sides.

1964 The Crystals performed on the British teen show, *Ready, Steady, Go!*, which was the English equivalent of *Soul Train* and *American Bandstand* rolled into one.

1987 The Impressions charted with "Can't Wait Til Tomorrow," reaching only #91 R&B. It was their fiftieth single to hit the R&B lists in an illustrious recording career that spanned twenty-nine years. The group is performing to this day.

1994 Lenny Kravitz was awarded the Best International Male Artist trophy at the thirteenth Brit Awards in London.

1996 Prince finally gave up the bachelor's life for the hand of a dancer named Mayte García. The wedding in a Minneapolis church was on Valentine's Day.

1998 The Isley Brothers were honored at the twenty-ninth NAACP Image Awards in Pasadena, CA, with the Hall of Fame Award.

The Isley Brothers

February

#1 R&B Song 1969: "Can I Change My Mind," Tyrone Davis

Born: James "Kokomo" Arnold, 1901; Brian Holland, 1941

1954 Joe Turner recorded the classic "Shake, Rattle & Roll," six months before Bill Haley's hit version.

1957 LaVern Baker began a U.S. tour with Chuck Berry, Fats Domino, Clyde McPhatter, the Five Keys, the Moonglows, Charles Brown, the Schoolboys, Ann Cole, and the Five Satins in Irving Feld's Greatest Show of 1957 rock package. The extravaganza would run through May 5 starting in Pittsburgh, PA, for eighty straight days and nights.

1961 Jackie Wilson was shot in his apartment in New York City by a female fan named Juanita Jones, apparently starved for the star's attention. In wrestling the gun from her, Wilson was hit in the stomach. Though he survived the ordeal, doctors were never able to remove the difficult-to-reach bullet.

1963 The Exciters, the Jive Five, Little Anthony, the Orlons, Jackie Wilson, the "5" Royales, and the Debonairs performed at the Syria Mosque in Pittsburgh, PA.

1964 As if he really needed the endorsement, Cassius Clay stated after defeating Sonny Liston for the world heavyweight championship that along with Cassius being the greatest, "Sam Cooke is the world's greatest rock 'n' roll singer, the greatest singer in the world."

1969 Vickie Jones was arrested on fraud charges after impersonating Aretha Franklin at a concert in Fort Myers, FL. Apparently the charade was impressive. No one in the audience asked for their money back.

1979 Donna Summer won the Best R&B Vocal Performance, Female category for "Last Dance" at the twenty-first Grammy Awards. George Benson won the Best R&B Vocal Performance, Male category for "On Broadway." He started out as a singer/guitarist prodigy who at ten years of age recorded for RCA's Groove Records division, cutting four songs including "It Should Have Been Me."

1993 "This is the crowning achievement of my career and they want to give it to me secretly. It's like I'm in the kitchen doing all the cooking and the waiters get all the credit. I cried…I've been waiting so long." This was the reaction from Little Richard upon hearing he was being given a Lifetime Achievement Grammy but would have to accept it at a dinner the night before. (See February 24).

47

February

16

#1 Song 1959: "Stagger Lee," Lloyd Price

Born: Bill Doggett, 1916; Otis Blackwell, 1932; Herman "Sonny" Chaney (the Jaguars), 1939; James Ingram, 1957

1956 Frankie Lymon & the Teenagers' second hit, "I Want You to Be My Girl" (#13 pop, #3 R&B), was recorded. Its B-side, "Who Can Explain?," reached #7 R&B.

1957 Ray Charles hit the R&B charts with "Ain't That Love," an eventual #8 hit. It became his seventeenth Top 10 R&B hit in a row. Ironically, his next single, "Swanee River Rock" would fail to reach the Top 10 (#14), but became his first pop chart single in November, reaching #34.

1959 The Coasters charted on the way to #2 R&B and pop with the novelty classic, "Charlie Brown." As big a hit as it was, the million seller was the first of four singles in a row to not make #1. The chart toppers before it were "Yakety Yak," "Young Blood," and "Searchin'."

1962 Pioneering vocalist Louis Jordan performed at the Ali Baba Club in St. Petersburg, FL. Meanwhile, the Edsels ("Rama Lama Ding Dong"), the Corsairs ("Smokey Places"), the Sensations ("Let Me In"), the Crystals ("There's No Other"), Bobby "Blue" Bland, and Erma Franklin (sister of Aretha) played the Apollo in New York.

1964 The Crystals embarked on a British tour backed by Manfred Mann.

1980 Legendary vocalist Charley Pride bounced onto the country charts with "Honky Tonk Blues," reaching #1. It was his twenty-third of twenty-nine #1 country smashes in a career as the most successful black country entertainer. Pride started out as a baseball player for the Memphis Red Sox in the Negro American League during the mid-'50s. The Mississippian was named Male Vocalist of the Year in 1971 and 1972 by the Country Music Association.

Charley Pride

February

#1 Song 1962: "Duke of Earl," Gene Chandler & the Dukays

Born: Orville "Hoppy" Jones (the Ink Spots), 1905; Tommy Edwards, 1922; Bobby Lewis, 1933; Mickey McGill (the Dells), 1937

1958 The Drifters, the Silhouettes, and the Dubs appeared at Houston's Municipal Auditorium for their Teenage Record Hop.

1958 Little Richard's "Good Golly Miss Molly" charted, reaching #10 pop and #4 R&B. It was Richard's fourteenth and last R&B Top 10 smash. Richard's piano introduction was inspired by the Jackie Brenston's 1951 R&B hit, "Rocket 88," which many historians consider the first rock 'n' roll record.

1958 The Monotones' classic rocker "Book of Love" (Mascot $225) was released.

1958 Chuck Berry's "Sweet Little 16" charted on its way to #2 pop.

1961 Brook Benton headlined at the Apollo Theater in New York City. Aretha Franklin, a newcomer to R&B, was the opening act.

1962 The Platters charted with "It's Magic," reaching only #91 pop, while becoming their last of thirty-five hits on the Top 100 while with Mercury Records. At the same time, the group toured Poland, becoming the first American vocal group to perform behind the Iron Curtain without a government subsidy. Nate Nelson, former lead of the Flamingos, also joined the group, who stated they would not perform in Atlanta, GA, until audiences became desegregated.

1973 The Jackson 5 charted in England with "Doctor My Eyes," reaching #9. The song was a cover of the Jackson Brown hit but was never issued in America.

1980 Muddy Waters won his sixth Grammy in nine years; all were in the same category, Best Ethnic & Traditional Recording.

1990 Actress/singer/rapper Queen Latifah made her chart debut with "Ladies First," reaching #64 R&B. Through 1998, she would manage to hit the charts fifteen times, though she was spending more time acting in films than recording.

February

18

#1 Song 1956: "The Great Pretender," the Platters

Born: Herman Santiago (Frankie Lymon & the Teenagers), 1941; Irma Thomas, 1941; Randy Crawford, 1952; Dr. Dre (Andre Young), 1965

1942 The Mills Brothers recorded what would become their biggest hit, "Paper Doll." Released in May, it took fourteen months to reach #1, but when it did, the single stayed there for twelve weeks, selling 6 million copies.

1950 Joe Liggins & His Honeydrippers charted with "Rag Mop," reaching #4 R&B. It was their eleventh of fourteen hits from 1945 to 1951. Their first hit, "The Honey Dripper," is the longest #1 all-time R&B hit, having spent eighteen weeks on top of the charts.

1950 Singer/songwriter/pianist Nellie Lutcher charted with "For You My Love," reaching #8 R&B. The last of the songstress's eleven hits, the song was a duet with Nat King Cole.

1956 The Romancers' "I Still Remember" ($75) and the Jayhawks' "Counting My Teardrops" ($200) were released. The Romancers' lead was young Bobby Freeman, later of "Do You Wanna Dance" fame. The Jayhawks went on to become the Vibrations.

1956 Frankie Lymon & the Teenagers' first single, "Why Do Fools Fall in Love" charted, reaching #6 pop and #1 (five weeks) R&B. The quintet had at various times called themselves the Premiers, the Earth Angels, the Coup De Villes, and the Ermines before becoming the Teenagers.

1956 The Flamingos, probably the finest vocal group of all time, made their chart debut with "I'll Be Home," reaching #5 R&B. They began recording in 1953 and though they only had eleven pop hits and nine R&B charters through 1970, many music historians believe their harmony and vocal style were without peer.

1984 Cameo hit the charts for the twenty-first time in seven years with what would become their biggest hit, "She's Strange" (#1 R&B for four weeks).

2001 Ed Wells, baritone and songwriter for the Six Teens, passed away. Wells formed the sextet singing group in Los Angeles, combining three teen girls and three teen boys from two Catholic schools, and wrote their first hit, "A Casual Look."

February

#1 R&B Song 1949: "Boogie Chillen," John Lee Hooker

Born: William McClain (the Cleftones), 1938; William "Smokey" Robinson (the Miracles), 1940; Bobby Rogers (the Miracles), 1940

1944 The Five Red Caps' debut chart 78, "I Learned a Lesson I'll Never Forget," hit the R&B list reaching #3 and #14 pop.

1949 Blind vocalist Al Hibbler hit the R&B charts with "Lover, Come Back to Me," reaching #9.

1955 Etta James charted with "The Wallflower" (sometimes called "Roll with Me Henry"), reaching #1 R&B for four weeks. The song was an answer record to Hank Ballard's "Work with Me, Annie," while Georgia Gibbs copied James's version for a pop version called "Dance with Me, Henry." James would go on to have thirty R&B hits with her last one being a cover of Big Brother and the Holding Company's (a.k.a. Janis Joplin and band) "Piece of My Heart."

1958 The Miracles' first single, "Got a Job," was issued on End Records. The song was an answer record to the Silhouettes' #1 hit, "Get a Job." Though the 45 did not chart, it was the start of the group's monumental career, which included forty-six pop and forty-eight R&B hits through 1978. It was also lead singer Smokey Robinson's eighteenth birthday.

1960 Dr. Jive's Rhythm & Blues Revue featuring the Flamingos, the Hollywood Flames, Barrett Strong, Johnny Nash, Nappy Brown, and Tiny Topsy took over the Apollo Theater in New York City for a raucous good-time show.

1960 Jimmy Jones, riding the charts with his new hit, "Handy Man," performed at the Uptown Theater in Philadelphia.

1974 Al Green received the award for Favorite Album Soul/R&B category at the Inaugural American Music Awards in Hollywood, CA.

1983 James Ingram and Patti Austin's "Baby, Come to Me" reached #1 on the pop charts after taking eighteen weeks to get there.

1966 The Isley Brothers' classic "This Old Heart of Mine" charted, reaching #12 pop (#6 R&B). Ron Isley would remake the song in a duet with Rod Stewart twenty-four years later, rising to#10 pop.

1994 The Jackson clan came together for the much-publicized Jackson Family Honors show at the MGM Grand in Las Vegas. Michael Jackson appeared but did not sing, much to the consternation of many paying customers. Dionne Warwick took time out from her Psychic Friends Network (where she was reportedly making seven figures a year) to appear with the flock.

February

#1 R&B Song 1943: "Apollo Jump," Lucky Millinder & His Orchestra

Born: Nancy Wilson, 1937

1954 The Flamingos' collectible, "Plan for Love" ($2,000) and the Clovers' "Little Mama" ($50) were released.

1956 Detroit's Riviera Theater hosted a show featuring Frankie Lymon & the Teenagers, the Five Keys, and the Jewels.

1960 Jimi Hendrix (originally named Johnny Allen Hendrix by his mother), a member of a local Seattle band called the Rocking Kings, performed at his first documented show at Washington Hall.

1991 B.B. King won the Best Traditional Blues Recording trophy for *Live at San Quentin* and MC Hammer won Best R&B Song and Best Rap Solo Performance awards at the thirty-third annual Grammy Awards ceremonies at New York's Radio City Music Hall for "U Can't Touch This." Upon hearing of the nomination from his publisher, sampled writer Rick James refused to go to the ceremonies, saying, "Every time I'm nominated for somethin' I lose. Why don't you go in my place?" Jay Warner did and Rick won.

1991 Chaka Khan and Ray Charles won Best R&B Performance by a Duo or Group with Vocal at the thirty-third annual Grammy Awards. The song was "I'll Be Good to You," and it was Charles's eleventh Grammy. Luther Vandross earned Best R&B Vocal Performance, Male honors.

1992 Jodeci peaked at #18 pop and #1 R&B with their debut album, *Forever My Lady*. All three of the doo-wop/R&B/new jack swing group's albums would reach #1 R&B over the next four years.

1999 Lenny Kravitz's "Fly Away" reached #1 in England thanks to its placement in a Peugeot car commercial that ran extensively throughout the British isles.

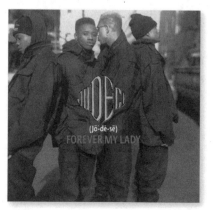

February

#1 R&B Song 1948: "I Love You, Yes I Do," Bull Moose Jackson & His Buffalo Bearcats

Born: Nina Simone, 1933; Bobby Charles (Robert Charles Guidry), 1938

1961 The Shirelles appeared on *American Bandstand* singing "Dedicated to the One I Love" and "Will You Love Me Tomorrow?"

1983 NBC-TV's *Late Night with David Letterman* featured an appearance by Sly Stone.

1987 Aretha Franklin charted in a duet with George Michael on "I Knew You Were Waiting." It was her first #1 in twenty years ("Respect," 1967).

1987 Ben E King's "Stand by Me" reached #1 in England after being used in a commercial for Levi's jeans. It was the third time the King classic had charted in Britain and the first time in almost twenty-six years. The #2 record at the time was Percy Sledge's "When a Man Loves a Woman," which not coincidentally was there due in great part to being in the same series of Levi's commercials.

1990 Chuck Berry's rock standard "Roll Over, Beethoven" was inducted into the National Academy of Recording Arts & Sciences (NARAS) Hall of Fame at the thirty-second annual Grammy Awards. As if that wasn't enough of an accolade for the icon, his *Chuck Berry—The Chess Box* earned Best Historical Album honors for its producer, Andy McKaie, of Universal Music. Also, John Lee Hooker's duet with Bonnie Raitt won for Best Traditional Blues Recording

1992 Natalie Cole performed at the famed Apollo Theater in New York City. She then donated her receipts to help save the financially strapped landmark.

1992 The Four Tops and the Temptations played at the Fox Theater in Detroit. What had started as a one-off reunion for Motown's twenty-fifth anniversary was so well received that the two groups began to tour together.

February

#1 R&B Song 1975: "Lady Marmalade," LaBelle

Born: Bandleader Big Al Sears, 1910; Ernie K. Doe, 1936; Bobby Hendricks (the Drifters), 1938; Robert Edwards (the Intruders), 1942

1951 The Clovers recorded "Don't You Know I Love You," their first of twenty-one R&B hits over the next nine years. Written by Atlantic Records president Ahmet Ertegun, he demo'd the song by singing into a Times Square recording booth microphone, since he could neither play an instrument nor write music.

1963 LaVern Baker headlined a show at Chicago's Regal Theater.

1964 A year and a half after their debut #1 hit, "Green Onions," Booker T. & the M.G.'s finally had their second chart single with "Mo-Onions," but it wasn't spicy enough for the hit list, only rising to #97 pop.

1969 David Ruffin, former lead of the Temptations, began his solo career with his chart debut, "My Whole World Ended (The Moment You Left Me)," which reached #2 R&B and #9 pop. He would eventually have sixteen more R&B charters through 1988.

1976 Florence Ballard, the original lead singer of the Supremes, died of a heart attack nine years after being forced out of the group. Though she sang on numerous hits, including nine #1 singles, Ballard passed away penniless, while living on welfare with her three children. The eulogy at her funeral was given by Reverend C.L. Franklin, Aretha Franklin's father, and the pall bearers were the Four Tops and Marv Johnson. She was only thirty-two.

1992 TLC charted with their debut recording "Ain't 2 Proud 2 Beg," reaching #2 R&B and #6 pop. The record consisted of samples from five acts including Bob James, James Brown, Kool & the Gang, Silver Convention, and Average White Band. One wonders if there was any room left for anything original.

TLC

February 23

#1 R&B Song 1946: "Buzz Me,"
Louis Jordan & His Tympany 5

Born: Blues guitarist Johnny
Winter, 1944; King Sun, 1967

1946 The Delta Rhythm Boys made their pop-chart debut with what would become their biggest hit (#17), "Just a-Sittin' and a-Rockin.' "

1952 The Mello-Moods, a dandy doo-wop group if there ever was one, charted with "Where Are You? (Now That I Need You)," reaching #7 R&B. A mint copy of this classic today would go for $5,000.

1957 The original version of "Little Darling," by the Gladiolas, was released (#41 pop, #11 R&B). Three years later the group would have the #1 record in America as Maurice Williams & the Zodiacs, singing "Stay."

1963 The Chiffons' mega-hit, "He's So Fine," charted today. It became the first vocal-group #1 in rock history to be produced by another vocal group, the Tokens. The record would remain #1 for four weeks.

1983 After twenty-one years of solo recording, Marvin Gaye finally got a Grammy when "Sexual Healing" won him the Best R&B Male Vocal Performance at the Grammy's twenty-fifth awards ceremony. Also finally winning after seventeen nominations was Lionel Richie as Best Pop Vocal Performance, Male for the song "Truly."

1989 Isaac Hayes was arrested and put in an Atlanta jail for nonpayment of child support and alimony to the tune of $346,300.

1991 Whitney Houston reached #1 with "All the Man That I Need"—amazingly, her ninth chart topper in five years. Her formula of recording old hits continued to pay off, as the original version was by Sister Sledge in 1982.

1994 Dionne Warwick attended a federal hearing by a Judiciary Juvenile Justice Sub-Committee in Washington, DC, which labeled gangsta rap as "pornography."

February

24

1967 Martin Luther King Jr. presented Aretha Franklin with the Southern Christian leadership Award at Cobo Hall in Detroit when the city declared it Aretha Franklin Day.

1973 Roberta Flack's "Killing Me Softly with His Song" topped the pop charts for the first of five weeks. Flack first heard the song as sung by Lori Lieberman on a TWA flight from Los Angeles to New York.

1978 Ray Charles performed "One of These Days" and a duet on "It's a Miracle" with Barry Manilow on *The Second Barry Manilow Special* TV show.

1982 James Ingram won a Grammy for Best Vocal R&B Performance, Male with his hit "One Hundred Ways." Of all the awards given out that night, his was the only one for an artist who never had an album out.

1987 Robert Cray performed with a collection of blues greats including B.B. King, Willie Dixon, Albert King, Dr. John, and others at the twenty-ninth annual Grammy Awards. He also won the Best Traditional Blues Recording category for the song "Showdown."

1993 L.A. Reid and Babyface received the Producer of the Year Award (which they had to share with Brian Eno and Daniel Lanois) at the thirty-fifth annual Grammy Awards in Los Angeles, mostly due to the success of Boyz II Men's "End of the Road" hit. The Boyz got their own award for "End" when they were named Best R&B Vocal Duo or Group. Meanwhile, Janet Jackson presented her brother Michael with the Grammy Legend Award.

1993 A justifiably disgruntled Little Richard stated at the Grammys, "I'm the innovator, I'm the emancipator, I'm the originator, I'm the architect of rock 'n' roll," when he was denied the opportunity to receive his award onstage. NARAS president Michael Greene, who told Richard there wasn't enough time during the telecast to make the presentation, *did* have enough time to make an incoherent, boring ten-minute speech himself.

1999 Sam Cooke was honored posthumously with the NARAS Lifetime Achievement Award at the forty-first annual Grammy Awards. Also honored were Smokey Robinson and Otis Redding, while Lauryn Hill received five Grammys including Best R&B Song and Best Female R&B Vocal Performance (for "Doo-wop (That Thing)"), Best New Artist, Album of the Year, and Best R&B album (for *The Miseducation of Lauryn Hill*).

February

#1 R&B Song 1984: "Encore,"
Cheryl Lynn

Born: Blues vocalist Ida Cox
(Ida Prather), 1896

1984 British jazz/R&B singer Sade charted in England with her debut "Your Love Is King," reaching #6. It would be almost a year before she would become known in America, but for a different song, "Smooth Operator."

1986 Dionne Warwick presented her cousin, Whitney Houston, with the Best Pop Vocal Performance, Female award at the twenty-eighth annual Grammys.

1992 Boyz II Men, who performed in their trademark '50s high-school matching garb and who would go on to be the most successful vocal group of the '90s, won the Best R&B Performance by a Duo or Group with Vocal category for their *Cooleyhighharmony* album at the thirty-fourth annual Grammy Awards at Radio City Music Hall, New York City. Natalie Cole, however, was the big winner, with Grammys for Record of the Year, Song of the Year, Traditional Pop Performance Album of the Year, and Best Engineered Album (nonclassical).

1992 James Brown and Muddy Waters each won the coveted Lifetime Achievement Award at the thirty-fourth annual Grammy Awards. Unfortunately for Waters, it was bestowed upon him almost nine years after he died.

1992 Tina Turner's British TV biopic, *The Girl from Nutbush*, aired on BBC1 in England.

1993 As if the previous year wasn't enough, James Brown was given the Lifetime Achievement Award at the fourth annual Rhythm & Blues Foundation Pioneer Awards in Los Angeles. The award was presented by MC Hammer. Also given pioneer awards that night were Floyd Dixon, Lowell Fulsom, Wilson Pickett, Carla Thomas, Little Anthony & the Imperials, Erskine Hawkins, and Martha & the Vandellas.

1997 Sade was arrested in Montego Bay, Jamaica for disorderly conduct, disobeying a policeman, and dangerous driving. In that particular incident she obviously was not a "smooth operator."

1999 Sarah Dash, Nona Hendryx, Cindy Birdsong, and Patricia Holt, better known as Patti LaBelle and the Bluebelles, appeared together for the first time in thirty-one years singing a stirring "You'll Never Walk Alone" at the Rhythm & Blues Foundation's Pioneer Awards in Los Angeles. The group was presented its award by five-time Grammy winner, Lauryn Hill.

February

26

#1 Song 1983: "Baby, Come to Me," Patti Austin & James Ingram

Born: Fats Domino (Antoine Domino Jr.), 1928; Erykah Badu (Erica Abi Wright), 1971

1983 Michael Jackson's *Thriller* album reached #1 and stayed there for thirty-seven weeks, selling more than 40 million copies. It was #1 in every western nation.

1985 Tina Turner won Record of the Year, Song of the Year, and Best Female Vocal Performance, all with the million seller, "What's Love Got to Do with It" at the twenty-seventh annual Grammys.

1985 "Chuck Berry is one of the most influential and creative innovators in the history of American popular music, a composer and performer whose talents inspired the elevation of rock 'n' roll to one of music's major art forms." Such was the tribute as Berry was honored by the twenty-seventh annual Grammy Awards NARAS committee when they bestowed upon him a Lifetime Achievement Award. Also that night, Jimmy Cliff became the first Jamaican artist to win a Grammy as the Best Reggae Recording category was instituted. He won for the song, "Reggae Night."

1990 Cornel Gunter of the Coasters was shot and killed while in his car in Las Vegas. He was scheduled to perform at the Lucky Lady Hotel that night.

1992 Aretha Franklin received the Lifetime Achievement Award and Bobby "Blue" Bland was honored at the Rhythm & Blues Foundation's third annual Pioneer Awards in New York.

1994 Toni Braxton's self-titled album reached #1 pop almost eight months after its first release. She was influenced by Chaka Khan, Stevie Wonder, Whitney Houston, and Quincy Jones.

1997 Soul divas Whitney Houston, Brandy, Mary, J. Blige, Toni Braxton, Aretha Franklin, Chaka Khan, and CeCe Winans sang a medley from *Waiting to Exhale* at the thirty-ninth annual Grammy Awards, held at New York's Madison Square Garden.

1998 The Five Satins were honored as pioneers at the Rhythm & Blues Foundation Awards in New York City. Gladys Knight & the Pips received a Lifetime Achievement Award (presented by Stevie Wonder) and the O'Jays received a Pioneer Award as presented by Gerald Levert, son of the group's lead singer, Eddie Levert.

February

#1 Song 1961: "Pony Time,"
Chubby Checker & the Dreamlovers

Born: Carl Anderson, 1945

1954 The Moonglows' magical "Secret Love" ($1,500) and the Royals' classic, "Work with Me, Annie," (#1 R&B) were issued. The Royals went on to become Hank Ballard & the Midnighters.

1961 Aretha Franklin made her pop chart debut with "Won't Be Long" on Columbia Records. It reached #76 and became the first of seventy-four hits for the "Queen of Soul" over the next thirty-three years.

1980 Michael Jackson was awarded the Best R&B Vocal Performance, Male Grammy at their twenty-second annual event for the song "Don't Stop Till You Get Enough."

1982 More than twenty-one years after their last chart single, Fred Parris & the Five Satins reached the pop charts, rising to #71 with "Memories of Days Gone By."

1993 After fourteen weeks at #1, Whitney Houston's "I Will Always Love You" became the longest-running chart topper, eclipsing Boyz II Men's 1992 smash, "End of the Road." Additionally, the 4 million selling single was #1 in more than a dozen countries. It became the second-largest-selling single in U.S. history, behind only "We Are the World" by USA for Africa.

1997 The Four Tops received the Pioneer Lifetime Achievement Award at the eighth annual Rhythm & Blues Foundation's ceremony at New York's Hilton Hotel. Also, Smokey Robinson & the Miracles reunited to accept a Pioneer Award.

1998 Janet Jackson was a guest on *The Rosie O'Donnell Show* and discussed the question on the world's collective mind—the position on her body of her tattoos.

Aretha Franklin

February

28

#1 R&B Song 1953: "Baby, Don't Do It," the "5" Royales

Born: Barbara Acklin, 1942; Cindy Wilson, 1957

1954 Spark Records of Los Angeles was formed and became home to the R&B group the Robins.

1968 Frankie Lymon, the voice that helped launch rock 'n' roll as well as a thousand sound-alikes, died in his grandmother's apartment in New York City's Harlem of a drug overdose. Though his youthful voice had lost its register, he was still recording and still hopeful. In fact, he had a recording session scheduled at Roulette Records the next day. Lymon was only twenty-five.

1975 Bobby "Blue" Bland and B.B. King's album, *Together for the First Time—Live*, was certified gold today by the RIAA. It was the first joint album for the artists, whose friendship went back to 1949 when Bland worked for King as a valet.

1976 Muddy Waters won the Best Ethnic or Traditional Recording award at the eighteenth annual Grammys. It was his third win in that category in five years.

1977 In an incident reminiscent of a despicable attack on Nat King Cole decades earlier, Ray Charles was assaulted onstage at a concert for disadvantaged youth by a lunatic who charged the stage carrying a rope and trying to strangle the blind vocalist.

1984 Michael Jackson won an amazing eight awards at the twenty-sixth annual Grammy celebration, including Producer of the Year (Non-Classical), shared with Quincy Jones; Record of the Year; Album of the Year; Best Rock Vocal Performance Male for "Beat It"; Best Pop Vocal Performance Male for *Thriller*; Best New R&B Song for "Billie Jean"; Best R&B Vocal Performance, Male; and Best Recording for Children for *E.T. The Extra-Terrestrial*.

1996 Stevie Wonder was honored at the thirty-eighth annual Grammy Awards with a Lifetime Achievement Award. He also won Best R&B Song and Best R&B Vocal Performance, Male trophies for "For Your Love."

1998 The album *Blues Brothers 2000*, from the film of the same name, reached #12 pop. An all-star performance by the so-called Louisiana Gator Boys (actually B.B. King, Bo Diddley, Lou Rawls, Clarence Clemons, Eric Clapton, Grover Washington, Billy Preston, and others) was a feature of the less-than-successful follow-up to the classic film, *The Blues Brothers*.

February

29

#1 R&B Song 1960: "Baby (You've Got What It Takes)," Dinah Washington & Brook Benton

Born: Ja Rule (Jeffrey Atkins), 1976

1964 The Temptations hit the pop charts for the first time with "The Way You Do the Things You Do," reaching #11. They would be regular residents of the Top 100 for twenty-seven years, amassing fifty-five hits during that time.

1964 Betty Everett charted with "The Shoop Shoop Song," which rose to #6.

1968 The Fifth Dimension's "Up, Up and Away" demolished the competition at the tenth annual Grammy Awards, grabbing Record of the Year, Song of the Year, Best Contemporary Single, Best Performance by a Vocal Group, and Best Contemporary Group Performance Vocal or Instrumental award categories. Aretha Franklin held her own when she won Best R&B Recording (for "Respect") and Best R&B Solo Vocal Performance, Female. Sam & Dave's "Soul Man" won Best R&B Group Performance Vocal.

1996 The Chantels were inducted into the Rhythm & Blues Foundation at its seventh annual awards dinner. One of the highlights of the evening was the pairing of awards presenter Patti Austin with Darlene Love and Staples Singers Mavis Staples belting out "Just One Look." Also honored was Bo Diddley with a Lifetime Achievement Award. A man who never won a Grammy, he used the occasion to state: "It's about time I won something."

The Fifth Dimension

March

#1 R&B Song 1969: "Everyday People," Sly & the Family Stone

Born: Harry Belafonte, 1927; Norman Connors, 1948

1957 Frankie Lymon & the Teenagers received $7,500 to perform at a carnival in Panama, a huge sum at the time.

1960 Saxman supreme, Red Prysock and his band performed at the Surf Club in Baltimore. Red was one of the great honkin' sax players of the day, playing on a variety of rock 'n' roll records while recording numerous albums for Mercury. He's best known for his rocking original, "Hand Clappin'" which had been the theme song for several radio shows over the decades.

1975 Aretha Franklin won her tenth Grammy Award with "Ain't Nothing Like the Real Thing" for Best R&B Vocal Performance. It was her eighth win in a row in that category. Unexpectedly, the Pointer Sisters won Best Country Vocal Performance by a Duo or Group for their hit, "Fairytale."

1986 James Brown's "Living in America" peaked at #4 on the Top 100 charts, becoming the second-biggest pop hit of his career. It was his ninety-eighth pop charter over thirty years and his first million seller in more than thirteen years. The song was the theme from the film *Rocky IV*.

1990 Janet Jackson began her first tour, the now famous Rhythm Nation World Tour 1990 at the Miami Arena, Miami, FL.

1992 Barry White performed at London's Nottingham Royal Center at the beginning of a tour of Britain.

1994 Curtis Mayfield received a Grammy Legend Award and Toni Braxton was awarded the Best New Artist and Best R&B Vocal Performance, Female trophy at the thirty-sixth annual Grammy Awards in New York's Radio City Music Hall for the song "Another Sad Love Song." Whitney Houston was also a big winner with three Grammys: Record of the Year; and Best Pop Vocal Performance Female for "I Will Always Love You"; and Album of the Year for *The Bodyguard*.

1995 Aaron Neville's duet with Trisha Yearwood on the Patsy Cline classic, "I Fall to Pieces," won Best Country Vocal Collaboration at the Grammy's thirty-seventh annual awards ceremony in Los Angeles.

March

#1 R&B Song 1946: "Hey. Ba-Ba-Re-Bop,"
Lionel Hampton & His Orchestra

Born: Lawrence Payton (the Four Tops), 1938

1955 Bo Diddley did his first demo in Chicago when he recorded "I'm a Man" and "You Don't Love Me."

1963 The Crystals performed at Chubby Checker's Limbo Party at San Francisco's Cow Palace, along with Marvin Gaye, Dee Dee Sharp, Bob B. Soxx & the Blue Jeans, Bobby Freeman, the Four Seasons, and H.B. Barnum with his thirty-piece orchestra.

1967 Ray Charles won the Best R&B Solo Vocal Performance, Male or Female of 1966 at the ninth annual Grammy Awards for "Crying Time."

1974 Gladys Knight & the Pips won Best Pop Vocal Performance by a Group for "Neither One of Us" and Best R&B Vocal Performance for "Midnight Train to Georgia" at the sixteenth annual Grammy Awards. The Temptations won Best R&B Performance for "Masterpiece."

1984 Gold Star Studios, the recording home of the Ronettes and the Crystals, was demolished to make way for a mini-mall featuring a Del Taco stand.

1988 Ray Charles was honored with a Lifetime Achievement Award at the thirtieth annual Grammy Awards ceremony. The accolades referred to Charles as "the father of soul, whose unique and effervescent singing and piano playing have personified the true essence of soul music in all his recorded and personal performances of basic blues, pop ballads, jazz tunes, and even country music." Fats Domino was also given a Lifetime Achievement Award along with being praised as "one of the most important links between rhythm and blues and rock and roll, a most influential performer whose style of piano playing and 'down home' singing have led the way for generations of other performers."

1994 Otis Blackwell, Clarence Carter, Don Covay, Bill Doggett, Ben E. King, Johnny Otis, Little Richard, the Coasters, the Shirelles' Mabel John, Earl Palmer, Irma Thomas, and Jerry Butler were honored with Pioneer Awards at the Rhythm & Blues Foundation's fifth annual awards at the Roseland Ballroom in New York City.

1995 Seven years to the day after earning a Lifetime Achievement Award from NARAS, the Grammy people, Fats Domino received the Ray Charles Lifetime Achievement Award from the Rhythm & Blues Foundation in Los Angeles at their sixth annual Pioneer Awards presentation. Also receiving awards were Lloyd Price and Cissy Houston, whose daughter, Whitney, made the presentation.

March

#1 R&B Song 1951: "Black Knight," Charles Brown & His Band

Born: Herman "Little Junior" Parker, 1927; Freddy King, 1934

1956 Singer/actress Gale Storm assaulted the hit list with a cover of Frankie Lymon & the Teenagers' #6 smash, "Why Do Fools Fall in Love?," reaching the Top 10 (#9). It was the first time a black act had beaten a white cover artist on the pop charts.

1958 Dee Irwin & the Pastels charted with their classic ballad, "Been So Long" (#24 pop, #4 R&B). The group formed at an Air Force base in Narsarssuak, Greenland. Irwin went on to have the hit "Swingin' on a Star" (#38 pop) in 1963, with uncredited Little Eva.

1958 The Chantels' "Every Night" was released. It reached #39 pop and #16 R&B.

1962 Chubby Checker squeezed still more mileage out of the "Twist" craze when he charted with "Slow Twistin'," an eventual #3 hit pop and R&B. The duet vocalist on the record was Dee Dee Sharp.

1973 Roberta Flack dominated the fifteenth annual Grammy Awards, winning Song of the Year and Record of the Year for "The First Time Ever I Saw Your Face," as well as Best Pop Vocal Performance by a Duo for "Where Is the Love?" with Donny Hathaway. Muddy Waters won the Best Ethnic or Traditional Recording prize for the second year in a row.

1984 Michael Jackson's single "Thriller" reached #4 pop and was the final of seven singles from the unprecedented best-selling album of the same name.

1985 Michael Jackson came face to face with his own image when he visited Madame Tussaud's famous waxworks in London for the opening of a display of his figure. Obviously in a jubilant mood, Jackson brought chaos and a traffic jam to the streets when he jumped on the roof of his car to wave at fans.

1988 Michael Jackson donated $600,000 from a recent concert to the United Negro College Fund.

1989 The Four Tops performed with Jay & the Americans, Sha Na Na, and Tommy James & the Shondells at the twenty-fourth annual Rock & Roll Revival Spectacular in New York's Madison Square Garden.

March

4

#1 R&B Song 1950: "I Almost Lost My Mind," Ivory Joe Hunter

Born: Bobby Womack, 1944; Miriam Makeba, 1952

1950 Billy Eckstine, known as "Mr. B," charted with "Sitting by the Window," reaching #6 R&B and #23 pop. Though known as a solo vocalist, he was often backed by the Quartones vocal group, as he was on this splendid recording.

1967 Aretha Franklin's Atlantic Records debut, "I Never Loved a Man," charted en route to #1 R&B for seven weeks and #9 pop, becoming her first of seventeen Top 10 pop hits. Atlantic had outbid Columbia for her contract with an offer of $25,000 after Columbia tried to break the artist doing standards, jazz, and soulless R&B from 1960 through 1965. Playing piano on many of her recordings, Franklin learned by listening to Eddie Heywood records.

1967 The Platters charted with "With This Ring," rising to #12 R&B and #14 pop. Their previous chart single, "I'll Be Home" was a remake of the Flamingos' 1956 hit with Nate Nelson singing lead. The interesting distinction was that Nelson was now the lead singer of the Platters and had charted with the same song eleven years earlier.

1972 The Stylistics charted with "Betcha by Golly Wow," reaching #2 R&B and #3 pop and becoming their biggest R&B hit.

1978 Former Stevie Wonder backup singer (with Wonderlove) Deniece Williams teamed with Johnny Mathis on "Too Much, Too Little, Too Late," which debuted on the pop listings today and eventually reached #1. It was Mathis's biggest hit since "Chances Are" in 1957.

1987 Tina Turner began her Break Every Rule tour starting in Munich, West Germany, which did predictably break every box office record in thirteen countries.

1993 "I feel like a queen," Patti LaBelle exclaimed as she was honored with a star on Hollywood's Walk of Fame.

Patti LaBelle

March

5

#1 Song 1983: "Billie Jean," Michael Jackson

Born: J.B. Lenoir, 1929; Tommy Tucker (Robert Higginbotham), 1933

1955 Jimmy Reed charted with "You Don't Have to Go," reaching #5 R&B. It was the first of nineteen R&B hits for the blues singer/guitarist through 1966.

1962 The Twist was still the world's biggest dance craze, and the Marvelettes made their contribution by singing "Twistin' Postman" on Dick Clark's *American Bandstand*.

1971 Aretha Franklin and Ray Charles performed at the Fillmore West, along with King Curtis & His Orchestra.

1977 The Supremes' "Let Yourself Go" became their last of forty-three R&B chart singles (#83).

1978 The rock 'n' roll film *American Hot Wax* debuted in theaters nationwide. Included in the film based on famous deejay Alan Freed was Chuck Berry playing himself, the ultimate parody.

1993 Patti LaBelle, Luther Vandross, and Natalie Cole cohosted the seventh annual Soul Train Music Awards.

1998 Toni Braxton was given the annual Echo Awards at the Congress Centrum, Hamburg, Germany for Best International Female Artist.

Chuck Berry

March

6

#1 R&B Song 1971: "Just My Imagination," the Temptations

Born: Walter "Furry" Lewis, 1893; Wes Montgomery, 1925; Sylvia Vanderpool (Mickey & Sylvia), 1936; Mary Wilson (the Supremes), 1944

1893 Legendary blues slide guitarist Furry Lewis was born today. In the early 1900s he played with W.C. Handy's Orchestra and was best known for his late '20s recordings of "Good Looking Girl Blues," "Cannonball Blues," "Rock Island Blues," and "Mistreatin' Mama." He played everything from medicine shows to riverboats with such artists as Blind Lemon Jefferson and Memphis Minnie.

1959 The "Ben E. King" Drifters' first recording session included "There Goes My Baby"(#2 pop, #1 R&B). It was the first R&B hit to use strings, though R&B acts had been occasionally using them since the early '50s.

1965 The Temptations' standard "My Girl" reached #1 pop and #1 R&B (for six weeks), making them the first male Motown group to hit the top spot.

1976 The Miracles' "Love Machine" reached #1 pop and #5 R&B, becoming their biggest hit since Smokey Robinson left in 1972 and subsequently their last Top 10 hit. The single would also reach #3 in Britain.

1976 Bobby Womack performed at the Hammersmith Odeon in London.

1977 A ninety-minute extravaganza, *An Evening with Diana Ross*, aired on American television. Most of the show was built around her stage act.

March

7

#1 R&B Song 1953: "(Mama) He Treats Your Daughter Mean," Ruth Brown

Born: Hamilton Bohannon, 1942

1957 The Tune Weavers standard "Happy Happy Birthday Baby" was recorded in a Boston studio.

1966 Tina Turner recorded her legendary vocal on Phil Spector's crowning achievement, "River Deep, Mountain High." Spector had already spent more than $22,000 creating the backing track and that didn't include the $20,000 he paid Ike Turner to stay *out* of the studio.

1969 Gladys Knight & the Pips performed in Amsterdam, the Netherlands, at the Grand Gala Du Disque, along with British legends the Moody Blues.

1985 USA for Africa's recording of "We Are the World" was released and sold 800,000 copies over the next two days.

1988 James Brown was presented with a special award for twenty years of innovation in dance music, by delegates from the World Deejay Convention at the Royal Albert Hall in London. Upon accepting the award he was greeted with a five-minute standing ovation. "They call me 'The Godfather of Soul.' None of the new generation can ever be godfather. The only people that qualify are myself and Sinatra," he said.

1997 Babyface was honored at the eleventh annual Soul Train Music Awards with the Sammy Davis Jr. Entertainer of the Year Award, which was presented to him by Will Smith.

1997 Legendary vocalist from the Wall of Sound era, Darlene Love, was awarded $263,500 in past-due royalties from her former producer and owner of Philles Records, Phil Spector. It took only about thirty years for her to get the judgment.

2000 The first black woman to conduct the symphony orchestras of Chicago, Los Angeles, Detroit and thirteen other American cities, Margaret Rosezarian Harris died of a heart attack today at age fifty-six. Originally a pianist, Harris gained her greatest acclaim as a conductor. She also worked on Broadway, most notably as music director of the musical *Hair*.

March

#1 R&B Song 1969: "Give It Up or Turn It Loose," James Brown

Born: Roxanne Shanté (Lolita Gooden), 1970

1969 The Fifth Dimension's "Aquarius/Let the Sun Shine" charted, becoming the group's first #1.

1970 Diana Ross made her solo debut, after leaving the Supremes, in Joe Lewis Arena in Detroit.

1975 The Temptations charted with "Shakey Ground," eventually reaching #1 R&B. It was their fourteenth and last chart topper.

1985 Whitney Houston's self-titled debut album reached #1 on the pop charts and stayed there for fourteen weeks. The album sold more than twelve million records worldwide, establishing her as a premier artist of the times though it took the album twelve months to climb to the top.

1993 Prince performed at the Sunrise Music Theater in Sunrise, FL. It was his first North American tour in five years.

1996 Tina Turner, known for legs that go on forever, was named the Hanes spokeswoman/model.

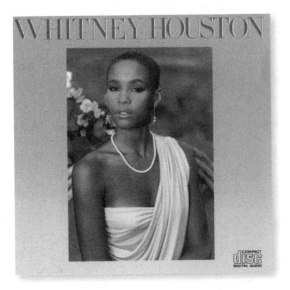

March

9

#1 R&B 1957: "Jim Dandy," LaVern Baker & the Gliders

Born: Lloyd Price, 1933; Laura Lee, 1945; Jeffrey Osborne, 1948

1957 Lloyd Price charted R&B on his birthday with "Just Because," reaching #3 while crossing over to pop for the first time, rising to #29. It was his sixth Top 10 R&B hit in a row and took him five years to hit the pop list.

1957 Fats Domino walked onto the hit list with "I'm Walkin'," and reached #4 pop and #1 R&B. It would be his third straight #1, including "Ain't That a Shame" and "Blue Monday." With each single replacing the other at the top spot, by the time "I'm Walkin' " dropped out of #1 in April, Domino had spent twenty-two consecutive weeks at the peak position.

1957 The "original" Drifters charted with "Fools Fall in Love," reaching #10 R&B and becoming the last of fifteen hits including three #1s ("Money Honey," "Honey Love," and "Adorable") by the group. Two years later, Ben E. King and his group, the Crowns, would become the "new" Drifters.

1959 Sam Cooke charted with "Everybody Likes to Cha Cha Cha," an eventual #2 R&B hit that helped to continue the cha-cha craze in America during the late '50s.

1962 An interesting cross-section of acts appeared at Chicago's Regal Theater when Duke Ellington & His Orchestra shared the stage with the Chantels and Gary "U.S." Bonds.

1968 Jackie Wilson reached #26 R&B and #49 pop with a remake of the Jerry Butler & the Impressions soul standard, "For Your Precious Love." Wilson's signature sound was highlighted by the backing of Count Basie's Orchestra.

2003 Hank Ballard, lead singer of the Midnighters and writer of such hits as "Work with Me, Annie," "Finger Poppin' Time," and "The Twist," died at his Los Angeles home. Ballard had thirteen pop charters from 1959 through 1962 and twenty-two R&B hits between 1953 and 1972. Though Chubby Checker's version of "The Twist" (with the Dreamlovers' backing vocals) was the standard, Ballard's version actually made it to #6 R&B and #28 pop as a B-side more than a year before Checker's hit. Dick Clark called it "the most important song in rock 'n' roll." Ironically, forty-four years earlier to the day, Ballard's "Teardrops on Your Letter" charted on its way to #4 R&B before the flip side took on a life of its own. The flip was "The Twist."

March

10

#1 Song 1973: "Killing Me Softly with His Song," Roberta Flack

Born: Dexter Tisby (the Penguins), 1935; Neneh Cherry, 1964; Jasmine Guy, 1964

1956 The Clovers and former Drifters lead Clyde McPhatter both re-signed with Atlantic Records.

1961 Rochelle & the Candles made it to the East Coast "Chitlin Circuit" performing as opening act for Sam Cooke at the Howard Theater in Washington, DC, on the basis of their current hit, "Once Upon a Time." Not only was Rochelle not a girl, he (Rochelle Henderson) wasn't even the lead singer. That privilege went to Johnny Wyatt, who sang the song in falsetto, fooling everyone from disc jockeys to swooning teen boys until the Los Angeles group came on stage.

1973 The Philadelphia trio First Choice attacked the Top 100 with "Armed and Extremely Dangerous" (#28). It became their biggest hit of five Top 100 singles.

1979 In a classic case of crossing the color line, James Brown performed at Nashville's Grand Ole Opry.

1990 Janet Jackson's "Escapade" spent its second of three weeks at #1 R&B. It was Jackson's sixth #1 in a row going back to November 1986 and "Control."

1995 Al Green appeared at the Hard Rock Hotel and Casino in Las Vegas on the venue's inaugural night.

71

March

#1 R&B Song 1967: "Love Is Here and Now You're Gone," the Supremes

Born: Fred Johnson (the Marcels), 1942; Bobby McFerrin, 1950; Cheryl Lynn, 1957; Gloria Lynn, 1957

1956 The Circle Theater in Cleveland, OH, featured the Turbans of "When You Dance" fame.

1960 Dinah Washington performed at the Regal Theater in Chicago while the Flamingos were knocking them out at the Lindewood Inn in Philadelphia.

1967 Arthur Conley charted with "Sweet Soul Music," rising to #2 pop and R&B. The song was produced by Otis Redding, who also rewrote it from the nucleus of a Sam Cooke song, "Yeah Man."

1970 The Fifth Dimension's "Aquarius/Let the Sun Shine In" won the Best Contemporary Vocal Performance by a Group and Record of the Year at the Grammy Awards' twelfth annual ceremonies.

1972 Dionne Warwick reached the Top 100 with "If We Only Have Love" (#84). It was her first chart single since leaving Scepter Records where she had thirty-eight hits.

1991 Janet Jackson, the youngest member of the Jackson clan, signed a $50 million contract with Virgin Records. The deal was for only two albums and was at the time the most lavish recording contract in history, though her brother Michael would soon eclipse her (see March 20).

2001 Bob "Chico" Edwards, guitarist for the Diablos, died. Edwards helped form the group at a Detroit high school in 1950 and played on all their sessions. Anyone who has heard "The Wind" and "Mind Over Matter" knows what an integral part his guitar work played in their sound. He was sixty-three.

March

12

#1 R&B Song 1949: "The HuckleBuck," Paul Williams & His Hucklebuckers

Born: Al Jarreau, 1940; Marlon Jackson (the Jackson 5), 1957

1960 Jackie Wilson performed on Dick Clark's nighttime version of his daily *American Bandstand*.

1966 The Drifters' "Memories Are Made of This" was released. The Dean Martin oldie reached #48 as their next-to-last of thirty-six Top 100 singles.

1969 Dionne Warwick won Best Contemporary Pop Vocal Performance, Female at the eleventh annual Grammy Awards with "Do You Know the Way to San Jose."

1977 "Uptown Festival," a disco medley of five Motown songs, charted, reaching #10 R&B and #25 pop. Though the group was listed as Shalamar there was no group. The recording was actually made by studio musicians and singers. Producer Dick Griffey put together a quickly-named trio (Jody Watley, Gerald Brown, and Jeffrey Daniels) to capitalize on the recording's success.

1977 The Gap Band charted with "Out of the Blue," reaching #42 R&B. It would be the first of thirty-three singles to reach the R&B hit list over the next eighteen years. The Oklahoma band formed by the three Wilson brothers—Charlie, Ronnie, and Robert—named the group after three Tulsa streets—Greenwood, Archer, and Pine. The brothers were cousins of funkster Bootsy Collins.

1991 Bell Biv DeVoe won the Best R&B Urban Contemporary Album of the Year, Male and the Contemporary Album of the Year, Male awards at the Soul Train Music Awards' fifth annual ceremonies at the Shrine Auditorium in Los Angeles.

1992 Barry White finished his latest tour at the Hammersmith Odeon in London.

Bel Biv DeVoe

March

#1 R&B Song 1954: "The Things That I Used to Do," Guitar Slim and His Band

Born: Blues singer Lightnin' Slim (Otis Hicks), 1913

1954 Muddy Waters charted with "I'm Your Hoochie Coochie Man," reaching #3 R&B. The classic blues tune became his biggest hit and eighth Top 10 R&B single in a row. In fact, the blues legend had sixteen chart hits and only one didn't make the Top 10. "Sugar Sweet" had to settle for a lowly #11. Waters's first recordings were not for a record company but for the Library of Congress and its roving archivist, Alan Lomax, who recorded Waters's "Country Blues" and "I Be's Troubled" in 1941.

1961 James Brown's magic number this day was eight as he charted with one of his earliest hits, "Bewildered," reaching #8 R&B. It spent eight weeks on the charts and was his eighth chart hit.

1961 "Find Another Girl" by Jerry Butler jumped on the R&B hit list, stopping at #10 (#27 pop). It was his second Top 10 hit since leaving the Impressions in 1958. The first was the classic "He Will Break Your Heart."

1963 "Foolish Little Girl" by the Shirelles hit the R&B charts, reaching #9 and #4 pop, while becoming their last of six Top 10 hits. During the group's 1963 performances they would often call upon a label mate to fill in when one of the women wasn't available. The backup vocalist was Dionne Warwick.

1965 The Ikettes, a female trio that spent most of its performance life as the backup singers/dancers for Ike & Tina Turner, charted with their own single, "Peaches 'N' Cream" (#36).

1976 The O'Jays' "Livin' for the Weekend" charted on its way to #1 R&B and the group's fifth #1 just as William Powell left due to cancer. His replacement would be Sammy Strain, an original member of Little Anthony and the Imperials.

1982 "Let It Whip" by the Dazz Band debuted on the R&B hit list, eventually reaching #1 and giving the Cleveland funk band their biggest of twenty-two chart singles from 1978 through 1998.

March

#1 R&B Song 1970: "Rainy Night in Georgia," Brook Benton

Born: Phil Phillips, 1931; Quincy Jones, 1933

1953 The Flamingos' debut single, "Someday, Someway," was issued. Their fledgling 45 is a $1,200 collector's treasure today.

1960 The Platters' album *Encore of Golden Hits* charted, reaching #6 on the Top 100 and spending 174 weeks on the pop list. The album was later certified gold in an era when gold meant one million copies sold as opposed to today where it only represents 500,000 copies.

1960 Sam Cooke performed in Montego Bay, Jamaica, to a sell-out audience that included two future stars, Bob Marley and Jimmy Cliff.

1972 Aretha Franklin received the Best R&B Vocal Performance, Female trophy at the Grammy Awards fourteen annual event for "Bridge Over Troubled Water." Muddy Waters won the Best Ethnic or Traditional Recording Award and Isaac Hayes came away a winner for Best Original Score Written for a Motion Picture when his "Theme from *Shaft*" won.

1987 James Ingram's duet with Linda Ronstadt, "Somewhere Out There," peaked at #2. It was from the animated film *An American Tail*.

2000 Though it was billed as the Supremes' reunion tour, Diana Ross was really the only original member when the promoters *insulted* Mary Wilson with an offer of $2 million while Ross was to get $20 million, according to TV's *Access Hollywood*. Undeterred, Ross went out with Scherrie Payne and Lynda Laurence, who weren't even in the group until years after Diana had left. Cindy Birdsong, original replacement for deceased Florence Ballard, wasn't even mentioned.

March

#1 R&B Song 1975: "Supernatural Thing—Part 1," Ben E. King

Born: Bertha "Chippie" Hill, 1905; Sam "Lightnin' " Hopkins, 1912; Sly Stone (Sylvester Stewart), 1944

1945 The first #1 pop album was by Nat King Cole.

1954 The Chords recorded the soon-to-be standard, "Sh-Boom," which became the first pop Top 10 hit (#5 pop, #2 R&B) by a rock 'n' roll/R&B vocal group.

1957 Frankie Lymon & the Teenagers arrived in London for a British tour. The Harlem teen quintet was the first rock 'n' roll vocal group to have a #1 record in England when "Why Do Fools Fall in Love" topped the U.K. charts in August 1956. Lymon also became the youngest headliner and the youngest British chart topper. The group spent two weeks in London featured at the London Palladium.

1966 James Brown earned the Best R&B Recording of 1965 for "Papa's Got a Brand New Bag" at the eighth annual Grammy Awards. It became his biggest R&B hit.

1969 The Isley Brothers' "It's Your Thing" charted on the way to #1 R&B and #2 pop. It would become their biggest hit of a career spanning five decades.

1978 The film *American Hot Wax* took off across the nation and included performances (both live and recorded) by the Spaniels, Chuck Berry, Jackie Wilson, the Moonglows, Maurice Williams & the Zodiacs, the Drifters, Little Richard, the Turbans, and the Cadillacs. The movie was based on the life of Alan Freed, who championed black music throughout his career.

1994 Babyface won the Best R&B Album, Male at the eighth annual Soul Train Awards for his CD *For the Cool in You* at Los Angeles' Shrine Auditorium. The show's hosts were Patti LaBelle, Gladys Knight, and Johnny Gill.

1998 VH-1 aired a one-hour special, *Behind the Music,* on Rick James.

1999 Charles Brown, Curtis Mayfield, and the Staple Singers were inducted into the Rock and Roll Hall of Fame at the fourteenth annual festivities in New York.

March 16

1957 The Heartbeats' "I Won't Be the Fool" and the Five Satins' "Oh, Happy Day" were released.

1962 Hank Ballard & the Midnighters charted pop for the last of thirteen times with "Do You Know How to Twist," their answer to Chubby Checker's version of their original hit "The Twist." The group then split up when the Midnighters became black Muslims and refused to perform for white audiences.

1970 Tammi Terrell, who had ten chart hit duets with Marvin Gaye, died of a brain tumor on stage, in Marvin's arms. She was only twenty-three.

1971 B.B. King won the Best R&B Vocal Performance, Male trophy at the thirteenth annual Grammy Awards for his hypnotic single, "The Thrill Is Gone." Dionne Warwick earned her second Grammy, Best Contemporary Vocal Performance, Female for her rendition of "I'll Never Fall in Love Again."

1994 A tribute concert, Swing Into Spring: a Harlem Tribute to Lionel Hampton (the legendary jazz vibraphonist), was held at New York's Apollo Theater with guest artists including George Benson.

1994 The other side of stardom is living with the risks that come with that stardom. Roberta Flack, who had been stalked on several occasions by a deranged New York cabdriver, was under siege while he attempted to get into her apartment and screamed: "I'll kill her if I see her." He was promptly arrested.

1995 Anita Baker and Babyface were at it again, co-hosting the ninth annual Soul Train Music Awards, this time with additional host, legendary diva Patti Labelle. Anita also received Best R&B/Soul Female Single and Best R&B Soul Female Album awards that night.

Marvin Gaye and Tammi Terrell

March

#1 R&B Song 1956: "Why Do Fools Fall in Love," Frankie Lymon & the Teenagers

Born: Nat King Cole (Nathaniel Adams Coles), 1919; Clarence Collins (the Imperials), 1941

1956 Howlin' Wolf charted with "Smokestack Lightning," reaching #8 R&B. Wolf was discovered by Ike Turner, who was acting as a talent scout for Chess and Modern records at the time.

1958 The Coasters recorded "Yakety Yak," which eventually reached #1 pop and R&B.

1958 United Artists Records acquired the rights to Lee Andrews & the Hearts as well as their new single, "Try the Impossible" (#33 pop).

1961 Chuck Jackson, Chubby Checker, the Drifters, Maxine Brown, and the Blue Notes performed at the Regal Theater in Chicago.

1966 Chuck Berry performed at the legendary Fillmore West in San Francisco with the Grateful Dead.

1967 Sam & Dave, Otis Redding, Carla Thomas, Booker T. & the M.G.s, Arthur Conley, Eddie Floyd, and the Mar Keys started a thirteen-date Soul Sensation '67 U.K. Tour at London's Finsbury Park, Astoria, England.

1967 The Jimi Hendrix Experience performed at the Star Club in Hamburg, West Germany, the legendary venue where the Beatles began their rise to fame.

1990 Dionne Warwick performed at the fifteenth anniversary celebration of her record label, Arista Records, at Radio City Music Hall in New York. She and other label performers would raise $2 million from the concert/fundraiser for AIDS organizations.

March

18

#1 R&B Song 1950: "Double Crossing Blues," Johnny Otis Quintette, the Robins & Little Esther

Born: Wilson Pickett (the Falcons), 1941; Helen Gathers (the Bobbettes), 1943; Irene Cara (Irene Escalera), 1959; Vanessa Williams, 1963; Queen Latifah (Dana Owens), 1970

1944 The Ink Spots charted with "Don't Believe Everything You Dream," from the motion picture *Around the World*, starring Kay Kyser. It reached #6 R&B and #14 pop.

1954 The Harptones appeared at the Apollo Theater.

1960 Dave "Baby" Cortez (of "Happy Organ" fame), the Coasters, the Isley Brothers, and Luther Bond performed on the Rocketship Revue at the Apollo Theater, hosted by New York's famed R&B disc jockey Jocko Henderson.

1970 Brook Benton's "Rainy Night in Georgia" reached #1 R&B and #4 pop. It was his seventh and last R&B #1. Not bad for a guy who started out as a truck driver.

1982 Former Harold Melvin & the Blue Notes lead singer Teddy Pendergrass was paralyzed from the neck down after his Rolls Royce flipped over while he was trying to avoid another car on a Philadelphia street. Adding to his woes came the news that his passenger, one Tenika Watson, was actually a transsexual nightclub act named John Watson.

1992 Donna Summer received a star on the Hollywood Walk of Fame.

1994 Lloyd Price was honored in his hometown of Kenner, LA, today when they renamed Fourth Street Lloyd Price Avenue.

Lloyd Price

March

#1 R&B Song 1966: "634-5789 (Soulsville, USA)," Wilson Pickett

Born: Clarence Paul (the "5" Royales), 1928; Clarence "Frogman" Henry, 1937; Walter Jackson (the Velvetones), 1938; Ruth Pointer (the Pointer Sisters), 1946

1955 Johnny Ace's posthumously issued "Pledging My Love" reached #17 pop today while continuing a run at #1 R&B for ten weeks starting February 12. The R&B standard was recorded by Elvis Presley more than twenty years later.

1962 Barbara George performed her one and only R&B chart record on *American Bandstand*. George was one of the few artists in music history to have her only chart single make #1. With her, it was all or nothing.

1969 The Flamingos' "Boogaloo Party" charted (#93). It was their only single among sixty-one releases to hit in England (#26).

1988 Michael Jackson bought the Sycamore Ranch in Santa Ynez Valley, CA. He reportedly paid more than $28 million for what would soon become known worldwide as the Neverland Ranch.

1993 Hugh Masekela, Philip Bailey, Gerald Albright, Chaka Khan, and Bobby Lyle started a twenty-six-night tour in Sacramento, CA, called, A Night on the Town.

1993 Mary J. Blige was awarded the Best New R&B Artist and Best R&B Album, Female for *What's the 411?* at the seventh annual Soul Train Music Awards in Los Angeles.

1996 Aaron Neville performed at the Angloa State Prison outside St. Francisville, LA.

2001 The Flamingos, along with Solomon Burke, were inducted into the Rock and Roll Hall of Fame.

March

20

#1 R&B Song 1943: "Don't Stop Now," Bonnie Davis

Born: Sister Rosetta Tharpe, 1921; Tracy Chapman, 1964

1948 Dinah Washington charted with Fats Waller's "Ain't Misbehavin'," reaching #6 R&B. The song was originally used in Waller's 1929 Broadway musical, *Hot Chocolates*.

1950 The Carols, a Ravens-styled quartet on Columbia, recorded their first single, "Please Believe in Me." In 1954, the Carols' bass lead and adoring Ravens fan Tommy Evans soon became the Ravens' new bass.

1965 The Temptations, Martha & the Vandellas, the Supremes, the Miracles, and Stevie Wonder began a twenty-one-date, twice-a-night tour of England as the Tamla Motown package in London at Finsbury Park.

1991 Michael Jackson trumped his sister Janet's $50 million record deal with his own Sony agreement that would be touted as the first billion-dollar entertainment contract starting with an $18 million advance just for his forthcoming *Dangerous* album. The deal included an unheard-of royalty of $2.08 per album, a $5 million advance for subsequent albums, and his own record, video, TV, and film complex.

1993 Rapper Dr. Dre reached #2 with "Nuttin' But a 'G' Thang," which heavily borrowed from the contents of the 1975 R&B hit "I Want'a Do Something Freaky to You," by Leon Haywood.

Michael Jackson's
Dangerous

March

21

#1 R&B Song 1970: "Call Me," Aretha Franklin

Born: Eddie "Son" House, 1902; Otis Spann, 1930; Russell Thompkins Jr. (the Stylistics), 1951

1930 Otis Spann, considered one of the finest blues piano players, was born today. He began in the '40s playing with the likes of Memphis Slim, Muddy Waters, and Roosevelt Sykes. His technical ability was mind-boggling, and his right hand was one of the fastest across the keys of anyone this side of Big Maceo. Over the years he played with artists as diverse as Chuck Berry, Sonny Boy Williamson, Fleetwood Mac, and Howlin' Wolf.

1959 The Platters' "Smoke Gets in Your Eyes" reached #1 in England, spending an amazing seventeen weeks in the British Top 10. The quintet would chart sixteen times in the United Kingdom over four years, including placing their hits "I'm Sorry" and "My Prayer" on the charts three times, each one making the Top 30.

1960 Rarely was an artist so versatile that he could have a two-sided hit with two so distinctly different recordings, but few were as great as Jackie Wilson. "Mr. Excitement" charted with the pop ballad "Night" (based on the classical melody "My Heart at Thy Sweet Voice" from Saint-Saëns's *Samson and Delilah*), reaching #3 R&B and #4 pop. The flip, "Doggin Around," a classic wailing blues number, reached #15 pop and spent three weeks at #1 R&B.

1963 Little Esther Phillips began a two-week engagement at Baltimore's Royal Theater.

1992 R. Kelly charted with "Honey Love," reaching #1 R&B and #39 pop. Known as a solo artist, Kelly actually recorded the song with his vocal group Public Announcement.

1998 Puff Daddy & the Family, featuring the Notorious B.I.G. and Busta Rhymes, charted with "Victory," reaching #13 R&B and #19 pop.

March

#1 R&B Song 1952: "Night Train," Jimmy Forrest & His All-Star Combo

Born: George Benson, 1943; Stephanie Mills, 1957; Jadakiss (Jayson Philips), 1975

1951 The Five Keys' first recording session included their first two singles, "With a Broken Heart" and the million-selling "Glory of Love."

1952 Ray Charles's "Kiss-a Me Baby" hit the R&B charts, rising to #8 for his third Top 10 hit in a row. An original copy of the single today would cost in the $300 range.

1980 Shalamar's "The Second Time Around" peaked at #8 pop and also reached #1 R&B to become their biggest hit in a career spanning ten years and twenty-two R&B chart singles. The group's lead, Howard Hewitt, would go on to solo success in the mid-'80s, while member Jody Watley (god-daughter of Jackie Wilson) became a solo star with hits like "Looking for a New Love."

1980 Soul balladeer Peabo Bryson charted with "Minute by Minute," reaching #12 R&B. Through 1993 the South Carolina native had forty-five hit 45s, including #1s "Show & Tell" and "Can't Stop the Rain."

1993 Sade performed at New York's Paramount Theater and must have felt quite comfortable as she did the whole show bare foot.

2001 Earl Beal, co-founder and baritone of the Silhouettes, died. He and lead singer Billy Horton formed the Philadelphia group in a pool hall in 1955. Beal suggested naming the group after the Rays' hit. They had only one chart record but it was a classic, "Get a Job," which went to #1 R&B and pop. Beal was seventy-six.

Peabo Bryson

March

#1 Song 1963: "Our Day Will Come," Ruby & the Romantics

Born: Granville "Sticks" McGhee, 1918; Chaka Khan (Yvette Marie Stevens), 1953

1957 The Platters charted with "I'm Sorry," reaching #11 pop and #15 R&B. Its B-side, "He's Mine," soared to #5 R&B and #23 pop, making that Platters single the sixth 45 in a row to have both sides chart on the pop Top 100.

1957 The Paragons' doo-wop classic "Florence" and the Coasters' "Youngblood" (#8 pop, #1 R&B) were released. "Youngblood" was around for eight years before becoming the Coasters hit. The term was "Brooklyn-eze" for "young chicks."

1957 "Lucille" by Little Richard charted, reaching #21 pop and #1 R&B. Out of Richard's first six singles, five had had both sides chart, including the flip of "Lucille," "Send Me Some Lovin' " (#3 R&B, #54 pop).

1959 The Fiestas hit the R&B charts with "So Fine" (#3, #11 pop), one of the first recordings acknowledged to be the start of the soul era.

1959 The Midnighters' "Teardrops on Your Letter" charted and stalled at #87 pop, but its B-side would go on to immortality as "The Twist."

1962 The Regal Theater in Chicago presented a dynamite lineup of Lloyd Price, Eddie Holland, the Crystals, Gene Chandler, Jimmy McCracklin, Solomon Burke, and Aretha and Erma Franklin.

1978 Bill Kenny, legendary lead singer of the pioneering Ink Spots, died.

1987 Luther Vandross and Dionne Warwick co-hosted the initial Soul Train Music Awards in Hollywood, CA. It was especially sweet for Vandross, who at age thirteen had seen Warwick perform and decided then and there on a music career. Vandross, who at one time worked as a clerk for S&H Green Stamps, spent several years doing backup vocals for artists like Barbra Streisand, Chaka Khan, Carly Simon, Ringo Starr, and Donna Summer before earning his solo success.

1994 The Staple Singers and Patti LaBelle performed at a joint benefit for the Rhythm & Blues Foundation and the Country Music Foundation at the Universal Amphitheater.

1999 Lauryn Hill began the first of three sold-out concerts at Madison Square Garden. The highlight was a duet with Mary J. Blige on "I Used to Love Him." She later donated $50,000 to a refugee fund-raising project.

March 24

#1 R&B Song 1962: "Twistin' the Night Away," Sam Cooke

Born: Billy Stewart (the Rainbows), 1937; Don Covay (Donald Randolph), 1938

1956 The El Capris' "(Shimmy, Shimmy) Ko Ko-Wop" was released. Four years later it became a hit for Little Anthony & the Imperials as "Shimmy, Shimmy Ko-Ko-Bop."

1956 The Platters charted with "(You've Got) The Magic Touch," reaching #4 pop and R&B. It would become their second million-seller of only three releases.

1956 "Later Alligator," by Bobby Charles, hit the R&B hit list going on to #14. The song was recorded by Charles in 1955, and with a name variation Bill Haley & the Comets had the pop hit as "See You Later Alligator" in 1956.

1958 Mahalia Jackson's version of "He's Got the Whole World in His Hands" was released.

1973 The O'Jays topped the pop and R&B charts with the message song, "Love Train," which also reached #9 in England.

1973 Eighteen years after their classic, "Close Your Eyes" came out, the Five Keys rerecorded it a cappella as a single for Bim Bam Boom Records.

Mahalia Jackson

2000 Al Grey, the heavy-swinging trombonist from the Count Basie Big Band, died at age seventy-four. Grey was one of the innovators of the "growl" style of playing that traced its roots to the Duke Ellington "jungle" sound of the '20s. He influenced rockers like Jimi Hendrix and played with legends such as Dizzy Gillespie, Lionel Hampton, Ella Fitzgerald, and Frank Sinatra. He appeared on almost 100 albums, including thirty of his own.

2000 Anthony Jackson, choreographer for Janet Jackson's Rhythm Nation Tour, also was responsible for the fancy footwork on the Judds' current tour. He was the first black choreographer to ever use that expertise for a country act.

March

25

1956 The Diablos appeared at Cleveland's Circle Theater.

1956 An all-star gospel show featuring the Soul Stirrers, Swan Silvertones, Swanee Quintet, the Holy Spiritualaires, the Five Blind Boys of Alabama, and the Jewel Gospel Singers brought 7,000 fans to the coliseum in Durham, NC.

1960 Jazzmen Horace Silver and Art Blakely performed along with Ray Charles and Dinah Washington at the Opera House in Chicago. Down the road, the Spaniels, Harvey (of the Moonglows), Etta James, Jerry Butler, Big Maybelle, and Wade Flemons were bringing down the house at the Regal Theater.

1967 Aretha Franklin's album *I Never Loved a Man (The Way I Love You)* reached #2, garnering "Lady Soul" her first gold album.

1967 One of the finest soul/doo-wop singles of the '60s, "Get Yourself Together," by the Caesars, charted, but the under-promoted 45 only reached #48 R&B.

1983 The Jackson 5 reunited, including Jermaine and Michael, for the anniversary show 25 Years of Motown at Los Angeles's Civic Center.

1985 Prince's *Purple Rain* soundtrack won the Oscar for Best Original Score at the annual Academy Awards show, and Stevie Wonder's "I Just Called to Say I Love You" was honored as Best Song. Wonder dedicated the award to Nelson Mandela.

1992 The National Association of Black-Owned Broadcasters gave Michael Jackson a Lifetime Achievement Award in Washington, DC.

1993 Bobby Womack performed a duet with Lulu on the British TV show, *Top of the Pops*.

March

#1 R&B Song 1988: "Man in the Mirror," Michael Jackson

Born: Rufus Thomas, 1917; Fred Parris (the Five Satins), 1936; Diana Ross (Diane Earl), 1944; Teddy Pendergrass (the Bluenotes), 1950

1955 The Hearts, one of the first rock 'n' roll female groups, stormed the R&B charts with their scintillating, powerhouse performance of "Lonely Nights," reaching #8. The record was also one of the first to have a talking bridge, and anyone who's heard that smokin' line "You great big lump o' sugar" will never forget the first in-your-face "attitude" hit. The group included Jeanette "Baby" Washington and Zell Sanders. Sanders went on to have her own J&S label, and produced the hit "Over the Mountain, Across the Sea," for Johnnie & Joe.

1959 The Coasters recorded "Along Came Jones" (#9 pop, #14 R&D).

1962 One-hit wonders Ronnie & the Hi-Lites performed their smash "I Wish That We Were Married" on *American Bandstand*. The Jersey City quintet reached #16 pop with twelve-year-old Ronnie Goodson singing lead on the tear-jerking ballad. Goodson was one of the youngest black vocal group leads—since Frankie Lymon in 1956—to have a hit.

1966 Marvin Gaye's "One More Heartache" reached #29 pop and #4 R&B. It was his fifteenth R&B hit in a little more than three years. The same month he would reportedly take a screen test to star in *The Nat King Cole Story*.

1985 Radio stations in South Africa boycotted all of Stevie Wonder's records the day after he dedicated his winning Oscar at the Academy Awards to Nelson Mandela.

1991 MC Hammer sold out the Tokyo dome in Tokyo, Japan in only six hours. The only other acts to accomplish that were Michael Jackson and the Rolling Stones.

1998 Patti LaBelle appeared at the Boston department store Filene's, while promoting her newest endeavor, Patti LaBelle's Signature Fragrance Collection.

2000 Ray Charles, Whitney Houston, Isaac Hayes, and Queen Latifah sang a special medley of previously-nominated Oscar songs at the Academy Awards presentation in Los Angeles.

March

#1 R&B Song 1961: "What's Going On," Marvin Gaye

Born: Sarah Vaughan, 1924; Walter "Bunny" Sigler, 1941; Brenda Knight (Gladys Knight & the Pips), 1941; Mariah Carey, 1970; André 3000 Benjamin (Outkast), 1975

1951 The Larks recorded their immortal ballad "My Reverie." Today an original copy goes for $8,000.

1954 The Spaniels' 45 "Goodnight Sweetheart, Goodnight" and the Tempo Toppers' "Always" were issued. The Tempo Toppers' lead vocalist was a newcomer named Little Richard.

1954 The Five Keys' collector's classic, "Someday Sweetheart," was released. An original 45 today is valued at about $1,000.

1965 The Miracles' classic doo-wop/soul ballad, "Ooo Baby Baby" charted, reaching #4 R&B and #16 pop.

1967 Fats Domino performed on his first British tour at London's Saville Theater with the Bee Gees and Gerry & the Pacemakers.

1971 Ike & Tina Turner's raucous remake of Creedence Clearwater Revival's "Proud Mary" reached #4 pop and #5 R&B, giving the tempestuous duo their first Top 5 hit. Ike, who began as a self-taught musician backing the likes of Sonny Boy Williamson, became a disc jockey at Clarksdale, MS's WROX radio station before graduating to talent scout for LA's Modern Records. He went on to discover B.B. King and Howlin' Wolf, whom he drafted for the label in 1952.

1993 Prince and Lenny Kravitz performed at New York's Apollo Theater singing Prince's "When You Were Mine." The concert was Prince's first at the famed venue and was a special invitation show for underprivileged children from the area.

March 28

1953 Willie Mae "Big Mama" Thornton charted with "Hound Dog," reaching #1 for seven weeks on the R&B hit parade.

1956 The Five Satins legendary love song, "In the Still of the Night" was released on its original label, Standord. It was soon reissued on the larger Ember label, reaching #24 pop, #3 R&B.

1967 The Murray the K Easter Show at the RKO theater in New York featured the Miracles.

1970 The Moments charted with "Love on a Two-Way Street," reaching #1 R&B for five weeks and #3 pop. The New Jersey trio had thirty-nine R&B hits between 1968 and 1988 but this was the biggest.

Willie Mae "Big Mama" Thornton

1974 Bluesman Arthur "Big Boy" Crudup died today after a massive heart attack. The man who launched Elvis Presley's career with his song "That's Alright Mama," had six chart hits in the '40s and performed with the likes of Sonny Boy Williamson, Elmore James, and Lightnin' Hopkins. He was so discontented and broke from his music-business experiences that he quit in the '50s to farm sweet potatoes in Mississippi. He was sixty-eight.

1981 Rick James charted with "Give It to Me, Baby," which would become his second R&B #1 (#40 pop).

1988 Tina Turner's Break Every Rule tour ended today in Osaka, Japan, after she performed 230 dates in twenty-five countries, playing to more than 3 million people.

March

29

#1 R&B Song 1969: "Runaway Child, Running Wild," the Temptations

Born: Camille Howard, 1914; Pearl Bailey, 1918

1951 The Ravens recorded "You Foolish Thing" for Columbia, now a $2,000 collectible.

1965 Dionne Warwick performed at London's Savoy Hotel in the intimate setting of a cabaret.

1975 LaBelle's "Lady Marmalade" reached #1 in America and became a million-seller. The group was formerly known as Patti LaBelle & the Blue Belles.

1980 The Spinners reached #2 pop and #6 R&B with the medley "Working My Way Back to You/Forgive Me Girl," the first time a medley of a hit and an original song had reached the Top 5. "Working" was originally a hit for the Four Seasons in 1966.

1980 Lionel Richie performed "Endless Love" at the Academy Awards' fifty-fifth annual ceremonies in Los Angeles.

1992 MTV began promoting its My Dinner with Michael Jackson contest in which 100 lucky contestants would have a dinner with the superstar in Los Angeles. More than 4 million people responded.

1996 Boyz II Men were honored with the Sammy Davis Jr. Award for Outstanding Achievements in the Field of Entertainment at the Soul Train tenth annual Music Awards, held at Los Angeles's Shrine Auditorium. The award was presented by Bill Cosby. Patti LaBelle was also honored with the Heritage Award and sang "Over the Rainbow." Hosting the show were Anita Baker, LL Cool J, and Brandy.

March

30

#1 R&B Song 1957: "I'm Walkin,'"
Fats Domino

Born: MC Hammer (Stanley Burrell),
1963

1953 The Crows' monumental hit, "Gee," was recorded at New York's Beltone Studios.

1963 Quincy Jones produced Lesley Gore's debut single, "It's My Party" today.

1963 The Chiffons reached #1 pop and R&B with "He's So Fine." The single spent four weeks in the top spot on both charts, becoming a million seller.

1967 Jimi Hendrix was about to perform on British TV's *Top of the Pops* when the engineer accidentally ran the backing track for an Alan Price record, "Simon Smith and His Amazing Dancing Bear" instead of "Purple Haze." Hendrix, without missing a beat, nonchalantly stated, "I don't know the words to that one, man."

1972 Berry Gordy Jr., founder of Motown Records, patented the name the Jackson 5, which would eventually force the group to change their names to the Jacksons when they signed with Epic Records in 1976.

1988 Gladys Knight & the Pips were honored with the Heritage Award at the second annual Soul Train Music Awards, coinciding with their thirtieth recording anniversary.

1989 After singing together as Gladys Knight & the Pips for thirty-seven years, Knight made her solo debut at Bally's Casino in Las Vegas.

Berry Gordy Jr.

1996 Two of the Isley Brothers, Ron and Ernie, along with R. Kelly, peaked at #4 pop with "Down Low (Nobody Has to Know)." The Isleys were an early influence on Kelly's career.

March

31

1945 Erskine Hawkins & His Orchestra charted with "Tippin' In," reaching #1 R&B for six weeks.

1956 The Coasters had their first chart single under their own name when "Down in Mexico" reached the R&B list today, eventually hitting #8. Two of the members, Bobby Nunn and Carl Gardner, had previously been with the Robins of *Smokey Joe's Café* fame.

1956 The King of Rock 'n' Roll, Elvis Presley, was also the king of the R&B charts...sort of. Elvis had thirty-five R&B hits from 1956 through 1963 starting today with the debut of "Heartbreak Hotel," which reached #3. He was the most successful white artist on the black charts and was #35 among the Top 500 R&B artists of all time. James Brown was #1.

1961 The Brooklyn Fox's Easter Extravaganza included performances by the Marcels, the Shirelles, Little Anthony & the Imperials, Maurice Williams & the Zodiacs, Carla Thomas, Ben E. King, the Olympics, Chuck Jackson, the Capris, the Isley Brothers, and Rosie, formerly of the Originals. All that for a couple of dollars.

1962 The Crystals' "Uptown" charted (#13) and became their only single featuring six members, as Lala Brooks replaced a pregnant Merna Girard, who hung on long enough to record at the session. The song was originally intended for Tony Orlando until producer Phil Spector convinced the writers it needed a female touch.

1967 The Jimi Hendrix Experience began its first tour at the Astoria Theatre in London, but the debut was short-lived as Hendrix was taken to a hospital for burns on his hands as a result of his new "gimmick" that included burning his guitar. The tour included American and British stars the Walker Brothers and Engelbert Humperdinck. Before the tour was over he would be playing his guitar with his teeth along with his nightly burn-the-guitar ritual, which would have theater owners up in arms.

1973 New York City (a vocal group from guess where) charted with the Thom Bell-produced "I'm Doin' Fine Now," reaching #14 R&B and #17 pop.

1991 Whitney Houston performed "The Star-Spangled Banner" at the Norfolk Naval Air Station for American soldiers returning from the Gulf War. Her recording of the anthem sold more than 750,000 records in only nine days.

#1 R&B Song 1956: "Drown in My Own Tears," Ray Charles & His Band

Born: Alberta Hunter, 1895; Amos Milburn, 1927; Rudolph Isley (the Isley Brothers), 1939

1960 In a great mix of the old and the new, Louis Jordan, Lenny Welch and the Four Tops performed at the Apollo Theater. The Tops were still four years away from their first hit and doing mostly jazz.

1972 B.B. King performed at the Mar Y Sol Festival in Puerto Rico with Emerson, Lake & Palmer, and the Allman Brothers.

1984 After a violent dispute, Marvin Gaye was shot to death by his ranting reverend father, Marvin Gaye, Sr., in their Los Angeles home. Marvin Jr. would have been forty-five the next day.

1989 B.B. King with U2 charted pop with "When Love Comes to Town," reaching #68 and becoming his last of thirty-six pop Top 100 entries.

1992 Boyz II Men and Hammer began the "Too Legit to Quit" tour in Hampton, VA.

1994 The O'Jays, the Whispers, and Levert performed at the Westbury Music Fair in Westbury, Long Island, NY.

1995 The Cameo funk era ended when their thirty-eighth chart single, "You Are My Love," barely scraped the R&B 100 (#99).

1996 Isaac Hayes—recording artist, musician, writer, producer, and actor—put on another hat when he became the new WRKS-FM disc jockey in their 6:00 a.m. to 10:00 a.m. slot.

Marvin Gaye

April

2

1961 The Shirelles began a major tour in Irving Feld's Biggest Show of Stars, 1961, starting in Philadelphia. Other acts included the Drifters, Fats Domino, Chubby Checker, and Bo Diddley.

1965 Dionne Warwick performed on Britain's *Ready, Steady, Go!* TV-show debut.

1966 Sarah Vaughan's cover of the Toys' hit "A Lover's Concerto" charted, reaching #63. It was the last of her thirty-three single successes.

1966 The Jazz Crusaders charted with Stevie Wonder's "Uptight (Everything Is Alright)," reaching #95 pop in their chart debut. The instrumental group formerly known as the Nighthawks would soon be known worldwide as simply the Crusaders. They would not reach the R&B charts for another six years.

1967 Wilson Pickett performed in Murray the K's Easter show, Music in the Fifth Dimension, at the RKO Theater in New York.

1983 Michael Jackson's "Beat It" charted R&B, reaching #1 on both the pop and R&B national singles charts. The lead guitarist on the session was Van Halen's Eddie Van Halen. The song was inspired by the Knack's "My Sharona."

Sarah Vaughan

#1 Song 1961: "Blue Moon," the Marcels

Born: Jimmy McGriff, 1936; Eddie Murphy, 1961

1959 England's BBC radio banned the Coasters' "Charlie Brown" because of its inclusion of the word "spitball."

1976 Billy Ocean's single, "Love Really Hurts Without You" charted, reaching #2 in England and #22 in America. Before hitting the charts, the West Indian vocalist worked as a tailor on London's Saville Row and later worked in a Ford Motor plant at night so he could record and write in the daytime.

1976 Diana Ross's "Love Hangover" sprinted onto the Hot 100, eventually settling in the top spot. It was her fourth solo #1 in six years.

1991 Queen Latifah, Big Daddy Cane, and Afrika Bambaataa appeared at Rap Portraits and Lyrics of a Generation of Black Rockers in New York, adding credibility to Afrika's (real name Kevin Donovan) reputation as a rap innovator.

1992 Prince started a tour at the Tokyo Dome, in Tokyo, Japan.

1996 MC Hammer (now known as Hammer) was also now known as "broke." He filed for bankruptcy today in Oakland, CA with debts of more than $10 million even though a 1991 *Forbes Magazine* list had him as the nineteenth highest paid entertainer.

April 4

#1 R&B Song 1981: "Being with You," Smokey Robinson

Born: Cecil Gant, 1913; Muddy Waters (McKinley Morganfield), 1915; Margo Sylvia (the Tune Weavers), 1936; Hugh Masekela, 1939; Major Lance, 1942

1958 The Platters' "Twilight Time" (#1 pop and R&B) was released.

1960 The Miracles' "You Can Depend on Me" was issued as their first Tamla (Motown) single. The B-side, "Way Over There," was the 45's second flip. The record originally had "The Feeling is So Fine" on the backside.

1964 Mary Wells's "My Guy" debuted on the Hot 100, rising to the top spot and making Wells the first Motown artist to have a #1.

1968 B.B. King, Jimi Hendrix, and Buddy Guy did an all-night blues stint in Virginia Beach, VA, on the evening of Martin Luther King Jr.'s assassination. They passed a hat to raise money for King's Southern Christian Leadership Fund.

1976 Brook Benton and the Stylistics performed in England at the De Montfort Hall, Leicester, at the beginning of an eleven-performance British tour that would end at the London Palladium on April 10.

1990 Phoebe Snow and Patti Austin performed at the first New York Rock & Soul Review at the Beacon Theater along with Michael McDonald and Donald Fagen of Steely Dan.

1992 MC Hammer signed an agreement to promote Kentucky Fried Chicken worldwide.

The Miracles

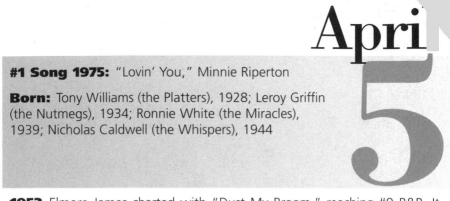

#1 Song 1975: "Lovin' You," Minnie Riperton

Born: Tony Williams (the Platters), 1928; Leroy Griffin (the Nutmegs), 1934; Ronnie White (the Miracles), 1939; Nicholas Caldwell (the Whispers), 1944

1952 Elmore James charted with "Dust My Broom," reaching #9 R&B. It was the first of many cover recordings by rock 'n' roll and blues artists to emanate from the rich catalog of blues great Robert Johnson, who made his last recordings in 1937.

1957 Frankie Lymon stated in an interview with Britain's Melody Maker magazine that "he preferred progressive jazz (Dave Brubeck, Stan Kenton, Ted Heath) to rock 'n' roll."

1958 Clyde McPhatter, Sam Cooke, Jimmy Reed, and many more performed at the start of an eighty-date tour called Irving Feld's Greatest Show of Stars, 1958 in Norfolk, VA.

1968 James Brown made a national TV plea for calm after the assassination of Martin Luther King Jr., and the subsequent riots in many cities. Its reassuring effect was followed by an official commendation from Vice President Humphrey.

1977 Richie Havens performed at a fund-raiser with John Sebastian and Jackson Browne to help endangered whales and dolphins. The Los Angeles concert raised more than $150,000.

1984 Michael Jackson took home the Best Video Award at the second annual American Video Awards for The Making of Michael Jackson's *Thriller*.

1985 USA for Africa's single "We Are the World" was played simultaneously over 5,000 radio stations around the world at 3:50 P.M. Greenwich Time.

1990 Michael Jackson visited the White House at President Bush's invitation.

1995 Whitney Houston's first album, *Whitney Houston*, was certified a 12-million-seller by the RIAA.

#1 Song 1963: "He's So Fine," the Chiffons

Born: Harmonica blues man Big Walter "Shakey" Horton, 1917

1956 Alan Freed's Easter show at the Brooklyn Paramount featured the Flamingos, the Platters, Frankie Lymon & the Teenagers, the Cleftones, the Valentines, and the Royaltones.

1957 Legendary recording honcho George Goldner started the Gone label, future home of acts like the Dubs, the Channels, the Shells, the Velours, and the Bobbettes.

1959 "It's Just a Matter of Time" by Brook Benton peaked at #3 on the pop charts. The deep baritone ballad characteristics of the song would set the style for Benton's hits throughout his career. Benton had already been a successful songwriter with hits like Nat King Cole's "Looking Back" and Clyde McPhatter's "A Lover's Question" in 1958.

1963 Fats Domino, who had fifty-eight R&B hits and fifty-nine pop charters through 1962 on Imperial Records, signed with ABC-Paramount Records. Not his best move, as it turned out he had only seven more chart records during the remainder of his recording career through 1968, with none reaching higher than #24 R&B ("Red Sails in the Sunset").

1963 Martha & the Vandellas charted with "Come and Get These Memories," reaching #6 R&B and #29 pop, and becoming their first of twenty-four pop hits through 1974. The group was first called the Del Phis but became the Vandellas after backing Marvin Gaye on "Hitch Hike." The name "Vandellas" came from a combination of Detroit's Van Dyke Street and Martha's favorite singer, Della Reese.

1991 Patti LaBelle performed on *Bob Hope's Yellow Ribbon Party* in honor of returning troops from the first Gulf War.

1992 The Marvelettes, the Supremes, the Temptations, the Four Tops, Jimmy Ruffin, Martha & the Vandellas, and Edwin Starr all sang at the Wembley Arena, Wembley, London.

1996 Mariah Carey's "Always Be My Baby" charted on its way to #1. It was her seventeenth hit in six years, eleven of which were #1.

#1 R&B Song 1968: "(Sweet, Sweet Baby) Since You've Been Gone," Aretha Franklin

Born: Billie Holiday (Eleanora Fagan), 1915; Charlie Thomas (the Drifters), 1937; Patricia Bennett (the Chiffons), 1947; Carol Douglas, 1948

1915 One of the all-time great blues singers, Eleanora "Billie" Holiday, was born today in Baltimore. She took her name from her favorite actress, silent-screen star Billie Dove, but her fans dubbed her "Lady Day."

1956 Little Richard's second 45 for Specialty Records, "Long Tall Sally," charted, reaching #1 R&B and #6 pop. The song was originally called "The Thing," and later, "Bald Headed Sally." Richard was encouraged by Lloyd Price to send his blues demos to Specialty's Art Rupe, who subsequently signed him. During Richard's early years he washed dishes at a bus station in between music gigs.

1956 The Diablos, the Moroccos, the Kool Gents, and the Daps brought down the house at the Madison Rink in Chicago.

1956 James Brown & the Famous Flames' fiery first 45 "Please, Please, Please" charted, reaching #5 R&B (and #105 pop), eventually selling more than a million copies.

1962 The Falcons' "I Found a Love" charted reaching #6 R&B (#75 pop). The lead singer was twenty-one-year-old Wilson Pickett, who was discovered as a replacement for Eddie Floyd when his neighbor Willie Schofield of the Falcons heard Wilson singing and playing guitar on his front porch.

1973 Gladys Knight & the Pips reached #2 pop and #1 R&B (for four weeks) with "Neither One of Us (Wants to Be the First to Say Goodbye)." Their fourth #1 R&B, the song was actually a country tune by Mississippi writer/artist Jim Wetherly.

Billie Holiday

April 8

#1 R&B Song 1972: "In the Rain," the Dramatics

Born: Carmen McRae, 1922; Jerome Louis "J.J." Jackson, 1941

1950 The Johnny Otis Orchestra, featuring Little Esther and Mel Walker on vocals, charted with "Mistrustin' Blues," reaching #1 for four weeks on the R&B charts. Otis's previous hit was "Double Crossing Blues" with Little Esther & the Robins (who would go on to be the core of the Coasters), which spent nine weeks at #1 R&B.

1958 The Platters left Los Angeles for a five-and-a-half-month tour of Europe through twenty-two cities in twelve countries.

1966 Otis Redding performed at Los Angeles's famed Whiskey A Go-Go. His label, Atlantic Records, recorded the evening's performance but did not release it until after Redding died.

1967 Wilson Pickett charted with "I Found a Love, Pt. 1," reaching #6 R&B, #32 pop. It was a remake of the hit he had in 1962 as lead of the Falcons, which coincidentally also reached #6 R&B.

1967 Peaches & Herb charted with their cover of the Five Keys' classic 1955 #5 R&B hit, "Close Your Eyes," reaching #4 and #8 pop.

1972 The ChiLites charted with "Oh Girl," which became their biggest hit and only #1. The Chicago quartet managed forty-three R&B hits from 1969 to 1998.

1978 George Duke arrived on the R&B hit list with "Dukey Stick (Part 1)," topping out at #4. The jazz/rock singer-keyboardist performed with a cornucopia of artists—from Cannonball Adderley to Frank Zappa's Mothers of Invention—before having his solo career take off in 1977.

#1 R&B Song 1955: "The Wallflower,"
Etta James & the Peaches

Born: Blues musician Mance Lipscomb, 1895;
Paul Robeson, 1898

1949 The Maxin Trio charted with "Confession Blues," reaching #2 on the R&B charts. The vocalist/pianist for the group was a young R.C. Robinson, who would soon become known as Ray Charles. It was his first chart single in a career that would last for seven decades. The blind eighteen-year old-began playing Nat King Cole Trio-styled jazz and blues in Seattle before recording.

1966 Sam & Dave charted with their soul standard-to-be "Hold On, I'm Comin,'" reaching #1 R&B and #21 pop. Twenty-two years later to the day Dave (David Prater) died when his car hit a tree in Syracuse, GA.

1974 Janet Jackson, youngest of the nine Jackson family siblings, and older sister LaToya made their performance debuts with the Jackson 5 at the MGM Grand Hotel in Las Vegas. Janet was seven years old and LaToya, seventeen.

1979 Donna Summer's "Last Dance" won an Oscar for Best Original Song at the fifty-first annual Academy Awards.

1982 Tina Turner performed at the Hammersmith Odeon in London. Amazingly enough, during this period in her comeback, the tremendously energetic and talented artist did not have a recording contract.

1992 Stevie Wonder performed "I'll Be Seeing You" on *The Tonight Show with Johnny Carson* as the legendary late-night talk-show host was retiring within a month. Carson's show was a longtime supporter of and performance venue for black artists and entertainers.

1994 Whitney Houston, Aaron Neville, and Branford Marsalis performed at Carnegie Hall in New York along with James Taylor, Elton John, and Sting among others at the fifth Rain Forest Benefit Concert.

Branford Marsalis

April

10

#1 R&B Song 1948: "King Size Papa," Julia Lee & Her Boyfriends

Born: Roscoe Gordon, 1928; Nate Nelson (the Flamingos), 1932; Danny Woods (the Chairmen of the Board), 1944; Kenneth "Babyface" Edmonds, 1959

1954 Billy Ward & the Dominoes' "Tenderly" and the Harptones' "My Memories of You" were released. Also, the Crows from Harlem, New York, jumped on the R&B hit list with "Gee," which many historians consider the first rock 'n' roll Top 10 pop hit. The record took off when a Los Angeles disc jockey began playing the record continuously because it was his girlfriend's favorite and they had just had a fight. She called him for fear he'd get fired, but "Huggy Boy" said: "I'm not taking it off until you come back here."

1956 During a performance for an all white audience in Birmingham, AL, Nat King Cole was beaten senseless while on stage.

1965 England's popular TV show *Juke Box Jury* welcomed Dionne Warwick as a guest panelist.

1971 Marvin Gaye—now more reflective and concerned after the death of his friend and singing partner, Tammi Terrell—wrote, produced, and recorded the anti-war, anti-pollution, anti-poverty anthem, "What's Going On," which reached #2 pop and #1 (for five weeks) R&B.

1992 The first album by Boyz II Men, *Cooleyhighharmony*, exceeded four million records sold and consequently became the biggest selling R&B vocal group record in music history.

1996 R. Kelly and LL Cool J performed at the Nassau Veterans Memorial Coliseum in Uniondale, NY.

1998 Prince performed with Larry Graham at the eleventh annual Essence Awards.

#1 R&B Song 1970: "ABC,"
the Jackson 5

Born: Richard Berry, 1935

1953 The Clovers received a gold disc for sales of 2 million records. The award was for the combined sales of their first nine singles up to their newest release, "Crawlin'."

1961 The Marcels recorded their second and third singles, "Summertime" and "You Are My Sunshine."

1961 John Lee Hooker was the featured act at Gerde's Folk City, the legendary folk and blues music venue in New York City. Hooker's opening act was a newcomer in his first appearance in the city, Bob Dylan.

1980 Barry White received an honorary degree from UCLA's Faculty Club in Recording Arts & Sciences.

1992 The Four Tops, Tina Turner, and the Temptations were grand-opening performers for Euro-Disney Amusement Park outside Paris, France.

1998 Stevie Wonder, Smokey Robinson, Ray Charles, James Ingram, Patti Austin, and Nancy Wilson appeared on *Quincy Jones...the First 50 Years*, a tribute to the legendary record producer that was televised on ABC-TV.

John Lee Hooker

Lester Cohen

April

12

#1 R&B Song 1969: "Only the Strong Survive," Jerry Butler

Born: Herbie Hancock, 1940

1963 The Drifters recorded a sensational Leiber/Stoller song, "Only in America." Unfortunately, due to racial unrest in the country, the group's vocals were lifted from the track and replaced by those of Jay & the Americans, who had the hit.

1964 Chubby Checker married a Miss World 1962 beauty queen from the Netherlands, Catharina Lodders.

1968 Jimi Hendrix dueted with Dusty Springfield on "Mockingbird" during her British TV show, *It Must Be Dusty*.

1969 The Fifth Dimension's "Aquarius/Let the Sun Shine In" topped the pop charts for six weeks while reaching #6 R&B. It became their biggest hit, selling more than three million copies, two million of those in just three months. Producer Bones Howe saw the separate songs performed in the Broadway show *Hair* and joined the two tracks together, with the group adding their vocals while performing in Las Vegas with Frank Sinatra.

1980 The Detroit Spinners, as they were known in England (actually the Spinners in the U.S.), topped the charts with "Working My Way Back to You/Forgive Me, Girl," making it their biggest British hit of ten charters there.

1986 Little Richard's "Great Gosh A'mighty (It's a Matter of Time)," from the Bette Midler/Richard Dreyfuss film *Down and Out in Beverly Hills*, reached #42 pop, and became Richard's last of twenty-one hits over thirty years.

1990 James Brown was transferred to Lower Savannah Work Center, Aiken County, GA, after serving fifteen months of his term in State Park Prison. While in prison, he counseled youths about drug abuse and was paid the standard minimum wage of $3.80 an hour. (See December 15.)

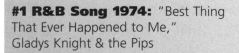

April

13

#1 R&B Song 1974: "Best Thing That Ever Happened to Me," Gladys Knight & the Pips

Born: Al Green, 1946; Peabo Bryson, 1951

1957 Richard Berry & the Pharaohs' original version of "Louie Louie" was released. It went relatively unnoticed until 1963, when the Kingsmen made it into one of America's all-time party records.

1963 Jackie Wilson's "Baby Workout" peaked at #5 pop but spent three weeks at #1 R&B. Meanwhile, across the Atlantic, Little Eva brought her "Locomotion" to the Olympia Theater in Paris.

1970 Dionne Warwick performed at London's Royal Albert Hall.

1985 "We Are the World" by USA for Africa reached #1 in America and stayed there for four weeks.

1999 Tina Turner, Whitney Houston, Mary J. Blige, TLC, and Cher performed at New York's Beacon Theater for VH-1's *Divas Live '99* show.

2000 Revlon sponsored their tenth-anniversary Carnegie Hall Benefit Concert to protect the rainforest, with performances by Gladys Knight, Martha Reeves, the Impressions, and Percy Sledge.

Gladys Knight

April 14

#1 R&B Song 1945: "Tippin' In,"
Erskine Hawkins & His Orchestra

Born: Sax man Gene "Jug" Ammons,
1925

1956 The Cleftones' classic, "Little Girl of Mine" (#57 pop and #8 R&B) was released.

1958 The Platters' "Twilight Time" charted on its way to #1 pop and R&B. The song was written by the group's manager, Buck Ram, in 1944, with the Three Suns, who had the original hit. Mercury Records created a film clip of the performance by the Platters and used it to promote the record to TV shows. In retrospect, it can be seen as the first promotional video.

1962 The Shirelles' "Soldier Boy" charted, becoming their biggest pop hit at #1 for three weeks and #3 R&B. The song, written in a country & western vein, was put together by the writers (Greenberg & Dixon) in a few minutes and tagged on at the end of a recording session. The track, done in about ten minutes, was instantly disliked by the group.

1967 An all-star, all–Stax Records package toured Europe, including Otis Redding, Sam & Dave, Arthur Conley, Eddie Floyd, Booker T. & the M.G.'s, and the Mar-Keys.

1969 Little Richard, Fats Domino, the Clara Ward Singers, Buddy Miles, and Jerry Lee Lewis, among others, performed on the NBC-TV special hosted by the Monkees, *33 1/3 Revolutions per Monkee*.

1973 Barry White charted with his first single under his own name with "I'm Gonna Love You Just a Little More Baby," reaching #3 pop and #1 R&B. White recorded in 1965 under the name Barry Lee on both Downey ("Man Ain't Nothing") and Veep ("Make It") labels.

1979 B.B. King toured the U.S.S.R. for a full month of concerts.

1991 The Pointer sisters performed on *Welcome Home America*, an ABC-TV tribute to American armed forces returning from the Gulf War.

April 15

#1 R&B Song 1978: "Too Much, Too Little, Too Late," Johnny Mathis & Deniece Williams

Born: Bessie Smith, 1895

1939 The Ink Spots—pioneers of pop who would harmonically branch into rhythm & blues—debuted on the charts with "If I Didn't Care," reaching #2. They would go on to have forty-six pop hits, but "If I" would become their signature song.

1944 The Nat King Cole Trio charted R&B with "Straighten Up and Fly Right," reaching #1 for an astonishing ten weeks while soaring to #9 pop. It was their third #1 in a row and was also their third chart record in a row. Nice way to start a career.

1950 The Johnny Otis Orchestra, with Little Esther on vocals, charted R&B with "Misery," reaching #9. Otis's band had eighteen R&B hits between 1948 and 1969, and are best remembered for their #9 1958 pop hit, "Willie and the Hand Jive," which also reached #3 R&B.

1956 Hartford, CT's State Theater held an all-star show featuring the Moonglows, the Cleftones, the Solitaires, the Willows, the Schoolboys, the Royaltones, and Dean Barlow & the Crickets.

1960 The Clovers, the Olympics, Robert & Johnny, Etta James, Santo & Johnny, and Ben E. King—in his first appearance after leaving the Drifters—performed at the Apollo Theater's Dr. Jive Rhythm & Blues Revue.

1972 Roberta Flack's "The First Time Ever I Saw Your Face" reached #1 and stayed there for six weeks. It was the longest-running #1 by a female solo artist since Gogi Grant's "The Wayward Wind" in 1956.

1993 Sade began a tour in Copenhagen, Denmark, that would include thirty-five shows, ending in London.

1994 James Brown performed at Radio City Music Hall in New York City to a sellout crowd of more than 4,000.

Bessie Smith

April
16

#1 R&B Song 1977: "At Midnight (My Love Will Lift You Up)," Rufus, featuring Chaka Khan

Born: Tony Williams (the Platters), 1928; Roy Hamilton, 1929

1949 Roy Milton charted R&B with "Hucklebuck," reaching #5. The singer, bandleader, and drummer (an unusual combination) charted R&B twenty-one times between 1946 and 1961. His first nineteen hits all made the Top 10.

1960 The latest installment of the Biggest Show of Stars '60 tour—including Joe Turner, Lloyd Price, Little Anthony & the Imperials, LaVern Baker, Clyde McPhatter, the Coasters, Jimmy Jones, Sammy Turner, and Jimmy Reed—began their travels at the Municipal Auditorium in Norfolk, VA.

1966 Percy Sledge entered the R&B hit list with what would become an all-time soul classic, "When a Man Loves a Woman," reaching #1 both pop and R&B.

1969 The Fifth Dimension's "Aquarius/Let the Sun Shine In" charted in England on its way to #11. The original American release, which was shortened for radio play and which omitted most of "Aquarius," was accidentally issued in England. The radio edit became the British hit and was never corrected.

1988 D.J. Jazzy Jeff & the Fresh Prince landed on the R&B hit list with "Parents Just Don't Understand," reaching #10 and #12 pop. It was the first of three Top 10 hits for the rappers, who were actually Jeffrey Townes and actor/rapper Will Smith.

1990 Anita Baker, Natalie Cole, Bonnie Raitt, and Mica Paris sang "Blowin' in the Wind" at Nelson Mandela—an International Tribute to a Free South Africa concert at Wembley Stadium in England.

D.J. Jazzy Jeff & the Fresh Prince

April 17

#1 R&B Song 1961: "One Mint Julep," Ray Charles

Born: Redman (Reggie Noble), 1970

1943 The Ink Spots charted with "I Can't Stand Losing You," reaching #1 for seven weeks. The legendary group was the precursor to rhythm & blues of the '50s. Between 1942 and 1948 they logged sixteen straight R&B Top 10 hits on what was then the Harlem Hit Parade and the race charts.

1948 Louis Jordan and His Tympany 5 jumped on the R&B hit list with "Reet, Petite and Gone," reaching #4. The song is likely where Berry Gordy got the idea for his song "Reet Petite," which became Jackie Wilson's solo hit debut.

1954 Detroit's Fortune label signed a young local group, the Diablos, whose falsetto-singing lead vocalist, Nolan Strong, became the emulated idol of one Smokey Robinson.

1957 An all-star show was held at the Regal Theater in Chicago including, the Dells, the Spaniels, Big Maybelle, Little Esther (Phillips), the Sensations, Junior Parker, Bobby "Blue" Bland, Nappy Brown, Solomon Burke, Annie Laurie, and Al Smith's Orchestra.

1965 Gospel singer Marie Knight prayed her way onto the R&B charts with the Julie London pop hit, "Cry Me a River," reaching #35. Knight had four hit singles from 1948 through 1965, a rare accomplishment for a gospel artist. Her biggest single was "Up Above My Head, I Hear Music in the Air," with Sister Rosetta Tharpe (#6) in 1948.

1971 Aretha Franklin's "Bridge Over Troubled Water" charted on its way to #1 R&B and #6 pop. Writer Paul Simon had previously stated that he wrote the song with Franklin in mind, though Simon & Garfunkel had the original hit a year earlier.

1971 "Want Ads" by the Honey Cone charted on its way to #1 pop and R&B. The female trio from Los Angeles consisted of a former Ikette, a former member of Bob B. Soxx & the Blue Jeans, and the sister of Blue Jeans member/Blossoms lead Darlene Love.

1980 Bob Marley performed before Prince Charles and President Mugabe in Salsbury, Zimbabwe, at their Independence Day celebrations.

April

#1 R&B Song 1953: "Hound Dog," Willie Mae "Big Mama" Thornton

Born: Clarence "Gatemouth" Brown, 1924

1953 Rufus Thomas entered the R&B charts with "Bear Cat," peaking at #3. The song was an answer record to Big Mama Thornton's hit, "Hound Dog," which would eventually be a huge hit for Elvis Presley. Rufus is the father of singer Carla Thomas.

1956 Jackie Wilson & the Dominoes recorded their first sides for Decca, including "St. Theresa of the Roses" and six others in Los Angeles.

1965 Little Richard performed at New York's famed Paramount Theater. A member of his backup group at the time was a young guitarist named Jimi Hendrix.

1970 The "New" Supremes, with Jean Terrell replacing Diana Ross, reached #10 pop and #5 R&B with their first release, "Up the Ladder to the Roof."

1981 Gary "U.S." Bonds's "This Little Girl" was released, reaching #11. It was written and co-produced for him by Bruce Springsteen, a longtime fan of Bonds. It was also Bonds's first hit in nineteen years.

1983 Marvin Gaye began what would become his last tour, starting in San Diego.

1993 B.B. King, Millie Jackson, and Bobby "Blue" Bland performed at the Westbury Music Fair, Westbury, NY.

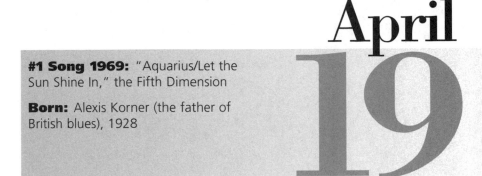

April 19

#1 Song 1969: "Aquarius/Let the Sun Shine In," the Fifth Dimension

Born: Alexis Korner (the father of British blues), 1928

1952 The Clovers' classic, "One Mint Julep," charted, rising to #2 R&B. Between 1951 and 1954, the Washington, DC, quintet scored fifteen straight R&B Top 10 winners. They hit the Top 10 four more times after their standard "Blue Velvet" only reached #14 R&B in 1955.

1956 Clyde McPhatter of the Drifters was discharged from the Army and began his solo career.

1975 The compilation album *The Best of the Stylistics* reached #1 in England, becoming the top-selling album of the year and the largest seller in Britain by a black act to date. It spent an amazing sixty-three weeks on the U.K. charts. It reached #13 R&B but only #41 pop stateside.

1980 Michael Jackson's "She's Out of My Life" single charted, reaching #10 pop and giving the King of Pop the distinction of becoming the first individual artist to have four hits from the same album, though he would later break his own record.

1991 Whitney Houston was accused of "terrorist threatening" and allegedly punching a man in the eye when the man tried to break up a fight between her brother Michael and a third man at a Radisson Hotel in Lexington, KY. The charges were later dismissed.

Whitney Houston

April 20

#1 R&B Song 1974: "TSOP (the Sound of Philadelphia)," MFSB featuring the Three Degrees

Born: Lionel Hampton, 1928; Ronald Mundy (the Marcels), 1940; Luther Vandross, 1951

1957 The Kingsmen's collector's classic "Don't Say You're Sorry" ($1,200) and the Dubs' standard "Don't Ask Me to Be Lonely" were released.

1959 The Falcons charted with "You're So Fine," reaching #17 pop and #2 R&B. The group originally included soul singer-to-be Eddie Floyd and lead singer Joe Stubbs, brother of the Four Tops' Levi Stubbs. Joe was later replaced in 1960 by a young vocalist named Wilson Pickett. "You're So Fine," along with the Fiestas' "So Fine" (which had charted two weeks earlier), are considered two of the first soul singles in a field that would dominate music in the '60s and '70s.

1963 James Brown's "Prisoner of Love" charted and soon became his first pop Top 20 hit (#18) after fifteen lesser Top 100 entries going back to 1956. Though the soul icon crossed over to pop an incredible 119 times through 1998, he never had a pop #1.

1968 Sly & the Family Stone peaked at #8 pop and #9 R&B, opening the door to a new style of rhythm and funk with elements of rock and jazz thrown in for good measure. Sly (Sylvester Stewart) recorded with a doo-wop group, the Viscaynes, in 1958, and later became a deejay in Oakland, CA, on station KDIA. He also produced hit records with the Beau Brummels, the Mojo Men, and Bobby Freeman during 1964 and 1965 before putting the Family Stone together.

1974 Diana Ross peaked at #5 in Britain with a remake of the Stylistics' hit, "You Are Everything," although her American fans never got to consider it as Motown didn't issue it stateside.

1990 Janet Jackson was honored with a star on the Hollywood Walk of Fame in Los Angeles.

Sly & the Family Stone

April 21

1956 Argo Records announced the signing of the Ravens (minus bass lead Jimmy Ricks), and the Six Teens' debut, "A Casual Look" (#25 pop, #7 R&B), was released. Meanwhile, Joe Turner, backed by the Cookies, entered the R&B charts with "Corrine, Corrina," reaching #2.

1958 The Shirelles charted for the first time with "I Met Him on a Sunday," reaching #49 pop. They were originally formed in junior high school as the Poquellos. The New Jersey teens renamed themselves the Shirelles, most likely after lead singer Shirley Owens Alston.

1958 Jackie Wilson charted for the first time R&B as a solo artist with "To Be Loved," reaching #7 and #22 pop. In England, it hit #27 in March, fell off the charts, and re-entered in May, peaking at #23, a practice that was common in Britain but unheard of in the States.

1961 Shep & the Limelites performed their hit "Daddy's Home" on *American Bandstand*. The song was a continuation of the Heartbeats' 1956 hit "A Thousand Miles Away." Not surprising since both were written by James Sheppard, who had been lead singer of both groups.

1962 Patti LaBelle & the Bluebelles hit the Hot 100 with a song they hadn't recorded: "I Sold My Heart to the Junkman" was actually done by the Starlets (featuring Dynetta Boone), who were signed to Chicago-based Pam Records. While touring in Philadelphia, they recorded "Junkman" for a used-car dealer, who issued the rocker as by his own unsuspecting Blue Belles. It rose to #15 as Patti & company rose to stardom while the Starlets drifted into obscurity.

1962 Tamla/Motown records issued the Marvelettes' single, "Playboy," an eventual #7 hit. A year earlier, the high school students, calling themselves the Marvels, auditioned for Motown boss Berry Gordy singing Chantels and Shirelles songs and were told to go home and come back when they graduated.

1974 The Pointer Sisters became the first pop act ever to perform at the San Francisco Opera House. The night's work was recorded for a live album that eventually reached #96 pop.

1997 Babyface was named among the twenty-five most influential people in America by *Time* magazine, which considered him the "yin to gangsta rap's yang."

April

22

#1 R&B Song 1944: "Main Stem," Duke Ellington & His Famous Orchestra

Born: Benjamin "Bullmoose" Jackson, 1919; Charles Mingus, 1922; Mel Carter, 1939

1959 Jackie Wilson appeared in the Alan Freed film, *Go, Johnny, Go!*, singing "You Better Know It." The movie premiered across the nation today. Also performing in the popular teen flick were Chuck Berry, the Flamingos, Harvey Fuqua (of Harvey & the Moonglows), and the Cadillacs.

1960 Marv Johnson, Ray Charles, Betty Carter, Tarheel Slim, and Little Ann performed at the Apollo Theater.

1964 Little Anthony & the Imperials recorded "I'm on the Outside Looking In" (#15 pop), their first hit in almost five years.

1972 Michael Jackson peaked at #2 pop and R&B with "Rockin' Robin." The song was a hit for Bobby Day & the Satellites in 1958 and coincidentally also reached #2. The song that kept Jackson out of #1 was Roberta Flack's "The First Time Ever I Saw Your Face."

Little Anthony & the Imperials

1973 Tina Turner began filming for the motion picture *Tommy* in her role as the *Acid Queen*. The former Annie Mae Bullock began singing at night with husband Ike while working in a hospital by day. Turner renamed her Tina because she reminded him of the star of the TV series *Sheena, Queen of the Jungle*.

1994 Brian McKnight and Chaka Khan sang "Bridge Over Troubled Water" at New York's Paramount Theater for the seventh annual Essence Awards.

1996 Ex-New Edition member Bobby Brown was unable to recite the alphabet today. This would normally have not been a big deal except Brown was in the middle of a sobriety test at the time and was subsequently booked for driving under the influence in Atlanta. To add to his chagrin, the woman in his car when he was pulled over was not his wife, Whitney Houston. No wonder he was laughing during his wedding vows. (See July 18.)

April 23

1949 "Trouble Blues" by Charles Brown charted on its way to #1 R&B for an amazing fifteen weeks. It became the fifth biggest R&B hit of all time. The recording spent twenty-seven weeks on the charts. Brown originally sang with Johnny Moore's Three Blazers and was married to vocalist Mabel Scott.

1949 The Orioles' "Tell Me So" hopped on the R&B charts, reaching #1. The Orioles charted eleven times between 1948 and 1953 with such standards as "Lonely Christmas," "It's Too Soon to Know," and "Crying in the Chapel."

1954 The Royals' single, "Work with Me, Annie" was issued, beginning the era of the "answer record." It became so popular (#22 pop, #1 R&B) that the group renamed themselves Hank Ballard & the Midnighters to avoid confusion with the "5" Royales.

1955 Al Hibbler charted with the inspirational recording, "Unchained Melody" from the motion picture Unchained. The record reached #1 R&B and #3 pop and was the definitive version of this oft-recorded song until the Righteous Brothers' blue-eyed soul version in 1965.

1988 Whitney Houston topped the pop charts with "Where Do Broken Hearts Go" while setting a record for most consecutive #1 singles. It was her seventh, beating out both the Bee Gees and the Beatles, who each had six in a row.

1990 A cappella specialists Take 6—along with Stevie Wonder, Patti Austin, Phoebe Snow, and James Taylor—performed at New York's legendary Carnegie Hall at a fund-raiser for Special Olympics Africa.

1995 Little Richard performed at the opening of Dolly Parton's Dollywood Amusement Park in Pigeon Falls, TN.

1997 The Four Tops received a star on the Hollywood Walk of Fame.

April

24

#1 R&B Song 1961: "Mother-in-Law," Ernie K-Doe

Born: Freddie Scott, 1933; Bernard Henderson (Hues Corporation), 1944; Robert Knight, 1945; Ann Kelly (Hues Corporation), 1947

1948 The Mills Brothers charted with "Shine," reaching #10 R&B. In 1932 the group had a pop hit with the same song (#7) with Bing Crosby singing lead, making it one of the few times in recorded history that an act had two Top 10 hits with the same tune in different recordings.

1954 The Diablos' debut, "Adios, My Desert Love," and the Chords' "Sh-Boom" were released. "Sh-Boom" was originally considered the "throw-away" B-side.

1976 Parliament (formerly the Parliaments) reached #5 R&B with "Tear the Roof Off the Sucker (Give Up the Funk)." It was the first of George Clinton & Parliament's seven Top 10 R&B hits. Not bad for a kid who started out working at the Uptown Tensorial Parlor, a Newark, NJ, barbershop.

1982 Stevie Wonder's duet with Paul McCartney, "Ebony and Ivory," reached #1 in Britain and would soon be #1 pop for seven weeks in the states (#8 R&B).

1982 Patti Austin's duet with James Ingram, "Baby, Come to Me," reached the Top 100 for the second time today. The record was first released almost a year earlier reaching only #73, but after being featured in the soap opera *General Hospital*, it was reissued and would eventually climb to #1. It would be Austin's only pop chart #1.

1992 Prince performed at the Sydney Entertainment Center in Sydney, Australia. It was the first of six sold-out shows.

Prince

April 25

#1 R&B Song 1987: "Sign of the Times," Prince

Born: Earl Bostic, 1913; Ella Fitzgerald, 1918; Albert King, 1923

1913 One of the great R&B "sax honkers," Earl Bostic, was born. He worked with many of the days greats including Lionel Hampton, Artie Shaw, Paul Whitman, Don Redman, and Louis Prima. His own band was a breeding ground for future jazz greats like Stanley Turrentine, John Coltrane, and Blue Mitchell. Bostic's biggest hits included "Flamingo" (#1, 1951) and "Temptation" (#10, 1948).

1953 Fats Domino had his seventh Top 10 R&B single in a row with "Going to the River" (#2). Of his first thirty chart 45s, an amazing twenty-eight would make the Top 10.

1962 The Untouchables ("Poor Boy Needs a Preacher") and the Checkmates (who wouldn't have a hit for seven years until "Black Pearl") began a long engagement at the Fremont Hotel in Las Vegas.

1964 Dionne Warwick's classic pop/R&B ballad "Walk on By" charted, reaching #6. It would also become a standard in England, reaching #9.

1970 Diana Ross "touched" the Hot 100 with "Reach Out and Touch (Somebody's Hand)." It reached #20 and was her first solo success since leaving the Supremes.

1970 In an unlikely combination, Wilson Pickett charted with the bubblegum-pop hit-makers the Archies' 1969 smash "Sugar Sugar." Pickett's version reached #4 R&B and a surprising #25 pop.

1973 Chuck Berry, Bruce Springsteen, and Jerry Lee Lewis played at the Cole Field House in Maryland, with Berry backed by Springsteen's band.

1992 Club Nouveau charted with "Oh Happy Day," which reached #45 R&B and became their last of eight hits, including the 1987 #2 hit, "Lean on Me." The recording had a twenty-two-member chorus aptly named the Oh Happy Day Choir.

2002 Lisa "Left Eye" Lopes of TLC was killed in a car accident. The singer/arsonist was thirty.

April

#1 R&B Song 1969: "It's Your Thing," the Isley Brothers

Born: "Ma" Rainey (Gertrude Pridgett), 1886; Blues guitarist Joseph Benjamin "J.B." Hutto, 1926; Maurice Williams (the Zodiacs), 1938; Claudine Clark, 1941

1957 Harry Belafonte signed for the then-unheard-of sum of $1 million with RCA Records. Known as the King of Calypso, Belafonte was actually from the Bronx.

1969 Dorothy Morrison & the Edwin Hawkins Singers hit the pop charts with the pure gospel song "Oh Happy Day," which broke all barriers on its way to #4 pop and million-selling status.

1975 Gladys Knight & the Pips' "The Way We Were" charted, becoming their thirty-third of forty-two Top 100 singles. The same day, the quintessential disco hit "The Hustle," by Van McCoy, entered the hit list, rising to #1 pop and R&B.

1975 Ben E. King peaked at #5 pop (#1 R&B) with "Supernatural Thing," his first Top 5 solo pop hit in almost fourteen years. Ben had been without a label when Atlantic Records President Ahmet Ertegun saw him performing at a Miami nightclub and asked him to re-sign with the organization. All of the ex-Drifters hits had been with Atlantic's subsidiary Atco records from 1961 through 1969.

1990 Aretha Franklin, who failed to appear in the show Sing Mahalia, Sing was ordered by a New York judge to pay restitution in the amount of $209,364.

1991 Three former Temptations lead singers (Eddie Kendricks, David Ruffin, and Dennis Edwards) banded together to go on tour in England, performing tonight at the Newport Center, Newport, Gwent, Wales.

1993 Bobby Brown and a young dancer were fined $850 for public lewdness while simulating a sex act at Augusta-Richmond's County Civic Center on January 13.

1994 R. Kelly and Salt-N-Pepa performed at the James L. Knight Center in Miami, FL.

April 27

#1 R&B Song 1957: "Lucille," Little Richard

Born: Maxine Brown (the Browns), 1932; Cuba Gooding (the Main Ingredient), 1944; Ann Peebles, 1947; Herb Murrell (the Stylistics), 1949

1960 The Biggest Show of Stars 1960 made a performance stop at the Lauderdale County Coliseum in Florence, AL, with performers including Little Anthony & the Imperials, Lloyd Price, Clyde McPhatter, Bo Diddley, Jimmy Reed, and the Coasters, among others.

1963 The Crystals soared onto the pop hit list with "Da Doo Ron Ron," an eventual #3 classic.

1972 The Chi-Lites hit #1 pop and R&B with their career establishing "Oh Girl." Lead singer Eugene Record was the husband of soul singer Barbara Acklin.

1974 The Impressions charted with "Finally Got Myself Together," reaching #1 R&B (#17 pop). It was their fourth and last #1 over eleven years, starting in 1963 with "It's All Right."

1984 Michael Jackson's incredible success and airwave "overkill" had its detractors and among them was radio WWSH in Philadelphia, which declared a "No Michael Jackson" weekend.

1990 B.B. King was hospitalized due to diabetes-related problems in Las Vegas. Within a month he would be back performing.

1991 Luther Vandross charted with "Power of Love/Love Power," reaching #1 R&B and #4 pop. The backing vocalists included Darlene Love and Cissy Houston.

1993 Aretha Franklin's first TV special was taped at New York's Nederlander Theatre and featured duets with Bonnie Raitt on "Since You've Been Gone," and "Natural Woman" with Raitt and Gloria Estefan. Also performing were Smokey Robinson (singing a duet with Aretha on "Just to See Her") and Elton John.

Luther Vandross

Matthew Rolston

April

28

#1 R&B Song 1962: "Mashed Potato Time," Dee Dee Sharp

Born: Emma Pought (the Bobbettes), 1942; Milan Williams (the Commodores), 1948

1956 The New York City doo-wop group the Willows entered the charts with the singing-group standard "Church Bells May Ring," reaching #11 R&B and #62 pop.

1958 The Drifters recorded their classic, "Drip Drop." It was the last charter (#58 pop) for the original group.

1958 The Charts' "You're the Reason," the Solitaires' "No More Sorrows," and the Spaniels' "Tina" were all released today.

1961 The Flamingos, the Vibrations, the Miracles, Shep & the Limelites' Jerry Butler, and Maxine Brown played Philadelphia's Uptown Theater while the Del Vikings performed on *American Bandstand*, also in Philly.

1963 Ray Charles performed at Carnegie Hall in New York City.

1990 MC Hammer (Stanley Burrell) charted with the dance-rap classic "U Can't Touch This," reaching #1 R&B (#8 pop). In its first week on the charts it reached #28, the highest position a rap song had achieved up to that time. The song appropriated the entire baseline of Rick James's "Superfreak," but thanks to the tenacious pursuit of his publisher, Jay Warner, James soon wound up with 50 percent of the ownership of the new song.

1991 Quincy Jones recorded his album *Hallelujah!*, a modern-day version of Handel's *Messiah*, at A&M Studios in Hollywood. On hand to sing on the album were Patti LaBelle and Stevie Wonder.

1995 Barry White performed at the Safari Park Garden Theater in Nairobi, Kenya, becoming the first Westerner to do so.

April 29

#1 Song 1972: "The First Time," Roberta Flack

Born: Duke Ellington, 1899; Big Jay McNeeley, 1927; Carl Gardner (the Coasters), 1928; Tammi Terrell (Thomasina Montgomery), 1946

1944 "G.I. Jive" by Louis Jordan charted, reaching #1 R&B for six weeks as well as #1 pop for two. Jordan's recordings hold the R&B record for most weeks at #1, an astounding 113 weeks.

1950 Johnny Otis & His Orchestra jumped on the R&B charts with "Cry Baby," reaching #6. The vocals were done by Mel Walker & the Bluenotes (not Harold Melvin's group).

1956 To capitalize on Elvis Presley's revival hit of "Money, Honey," Atlantic Records reissued Clyde McPhatter & the Drifters' three-year-old original in both the pop and R&B markets.

1957 "The Negro disk jockey, once considered a rarity on the nations airwaves, has become almost commonplace in this day and age," Ellis Waters stated today in the new Negro men's magazine, *Duke*. The writer continued: "There are now more than 500 Negro platter spinners on the air across the nation." He described disc jockeying as the "newest Negro industry," a $250 million annual business.

1960 Sam Cooke began a week's engagement at New York's Apollo Theater.

1967 Cindy Birdsong (Patti LaBelle & the Blue Belles) made her stage debut as a replacement for Florence Ballard in the Supremes at the Hollywood Bowl in a benefit concert for the UCLA School of Music. Also performing was the Fifth Dimension.

Duke Ellington

April 30

#1 R&B Song 1966: "Get Ready," the Temptations

Born: Mabel Scott, 1915

1949 John Lee Hooker charted with "Hoogie Boogie," which reached #9 R&B. Considering contracts an acquired taste he had not acquired, Hooker recorded for anyone with the money and between 1949 and 1954 he had seventy singles out on twenty-one labels under no less than ten very diverse names, such as Birmingham Sam & His Magic Guitar, Little Pork Chops, Delta John, John Lee Hooker, and the ever popular the Boogie Man.

1949 Billy Eckstine entered the R&B hit list with "Caravan," reaching #14 and #27 pop. The singer/trombonist had his own band before going solo in 1947, a who's who of legendary talent that included Charlie Parker, Sarah Vaughn, Dizzy Gillespie, Miles Davis, and Gene Ammons. Including his band releases, "Mr. B," as he was respectfully known, had eighteen hits between 1944 and 1976.

1966 The Platters' "I Love You 1,000 Times" charted, reaching #6 R&B and #31 pop, their first hit in four years.

1983 Muddy Waters, the crown prince of Chicago blues, died of a heart attack at his Chicago home while sleeping. The man who started out driving a truck for a Venetian-blind company had driven blues to a new level of acceptance with his resonant, deep voice and biting electric guitar style. Waters was sixty-eight.

1990 Prince performed at Rupert's Nightclub in Golden Valley, MN as a preview of his new Nude Tour. The show was also a fund-raiser, with the $100 admission going to the family of his bodyguard, who had died earlier in the month.

1994 James Brown performed "Get on Up" with Jeffrey Osborne, Jim Belushi, Dan Aykroyd, Bruce Springsteen, and Magic Johnson, among others, at the inaugural night of the House of Blues, Los Angeles.

1994 The Staple Singers performed at the twenty-fifth annual New Orleans Jazz & Heritage Festival.

May

#1 R&B Song 1971: "Never Can Say Goodbye," the Jackson 5

Born: Ada Brown, 1890; Big Maybelle (Maybelle Louise Smith), 1924; Marion "Little Walter" Jacobs, 1930; Reather Dixon (the Bobbettes), 1944; Ray Parker Jr. (Raydio), 1954

1948 Wynonie Harris bounced onto the R&B hit parade with "Good Rockin' Tonight," reaching #1. Six years later, Elvis Presley would make the song his own at the start of his legendary career, which was heavily influenced by artists like Harris.

1961 The Edsels' "Rama Lama Ding Dong" debuted on the pop charts, rising to #21. It was originally issued three years earlier but went nowhere.

1965 The Supremes leaped onto the charts with "Back in My Arms Again," their fifth #1 in a row.

1965 Solomon Burke had his biggest hit when "Got to Get You Off My Mind" reached #1 R&B for three weeks and peaking at #22 pop. Originally signed to Apollo Records in 1955, he temporarily retired from music to become a mortician.

1971 Wilson Pickett charted with "Don't Knock My Love, Part 1," reaching #1 R&B and #13 pop and becoming his last of five #1s. He had just returned from performing in Ghana, Africa, for that country's independence celebration.

1973 Marvin Gaye performed at the Kennedy Center in Washington, DC. Earlier in the day, the city declared it Marvin Gaye Day.

1993 Shirley Owens Reeves of the Shirelles received the Lifetime Achievement Award at the opening of the doo-wop Hall of Fame of America in Providence, RI.

1998 The Vocal Group Hall of Fame and Museum opened in Sharon, PA. By October, the hall would induct fourteen groups into the shrine, eight of which were legendary black acts. (See October 30.)

Solomon Burke

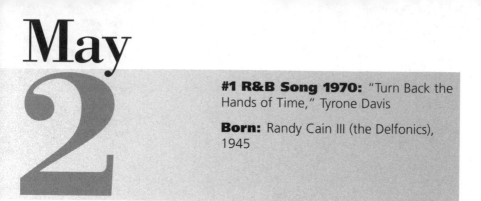

May

2

#1 R&B Song 1970: "Turn Back the Hands of Time," Tyrone Davis

Born: Randy Cain III (the Delfonics), 1945

1956 The Joytones, one of rock 'n' roll's first girl groups, recorded their single "Gee, What a Boy." The 79-cent single is a $300 collectible today.

1960 Ben E. King, lead singer of the Drifters, was fired by his manager George Treadwell when he asked for a raise.

1960 Etta James reached the Hot 100 with "All I Could Do Was Cry," (#33) her first of twenty-eight hits over the next ten years.

1970 The modest chart success of "Killer Joe" (#47 R&B, #74 pop) was the start of Quincy Jones's illustrious career as he went on to have twenty-eight R&B and thirteen pop hits through 1999. His contributions as an arranger and producer for other artists such as Michael Jackson earned Jones a Grammy Living Legends Award in 1990.

1981 Rick James charted with his album *Street Songs*, reaching #3 pop and an amazing #1 R&B for twenty weeks. James, who was the nephew of the Temptations' bass, Melvin Franklin, originally formed the soul/rock band, the Myna Birds, whose membership included Neil Young (Crosby, Stills Nash & Young) Bruce Palmer, and Goldie McJohn. Palmer later joined Young in Buffalo Springfield and McJohn joined Steppenwolf. *Street Songs* stayed on the pop charts for seventy-four weeks and the R&B hit list for seventy-eight.

1989 Michael Jackson was nearly arrested today when he showed up at a Simi Valley, CA, jewelry store wearing a wig, fake teeth, and a false mustache to do some innocent shopping. The security guard alerted police to the potential thief as the embarrassed star removed his disguise in order to satisfy three carloads of cops.

1991 B.B. King's Memphis Blues Club (owned by the blues great) opened on Beale Street in Memphis, TN.

1991 Lenny Kravitz performed at the Apollo Theater in Manchester, England, at the beginning of an eight-date British tour.

1994 The Shirelles were inducted into the Rhythm & Blues Foundation with a Pioneer Award and performed "Dedicated to the One I Love" for the first time in seventeen years.

May 3

#1 R&B Song 1952: "5-10-15 Hours," Ruth Brown

Born: James Brown, 1933

1947 Erskine Hawkins & his Orchestra charted with "Hawk's Boogie," reaching #2 R&B. The bandleader, composer, and trumpet player from Birmingham, AL, reached the R&B hit list twelve times between 1942 and 1950.

1950 Muddy Waters, recently signed to Chess Records of Chicago, had his first single for them, the venerable "Rolling Stone." Though it did not chart, the recording became well known among musicians and made its way across the Atlantic to the blues-hungry British rock 'n' rollers of the '60s. In fact, one act went so far as to name themselves after the song.

1959 Florence Greenberg, a Passaic, NJ, housewife who discovered the Shirelles, opened her own Scepter Records in New York and signed the girls after they charted on Decca with "I Met Him on a Sunday." The Shirelles would go on to have twenty-five more pop hits and twenty R&B charters all on Scepter, which would also become the home of Dionne Warwick and Chuck Jackson.

1963 The Drifters, Sam Cooke, Dionne Warwick, the Crystals, Jerry Butler, Little Esther, Dee Clark, and Solomon Burke performed at Pittsburgh's Syria Mosque.

1969 Jimi Hendrix was arrested at Toronto International Airport in Toronto, Canada, for possessing heroin. He was later released on $10,000 bail.

1980 Larry Graham charted with "One in a Million You," reaching #1 R&B and #9 pop for his biggest solo hit. Graham had formerly been a member of Sly and the Family Stone and later, Graham Central Station.

1997 Michael Jackson went to visit his concert promoter Marcel Avram. That was nothing unusual except for the fact that Avram was in Stadelheim Prison in Munich, Germany, at the time on charges of tax evasion.

May

4

#1 R&B Song 1968: "I Got the Feelin'," James Brown

Born: Tyrone Davis, 1938; Nick Ashford (Ashford & Simpson), 1943; Sigmund Esco "Jackie" Jackson (the Jackson 5), 1951

1946 Billy Eckstine charted with "Prisoner of Love," reaching #3 R&B and #10 pop. The song would later be passionately revived in James Brown's electric version.

1962 The latest edition of the Biggest Show of Stars 1962 tour began at Pittsburgh's Syria Mosque, featuring Fats Domino, Don & Juan, Brook Benton, the Impressions, and Gene Chandler.

1967 The Jimi Hendrix Experience peaked at #3 with "Purple Haze" on the British charts, their second Top 10 hit in a row.

1991 Crystal Waters, niece of legendary vocalist Ethel Waters, vaulted onto the Top 100 with "Gypsy Woman."

1992 In order to get his battered girlfriend to drop charges against him, Wilson Pickett paid a $6,500 fine along with $3,500 to the battered women's shelter she was staying in.

1994 Toni Braxton was named the World's Best-Selling R&B Newcomer of the Year at the sixth World Music Awards in Monte Carlo, Monaco, while Whitney Houston received the World's Best-Selling Pop Artist of the Year, Female Recording Artist of the Year, American Recording Artist of the Year, R&B Artist of the Year, and Overall Recording Artist awards.

Toni Braxton

May 5

1945 Bluesman Arthur "Big Boy" Crudup's chart debut was "Rock Me Mama," an eventual #3 R&B. Crudup started singing with the gospel group the Harmonizing Four and was discovered by an Okeh Records A&R man while playing on a Chicago street corner.

1953 The legendary vocal group the Spaniels recorded their first 45, "Baby, It's You." The single is now a $4,500 rarity.

1969 Stevie Wonder received the Distinguished Service Award from the President's Committee on Employment of Handicapped People by President Nixon at the White House.

1979 "We Are Family" by Sister Sledge charted, reaching #1 R&B and #2 pop. Background vocals were added by Luther Vandross, who watched and learned how his older sister did it when Patricia Vandross was a member of the '50s hit group the Crests.

1988 Michael Jackson became the first non-Russian to appear on Soviet television endorsing a product.

1989 Natalie Cole appeared at the John Lennon Tribute Concert singing "Lucy in the Sky with Diamonds" and "Ticket to Ride." The event was held at the Pier Head Arena in Merseyside, England.

1990 En Vogue charted with "Hold On," (#2) their first of twelve hits through 1996.

1995 In a campaign for Major League Baseball, Aretha Franklin appeared with the Detroit Tigers singing "Take Me Out to the Ball Game" in their promotional video while LL Cool J did the same with the Seattle Mariners.

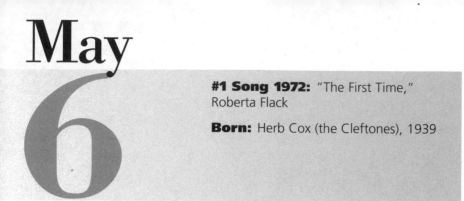

May

#1 Song 1972: "The First Time," Roberta Flack

Born: Herb Cox (the Cleftones), 1939

1944 The King Cole Trio charted with "I Can't See for Lookin'," reaching #2 R&B and #24 pop. The trio would have twenty-five hits between 1942 and 1950 before their leader Nat King Cole would permanently go solo.

1950 Joe Liggins & His Honeydrippers came up with one of the biggest hits of the '40s when "Pink Champagne" charted, intoxicating its listeners to the tune of #1 R&B for thirteen weeks (#30 pop).

1950 Amos Milburn, a Houston, TX, blues artist, charted with "Walking Blues," reaching #8 R&B. With Milburn it was all or nothing, as he had nineteen straight Top 10 R&B hits, including four #1s from 1948 to 1954. His biggest success was his first charter, "Chicken Shack Blues."

1960 Sam Cooke performed at the Howard Theater in Washington, DC, while the Platters were in San Francisco at Fack's #2 Club.

1972 Billy Preston charted with his biggest hit, "Outa-Space," reaching #1 R&B and #2 pop.

1990 Aaron Neville performed at the Jazz & Heritage Festival's twenty-first annual show in New Orleans.

1992 Whitney Houston performed on her first network TV special, *Whitney Houston—This Is My Life*, on ABC-TV. The show was produced by her own Nippy Inc. production company. Nippy was her nickname as a child.

1997 George Clinton and the Parliament/Funkadelic army were inducted into the Rock and Roll Hall of Fame at their twelfth annual induction ceremonies. The event was held at the hall's Cleveland home for the first time. Among Clinton's pre-music-career jobs, he was the foreman of a New Jersey Hula Hoop factory. Probably how he developed that great stage presence.

May 7

#1 R&B Song 1955: "I've Got a Woman,"
Ray Charles & His Band

Born: Jimmy Ruffin, 1939,
Thelma Houston, 1946

1953 Clyde McPhatter signed with Atlantic Records as lead singer of the Drifters.

1954 Clyde McPhatter of the Drifters was drafted into the Army, but was lucky to be stationed in Buffalo, NY. On weekends he would bus in for gigs with the group.

1955 Bo Diddley charted with his homage to himself, "Bo Diddley," reaching #1 R&B and beginning a legendary career that pushed him into the Rock and Roll Hall of Fame in 1987.

1966 After going without a Top 10 hit for almost three years, the Chiffons came back strong when "Sweet Talking Guy" charted on its way to #10 pop. The song was co-written by Doug Morris, who went on to become president of Universal Music Group, parent of UNI and MCA Records.

1968 Aretha Franklin made her first tour of Europe. While at the Olympia Theatre in Paris, her performance was recorded for a future album.

1988 Terence Trent D'Arby reached #1 pop and R&B with "Wishing Well." The malcontent who often denounced his home country of America apparently wised up in a later interview when he refused to comment, saying: "Every time I open my mouth, I ruin my career."

Terence Trent D'Arby

Chris Cuffaro

May 8

#1 R&B Song 1943: "I Can't Stand Losing You," the Ink Spots

Born: Robert Johnson, 1911; Philip Bailey (Earth, Wind & Fire), 1951

1943 Duke Ellington & His Orchestra charted with "Don't Get Around Much Anymore," reaching #1 R&B and #8 pop. The often-recorded hit was originally titled "Never No Lament."

1961 Darlene Love & the Blossoms—who were the premier vocal back-up singers for everyone from Elvis to Dionne Warwick—finally earned some attention with a single of their own when "Son-in-Law" charted, reaching #79 pop. It was their only Top 100 single and the answer record to Ernie K-Doe's "Mother-in-Law."

1963 Darlene Love made a rare TV appearance when she performed on Dick Clark's *American Bandstand* singing her current hit, "(Today I Met) The Boy I'm Gonna Marry."

1964 Little Richard performed on the British TV show, *Ready, Steady, Go!* along with Carl Perkins and the Swinging Blue Jeans.

1968 James Brown attended a dinner at the White House, at the invitation of President and Mrs. Johnson,

1992 a monument was dedicated to "Muddy Waters, master of the blues," in Rolling Fork, MS, by local officials.

1992 The Dixie Cups of "Chapel of Love" fame reunited and performed at Radio City Music Hall in New York for WCBS-FM's twentieth anniversary concert.

1996 The eight annual World Music Awards in Monte Carlo, Monaco, bestowed honors upon Michael Jackson, including awards as World's Best-Selling Album of All-Time (for *Thriller*), World's Best-Selling Male Pop Artist, American Male Recording Artist, and World's Best-Selling R&B Artist. Also honored with a Lifetime Achievement Award was Diana Ross. Best Pop Group and Best R&B Group kudos went to TLC.

May 9

#1 R&B Song 1987: "There's Nothing Better Than Love," Luther Vandross

Born: Dave Prater Jr. (Sam & Dave), 1937

1953 Billy Ward & the Dominoes' "These Foolish Things" was released. It became their ninth Top 10 R&B hit (#5) in three years.

1959 Jackie Wilson's "That's Why (I Love You So)" topped off at #2 R&B and #13 pop. Wilson was originally intent on being a boxer and was in fact the Amateur Golden Gloves Welterweight champ at sixteen in 1950 under the name Sonny Wilson; he made the cut by purporting to be eighteen. His mother insisted he pursue a less dangerous profession such as singing. He started with a non-recording group called the Thrillers that included Hank Ballard (later of the Rock and Roll Hall of Famers, the Midnighters).

1962 While singing lead with the Dixie Flyers, Dionne's sister, Dee Dee Warwick, sailed onto the Hot 100 with "She Didn't Know" (#70 pop).

1964 Chuck Berry began his first British tour, performing with the Animals, the Nashville Teens, the Swinging Blue Jeans, and others at the Astoria Theater, Finsbury Park, London.

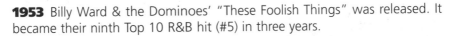

Jackie Wilson

1992 Rapper Snoop Doggy Dogg made his R&B chart debut with "Deep Cover," reaching #46. The recording actually read, "Dr. Dre Introducing Snoop Doggy Dogg," and was from the film of the same name. Snoop would go on to become a rap icon with forty-four R&B charters through 2003.

May
10

#1 R&B Song 1975: "Get Down, Get Down (Get on the Floor)," Joe Simon

Born: Larry Williams, 1935

1957 The Jive Bombers of "Bad Boy" fame recorded their unique version of the 1928 song "Cherry."

1963 The obscure Chuck Berry tune "Come On" became the first single recorded by the Rolling Stones.

1975 The Commodores' "Slippery When Wet" charted, becoming their first pop Top 20 hit (#19) and first R&B #1. The group began their career playing the club circuit, but unlike most acts, it wasn't the local club circuit. They started in French resorts like St. Tropez.

1975 Bob Marley and the Wailers charted with their *Natty Dread* album, reaching #92. It was the first of seventeen chart albums through 1995. The band was originally called the Wailin' Wailers because they used to start out crying. Marley worked alternatively as a forklift driver, a waiter, a Chrysler assembly-line worker, and a lab assistant at DuPont Chemicals before succeeding as a reggae star.

1980 Charley Pride jumped on the country charts with "You Win Again," reaching #1. Pride, the most popular black artist in country music history would go on to have an extraordinary sixty-seven hits between 1966 and 1989. Although his music was overwhelmingly country, he managed to cross to the pop charts eleven times, including his biggest hit, "Kiss an Angel Good Mornin,'" which reached #1 for five weeks country and #21 pop.

Bob Marley's
Natty Dread

May 11

#1 R&B Song 1959: "It's Just a Matter of Time," Brook Benton

Born: Coronet player Joe "King" Oliver, 1885

1956 R&B invaded Chicago for the first all-star show when the Flamingos, Drifters, Platters, Frankie Lymon & the Teenagers, and the Teen Queens tore up the International Amphitheater.

1962 In a blockbuster show put on by legendary Pittsburgh disc jockey Porky Chedwick, the Civic Arena was rocked by the Drifters, Jerry Butler, Jackie Wilson, the Flamingos, the Jive Five, Bo Diddley, Patti LaBelle & the Bluebelles (then only known as the Bluebelles), the Coasters, the Marvelettes, the Skyliners, Kelly Lester, Big Maybelle, the Carousels, Gene Pitney, and Bobby Vinton. The average ticket price for the spectacular was under $3 with 13,000 fans in attendance.

1968 The Raelettes entered the R&B charts with "I'm Getting' Long Alright," reaching #23. The group was originally called the Cookies and were Ray Charles's backing vocalists through the mid-'60s. Some of the outstanding vocalists in the group included Minnie Riperton, Merry Clayton, Clydie King (Brown Sugar), and Mable John.

1974 Tavares, a quintet from Bedford, MA, jumped on the charts with "Too Late," peaking at #10 R&B. The five were all brothers who would have twenty-seven hits over a ten-year span from 1973 to 1983.

1981 Bob Marley died of lung cancer in Miami at the age of thirty-six.

1985 Whitney Houston charted solo for the first time on the pop charts with "You Give Good Love," reaching #3 and becoming her first of eight R&B #1s. Whitney is the daughter of Cissy Houston and cousin of Dionne and Dee Dee Warwick. Before her solo career started she was a model for *Glamour* magazine and graced the cover of *Seventeen*.

1989 Anita Baker cohosted, with Dick Clark, the twentieth annual Songwriters Hall of Fame awards ceremony at Radio City Music Hall in New York.

1989 The ever-versatile, ever-surprising Ray Charles performed his song, "A Fool for You" with the New York City Ballet at Lincoln Center.

May

#1 R&B Song 1979: "Reunited,"
Peaches & Herb

Born: Jay Otis Washington (the
Persuasions), 1941

1945 Known as Lady Day, Billie Holiday charted R&B (#5) with "Lover Man (Oh, Where Can You Be?)." It was her first and only R&B hit but her last of thirty-nine pop hits that started in 1935. The film *Lady Sings the Blues*, starring Diana Ross was based on Holiday's life.

1956 The Flamingos' "A Kiss from Your Lips" and the Penguins "Dealer of Dreams" were issued.

1962 The Temptations charted for the first time with "Dream Come True," reaching #22 R&B, though it was the flip, "Isn't She Pretty," that was the portent of things to come from this Hall of Fame quintet.

1963 Ray Charles & the Raelettes began their first British tour in London's Finsbury Astoria.

1965 After three R&B chart singles with Lloyd Price's Double L label, Wilson Pickett's contract was bought by Atlantic Records. He would go on to have his greatest success with Atlantic, racking up thirty-five R&B hits between 1965 and 1973.

1979 Originally known as the gospel group the Heavenly Sunbeams, the Emotions (paired with Earth, Wind & Fire) charted with "Boogie Wonderland" (#6), their last of nine Hot 100 discs.

1993 Honored at the fifth annual World Music Awards in Monte Carlo, Monaco, Michael Jackson received awards as World's Best-Selling Pop and Overall Artist of the Year, Best-Selling U.S. Artist of the Year, and World's Best-Selling Artist of the Era. Boyz II Men were christened International New Group of the Year and performed their international hit, "End of the Road." Tina Turner was given an Outstanding Contribution to the Music Industry award.

May

13

#1 R&B Song 1967: "Jimmy Mack,"
Martha & the Vandellas

Born: Maxine Sullivan, 1911; Harold Winley
(the Clovers), 1933; Candi Staton, 1940; Mary
Wells, 1943; Carolyn Franklin, 1944; Stevie
Wonder (Steveland Hardaway Judkins), 1950

1952 The Royals signed with Federal Records and went on to have thirteen hits after they changed their name to Hank Ballard & the Midnighters.

1957 The Dell-Vikings signed with Mercury Records. The Spaniels' "Everyone's Laughing" ($60) and the Diablos' "Can't We Talk This Over" ($80) were released.

1960 Frankie Lymon (without the Teenagers), Shirley & Lee, Robert & Johnny, Billy Bland, Major Lance, Barrett Strong, and Irma Thomas performed on a bill together with backing by Ernie Fields's band at the Regal Theater in Chicago.

1961 Hank Ballard & the Midnighters, Clyde McPhatter, Sam Cooke, the Olympics, and Aretha Franklin appeared at the Kiel Auditorium in St. Louis.

1971 Reaching his twenty-first birthday, Stevie Wonder was paid all of his childhood earnings while with Motown. Well…not really. He earned more than $30 million but received only one million, resulting in new negotiations with the Berry Gordy company and the establishment of Wonder's own publishing and production companies.

1989 Stevie Wonder spent his thirty-ninth birthday on stage at Wembley Arena in London.

1996 Patti LaBelle taped a TV special with the Boston Pops Orchestra.

Stevie Wonder

May
14

#1 R&B Song 1983: "Candy Girl," New Edition

Born: Shanice Wilson, 1973

1951 The Dominoes recorded two of their best, "That's What You're Doing to Me" (#7 R&B, $400) and "These Foolish Things" (#5 R&B, $300).

1951 Bluesman Howlin' Wolf recorded one of his earliest sessions at Sam Phillips's legendary Sun Studios in Memphis. The session included his early classics "Moanin' at Midnight" and "How Many More Years," which would become both sides of his first chart single.

Howlin' Wolf

1955 The Five Keys' single, "The Verdict" (#13 R&B) was released.

1969 Little Anthony & the Imperials recorded two standards, "Ten Commandments of Love" (#82 pop), originally by the Moonglows, and "Out of Sight, Out of Mind" (#38 R&B, #52 pop), first done by the Five Keys.

1984 Michael Jackson received a Presidential Humanitarian Award at the White House from President and Mrs. Reagan. Jackson wore a military-styled uniform jacket to the proceedings, which he had asked for and was given by an elevator operator in New York.

1988 L.A. Reid and Babyface's group the Deele charted its last of eight singles when "Shoot 'Em Up Movies" reached the R&B Top 100 on its way to #10. Within a year, Babyface would begin his highly successful solo career.

1988 The Coasters, with original members Carl Gardner, Cornelius Gunter, Will Jones, and Billy Guy, performed at Atlantic Records' fortieth anniversary concert at Madison Square Garden in New York City. Sam of Sam & Dave, in duet with Dan Aykroyd—whose *Blues Brothers* film resurrected many of Sam & Dave's classic songs—also performed, as did the Spinners.

1994 While visiting the Great Wall of China, B.B. King was on hand to open the first Hard Rock Cafe in Beijing. Meanwhile, Janet Jackson performed on NBC-TV's *Saturday Night Live*.

May

15

#1 Song 1976: "Boogie Fever,"
the Sylvers

Born: Corinthian "Kripp" Johnson
(the Del-Vikings), 1933;
Lenny Welch, 1938

1954 The Dreamers' first single, "Maybe You'll Be There" was issued under the group's new name, Lee Andrews & the Hearts.

1956 The Teenagers' third single, "I Promise to Remember" was recorded. It was a cover of Jimmy Castor & the Juniors' recent release. Castor sounded so much like Frankie Lymon that years after Lymon died, Castor joined the Teenagers as lead singer.

1961 Gladys Knight & the Pips became the first act in history to have two different versions of the same song on the charts at the same time when "Every Beat of My Heart" hit the pop Top 100. First recorded for Huntom and licensed to VeeJay (#6 and #1 R&B), they rerecorded it for Fury (#45 and #15 R&B) and both raced up the hit list starting today.

1961 The Dukays' debut single, "The Girl's a Devil," charted, reaching #64 pop while missing the R&B charts altogether. Their lead singer was Gene Chandler, who would soon become famous for hitting with "Duke of Earl."

1963 Ray Charles won the Best R&B Recording Award at the fifth annual Grammy Awards for his classic country pop single, "I Can't Stop Loving You."

1965 Barbara Mason's Hot 100 debut, "Yes, I'm Ready" (#5), was followed by ten more soulful singles over the next ten years.

1965 The Four Tops charted with, "I Can't Help Myself." It went on to million-selling status, reaching #1 R&B for nine weeks and #1 pop for two. The song knocked another Motown group, the Supremes, out of the top spot when the Tops' hit replaced "Back in My Arms Again." The quartet were originally called the 4 Aims but changed it to avoid confusion with the Ames Brothers.

1992 Boyz II Men, Hammer, and Jodeci performed at Madison Square Garden in New York.

May

16

#1 R&B Song 1981: "A Woman Needs Love (Just Like You Do)," Ray Parker Jr. & Raydio

Born: Betty Carter, 1930; Barbara Lee (the Chiffons), 1947; Brenda Lee Jones (the Chiffons), 1947; Janet Jackson, 1966

1956 Vee Jay Records signed the legendary Sonny Til & the Orioles with an announcement it was taking the group pop.

1983 The Temptations and the Four Tops sang on Motown's twenty-fifth anniversary and Smokey Robinson & the Miracles reunited for the show, which was televised on NBC-TV. The Supremes (Diana Ross, Mary Wilson and Cindy Birdsong) also reunited for the event and, appropriately, sang "Someday We'll Be Together." Stevie Wonder sang "You Are the Sunshine of My Life."

1985 Manager Ken Kragen—who developed the idea for the "We Are the World" recording to raise money for African relief—was handed a check for $6.5 million in royalties from Columbia Records President, Al Teller. The song merchandising rights and album would go on to raise in excess of $50 million.

1989 Janet Jackson was harassed by fans when she took a VIP tour of Universal Studios. Adding insult to injury, the fans believed they were hounding her brother Michael. He, on the other hand, went unnoticed on the tour while wearing a disguise.

1991 Ray Charles became one of the first celebrities to be enshrined at the Atlanta Celebrity Walk, along others such as Hank Aaron, Martin Luther King Jr., Jimmy Carter, Andrew Young, and Margaret Mitchell.

1992 Stevie Wonder began his aptly titled, European Natural Wonder tour in Switzerland.

Ray Charles

May 17

#1 R&B Song 1947: "I Want to Be Loved," Savannah Churchill & the Sentimentalists

Born: Taj Mahal (Henry St. Claire Fredericks), 1942; George Johnson (Brothers Johnson), 1953

1942 Bluesman Taj Mahal was born today. The New Yorker was a University of Massachusetts graduate in animal husbandry but was more drawn to blues singing and was a regular performer at the Fillmore East and West, as well as the Newport Jazz Festival.

1952 Lloyd Price charted with his debut single, "Lawdy Miss Clawdy," on Specialty Records, reaching #1 R&B for seven weeks. He was originally turned down by Imperial Records, who instead signed fellow New Orleans musician Fats Domino. Meanwhile, Domino played piano on Price's "Lawdy." Price would go on to have twenty-three R&B hits through 1976 and is considered a pioneering R&B influence today.

1957 The Spaniels and the Dells appeared at Chicago's Regal Theater.

1960 Fats Domino performed at the Memorial Auditorium in Dallas, TX, but his appearance cost him more than he made. Thieves rifled his dressing room, absconding with $1,300 of the Fat Man's money while he was onstage doing "Ain't That a Shame."

1969 Junior Walker & the All-Stars charted with "What Does It Take (To Win Your Love)," reaching #1 R&B and #4 pop. The recording featured one of the most popular and recognizable sax solos in R&B and soul history and helped take the recording to million-selling status.

1978 Donna Summer's film *Thank God It's Friday* premiered in Los Angeles.

1986 Run-D.M.C., a trio in the early days of rap, stormed onto the R&B hit list with "My Adidas," peaking at #5 while becoming their eleventh of twenty-six chart climbers through 2000.

May

#1 Song 1959: "Kansas City," Wilbert Harrison

Born: "Big" Joe Turner, 1911; Feliciano "Butch" Tavares (Tavares), 1953

1957 Pittsburgh's WJAS disc jockey Barry Kaye hosted a two-hour rock 'n' roll show at the Syria Mosque featuring the Moonglows, Otis Williams & the Charms, and the Clovers.

1959 "Along Came Jones" was the Coasters' seventh chart single, all written by their producers, Leiber & Stoller.

1959 Lloyd Price charted with "Personality," reaching #1 R&B for four weeks and #2 pop. Though not his biggest hit, the song became a career-defining single.

1959 A young chicken plucker in Philadelphia with a penchant for imitating other acts' vocal styles had his first single chart today as "The Class" reached #38 pop. The artist was Chubby Checker (Earnest Evans) who was renamed by Dick Clark's wife Bobby because she felt he resembled Fats Domino. The hit started out as a recorded Christmas greeting when the Clarks asked Cameo Records honcho Kal Mann to come up with a novelty record they could send to friends for the holiday. The result was "The Class" and the unusual debut was sent out as a musical holiday card in December 1958.

1985 Sade reached #5 pop and R&B with "Smooth Operator." The former model of English/Nigerian descent was a member of the eight-member funk band Pride before establishing her own group called Sade, which most people thought was the name of a solo artist.

1988 James Brown, a member of the President's Council Against Drugs, spent the night in jail after a car chase in Aiken County, SC, not far from his home. It was the Godfather of Soul's fifth arrest in ten months. The counts included resisting arrest, assault, possession of PCP and illegal weapons. Any similarities between James Brown and Bobby Brown are strictly coincidental.

May

#1 Song 1962: "Soldier Boy,"
the Shirelles

Born: Grace Jones, 1952

1956 The Cleftones entered the R&B charts with the rock 'n' roll standard-to-be, "Little Girl of Mine," reaching #38 and #57 pop.

1958 Alan Freed took his R&B records with him when he joined New York's WABC-radio one week after quitting his position at WINS. The same day, the Clovers signed with Poplar Records after seven years with Atlantic, the Drifters' classic, "Drip Drop" (#58 pop), was released, and Jerry Butler & the Impressions' debut disc, "For Your Precious Love" (#11 pop), came out.

1958 Bobby Freeman, former lead singer of the Romancers, went solo and charted with "Do You Want to Dance," which reached #2 R&B and #5 pop. The song went on to become a rock 'n' roll standard.

1960 Ben E. King recorded his last sides with the Drifters before going solo. They included "I Count the Tears" (#17 pop, #6 R&B) and the epic "Save the Last Dance for Me" (#1 pop and R&B).

1968 The Fifth Dimension performed on *The Ed Sullivan Show* singing "Stone Soul Picnic."

1973 Stevie Wonder hit #1 pop and #3 R&B with "You Are the Sunshine of My Life."

1979 Former lead of the R&B/rock group, Rotary Connection, Minnie Riperton hurdled the Top 200 with "Minnie"(#29), the fifth of six solo album successes between 1974 and 1980. The same day, quintessential white funkster Teena Marie charted with her debut single, "I'm a Sucker for Your Love," reaching #8 R&B. The record was produced by Rick James.

1984 On the third anniversary of his death, Island Records issued the Bob Marley compilation album *Legend*, which reached #1 in Britain on its first week of release and stayed on the charts for an incredible 129 weeks.

May

20

#1 R&B Song 1972: "I'll Take You There," the Staple Singers

Born: Frederick Earl "Shorty" Long, 1940

1955 Ruth Brown's hit, "Mama, He Treats Your Daughter Mean," was banned in Britain. British Broadcasting felt it might encourage wife beating.

1957 The Channels' "I Really Love You" was released.

1957 Roy Brown charted with his last of sixteen R&B chart hits, a cover of Fats Domino's "Let the Four Winds Blow" reaching #5 and #29 pop. Brown was best known for his chart toppers "Long About Midnight" and "Hard Luck Blues."

1960 The Flamingos, the Crests, and Sam Cooke performed at the Tivoli Theater in Chicago.

1978 Quincy Jones landed on the R&B hit list with "Stuff Like That," reaching #1 and #21 pop. Similar to his predecessor Johnny Otis, Jones used guest vocalists on the recordings with his orchestra. The vocals for "Stuff" were by Chaka Khan and Ashford & Simpson.

1978 Rick James's first single as a member of the Motown family, "You and I," charted, reaching #1 R&B and #13 pop, becoming his first gold disc. Rick, whose real name was James Johnson, played with a blues group in London called the Main Line in 1970 before signing to Motown's Gordy label. He was motivated by acts like Sly Stone, the Drifters, and George Clinton, all of whom inspired the style of music he created and called funk 'n' roll.

1989 Rick James, the King of Punk Funk, charted with "This Magic Moment/Dance with Me," reaching #74 R&B. The recording was a medley of two late '50s Drifters hits and the only songs of his career that he charted with but didn't write. It was also his last of twenty-seven career singles charters.

May 21

1955 Chess Record's new artist Chuck Berry recorded his first single, "Ida Red." During the session, producer Leonard Chess decided to rename it "Maybellene." His basic style of uptempo blues driven by a guitar rhythm with a country rockabilly influence would make Berry a pioneer in rock 'n' roll and R&B.

1955 The Four Knights' first Top 100 single, "If I May," charted (#8 pop). One of the group's four hits was "My Personal Possession" (#21 pop), with Nat King Cole singing lead.

1963 Stevie Wonder recorded what would become his first hit, "Fingertips Pt. 2." It was a live concert that was taped at Chicago's Regal Theater for his *12 Year Old Genius* album.

1981 A worldwide reggae legend, Bob Marley was especially revered in his hometown of Kingston, Jamaica, where he was buried with full state honors. In his casket he had a guitar in one hand and a bible in the other.

Stevie Wonder

1983 Anita Baker debuted on the R&B charts with "No More Tears," which reached #49. She would go on to have twenty-one R&B chart singles through 1995. Meanwhile, Prince's "Little Red Corvette" reached #6 pop and #15 R&B.

1996 Babyface was named Songwriter of the Year at BMI's fourth annual pop awards ceremony in Los Angeles for the song "I'll Make Love to You." The tune was the most-performed work two years running, a first among songwriters.

May

#1 R&B Song 1954: "Work with Me Annie," Hank Ballard & the Midnighters

Born: Roscoe Robinson, 1928; Jimmy Keyes (the Chords), 1930; Johnny Gill, 1966

1928 Gospel/soul singer Roscoe Robinson was born. He performed with the Fairfield Four, the Five Blind Boys of Mississippi, and the Highway Q.C.'s before having four R&B chart successes in the mid-'60s, most notably, "That Enough" (#7).

1954 The Royals reached the top of the R&B charts with "Work with Me, Annie." Due to their first success after ten strong but mostly overlooked ballad singles, they had to change their name to Hank Ballard & the Midnighters to avoid confusion with the "5" Royales on Apollo. The hit spawned "The Wallflower," by Etta James, and "Dance with Me Henry," by Georgia Gibbs.

1971 Richie Havens's "Here Comes the Sun" reached #16 on the pop Top 100, earning the folk artist his only chart appearance. The song was originally recorded by the Beatles.

1976 Donna Summer reached #52 pop with "Could It Be Magic," originally recorded by Barry Manilow and given to Summer by Manilow's publisher, Jay Warner.

1980 Electric Ladyland Studios was robbed of four gold albums, all belonging to Jimi Hendrix.

1993 Salt-N-Pepa performed at a benefit to raise money for AIDS patients called LIFEbeat's Counteraid. They had intended to become nurses but wound up as telephone sales operators before striking gold as a rap act.

1999 The Temptations charted with "How Could He Hurt You," their eighty-seventh and last R&B charter of the century, reaching #57. The group had its first R&B hit thirty-seven years earlier and by this time, only Otis Williams remained from the original group.

May 23

#1 Song 1964: "My Guy," Mary Wells

Born: Robert "Bumps" Blackwell, 1918; Arthur Gunter, 1926; General Norman Johnson (Chairmen of the Board), 1943

1960 Ella Fitzgerald charted R&B with "Mack the Knife," reaching #6. The song was recorded in West Berlin, Germany, with the Paul Smith quartet doing backup vocals. Despite the huge success of the Bobby Darin pop version, which hit the Top 100 nine months ahead of Fitzgerald's pop chart debut, her version still impressively reached #27.

1960 First recorded by the Spaniels in 1958, "A Rockin' Good Way" bounced onto the Hot 100 for Dinah Washington in a duet with Brook Benton while rockin' its way to #7.

1964 Millie Small charted with her soon-to-be hit, "My Boy Lollipop" (#2 U.S. & U.K.). The harmonica part was played by a nineteen-year-old then–*folk singer* named Rod Stewart.

1981 After Smokey Robinson's song "Being with You" was turned down for Kim Carnes, he recorded it himself and it reached #2 pop today. He was kept from the top spot by (you guessed it) Kim Carnes's "Bette Davis Eyes."

1995 Donna Summer performed in Sao Paolo, Brazil.

Ella Fitzgerald

May

24

#1 Song 1975: "Shining Star," Earth, Wind & Fire

Born: Patti LaBelle (Patricia Holt), 1944

1947 The Hadda Brooks Trio charted with "That's My Desire," reaching #4 R&B.

1947 Lionel Hampton & His Septet entered the R&B charts with "Blow Top Blues," peaking at #5. The vocalist on the record was young jazz great Dinah Washington, who would record the song again solo in 1952, coincidentally reaching #5 again.

1952 Clyde McPhatter & the Dominoes charted with "Have Mercy Baby," which scaled the hit list, reaching #1 R&B for an impressive ten weeks. A year before, the group had one of the century's biggest hits when their "Sixty Minute Man" spent fourteen weeks at #1 becoming the seventh-biggest hit of all time on the R&B charts. "Have Mercy Baby" was no slouch either, coming in at #30 all-time.

1961 The Monotones recorded their last single, "Daddy's Home, But Mama's Gone," an answer record to Shep & the Limelites' hit, "Daddy's Home."

1969 The Emotions charted with "So I Can Love You," their debut disc on both the pop (#39) and R&B (#3) charts. The trio of Hutchinson sisters went on to have thirty R&B hits through 1984.

1970 B.B. King and Albert King (no relation) performed on the last night of their four-night stand at the Fillmore West in San Francisco.

1993 Dionne Warwick performed at ASCAP's tenth annual Pop Awards at the Beverly Hilton Hotel in Beverly Hills, CA, performing Bacharach & David songs.

May

25

#1 Song 1963: "If You Wanna Be Happy," Jimmy Soul

Born: Donnie Elbert, 1936; Lauryn Hill, 1975

1951 The first R&B hit to crossover to the pop Top 20 was Billy Ward & the Dominoes' "Sixty Minute Man" (#17).

1956 British bandleader Ted Heath stated upon his return from a U.S. tour that: "Rock 'n' roll is mainly performed by colored artists for colored people and is therefore unlikely to ever prove popular in Britain."

1959 Dinah Washington made her pop chart debut with "What a Difference a Day Makes" (#8). By 1963, she would have twenty more. Meanwhile, the Chiffons' "One Fine Day" was released, eventually reaching #5 pop and #6 R&B.

1963 Otis Redding charted pop with his first release, "These Arms of Mine," reaching #85 and #20 R&B. Redding, who was influenced by Little Richard, began as a member of the band Johnny Jenkins & the Pinetoppers and was often their chauffeur.

1974 The Commodores, a band known for their romantic ballads, opened their career by charting with the rapid fire instrumental, "Machine Gun," which reached #7 R&B and #22 pop. The group started out as members of two bands, the Mighty Mystics and the Jays, at Tuskeegee Institute in Alabama. One can only wonder what the group's members thought when they learned their recording became famous in Nigeria as the sign off for TV stations after the national anthem. Must have been a military government.

Dinah Washington

1990 Barry White began his first world tour in seven years starting in St. Louis, MO, along with a thirty-piece orchestra.

May

#1 R&B Song 1973: "I'm Gonna Love You Just a Little More," Barry White

Born: Mamie Smith, 1883, Miles Davis, 1926; Lenny Kravitz, 1964

1956 The Clovers' "Love, Love, Love" (#4 R&B) and the Magnificents' "Up on the Mountain"(#9 R&B) were released.

1965 Howlin' Wolf performed on the TV show *Shindig* along with the Rolling Stones, who specifically requested he appear with them. They did his first and biggest hit, "How Many More Years."

1968 The Jackson 5 signed to Motown Records. Among the draconian terms was a clause prohibiting their recording for another label until five years after the Motown contract was over. They were to be paid $12.50 for each released song, along with a small royalty. Motown President Berry Gordy intended to label their music "soul bubblegum." Luckily, the label didn't stick.

1979 British-born Maxine Nightingale, who starred in *Jesus Christ Superstar* and *Godspell*, hit the Top 100 with "Lead Me On" (#5).

1990 Michael Jackson received *Billboard* magazine's Music of the '80s poll awards, including Black Artist of the Decade, Black Single of the Decade ("Billie Jean"), Pop Album of the Decade (*Thriller*), and Black Album of the Decade (*Thriller*).

1990 Lenny Kravitz performed at Dodger Stadium as the opening act for David Bowie. Inspired by the likes of Led Zeppelin, James Brown, Bob Marley, and Jimi Hendrix, Kravitz originally performed under the name Romeo Blue.

1994 The world is still scratching their collective heads over this one: The King of Pop and the daughter of the King of Rock 'n' Roll were married today. Lisa Marie Presley and Michael Jackson tied the knot in La Vega, Dominican Republic. Obviously proud of their union, the two denied for two months that it had ever happened.

1994 The Stylistics performed at the Apollo Theater Hall of Fame concert.

May

27

#1 R&B Song 1957: "School Day," Chuck Berry

Born: Ramsey Lewis, 1935

1944 Drummer Cozy Cole & His All-Star Band charted with "Just One More Chance," reaching #10 R&B. It would be fourteen more years before Cozy would chart again, this time with the rock 'n' roll instrumental standard, "Topsy Part 2."

1954 Twenty days after Uncle Sam called Clyde McPhatter, the Drifters' "Honey Love" was released. It became their second #1 R&B hit of three releases.

1957 The Cellos' doo-wop novelty, "Rang Tang Ding Dong" slipped onto the charts, reaching #62. The same day, the Dominoes' "Stardust" was released (#12 pop, #5 R&B).

1960 Jackie Wilson broke the attendance record at the Apollo Theater in New York while performing for a week. Meanwhile, the Philadelphia Arena hosted a rock 'n' roll extravaganza featuring LaVern Baker, the Coasters, Lloyd Price, Little Anthony & the Imperials, Bo Diddley, Jimmy Jones, Sammy Turner, and Jimmy Reed.

1963 Ruth Brown appeared at the Café Tia Juana in Cleveland. Brown was once asked by a reporter, "At what point did rhythm & blues start becoming rock 'n' roll?" Without hesitation she fired back, "When the white kids started to dance to it."

1990 B.B. King performed at the Valley Forge Music Fair in Devon, PA, before a sell-out crowd.

B.B. King

May

#1 Song 1966: "When a Man Loves a Woman," Percy Sledge

Born: Saxman Andy Kirk, 1898; Aaron Thibeaux "T. Bone" Walker, 1910; Papa John Creach, 1917; Gladys Knight, 1944

1949 Wynonie Harris charted with the carousing classic "Drinkin' Wine, Spo-Dee-o-Dee," reaching #4 R&B.

1949 Louis Jordan jumped on the R&B hit list with "Cole Slaw," peaking at #7. It was Jordan's forty-sixth hit in six and a half years.

1954 Apollo Records formed the subsidiary Lloyds label and signed the Larks, who had re-formed after previously being with Apollo and breaking up.

1962 The Miracles performed their new single "I'll Try Something New" on *American Bandstand*, reaching #11 R&B and #39 pop after the show's exposure.

1983 Gladys Knight's "Save the Overtime (for Me)" reached #1 R&B and gave Knight her first #1 in almost nine years.

1983 The New Edition's first single, "Candy Girl," reached #1 in England and #46 pop stateside. It would soon be #1 R&B as well.

Gladys Knight

150

May

29

#1 R&B Song 1943: "Don't Get Around Much Anymore," Duke Ellington & His Orchestra

Born: Sylvia Vanderpool (Mickey & Sylvia), 1936; Maureen "Rebbie" Jackson, 1950; LaToya Jackson, 1956

1943 The legendary Mills Brothers charted with "Paper Doll," which reached #2 R&B and #1 pop for an astounding twelve weeks.

1958 Little Anthony & the Imperials recorded their immortal "Tears on My Pillow" (#4 pop, #2 R&B), their first million-seller. They started the session as the Chesters and left the studio as the Imperials. When disc jockey Alan Freed began playing the single, he christened the group Little Anthony & the Imperials, and within a month all new copies of the 45 read Little Anthony & the Imperials.

1959 The Drifters, Ray Charles, Ruth Brown, Jimmy Reed, and B.B. King, among others, performed at the R&B Festival at Herndon Stadium in Atlanta, GA. King was playing an average of 300 shows a year and would continue to do so into the '90s.

1961 "Quarter to Three," the raucous party record sung by Gary "U.S." Bonds (formerly of the doo-wop group, the Turks) and produced in Frank Guida's New Orleans record-store back-room recording studio on primitive equipment jumped on the R&B charts on its way to #3 R&B and #1 pop. The song was originally an instrumental named "A Night with Daddy G" until Guida added lyrics. The tune was reportedly recorded while Bonds and the band were heavily intoxicated. How much more could be working against you? Ah, the good old days when anything could happen and often did. The song went on to sell more than a million copies.

1965 Sam Cooke's "When a Boy Falls in Love" was released (#52). His fortieth chart single, it was issued six months after he died.

1993 Janet Jackson's album *Janet* reached #1 in England. The recordings included a diverse guest-artist list, including Public Enemy's Chuck D and opera singer Kathleen Battle.

May

30

1953 Collector's favorites "You Are My Only Love," by the Cardinals ($400), and the incredibly rare "These Foolish Things," by the Five Keys ($4,000), were released.

1960 James Brown's remake of the "5" Royales' "Think" charted, going on to #7 (#33 pop). At this point in his career, Brown's label began issuing a single of his every two or three months for the next ten years. It was meant to satisfy the legion of fans who packed his seemingly nonstop performances. No wonder he was nicknamed "the hardest-working man in show business."

1964 Dionne Warwick made her debut in England appearing on BBC-TV's *Top of the Pops*.

1977 At the Mohammad Ali Invitational Track Meet at Cerritos College in Cerritos, CA, Marvin Gaye outpaced Tony Orlando and the host, Ali, in the race.

1990 B.B. King was honored at the Songwriters Hall of Fame's twenty-first annual induction dinner with a Lifetime Achievement Award, while Smokey Robinson was inducted by Whitney Houston at the Hilton Hotel in New York.

1992 Michael Jackson granted his first interview in six years when he told Ebony magazine: "I haven't scratched the surface yet of what my real purpose is for being here."

1992 Bell Biv DeVoe charted en-route to #1 R&B with "The Best Things in Life Are Free," their third #1 in two years. Janet Jackson and Luther Vandross also contributed vocals to the hit, which was from the film *Mo' Money*.

1996 One of England's most revered female vocalists, Joan Armatrading was honored at the forty-first Ivor Novello Awards with the Outstanding Contemporary Song Collection award in London.

May 31

1952 Roy Milton charted with "So Tired," reaching #6 R&B. The title pretty much summed up Milton's feelings, since he charted nineteen times in the Top 10 while never having a #1. He had three #2's including his biggest hit, the aptly titled "R.M. [Roy Milton] Blues" in 1946.

1954 The Clovers opened at Emerson's in Philadelphia.

1961 Chuck Berry opened his own amusement park outside St. Louis called Berry Park.

1970 Wilson Pickett charted with "Born to Be Wild," a cover of the Steppenwolf hit from the previous year. It was Pickett's twenty-fifth R&B hit. Wilson once stated: "I imagine there's all kinds of screams that guys are doin' [that] are off-key. Like James [Brown], he'll scream between the notes. He screams, but nobody ever knows what key he's in. But I scream on key."

1991 Diana Ross performed at the Mid-Hudson Civic Center in Poughkeepsie, NY, on the first night of her world tour. It was an encouraging start as she broke the house attendance record previously held by John Denver.

1995 Luther Vandross performed at the Summer Pops Bowl Amphitheater in San Diego, CA.

Diana Ross

June

#1 R&B Song 1974: "Be Thankful for What You Got," William DeVaughn

Born: Ada Jones, 1873; Marie Knight, 1925

1946 The Ink Spots, pioneers of what would become R&B, entered the charts with yet another hit, "The Gypsy," reaching #1 R&B for three weeks while spending thirteen weeks at the top of the pop charts.

1959 The Flamingos' fabulous "I Only Have Eyes for You" charted on its way to #11 pop, #3 R&B, and immortality.

1960 The Hitmakers of 1960 tour started at the Gardens in Cincinnati, OH. These late '50s and early '60s tours were usually a series of grueling one-nighters, and it was not uncommon for acts to perform several times a day. The artists on this travelogue were the Drifters, Ruth Brown, Ray Charles, Billy Bland, bongo pro Preston Epps, Marv Johnson, Ray Bryant, Doc Bagby, and, for a change of pace, comedian Redd Foxx.

1960 The Flamingos performed on Dick Clark's *American Bandstand* daytime show singing one of their rare uptempo tunes, "Nobody Loves Me Like You."

1962 The "5" Royales, Jackie Wilson, Big Maybelle, and the Corsairs entertained New York's Apollo Theater crowd tonight.

1963 The Chiffons, a quintet of teenagers from the Bronx, NY, charted with "One Fine Day," which went on to #5 pop. The recording was originally done by Little Eva of "Locomotion" fame and produced by the song's composers, Gerry Goffin and Carole King, for the Tokens, who were the Chiffons' producers. The Tokens decided to acquire the recording and subsequently erased Little Eva's vocal, replacing it with the Chiffons.

1991 Temptations lead singer David Ruffin died of a drug overdose at the University of Pennsylvania Hospital.

1991 Seal's self-titled debut album reached #1 in Britain during its first week on the charts. The background vocals were by Wendy & Lisa.

1994 The Songwriters Hall of Fame held their twenty-fifth annual awards in New York and honored Lionel Richie by inducting him.

June 2

#1 Song 1962: "I Can't Stop Loving You," Ray Charles

Born: John Carter (the Flamingos), 1933; Otis Williams (the Charms), 1936; William Guest (the Pips), 1941

1956 The Four Tops' first single, "Could It Be You" ($200), was issued. The same Tops are still together forty-nine years later.

1961 Carla Thomas and Bobby Lewis appeared on *American Bandstand*. Lewis sang his hit "Tossin' and Turnin'," which would go on to be the #1 record of the year.

1962 In an interesting evening mixing jazz, R&B, and big-band swing, Lionel Hampton & His Orchestra, LaVern Baker, and the Dave Brubeck Quartet performed in Atlanta, GA.

1972 Lloyd Price, Shirley & Lee, Little Richard, the Cleftones, the Exciters, Danny & the Juniors, and a reunited Dion & the Belmonts performed a rock 'n' roll spectacular at New York's Madison Square Garden.

1981 Prince made his performance debut in London's Lyceum Ballroom. The crowd, however, was so small that the rest of his tour was canceled and his ego was so bruised that he refused to tour in Britain for another five years.

1984 Whitney Houston charted for the first time with "Hold Me," a duet with Teddy Pendergrass. The record reached #5 R&B (#46 pop) and would be the start of forty-five R&B charters through 2003. Before recording on her own, Houston was a background singer for Chaka Khan and Lou Rawls.

1990 Mariah Carey assaulted the Hot 100 with "Vision of Love," her first of five straight #1s.

1993 Ray Charles received the Songwriters Hall of Fame Lifetime Achievement Award from Billy Joel at the twenty-fourth annual induction ceremonies in the Sheraton Hotel in New York City.

1998 Luther Vandross and Mariah Carey joined Patti LaBelle for her Patti LaBelle in Concert on Broadway at the Hammerstein Ballroom in New York. The show would later be aired on PBS-TV.

June

3

#1 Song 1957: "Young Blood," the Coasters

Born: Memphis Minnie (Lizzie Douglas), 1896; Curtis Mayfield (the Impressions), 1942; Eddie Holman, 1946; Deniece Williams (June Deniece Chandler), 1951

1957 The Isley Brothers' first single, the doo-wop-styled "The Angels Cried" (Teenage Records), was released. It would be two years before they would have their first hit, "Shout."

1967 Aretha Franklin's "Respect" topped the pop charts for two weeks and the R&B list for eight, giving Franklin her second million seller. The song was originally a hit (#4 R&B) for Otis Redding in 1965.

1967 The Fifth Dimension charted with "Up, Up and Away," which became their first million seller, reaching #7. The light, lilting, pop feel of the recording was such that it never got near the R&B charts. In fact, the all-black group charted almost twice as much pop (thirty times) as R&B (seventeen) during their ten-year hit-list career.

1967 The Jimi Hendrix Experience reached the British Top 10 for the third time in a row when "The Wind Cries Mary" peaked at #6 today. The unusual aspect of an American artist having hits in England while going unrecorded in the U.S. was not lost on Reprise Records, who would finally sign Hendrix.

1967 The Staples Singers charted with "Why? (Am I Treated So Bad)," reaching #95 pop. It was the first Top 100 single for the family of gospel-turned-R&B vocalists, who would have eighteen charters through 1992.

1972 The Staples Singers had their first of two #1 pop hits and three #1 R&B smashes when "I'll Take You There" reached the top spot today. Nineteen years later, lead singer Mavis Staples would have a hit with it, this time as lead with Bebe and Cece Winans, reaching #1 R&B once again.

1990 Michael Jackson, experiencing chest pains later diagnosed as a rib-cage disorder, was admitted to St. John's Hospital in Santa Monica, CA.

June

4

#1 R&B Song 1966: "It's a Man's, Man's, Man's World," James Brown

Born: Leroy Hutson, 1945; El DeBarge (DeBarge), 1961

1955 The Miracles recorded their first single, "I Wanted You," at Radio Recorders in Hollywood. While considering a new name in engineer Bob Ross's office, comedian Stan Freberg came in. Posed with the question, he sat down, unwrapped a candy bar, finished it and said, "The Jaguars," and left. The group then became the Jaguars of "The Way You Look Tonight" fame.

1983 Donna Summer entered the charts with the women's national anthem of the '80s, "She Works Hard for the Money" reaching #1 R&B for three weeks and #3 pop.

1988 Armed with an anthropology degree from Tufts University (just in case), folk/R&B artist Tracy Chapman didn't need it when she cruised onto the charts with "Fast Car" (#6), her first of five hits through 1996.

1991 The Shirelles performed at Los Angeles's Pantages Theater in the Celebrate the Soul of American Music concert to raise money for Supreme Court Justice Thurgood Marshall's scholarship fund.

1992 Dionne Warwick sang at the Hammersmith Odeon in London at the end of a ten-performance trip through England.

1994 Seal's second album reached #1 in England on its first week on the charts. It took him over two years to make the record.

SEAL

June 5

#1 R&B Song 1971: "Want Ads," the Honey Cone

Born: Floyd Butler (Friends of Distinction), 1941; Ronnie Dyson, 1950; Brian McKnight, 1969

1954 The Drifters' "Honey Love" (#40 pop, #1 R&B; $50.00), the Midnighters' "Sexy Ways" (#2 R&B; $80.00), and the Moonglows' blues classic, "I Was Wrong" ($800) were released.

1964 The Chiffons began a tour starting in San Bernadino, CA, as the opening act for the Rolling Stones on their debut American tour.

1974 Sly Stone (Sylvester Stewart) married Kathy Silva on stage at Madison Square Garden in New York City prior to a concert by his group, Sly & the Family Stone. It lasted five months (the marriage, not the concert.)

1982 The Temptations' reunion album reached #37 pop and included all of 1964's original members, including Eddie Kendricks. In his enthusiasm to get into the music business, Kendricks forged his brother's signature on an $82 income tax refund check to have traveling money to Detroit.

1993 Mariah Carey married Sony Music president Tommy Mottola at St. Thomas Episcopal Church in New York. Among the guests were Barbra Streisand, Bruce Springsteen, and Billy Joel.

1993 Richie Havens performed at UCLA in Los Angeles in the Troubadours of Folk Festival.

1994 Donna Summer performed with the Nashville Symphony at the town's Summer Lights Arts Festival.

Mariah Carey

June 6

#1 R&B Song 1970: "Love on a Two-Way Street," the Moments

Born: Levi Stubbs (the Four Tops), 1936; Gary "U.S." Bonds (Gary Anderson), 1939

1956 The Platters' beautiful standard, "My Prayer" (#1 pop and R&B), was released

1960 Sam Cooke's "Wonderful World" charted en route to #2 R&B (#12 pop). It was his last hit for the independent Keen label before he went on to RCA for major money and began writing gospel-inflected songs with more blues influence.

1963 Little Miss & the Muffets (originally called the Meltones) topped the Hot 100 with "Chapel of Love," but thanks to a last-minute name change they became known to the world as the Dixie Cups.

1970 Bo Diddley and Chuck Berry headlined the Hampden Scene '70 concert in Glasgow, Scotland.

1971 Gladys Knight & the Pips were the last pop or R&B act to appear on *The Ed Sullivan Show*.

1992 Earth, Wind & Fire performed on the Great Lawn of Central Park in New York City at the Earth Pledge Concert to save the environment.

1993 The biopic, *What's Love Got to Do with It*, based on Tina Turner's life and her 1986 autobiography, premiered.

1994 Stevie Wonder performed at the twentieth-anniversary concert for the Duke Ellington School of the Arts and then donated his harmonica to the Hard Rock Cafe in Washington, DC.

June

7

#1 R&B Song 1975: "Love Won't Let Me Wait," Major Harris

Born: Billy Butler (the Enchanters), 1945; Prince (Prince Rogers Nelson), 1958

1979 Chuck Berry performed at the White House by the special request of President Carter. A month later (July 10), he was sentenced to four months in jail for income-tax evasion.

1980 Joan Armatrading hit the Top 200 albums with her fifth and biggest success, *Me, Myself, I*. It reached #28. Though she charted twelve times on the album Top 200, Armatrading never had a single on the R&B charts. Lack of commercial product was her eventual undoing in America.

1980 Bob Marley and the Average White Band performed at the Summer of '80 Garden Party at the Crystal Palace Concert Bowl in London.

1993 Chuck Berry was among those who attended the ground-breaking ceremony of the Rock and Roll Hall of Fame in Cleveland, OH.

1993 Prince, who turned thirty-five today, decided to celebrate by changing his name to a symbol that doesn't exist on a computer keyboard. The press began calling him the Artist Formerly Known as Prince. (Maybe they should have just referred to him as $.)

1997 New Edition's "One More Day" charted en route to #22 R&B and #61 pop. It would be the last of twenty-five R&B hits for the quintet since starting in 1983.

June

8

#1 R&B Song 1968: "Ain't Nothing Like the Real Thing," Marvin Gaye and Tammi Terrell

Born: Sherman Garnes (the Teenagers), 1940

1946 The King Cole Trio featuring Nat Cole charted with "(Get Your Kicks On) Route 66," reaching #3 R&B and #11 pop. It was their twelfth hit, all but one of which reached the Top 5. The "failure" was a B-side titled: "I Realize Now," which "only" made #9.

1956 The Cadillacs drove into Detroit for a three-day performance at the Motorama, while in New York, Clyde McPhatter made his last appearance with the Drifters at the Apollo Theater.

1959 An obscure group called the Parliaments had their first single, the beautiful, plaintive ballad "Lonely Island" issued on the Flipp label. Though the record went nowhere, the New Jersey doo-wop group would develop into one of the funkiest aggregations to ever storm a stage, Parliament/Funkadelic, with brain trust George Clinton at the helm just as he was on that "Lonely Island" debut.

1985 The Mary Jane Girls peaked at #7 pop for three straight weeks (#3 R&B) with the infectious dance hit "In My House," which was written and produced by Rick James.

1991 Diana Ross showed another side of her talents when she filled in for a British disc jockey on BBC–Radio I in London for a week.

1996 The Fugees with lead vocalist Lauryn Hill reached #1 in England with "Killing Me Softly," a remake of Roberta Flack's hit from 1973. A week later it became the first single to reach #1 in Germany in its first week on the charts. In contrast, it never made the U.S. pop or R&B Top 100 lists, though it did reach #2 in pop airplay.

June

9

#1 R&B Song 1979: "We Are Family," Sister Sledge

Born: Johnny Ace (John Alexander), 1929; Jackie Wilson (the Dominoes), 1934

1956 The Five Satins' immortal "In the Still of the Night" was picked up from the tiny Standord label and released on Ember while the Six Teens' "A Casual Look" charted en route to #25 pop, #7 R&B.

1958 Johnny Mathis's *Greatest Hits* album reached #1. It remained there for what was then a record 490 weeks (almost ten years).

1962 The Orlons leaped onto the Hot 100 with "Wah-Watusi," rising to #2 pop and becoming their third straight Top 5 hit.

1962 Carole King's babysitter, Little Eva, had her first single released. It became the rock 'n' roll standard "Locomotion," a worldwide #1.

1990 MC Hammer's album, *Please Hammer Don't Hurt 'Em*, reached #1 pop and stayed there for an amazing twenty-one weeks. It had the longest run at #1 or #2 of any album since 1963. The album was ten-times platinum and stayed in the Top 200 for 108 weeks. Not a bad reimbursement for an album that cost $10,000 to make.

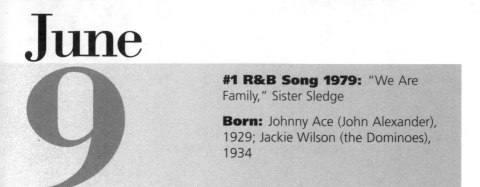

1990 Bell Biv DeVoe peaked at #3 pop with their debut single, "Poison." The mixture of hip-hop, doo-wop, and soul became the first of nine R&B hits through 1993. The trio was formerly the nucleus of the teen pop R&B group New Kids on the Block.

1994 After an argument, TLC member Lisa "Left Eye" Lopes accented her displeasure by setting fire to her boyfriend's (professional football player Andre Rison) $2 million mansion. (And you thought TLC meant "tender loving care"). The star was rewarded with a five-year "probation" sentence.

1998 Stevie Wonder performed in Modena, Italy, at the Pavarotti & Friends concert for his War Child Charity.

June

10

#1 Song 1967: "Respect," Aretha Franklin

Born: Hattie McDaniel, 1895; Howlin' Wolf (Chester Arthur Burnett), 1910; Gerald Gregory (the Spaniels), 1934; Shirley Alston (the Shirelles), 1941; Faith Evans, 1973

1957 The Bobbettes' immortal "Mr. Lee" (#6) was released today along with such doo-wop standards as "Happy Happy Birthday Baby" by the Tune Weavers and "Desiree" by the Charts.

1967 An interesting mix of talent performed at the Fantasy-Faire and Magic Mountain Music Fest in Mount Tamalpais, CA, including the Miracles, Dionne Warwick, Jefferson Airplane, and the Doors.

1972 Chuck Berry's album *The London Chuck Berry Sessions* charted on its way to #8 pop, the most successful album of his career. One side of the recording consisted of sides cut in a London studio with the Faces, while the other side was a live and unauthorized (by Berry) recording with the Average White Band at the Lanchester Arts Festival in Coventry, England.

1978 George Benson's remake of the Drifters' 1963 hit, "On Broadway," leveled off at #7 on the pop charts. Ironically, the Drifters' version fifteen years earlier also reached #7, but on the R&B charts.

1991 Stevie Wonder and Aretha Franklin sang at the burial of Temptations' lead singer David Ruffin. Michael Jackson paid for the funeral.

1991 The *James Brown—Living in America* live pay-per-view TV special aired. The show featured Bell Biv DeVoe, Hammer, En Vogue, and C&C Music Factory, among others.

1996 Diana Ross performed at Boston Symphony Hall at a benefit for the Anti-Defamation League. The diva raised $450,000.

1998 Diana Ross received the Hitmaker Award at the Songwriters Hall of Fame's twenty-ninth annual awards in New York. The presentation was made by Whitney Houston. It's interesting to note that Ross never wrote any of her hits and neither did her presenter. (Maybe they ran out of writers to honor.)

June 11

#1 R&B Song 1955: "Ain't It a Shame," Fats Domino

Born: Clarence "Pine Top" Smith, 1901; James "Pookie" Hudson (the Spaniels), 1934; Wilma Burgess, 1939

1949 Ella Fitzgerald and Louis Jordan charted with their duet, "Baby, It's Cold Outside," reaching #6 R&B and #9 pop. It was from the film *Neptune's Daughter*, starring '40s swimming star Esther Williams.

1954 The Spaniels made their debut appearance at the Apollo Theater.

1955 Fats Domino's "Ain't That a Shame" reached #1 R&B and stayed there for eleven weeks while becoming his first single to cross over to pop at #10. It took him five years and fourteen singles to make the pop charts.

1977 The Spinners performed at San Diego's Kool Jazz Festival.

1988 Chubby Checker performed at Nelson Mandela's seventieth-birthday concert at Wembley Stadium in England. Also performing were Natalie Cole (in a rare live performance), Al Green, Ashford & Simpson, Tracy Chapman, and the artist she emulated, Joan Armatrading. Stevie Wonder's synthesizer programs were stolen before the event yet he performed as well.

1994 Seal charted with "Prayer for the Dying," reaching #21 pop. The song must have been a reflection of his time in Los Angeles the previous year, during which he was a witness to a shooting in a Hollywood pool hall, almost died in a rollover in his Range Rover, and contracted pneumonia.

1996 Barry White performed at the Harborlights Pavillion near Boston. Droning overhead was a plane pulling a banner that said, "Barry, call the two chicks at WRKO." No, it wasn't an elaborate pickup attempt. The "two chicks" were Laurie Kramer and Leslie Gold, who had a talk show called *Two Chicks Dishing*, and who had just spent $1,800 of their station's money to get White's attention. Surprisingly, the personable performer called them and did an interview.

June

12

#1 Song 1965: "Back in My Arms Again," the Supremes

Born: Lyn Collins, 1948

1954 The collectors' items "Three Coins in the Fountain" by the Dominoes ($50), the Robins' "Riot in Cell Block #9" ($300), and the Checkers' "Over the Rainbow" ($400) were released.

1961 Ben E. King's immortal "Stand by Me" reached #4 pop and #1 R&B for four weeks. The song was based on the gospel song "Lord, Stand by Me."

1971 Roberta Flack first charted with "You've Got a Friend" (#29 pop). She reached the Top 100 a total of eighteen times over the next twenty years.

1982 Gary "U.S." Bonds charted with his last of eleven pop hits since 1960. The song, "Out of Work" reached #21, but thanks to nostalgia tours and oldies shows, Bonds rarely was out of work.

1982 Afrika Bambaataa charted with the "Planet Rock," a trend-setting mixture of European electronic music, in the vein of Kraftwerk and Tangerine Dream, and New York street rap. Bambaataa, a former street-gang member, rode the success of the single to more than a million sales despite its reaching only #48 on the national Top 100. The recording featured a heavy dose of riffs lifted from Kraftwerk's "Trans-Europe Express."

1992 Even though she had suffered chronic back pain that caused her to collapse at Los Angeles International Airport, Dionne Warwick still had the temerity to attend and perform at her record-company president's (Clive Davis) Man of the Year honors at New York's Waldorf-Astoria, where she sang "That's What Friends Are For" with Whitney Houston.

Dionne Warwick

June

#1 R&B Song 1987: "Rock Steady," the Whispers

Born: Bobby Freeman (the Romancers), 1940

1953 "Ain't That Good News" by the Tempo Toppers was released. The group's lead singer was a new vocalist named Little Richard.

1960 Clyde McPhatter signed with Mercury Records after having recorded for Atlantic Records with the Drifters and been solo for seven years.

1969 Trumpeted as the biggest-ever soul music festival to date, Sam and Dave, Aretha Franklin, Ray Charles, Percy Sledge, the Staple Singers, Reverend James Cleveland, Johnny "Guitar" Watson, Clara Ward, and more performed at Soul Bowl '69 at the Astrodome in Houston.

1970 The Three Degrees' chart debut, "Maybe," reached #4 R&B and #29 pop. The recording was a remake of the Chantels' 1958 standard.

1972 The Drifters' original lead singer, Clyde McPhatter, died. He was considered by many as one of rock 'n' roll's greatest voices. Elvis Presley frequently stated that he wished his voice were the equal of McPhatter's.

1981 Almost twenty years after his last chart appearance, Gary "U.S." Bonds reached #11 on the pop Top 100 with "This Little Girl," a song produced for him by Bruce Springsteen and Miami Steve Van Zant. Bonds met Springsteen three years earlier while working at the Red Baron, a New Jersey club. He pulled Springsteen—a long-time fan who frequently performed "Quarter to Three"—onstage out of the audience to sing with him. Springsteen proposed that Bonds and Van Zandt work on a comeback album eventually called *Dedication*, from which "This Little Girl" was pulled as a single.

1992 Luther Vandross and Janet Jackson's duet "The Best Things in Life Are Free" peaked at #10 pop and became Janet's seventh #1 R&B.

2005 Michael Jackson was acquitted of ten counts of child molestation and conspiracy in Santa Barbara, CA, in one of the most highly-publicized trials since the O.J. Simpson murder trial.

2005 Destiny's Child announced that the group was breaking up. Since its debut in 1997, the trio has reportedly sold more than 40 million records.

June 14

1952 The Dominoes were so hot that they were booked at a Washington, DC, auditorium for an afternoon performance and then flew to New Orleans for an evening show.

1961 The Cleftones performed on *American Bandstand* singing their hit, "Heart & Soul," while the Flamingos were in Chicago appearing at Robert's Show Club.

1976 An Evening with Diana Ross began its performance tour at the Palace Theater in New York.

1980 Singer/dancer/actress/pianist Irene Cara earned her first taste of stardom when "Fame" (from the film *Fame*) vaulted onto the Top 100. The #4 smash was the first of her eight hits through 1984.

1980 "The Breaks (Part 1)" by Curtis Blow was issued, eventually reaching #4 R&B and consequently becoming the first rap record certified as a million seller by the RIAA. Blow studied voice at the High School of Music and Art and Communications at New York City College and began rapping while a deejay in Harlem clubs in 1976.

1986 Patti LaBelle, in a duet with Michael McDonald, topped the pop charts with "On My Own." The song was recorded by each singer in separate studios 3,000 miles apart. In fact, the two did not meet until they performed the song together on Johnny Carson's *Tonight Show*.

1998 B.B. King was honored as the official Ambassador of Music to represent America at the World Expo '98 in Lisbon, Portugal.

Irene Cara

167

June

15

#1 R&B Song 1968: "Think," Aretha Franklin

Born: Ice Cube (O'Shea Jackson), 1969

1953 The Flamingos performed at Gleason's Night Club in Cleveland as the Five Flamingos. They continued performing under that name for the next two years even though they were recording since 1954 as the Flamingos.

1974 The jazz/funk group Rufus charted, reaching #3 pop with "Tell Me Something Good," which was originally recorded by Stevie Wonder. The group was first called Ask Rufus and their lead singer would go on to stardom as a solo act. It was Chaka Khan.

1974 The Stylistics' "You Make Me Feel Brand New" reached #2 pop and #5 R&B, giving them their fifth and last million seller.

1977 Marilyn McCoo & Billy Davis, formerly of the Fifth Dimension, began co-hosting a summer TV variety show called *The Marilyn McCoo and Billy Davis Jr. Show*. It would run for only six weeks.

1982 The Five Satins performed "Memories of Days Gone By" on *American Bandstand*. It was their first chart hit in twenty-one years.

1991 Stevie Wonder, Gladys Knight, and Dionne Warwick performed at a benefit concert for the family of the late Temptations lead singer, David Ruffin.

1993 Diana Ross performed "God Bless the Child" at the first Apollo Theater Hall of Fame concert from the historic venue, and Ben E. King sang "Save the Last Dance for Me," the song he made famous as lead of the Drifters. Teddy Pendergrass also performed, singing "Close the Door," his #1 hit from 1978.

Marilyn McCoo & Billy Davis

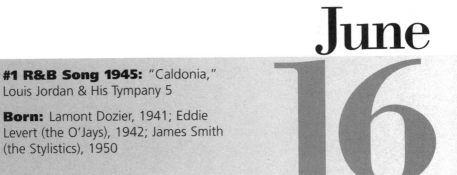

June 16

#1 R&B Song 1945: "Caldonia,"
Louis Jordan & His Tympany 5

Born: Lamont Dozier, 1941; Eddie
Levert (the O'Jays), 1942; James Smith
(the Stylistics), 1950

1958 The Danleers' summertime classic, "One Summer Night" (#7 pop, #4 R&B), was released.

1960 The Platters performed for the first time without longtime lead Tony Williams as Sonny Turner took over for his debut with the group at the Lotus Club in Philadelphia.

1962 The Isley Brothers charted with "Twist and Shout," reaching #2 R&B and #17 pop. The song was originally recorded by the Top Notes on Atlantic in 1961.

1976 A summer variety series featuring the Jackson family called *The Jacksons* debuted on CBS-TV for a four-week run. Along with the Jackson 5 were the group's sisters Rebbie, LaToya, and youngest member Janet.

1979 Donna Summer's "Bad Girls" hit #1 pop (for five weeks) and R&B, making it her biggest Top 100 hit.

1984 Tina Turner's *Private Dancer* album charted, reaching #3 (#1 R&B) and becoming such a huge hit that it stayed in the Top 10 for ten months. It also sold more than 10 million copies worldwide. In Britain it reached #2. Not bad for her first album without ex-husband Ike.

1992 Prince performed at Earls Court in London as part of his most recent tour.

1995 Diana Ross performed in Moscow at the Kremlin Palace of Congresses.

1998 ASCAP's first Rhythm & Soul Heritage Award was given to Chaka Khan at their eleventh annual Rhythm & Soul Awards in New York.

June 17

1957 The Del-Vikings' doo-wop classic "Whispering Bells" was released and reached #9 Pop and #5 R&B. The same day Atlantic Records signed the teen sextet the Bobbettes, whose "Mr. Lee" was released a week before, and the Moonglows' "Please Send Me Someone to Love" was issued.

1957 "Jenny Jenny" by Little Richard charted, reaching #14 pop and #2 R&B. It was Richard's eleventh Top 10 R&B single in less than a year and a half.

1965 In what would seem to be a miscasting, Chuck Berry and Muddy Waters performed at the first New York Folk Festival at Carnegie Hall in New York.

1967 Otis Redding, backed by Booker T. and the M.G.'s, performed at the Monterey International Pop Festival in Monterey, CA. He followed Jefferson Airplane as the evening's closing act.

1978 Al Green won the Tokyo Music Festival's Grand Prize (along with $14,000) for his passionate performance of the song "Belle," a record that only reached #83 pop in the states.

1978 The Commodores charted with "Three Times a Lady" on its way to #1 both pop and R&B. The Lionel Richie song was inspired by his parents' romantic longevity and their thirty-seventh wedding anniversary. The group credits their name to flipping open a dictionary and William King blindly pointing his finger somewhere on a page.

1994 The Jackson 5's first single, "Big Boy," originally released in 1968 on Steeltown Records, was reissued by the owner of Steeltown, who had misplaced the masters for more than twenty-six years. He eventually found them in his pantry.

1995 Michael and Janet Jackson's duet on "Scream" reached #5 in its debut week on the pop charts, the highest debut of any single up to that time. A week earlier the single had reached #3 in England in its first week on the charts.

June 18

1938 Ella Fitzgerald stormed onto the hit list with "A-Tisket, A-Tasket." It settled in at #1 for an amazing ten weeks, becoming her biggest hit.

1966 Ike & Tina Turner's (actually only Tina) thundering "River Deep, Mountain High" reached only #88 pop. Even though the British had a much greater appreciation of it (#3 U.K.), its failure in America so demoralized its producer, Phil Spector, that he withdrew from production for several years.

1967 The Jimi Hendrix Experience made their American performance debut at the now-legendary Monterey Pop Festival in Monterey, CA. After playing "Like a Rolling Stone" and "Wild Thing" and setting fire to and smashing his guitar, the crowd went wild. The trio was only booked on the show due to the insistence of Paul McCartney.

1988 Choreographer Paula Abdul punched her way onto the charts with "Knocked Out" (#41), her first of fourteen hits through 1995.

1995 Robert Cray performed in front of an audience of more than 72,000 people as the opening act for the Rolling Stones in Landgraaf, the Netherlands.

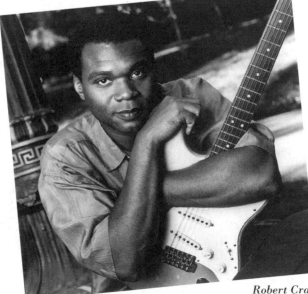

Robert Cray

June

19

#1 Song 1965: "I Can't Help Myself," the Four Tops

Born: Shirley Goodman (Shirley & Lee), 1936; Paula Abdul, 1962

1937 Blues great Robert Johnson had his second recording session, this time in a warehouse in Dallas, TX, recording such originals as "From Four Til Late" and "Stones in My Passway." Johnson—who was influenced by Ike Zimmerman, Willie Brown, Charley Patton, and Son House—stated that his ability was based on a pact he made with the devil that was consummated on a Mississippi crossroads one night at midnight.

1954 The Scarlets' "Dear One" ($150) was issued. They later became the nucleus of the Five Satins.

1961 The Chanters' "No, No, No" charted, reaching #41 pop, #9 R&B more than three years after its initial release and two years after the group broke up.

1971 The Isley Brothers' "Love the One You're With" charted, reaching #3 R&B (#18 pop). The cover of Stephen Stills's recent hit was their first R&B Top 10 single in more than two years.

1980 Donna Summer became the first act signed to former William Morris Agency mailroom boy David Geffen and his Geffen Records.

1993 Though Ray Charles's *My World* album reached only #145 on the Top 200 album charts, it represented a far greater and rarer accomplishment. It gave Charles his sixth consecutive decade in which he had placed recordings on the charts. When his posthumous album *Genius Loves Company* charted in 2004, it gave Ray an unprecedented seven decades of hits.

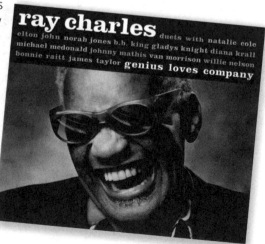

June

20

#1 R&B Song 1953: "Help Me Somebody," the "5" Royales

Born: Lionel Richie, 1949

1953 Beautiful R&B ballads were the norm in the early '50s. Too bad so many went unnoticed, though they're now sought-after collectors' items like the Five Willows' "My Dear Dearest Darling" ($300), which was released today. *Billboard* "Buys of the Week" included "If I Can't Have You," the Flamingos' debut 45 ($2,000), and the Crickets' "For You I Have Eyes" ($200).

1964 James Brown, Otis Redding, Solomon Burke, Joe Tex, and Garnett Mimms performed at the Summer Shower of Stars tour at the Donnelly Theatre, Boston, MA.

1973 Though bedridden at the time, Little Richard choose to perform on *Dick Clark's 20th Anniversary American Bandstand* TV show.

1979 *The Blues Brothers* film opened throughout America. Some of the movie's highlights included Aretha Franklin's portrayal of a crusty waitress, singing her 1968 hit, "Think"; James Brown's performance as a hypnotic dancing and singing preacher; Ray Charles and the Blues Brothers' rockin' "Shake a Tail Feather"; and John Lee Hooker's rough and raw version of "Boom Boom."

1986 Tina Turner performed in the Prince's Trust concert in London along with Elton John and Eric Clapton.

1991 Bell Biv DeVoe performed on James Brown's *Living in America* live cable special.

1994 Aretha Franklin performed at the White House in Washington, DC, for President and Mrs. Clinton.

1997 Lawrence Payton of the Four Tops died today of liver cancer at his Southfield, MI, home. It was the first time in forty-four years that the Tops would be without an original member, as the same four men stayed together until Payton's death. He was never replaced, and the three remaining original members are still performing as the Tops. Payton was fifty-nine.

June

#1 R&B Song 1975: "Give the People What They Want," the O'Jays

Born: Carl White (the Rivingtons), 1932; Ocie Lee "O.C." Smith, 1932; Mitty Collier, 1941; Brenda Holloway, 1946

1964 B.B. King performed at Chicago's Regal Theater. The live recording of that concert became the classic *Live at the Regal* album the following year.

1978 Aretha Franklin performed in Las Vegas for the first time in eight years.

1990 Little Richard Day was proclaimed in Los Angeles as the rock icon was given a star on the Hollywood Walk of Fame. About this time he stated: "I believe my music is the healin' music. I believe my music can make the blind see, the lame walk, the deaf and dumb hear and talk, because it inspires and uplifts people. It regenerates the heart, makes the liver quiver, the bladder splatter, and the knees freeze. I'm not conceited either."

1997 Actor and rapper Will Smith debuted on the R&B charts as a solo with "Men in Black" from the film, which he starred in. The record reached #9 on the airplay charts. Smith was originally half of the duo D.J. Jazzy Jeff & the Fresh Prince and starred in the TV show *Fresh Prince of Bel-Air* (so you can surmise which half he was).

1997 2Pac (Tupac Shakur) attacked the R&B hit list with "Smile," reaching #4 and #12 pop. The hard-core rapper had died almost a year earlier when he was shot to death in a drive-by attack in Las Vegas. Like many rappers, 2Pac had more chart success after his demise than before as he reached the R&B Top 100 thirty-four times through 2004, twenty of those after expiring.

1998 Bobby Brown was arrested at the Beverly Hilton Hotel, Beverly Hills, CA, on suspicion of misdemeanor sexual battery after a purported occurrence at his pool.

2001 Blues legend John Lee Hooker—one of the few remaining links to the classic R&B and blues style that developed into the foundation of rock 'n' roll—died of natural causes at his home in Los Altos, CA. He had performed on more than 100 albums in a career that covered more than half a century. He influenced artists including Eric Clapton, the Rolling Stones, ZZ Top, Bonnie Raitt, and Jimi Hendrix.

#1 R&B Song 1985: "Rock Me Tonight" Freddie Jackson

Born: Ella Johnson, 1923; Verne Allison (the Dells), 1936; Chuck Jackson, 1937; Jimmy Castor (the Juniors), 1943

1959 Jackie Wilson charted with "I'll Be Satisfied," reaching #6 R&B and #20 pop. It was his fourth Top 10 hit in a row. He would go on to have ten in a row through 1961 and eventually chart forty-seven times on the R&B hit list through 1975.

1963 Little Stevie Wonder's "Fingertips, Part 2" became the thirteen-year-old's first of sixty-five pop-chart records through 2002.

1963 The Four Pennies charted en route to #67 pop with a Chiffons-styled takeoff of the Crystals' "Uptown," called "My Block." One reason for the style similarity was because the Four Pennies were the Chiffons. With their current hit "One Fine Day" riding up the charts, the group's producers were so enamored of "My Block" that they didn't want to wait months to release it as another Chiffons song, so they just renamed the group, at least for the one release.

1968 Sly & the Family Stone performed at the Fillmore West in San Francisco.

1969 The Impressions, Ike & Tina Turner, and Santana performed at Fillmore West in San Francisco, a venue known for hosting mostly rock bands.

The Impressions

June

#1 Song 1979: "Hot Stuff," Donna Summer

Born: Helen Humes, 1913

1956 Shirley & Lee's immortal "Let the Good Times Roll" was issued (#20 pop). The same day, doo-wop standards "Can't We Be Sweethearts" by the Cleftones ($40), "Your Way" by the Heartbeats ($200), and "Castle in the Sky" by the Bop Chords ($200) were released.

1958 The Shields' "You Cheated" (#12 pop, #11 R&B) was issued.

1970 Chubby Checker was arrested when police found marijuana in his car in Niagara Falls, NY.

1979 Chic's "Good Times" charted on its way to #1 R&B for six weeks and #1 pop for one week.

1983 Miles Davis, Ray Charles, and B.B. King, among others, performed at New York's Kool Jazz Festival.

1991 Michael Jackson left for home after a stay in Bermuda, where, among other things, he played with film star Macauley Culkin.

1997 Brandy appeared in the lead role of the ABC/Disney-TV production of *Cinderella*. She also had a part in the hit teen-horror flick, *I Know What You Did Last Summer*.

Brandy

June

24

#1 R&B Song 1957: "C.C. Rider," Chuck Willis

Born: Eugene Mumford (the Larks, the Dominoes), 1925; Garland Green, 1942

1957 The Flamingos signed with Decca Records and the Velours' "Can I Come Over Tonight" ($200) was issued.

1960 John Lee Hooker performed at the second annual Newport Folk Festival in Newport, RI, while the Flamingos, the Five Satins, Sonny Boy Williamson, and Marv Johnson played the Apollo Theater in New York.

1964 Sam Cooke headlined a two-week stay at New York's famed Copacabana Club. Cooke had previously played the Copa in 1958 but as an opening act to Jewish comedian Myron Cohen.

1966 Percy Sledge, Sam & Dave, Patti LaBelle & the Blue Belles, Garnett Mimms, and Otis Redding began a grueling one-nighter's tour schedule of forty-six performances in Greensboro, NC.

1978 Rick James debut album *Come Get It!* charted, reaching #3 R&B and #13 pop. James's first recordings were made in Toronto, Canada, in June of 1975 when he recorded a prophetic one-off single for Quality entitled "(I Wanna Be a) Hollywood Star" under the name Gorilla.

1978 Janice Marie Johnson led A Taste of Honey onto the charts with "Boogie Oogie Oogie." It finally stopped "boogying" at #1.

1989 Aretha Franklin and Whitney Houston's duet "It Isn't, It Wasn't, It Ain't Never Gonna Be" was released. It became Franklin's seventy-second chart rider (#41) and Houston's twelfth, though it was the only single of her first fourteen that did not reach the Top 5.

1995 Michael Jackson's *HIStory: Past, Present and Future, Book I* album debuted at #1 in England and would be #1 in America within two weeks.

June

#1 R&B Song 1955: "Bo Diddley," Bo Diddley

Born: Clifton Chenier, 1925; Bobby Nunn (the Coasters), 1936; Eddie Floyd (the Falcons), 1935; Harold Melvin (the Blue Notes), 1939; Johnnie Richardson (Johnnie & Joe), 1940

1925 Clifton Chenier, known as the king of zydeco music, was born in Montgomery, AL. The accordion player (along with his Red Hot Louisiana Band) was considered an international ambassador of zydeco culture and received a Grammy for his album *I'm Here* in 1984.

1949 Louis Jordan charted with "Every Man to His Own Profession," reaching #10 R&B. It was the forty-seventh of fifty-seven hits he would have through 1951. He ranks as the #1 R&B artist of the '40s.

1955 The Nutmegs, the Ravens, and the Cardinals joined Bill Haley & the Comets in concert at the Philadelphia Arena.

1961 The Shirelles, Etta James, Gene McDaniels, the Flairs, Tony Williams (of the Platters), Clarence "Frogman" Henry, and B.B. King performed in Alan Freed's Spectacular at Los Angeles's Hollywood Bowl along with Brenda Lee, Jerry Lee Lewis, and the Diamonds, among others. A front-row seat set you back $4.00.

Clifton Chenier

June

26

#1 Song 1961: "Quarter to Three,"
Gary "U.S." Bonds

Born: Blues singer "Big Bill"
Broonzy (William Lee Conley), 1893;
Billy Davis Jr. (the Fifth Dimension),
1940

1893 "Big Bill" Broonzy—one of Chicago's early blues guitar influences—was born today. Broonzy started recording in 1927 and had a hit with "Big Bill's Blues." By the '50s he was billing himself as "the last blues singer."

1954 One of the first singles by the Platters, "Tell fhe World" ($200), was released.

1961 The Spinners' debut single, "That's What Girls Are Made For," charted, reaching #5 R&B and #27 pop. The quintet was discovered by Moonglows leader/producer Harvey Fuqua at Detroit's Make Way for Youth show, and it was Fuqua who sang the lead on this and their follow-up single, "Love (I'm So Glad) I Found You."

1964 The Supremes, the Shirelles, the Crystals, and Major Lance, among others, performed at the Fairgrounds Grandstand in Allentown, PA, on Dick Clark's Caravan of Stars tour.

1965 Wilson Pickett's "In the Midnight Hour" charted, reaching #1 R&B, #21 pop. It was the first of five #1s for "the wicked Pickett," a nickname he earned at the Atlantic Records office for his affection for the label's ladies.

1993 Stevie Wonder performed with Prince at the Purple One's Grand Slam Club in Los Angeles.

June

#1 R&B Song 1981: "Give It to Me Baby," Rick James

Born: Rosalie Allen (Julie Marlene Bedra), 1924

1953 Jackie Wilson made his recording debut with the Dominoes, cutting "You Can't Keep a Good Man Down" ($100). Meanwhile, R&B standards "Gee" by the Crows (#14 pop, #2 R&B, $400) and "I Cover the Waterfront" by the Orioles ($1,200) were released.

1960 Lonnie Johnson, an originator and founding father of modern guitar blues performed at the Playboy Club in Chicago. The innovative Johnson, who played with the likes of Louis Armstrong and Duke Ellington going back to the '20s, was recently found working as a janitor in a Philadelphia hotel.

1964 The Valentinos charted with "It's All Over Now," reaching only #94 pop. The group was actually Bobby Womack and his brothers, who started out as the gospel group, the Womack Brothers. Bobby's song, however. would gain immortality as an early hit for the Rolling Stones.

1970 The Jackson 5 hit #1 with "The Love You Save," thus becoming the first artists to reach the top pop spot with their first three charters.

1987 Whitney Houston's "I Wanna Dance with Somebody" hit #1, while her album *Whitney* became the first album by a female singer to debut on *Billboard*'s chart at #1.

1992 Michael Jackson began his latest world tour in support of the album *Dangerous* in Munich, West Germany. A European-only TV program was taped and included two of Michael's performances live from the concert.

1996 The Fugees appeared at the free Hoodshock concert in New York. A man began firing a gun and numerous onlookers where hospitalized.

June 28

#1 R&B Song 1952: "Have Mercy Baby," the Dominoes

Born: Blues singer David "Honey Boy" Edwards, 1915

1947 Louis Jordan entered the R&B hit list with "I Know What You're Putting Down," reaching #3.

1947 Ella Fitzgerald and the Andy Love Quintet (a vocal group) charted with a beautiful version of "That's My Desire," reaching #3 R&B.

1957 An all-star show at the Apollo Theater included the Jesters, the Charts, the Heartbeats, the Velours, and the Sensations.

1965 The Temptations, Dionne Warwick, the Supremes, Martha & the Vandellas, the Ronettes, and the Four Tops performed on the *It's What's Happening, Baby* special on CBS-TV.

1986 Sade and Hugh Masekela performed at an anti-apartheid concert at Clapham Common in London. Also appearing were Sting, Boy George, Elvis Costello, and Peter Gabriel, among others. Nearly a quarter of a million people attended.

1990 Tina Turner became the first woman and only the second rock 'n' roll act (Pink Floyd being the other) to perform at the Palace of Versailles in France.

1996 R. Kelly was involved in a fight at a health club in Lafayette, LA, and as if his day couldn't get any worse, the local Cajundome's Commission commandeered his and his band's equipment for ostensibly failing to fulfill a commitment to perform a concert.

Hugh Masekela

June

1946 Louis Jordan and Ella Fitzgerald charted with their duet on the rousing "Stone Cold Dead in the Market (He Had It Coming)," reaching #1 R&B for five weeks and #7 pop.

1953 The Drifters recorded their first song today, "Lucille," which would become their third R&B chart hit (#7).

1956 The Channels recorded their classic "The Closer You Are" ($250). Sharing the session (to save money) were label mates the Continentals, who then recorded their beautiful ballad "Dear Lord" ($30).

1963 James Brown's first album, *Live at the Apollo*, debuted on the pop charts today, eventually rising to #2. As with his pop singles, even though he had enormous chart success, he never had a #1 pop album. Though Brown would go on to have forty-nine albums hit the pop charts through 1988, *Live* would remain his all-time biggest success and would be considered a milestone in the development of live albums for years to come.

1968 Pigmeat Markham, one of the few comedians to hit the singles charts, did it today with "Hear Comes the Judge," which reached #4 R&B and #19 pop. The title line was from a recurring gag on TV's *Rowan & Martin's Laugh-In* show.

1985 Whitney Houston stormed onto the singles chart with "Saving All My Love for You," an eventual #1 pop and R&B. She would go on to have eleven pop #1 singles through 2002. The song was originally done in 1982 by Marilyn McCoo & Billy Davis, formerly of the Fifth Dimension.

1985 The Mary Jane Girls entered the R&B charts with "Wild and Crazy Love," reaching #10 and #42 pop. It was their follow-up to their breakthrough hit, "In My House," which reached #3 R&B and #7 pop. Both were written and produced by Rick James.

1991 Dionne Warwick, Chaka Khan, En Vogue, Levert, and Dianne Reeves, among others, performed on the *Celebrate the Soul of American Music* TV show.

June

30

#1 R&B Song 1951: "Sixty Minute Man," the Dominoes

Born: Lena Horne, 1917; Florence Ballard (the Supremes), 1943; William Brown (Ray, Goodman & Brown), 1946; Stanley Clarke, 1951

1953 The Orioles' legendary "Crying in the Chapel" (#11 pop, #1 R&B) was recorded.

1956 Aladdin Records sued the Five Keys for breach of contract when the quintet signed with Capital Records. The same day, the Velours' debut 45, "My Love Come Back" ($200) was issued.

1972 Stevie Wonder performed in Vancouver, British Columbia, as the opening act for the Rolling Stones on an eight-week North American tour.

1984 The Jackson 5 charted with "State of Shock," which featured a duet by Michael Jackson and the Rolling Stones' Mick Jagger. It reached #3 pop and #4 R&B.

1989 Bobby Brown made a personal appearance at the HMV store on London's Oxford Street and police had to close off the thoroughfare as 4,000 fans attempted (among other things) to get his autograph. During the near-riot scene, six fans were hospitalized and one was brought back to life (so to speak) by a kiss from the star.

1990 Mariah Carey's self-titled debut album charted. It would take the ten-song collection thirty-six weeks to make #1.

1995 Boyz II Men, Mary J. Blige, and Montell Jordan performed at the Starwood Amphitheater in Antioch, TN.

1995 Brandy, Blackstreet, Notorious B.I.G., Naught by Nature, and Method Man, among others, performed at the Byrne Meadowlands Arena in East Rutherford, NJ, at the Hot 97 Summer Jam.

1997 George Clinton, Cypress Hill, and Erykah Badu began the House of Blues Smokin' Grooves tour at the Great Woods Center for the Performing Arts in Mansfield, MA. Badu originally performed under the name M.C. Apples in a rap trio before becoming part of the duo Erykah Free.

July

#1 R&B Song 1978: "Stuff Like That," Quincy Jones

Born: Gospel pioneer "Georgia" Tom" Dorsey, 1899; Willie Dixon, 1915; Bobby Day (the Hollywood Flames), 1930; Syl Johnson, 1939; June Montiero (the Toys), 1946; Evelyn "Champagne" King, 1960; Melissa Arnette "Missy" Elliott, 1971

1954 The Ink Spots began a stint at the Trocadero on Hollywood's Sunset Strip.

1957 A Philadelphia radio station with only 250 watts of power began repeat plays of the Tune Weavers' new release, "Happy, Happy Birthday Baby." By October it was #1.

1960 The Jesters, Ben E. King, Ruth Brown, Jimmy Jones, and the Olympics performed on one of disc jockey Jocko Henderson's Jocko's Rocketship Revue at New York's Apollo Theater.

1971 James Brown and his entire catalog of two decades worth of recordings were signed to Polydor Records.

1972 The Trammps entered the R&B hit list with the scintillating disco cover of the Coasters' "Zing Went the Strings of My Heart," reaching #17. The group from Philadelphia formerly recorded under the name the Volcanos.

1978 Martha & the Vandellas reunited for the first time in ten years for a benefit concert for actor Will Geer in Santa Cruz, CA.

1992 Vanessa Williams and Dinah Washington's goddaughter, Patti Austin, performed at a fund-raiser for the Hollywood Women's Political Committee. Austin, a veteran performer since her teens, had over the years toured and performed on TV with such notables as Sammy Davis Jr., Connie Stevens, Quincy Jones, Roberta Flack, Harry Belafonte, and Bobby Darin.

1998 The Dixie Hummingbirds, Stevie Wonder, and Paul Simon appeared on TV's *Late Show with David Letterman*.

#1 R&B Song 1966: "Ain't Too Proud to Beg," the Temptations

Born: Paul Williams (the Temptations), 1939

1954 Lillian Leach, one of the premier R&B lead singers of the '50s, and her group the Mellows signed to Jay Dee Records.

1962 Jimi Hendrix, now a member of Bobby Taylor & the Vancouvers, performed at Dante's Inferno Club in Vancouver, British Columbia. He was previously playing with Bob Fisher & the Barnevilles, who toured America backing acts like the Impressions and the Marvelettes.

1966 Dionne Warwick had her first charter after a drought of three and a half years when "Trains, Boats and Planes" cruised onto the hit survey (#22 pop).

1974 The man who brought bass singing into prominence in the '40s and '50s, Jimmy Ricks of the Ravens, died.

1982 DeFord Bailey, the first star of the Grand Ole Opry, died. Known as "the harmonica wizard," Bailey was a fixture on Nashville's WSM Barn dance radio show in 1927 and its most popular performer. After one particularly scintillating performance of his classic "Pan American Blues," radio announcer George Hay stated, "For the last hour we have been listening to music largely from Grand Opera, but from now on we will present the Grand Ole Opry." The Opry and its first star were born.

1986 Prince's second film, *Under the Cherry Moon*, debuted nationwide.

1988 Chubby Checker & the Fat Boys charted R&B with "The Twist (Yo, Twist.)," reaching #40 R&B and #16 pop. It would be the last of Checker's thirty-five pop hits and eighteen R&B entries, a streak that started in 1959. The record reached #2 in England and was a hit throughout Europe, just as his original "Twist" from twenty-eight years earlier had been.

1988 "Dirty Diana" by Michael Jackson reached # 1, becoming his fifth chart-topper in a row and the first time an artist had five #1s from the same album (*Bad*).

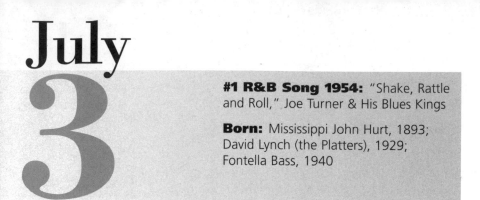

#1 R&B Song 1954: "Shake, Rattle and Roll," Joe Turner & His Blues Kings

Born: Mississippi John Hurt, 1893; David Lynch (the Platters), 1929; Fontella Bass, 1940

1948 Sarah Vaughan reached the Top 100 with "Nature Boy" on her way to #9 pop. It was the first of thirty-three hits through 1966 for the jazz vocalist known as "the Divine One."

1954 Collectibles by the Thrillers ("Lizabeth," $400) and the Hawks ("It Ain't That Way," $100) were released.

1961 The Chantels' biggest hit, "Look in My Eyes," charted today on its way to #14 pop and #6 R&B. It beat out their legendary standard "Maybe" by one chart position pop, though "Maybe" was the bigger R&B hit (#2).

1963 LaVern Baker performed at the Riviera Hotel in Las Vegas. It was her first Vegas booking after fifteen years in show business and eighteen pop chart singles.

1965 Otis Redding's "I've Been Loving You Too Long" peaked at #21 pop, #2 R&B, becoming his first big hit. Redding wrote the song with Jerry Butler in a Buffalo, NY, hotel room.

1967 The Jimi Hendrix Experience performed at New York's the Scene with Tiny Tim. Apparently the booking agent had never seen either act; if he had, he would have been out of his mind to pair them on the same bill.

1969 The Newport Jazz Festival opened its doors to rock and R&B artists for the first time. Taking part in the performance festivities were James Brown, Sly & the Family Stone, and others.

1971 Earth, Wind & Fire's chart debut, "Love Is Life," went on to #43 R&B, setting the stage for a career that would still be going strong in the twenty-first century. The group, an outgrowth of the Chicago band the Salty Peppers, went on to have thirty-five pop chart singles through 1993.

#1 R&B Song 1953: "Please Love Me,"
B.B. King & His Orchestra

Born: Bill Withers, 1938; Annette Sterling
(Martha & the Vandellas), 1943; Jesse Lee
Daniels (Force M.D.'s), 1963

1960 The Voicemasters jumped onto the R&B hit list with "Everything About You," reaching #18. The group consisted of David Ruffin (later of the Temptations), Lamont Dozier (later of Holland, Dozier & Holland), and three members who would go on to form the nucleus of the Originals.

1970 Jimi Hendrix, B.B. King, the Chambers Brothers, Jethro Tull, and Rare Earth, among others, performed at the Second Atlanta International Pop Festival at the Middle Georgia Raceway near Byron, GA. The crowd reportedly numbered more than 200,000.

1974 Barry White married Glodean James, a member of the vocal group Love Unlimited, for whom Barry wrote and produced.

1976 On the bicentennial of America's birth, Bob Marley's "Roots, Rock, and Reggae" charted, becoming his biggest pop hit at #51.

1993 The Four Tops performed at the Meadow Brook Music Festival in Rochester, MI, for their Independence Day show.

1997 Roberta Flack performed in Boston at the Hatch Shell with the Boston Pops Orchestra.

1998 Aretha Franklin charted for the ninety-seventh time when "Here We Go Again" hit, eventually reaching #24 R&B. Her R&B chart totals included twenty #1s over the thirty-eight-year period.

1998 Lionel Richie performed at London's Hyde Park in the Prince's Trust Charity concert, Party in the Park.

The Four Tops

July 5

#1 Song 1986: "There'll Be Sad Songs," Billy Ocean

Born: Blues singer Smiley Lewis (Overton Amos Lemons), 1913

1958 Ray Charles performed at the Newport Jazz Festival in Newport, RI. Atlantic Records recorded the performance for a live album.

1961 Dick Clark's *American Bandstand* welcomed a rare blues guest when Slim Harpo came on and sang "Rainin' in My Heart."

1962 Little Eva introduced "The Locomotion" to a national TV audience via *American Bandstand*, helping to take the record to #1. Before recording the song, Eva was the babysitter for songwriter Carole King.

1969 Chuck Berry performed on the same bill as the Who at the Pop Proms in the Royal Albert Hall in London. The Albert Hall banned rock 'n' roll after over-zealous fans charged the stage.

1969 Comedienne Moms Mabley charted with her version of "Abraham, Martin & John," reaching #18 R&B and #35 pop. Probably the oldest artist ever to have a hit that wasn't posthumous, Mabley was seventy-five at the time.

1980 Teddy Pendergrass's "Can't We Try," from the Meatloaf film, *Roadie*, charted, reaching #3 R&B. His European tour had recently been canceled due to a reported affair with the wife of Marvin Gaye, who was to tour Britain at the same time.

1986 Janet Jackson's *Control* album soared to #1, making the twenty-year-old the youngest artist since thirteen year-old Little Stevie Wonder to top the album Top 200.

1987 Ben E. King performed with George Harrison, Ringo Starr, and Elton John at the fifth annual Prince's Trust Rock Gala at London's Wembley Arena.

1997 Brooklyn rapper, Lil' Kim charted with "Not Tonight" reaching #33 R&B and #6 pop with the recording help of Missy "Misdemeanor" Elliott, Lisa "Left Eye" Lopes, Da Brat, and Angie Martinez. Kim would go on to have twenty-two R&B hits through 2004 and a conviction for lying to a grand jury, perjury, and conspiracy in an investigation into a shooting.

July 6

#1 Song 1974: "Rock the Boat," the Hues Corporation

Born: Della Reese (Delloreese Patricia Early), 1931; Gene Chandler (Eugene Dixon, the Dukays), 1937; Jan Bradley, 1943; Phyllis Hyman, 1950; 50 Cent (Curtis Jackson III), 1976

1946 Buddy Johnson & His Orchestra, with Arthur Prysock on vocals, charted with "They All Say I'm the Biggest Fool," reaching #5 R&B.

1946 The Ink Spots entered the R&B charts with the oft-recorded "Prisoner of Love," reaching #5 and #9 pop.

1963 Anita Humes & the Essex, a vocal group made up of five U.S. Marines, topped the singles charts with "Easier Said Than Done." The group needed special permission from the Defense Department to perform off-base.

1963 The Cookies' "Will Power" charted (#72 pop). Though the female trio had four pop and four R&B charters, they were mostly a backup group for the likes of Neil Sedaka, Carole King, and Little Eva. An earlier incarnation in the '50s became Ray Charles' background vocalists the Raelettes, but as the Cookies they reached #9 R&B with "In Paradise" in 1956.

1963 Chubby Checker, the Percells, Dee Dee Sharp, and the Earls performed at New York's Polo Grounds prior to a Mets baseball game.

1974 The Persuasions, popularly known as a "niche" a cappella group, charted with instrumentation when "I Really Got It Bad for You" hit the R&B charts, reaching #56.

1984 The Jackson 5 began their Victory Tour at Arrowhead Stadium in Kansas City, MO. Actually, it was the Jackson 6, as all of the brothers shared the stage for the first time in eight years.

1991 James Brown and B.B. King performed in Zagreb, Yugoslavia, while on a European tour.

Della Reese

July

7

#1 R&B Song 1951: "Rocket 88," Jackie Brenston & His Delta Cats (with Ike Turner)

Born: Lloyd "Tiny" Grimes, 1916; Michael Henderson, 1951

1956 The Teenagers' "I Promise to Remember" was released, eventually reaching #10 R&B and #57 pop.

1956 Little Richard's "Rip It Up" charted, reaching #17 pop and becoming Richard's second #1 R&B single. Richard was so hot that even his B-sides were becoming hits: "Ready Teddy" made #8 R&B (#44 pop), and his last single's flip side, "Slippin' and Slidin'," hit #2 R&B (#33 pop).

1957 The Coasters opened for a week at the Apollo Theater.

1984 Prince topped the pop and R&B charts with "When Doves Cry," which went on to be the best-selling single of the year.

1990 Public Enemy charted with "Brothers Gonna Work It Out," reaching #20 R&B. Their name was said to have showed up in a subsequent FBI report to Congress regarding "Rap Music and Its Effects on National Security."

1995 The Neville Brothers played the annual Montreux Jazz Festival in Montreux, Switzerland.

1997 Michael Jackson's *Thriller* album reached the 25 million sales mark, as ratified by the RIAA.

July 8

#1 R&B Song 1972: ("If Loving You Is Wrong) I Don't Wanna Be Right," Luther Ingram

Born: Louis Jordan, 1908; Billy Eckstine, 1914

1908 Louis Jordan—considered to be the father of rhythm and blues—was born today. With his Tympany Five (which actually had nine members) Jordan became the opening act for the Mills Brothers in 1938. His innovative and humorous style led him to become the most popular R&B recording act of the '40s, with fifty-seven hits between 1942 and 1951. His jump blues and jazz fusion paved the way for R&B's influence on rock 'n' roll.

1950 Nat King Cole entered the R&B hit list with one of his best-loved recordings, "Mona Lisa," reaching #1 for four weeks and topping the pop charts for eight. The song was from the Alan Ladd film Captain Carey.

1963 Little Stevie Wonder performed "Fingertips, Part 2" on *American Bandstand.*

1972 The O'Jays charted with "Backstabbers," reaching #1 R&B and #3 pop, their first of a career ten R&B chart toppers.

1995 TLC's "Waterfalls" reached #1 pop for seven weeks and #4 R&B. It was the trio's second of four #1s, including "Creep," "No Scrubs," and "Unpretty."

July
9

#1 R&B Song 1977: "Best of My Love," the Emotions

Born: Joe Liggins, 1916; Don McPherson (the Main Ingredient), 1941; Gwen Guthrie, 1950

1955 The Harptones' brilliant "Life Is But a Dream" was released. Though they were never a major chart success, the group's incredible R&B/jazz harmonies influenced dozens of groups, including the Crests, the Marcels, and the Brooklyn Bridge.

1966 The Intruders debuted with "United" (#14 R&B). They went on to have twenty-four hits through 1975, including the #1 "Cowboys to Girls" in 1968.

1983 Jerry Butler, who had a succession of hit duets with females (Brenda Lee Eager, Betty Everett, and Thelma Houston), hit the R&B charts with Patti Austin on "In My Life" (#92). It was the last of his fifty-nine charters.

Jerry Butler

July 10

#1 Song 1961: "Tossin' & Turnin,'"
Bobby Lewis

Born: Bandleader Noble Sissle, 1899; Blues
vocalist Ivie Anderson, 1905

1954 WHBQ, a Memphis radio station, began playing Arthur "Big Boy" Crudup's song "That's All Right Mama" as recorded by a young singer named Elvis Presley, thus jump-starting the career of the most successful solo act in pop history. Presley later recorded Crudup's "So Glad You're Mine," which Arthur had taken to #3 R&B in 1946.

1954 Clyde McPhatter & the Drifters reached #1 R&B with "Honey Love" despite the fact that several stations banned the record, including Memphis radio WDIA, for having "overtly sexual" lyrics.

1966 James Brown performed at the Los Angeles Sports Arena while a riot was in full swing outside because an overflow of fans was denied entry to the sold-out show.

1975 Gladys Knight & the Pips began their own four-week summer replacement TV show on NBC.

1989 The Shirelles appeared in Nashville, but not to sing in the usual sense. They were in federal court suing local Gusto Records over improper payments of royalties on reissued hits. Ten months later, they won.

1993 While on a European tour, Chaka Khan performed at the Montreux Jazz Festival in Montreux, Switzerland, and continued on to the JVC Jazz Festival in Nice, France, and the North Sea Jazz Festival in the Hague, the Netherlands.

1993 Cypress Hill charted with "Insane in the Brain," reaching #19 pop and #27 R&B, making it the most successful single of their career. The rap trio named themselves after a Los Angeles street.

July 11

1897 Blind Lemon Jefferson—an innovative blues musician and founder of the Texas blues style—was born today. His formula was a combination of Tex-Mex flamenco guitar and a starting and stopping rhythm style mixed with Chicago blues. He was best remembered for songs like "Matchbox Blues," "Mean Jumper Blues," and "Jack of Diamonds." Recording for Paramount, he had forty-three 78s released, a vast catalog for the times. He is considered the first of the legendary male blues stars of the '20s.

1953 The flip side of the Flamingos' debut single ("If I Can't Have You"), "Someday, Someway," broke out in Los Angeles.

1987 The Temptations sang backup vocals for actor Bruce Willis's passable version of the Drifters' 1964 hit, "Under the Boardwalk." Though it only reached #59 pop in America, the Brits loved it to the tune of #2.

1992 Jazz prodigy Patti Austin and Vanessa Williams performed at the Hollywood Women's Political Committee fund-raiser.

1995 Donna Summer sang at the Nautica Stage in Cleveland, OH, at the start of a U.S. tour.

Patti Austin

194

July

12

#1 R&B Song 1952: "Lawdy Miss Clawdy," Lloyd Price & His Orchestra

Born: Sam "The Man" Taylor, 1934; Jay "Jaybird" Uzzell (the Corsairs), 1942; Jerry Williams Jr., 1942; Tracie Spencer, 1976

1951 The Clovers recorded their soon-to-be second #1 R&B hit in a row, "Fool, Fool, Fool."

1952 The Chicago vocal quartet the Four Blazes charted with "Mary Jo," reaching #1 R&B for three weeks. But the B-side, a smooth version of "Mood Indigo," was the real gem.

1956 Shirley & Lee sang at the Carrs Beach Amphitheater in Maryland along with the Teenagers, the Cleftones, Carl Perkins, and the Spaniels. More than 8,000 lucky fans got in to see them while an unlucky 10,000 were turned away.

1960 Frankie Lymon appeared on Dick Clark's *American Bandstand* for the first time since 1958, and without the Teenagers, as he sang "Little Bitty Pretty One."

1980 Diana Ross bounced onto the Hot 100 with "Upside Down" (#1). It was her fifth solo chart topper in ten years.

1989 The Disney Channel announced it was doing *Mother Goose Rock 'n' Rhyme*. Included in the cast was Old King Cole himself, Little Richard.

1995 The O'Jays performed at the Universal Amphitheater in a benefit called Let's Stamp Out AIDS.

July

13

#1 R&B Song 1946: "The Gypsy," the Ink Spots

Born: Johnny Funches (the Dells), 1935

1954 The Dominoes began a two-week stint at Las Vegas's Sahara Hotel.

1959 The Eternals charted with their debut 45, "Rockin' in the Jungle," an eventual R&B novelty standard even though it only reached #78 pop.

1959 Sam Cooke's dreamy yet bouncy ballad, "Only Sixteen," reached its chart plateau at #28 pop, while peaking at #13 R&B. Still, it became one of his most popular songs and the epitome of '50s pop culture. The song was written by Barbara Campbell, who wasn't a writer. It was the odd pseudonym for Cooke, Herb Alpert, and Lou Adler, using Sam's wife's maiden name.

1963 Stevie Wonder's *The Twelve Year Old Genius* charted, becoming #1 pop and making Stevie the first artist to top the album, R&B singles, and Hot 100 singles charts at the same time.

1963 In an era when blues artists did not fare well on the pop album charts, Bobby "Blue" Bland landed there with his set *Call on Me/That's the Way Love Is*, which would eventually reach #11. Remarkably, the album never charted R&B. Bobby would put eleven albums on the pop charts through 1979.

1974 Gladys Knight & the Pips' "On and On" became their fourth consecutive gold 45 when it peaked at #5 pop. It reached #2 R&B.

1985 B.B. King, Patti LaBelle, the Four Tops, Tina Turner, Lionel Richie, David Ruffin, and Eddie Kendrick were among the stars who performed at Live Aid at Philadelphia's JFK Stadium. Teddy Pendergrass also performed. It was his first live performance since being paralyzed in a car accident in 1982.

1993 Fats Domino and Ray Charles performed at the Westfalenhalle 1 in Dortmund, Germany, on their European tour.

#1 R&B Song 1979: "Ring My Bell," Anita Ward

Born: Clifford & Claude Trenier, 1919; Lowman Pauling (the "5" Royales), 1926; Ty Hunter (the Voice Masters), 1940

1954 Lillian Leach & the Mellows recorded their doo-wop standard, "Smoke From Your Cigarette," now a $250 collector's item.

1956 One of the first R&B vocal group albums to successfully cross over to pop, *The Platters* charted, reaching #7. The same day, their single "My Prayer" (originally done by the Mills Brothers) charted on its way to #1 pop (two weeks) and #1 R&B (five weeks). It was their third million-seller out of only four releases. The group, led by the pristine tenor of Tony Williams (who was working as a parking-lot attendant when he first started), was the most popular group of the '50s. They went on to have almost twice as many pop hits as R&B (forty to twenty-one) through 1967.

1958 The Drinkard Singers' (RCA) spiritual 45, "Rise, Shine," was issued. The group consisted of Dionne Warwick, Cissy Houston (Whitney's mother), Dee Dee Warwick (Dionne's sister), and Judy Clay.

1984 Prince's *Purple Rain* album, from the film of the same name, charted on its way to #1 pop for an astounding twenty-four weeks. It would go on to sell more than 10 million copies in the U.S. alone.

1992 Aretha Franklin sang "The Star-Spangled Banner" at the second night of the Democratic National Convention.

1992 The Pointer Sisters performed at the Valley Forge Music Fair in Devon, PA.

July 15

#1 R&B Song 1967: "I Was Made to Love Her," Stevie Wonder

Born: Millie Jackson, 1944

1952 An eight-year-old girl won $2,000 and a gold cup for her rendition of "Too Young" on *Ted Mack's Amateur Hour*. The child was Gladys Knight.

1957 The Five Satins entered the R&B hit list with their soon-to-be standard, "To the Aisle," reaching #5 and #25 pop. The lead singer was emergency lead Bill Baker, drafted from the Connecticut group the Chestnuts, as the Satins' regular frontman, Fred Parris, had received a real draft notice, courtesy of Uncle Sam.

1957 A Harlem street gang named the Charts charted with their sensuously smoking single "Desiree" (#88 pop). The same day, New York's quintessential doo-woppers, the Jesters, charted pop with their first 45, "So Strange" (#100 pop).

1963 Dick Clark's Caravan of Stars began its cross-country tour with Big Dee Irwin, Barbara Lewis, the Crystals, Ruby & the Romantics, the Tymes, the Orlons, Bob B. Soxx & the Blue Jeans, Gene Pitney, and the Dovells, among others.

1972 The Main Ingredient reached the R&B charts with "Everybody Plays the Fool" (#2 R&B, #3 pop), which would become their biggest of twenty R&B charters through 1990. The group's lead singer, Cuba Gooding, is the father of actor Cuba Gooding Jr.

1978 L.T.D. jumped on the R&B charts with "Holding On (When Love Is Gone)," reaching #1 R&B (#49 pop). The group's lead singer at the time would go on to have twenty-three hits of his own. His name is Jeffrey Osborne.

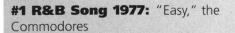

July 16

1949 Blues singer Memphis Slim entered the R&B charts with "Blue and Lonesome," peaking at #2. It was the third of Slim's seven hits, starting in 1948 with his biggest record, "Messin' Around" (#1 R&B).

1959 The Coasters' memorable novelty, "Poison Ivy" (#7 pop, #1 R&B), was recorded.

1972 Smokey Robinson appeared with the Miracles for the last time at a concert at the Carter Barron Center in Washington, DC, leaving to pursue a solo career. He had been with them for eighteen years.

1983 Jazz pianist Herbie Hancock charted with "Rockit," which reached #6 R&B, making it the biggest of his sixteen hits between 1974 and 1988. Hancock played with Miles Davis from 1963 through 1968 before going on his own.

Herbie Hancock

July 17

#1 R&B Song 1954: "Honey Love," the Drifters

Born: Peppermint Harris (Harrison D. Nelson Jr.), 1925; Diahann Carroll (Carol Diann Johnson), 1935; Regina Belle, 1963

1943 The Four Vagabonds charted R&B with one of the most beautiful ballads of the '40s, "It Can't Be Wrong," reaching #3. The superb quartet from St. Louis never had another hit.

1954 The Clovers, the Hollywood Flames, the Crows, the Chords, the Robins, and the Four Tunes appeared at the annual Rock 'n' Roll Jubilee held at Hollywood's Shrine Auditorium.

1961 The Shirelles' "What a Sweet Thing That Was" charted a week after it's a-side, "A Thing of the Past" did the same thing. Consequently, the songs killed each other off on the race up the pop charts, with "What" reaching #54 and "Thing" halting at #41.

1965 The Four Tops began their first tour of Europe with sellout shows in London. The British part of their tour was handled by Beatles manager Brian Epstein.

1967 In one of the most bizarre performance pairings in history, the Monkees appeared at Forest Hills Stadium in New York with show opener Jimi Hendrix.

1991 Little Richard was quoted in *USA Today* saying, "If I had been white, there never would have been an Elvis Presley."

1994 Whitney Houston performed at the World Cup soccer finals between Italy and Brazil at the Rose Bowl in Pasadena, CA.

July 18

1953 The Dominoes' "You Can't Keep a Good Man Down" (#8 R&B) was released. It became their tenth Top 10 hit.

1953 Johnny Ace & the Beal Streeters (named after the famous Memphis Street) had their second #1 when "The Clock" topped the R&B charts for five weeks. The Beale Streeters included, at various times, Earl Forest, Junior Parker, and Bobby "Blue" Bland.

1964 The Dixie Cups charted with "People Say," an eventual #12 pop hit. Though they had five chart singles in the mid-'60s, their music was considered so light that they never charted R&B.

1972 Sly & the Family Stone apparently parked in the wrong place as police searched their motor home on Santa Monica Boulevard in Santa Monica, CA, and found two vials of illegal drugs along with two pounds of marijuana. The group members were promptly arrested.

1975 Bob Marley performed at the Mecca Lyceum in London.

1992 Whitney Houston married Bobby Brown, former member of New Edition, at her Mendham, NJ, home. One of his friends from the group noted that when the "until death do you part" section of the vows was reached, Brown was laughing.

Bob Marley

July
19

#1 R&B Song 1969: "What Does It Take (To Win Your Love)," Junior Walker & the All-Stars

Born: Vaudeville singer Butter Bean (Jody Edwards), 1895

1958 George Treadwell, the Drifters' manager, walked backstage at the Apollo Theater, fired his group, walked across to the dressing room of the group's opening act, the Crowns, hired them, and then christened *them* the Drifters. The Crowns' lead singer was Ben E. King.

1975 George "Bad" Benson's debut solo single, "Supership," peaked at #98 on the R&B chart. Benson originally sang lead for a Pittsburgh vocal group the Altairs, who released the 45 "If You Love Me" (Amy Records) in 1959, when George was only sixteen years old. Despite the poor start, he would go on to have twenty-five R&B charters through 1988, including two #1s, "Give Me the Night" and "Turn Your Love Around."

1975 Esther Phillips charted with "What A Difference A Day Makes" reaching #10 R&B and #20 Pop. It was her nineteenth R&B hit and her first top ten in thirteen years years since "Release Me" hit No. 1 (#8 Pop) in 1962.

1990 Dionne Warwick appeared at the Greek Theater in Los Angeles alongside Johnny Mathis.

1994 Rick James was sentenced to five years plus in prison for assaulting two women and for cocaine use. He would serve his time at Fulsom Prison in California.

Rick James

#1 R&B Song 1974: "My Thang," James Brown

Born: Billy Guy (the Coasters), 1936

1967 The Jimi Hendrix Experience recorded at New York's Mayfair Recording Studios with the Sweet Inspirations (Elvis Presley's and Aretha Franklin's background singers) doing backup vocals on "Midnight Lamp." Hendrix played the harpsichord, but there's no report as to whether or not he tried to burn it.

1968 The Soul Clan, a one-off recording by five of R&B's top stars, including Ben E. King, Joe Tex, Don Covay, Arthur Conley, and Solomon Burke, charted R&B with "Soul Meeting." Despite the star power, the record only reached #34.

1971 The Commodores were the opening act for the Jackson 5 at the Coliseum in Charlotte, NC.

1978 The O'Jays performed at Los Angeles's Greek Theater on their twentieth anniversary.

1990 Luther Vandross performed at the Westbury Music Fair to a sold-out crowd.

1991 Patti LaBelle joined forces with Dionne Warwick and Gladys Knight for "Superwoman," a cut on Knight's new *Good Woman* album, which charted today and eventually reached #45.

1995 TLC's album *Waterfalls* headed toward nine million sales while the group (which obviously didn't know how to mange its money) filed for Chapter 11 bankruptcy today.

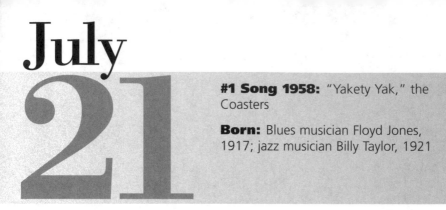

July 21

#1 Song 1958: "Yakety Yak," the Coasters

Born: Blues musician Floyd Jones, 1917; jazz musician Billy Taylor, 1921

1955 The Cadets charted with their rock 'n' roll novelty, "Stranded in the Jungle" (#4 R&B, #15 pop). A year earlier, their balladeer alter egos the Jacks had a hit with "Why Don't You Write Me," which reached #3 R&B and #82 pop. This Jekyll-and-Hyde persona would continue for several years, with the group being balladeers as the Jacks and purveyors of rock 'n' roll as the Cadets.

1958 The Dell-Vikings' cover of "You Cheated" was released, along with the Miracles' "Money" and the Videos' classic "Trickle, Trickle."

1961 The Supremes' second single, "Buttered Popcorn," was released, with Florence Ballard singing lead. The group was still more than a year away from its first chart 45, "Your Heart Belongs to Me."

1962 John Lee Hooker's "Boom Boom" reached #60 pop (#16 R&B), becoming his only 45 in the pop Top 100. It was also his last of nine R&B hits starting in 1949.

1988 James Brown received a two-year suspended sentence and a $1,200 fine for resisting arrest, carrying a gun, and drug possession. (See May 18.)

1990 En Vogue reached #2 pop with "Hold On," their debut disc. Former Commodores member Thomas McElroy and partner Denzil Foster, who wanted to invent a funky, contemporary version of the Supremes, put the female quartet together.

En Vogue

July

22

Born: George Clinton, 1940; Keith Sweat, 1961

1957 B.B. King charted pop for the first time with "Be Careful with a Fool" (#95). He had already had eighteen R&B charters; it took him six years to cross over. He would go on to have thirty-six pop singles on the hit list through 1989.

1960 Screamin' Jay Hawkins, the Five Satins, Joe Turner, Ben E. King, Faye Adams, Nappy Brown, and Annie Laurie (who had an R&B hit with "Since I Fell for You" in 1947) appeared at Chicago's Regal Theater.

1961 Singer and songwriter Keith Sweat was born. The balladeer began working as a Wall Street brokerage assistant and graduated to soulful love songs for a new generation. Influenced by singing groups such as the Emotions and the Sylvers, Sweat managed twenty-nine R&B charters and eighteen pop winners through 2002.

1969 Aretha Franklin was arrested and fined $50 for creating a disturbance in a Detroit parking lot. Upon leaving, she expressed her frustration by running over a road sign.

1983 Diana Ross gave a free concert in New York's Central Park after the previous night's concert was washed out by heavy wind and rain.

1991 Bobby Womack performed at London's Hackney Empire.

1998 Cypress Hill, Busta Rhymes, Canibus, Wyclef Jean, and Public Enemy, among others, performed at the third annual Smokin' Grooves tour at the Darien Lake Performing Arts Center, Darien Center, NY.

July

23

#1 R&B Song 1949: "Trouble Blues," the Charles Brown Trio

Born: Cleve Duncan (the Penguins), 1935

1962 The Shirelles charted with "Welcome Home Baby," a logical sequel to their last hit, "Soldier Boy." The single made it to #20 R&B and #22 pop. Soon after, a publisher offered the group's manager, Florence Greenberg, a new tune as a follow-up called "He's a Rebel." Florence turned it down, and the Crystals went on to have a #1 hit with it.

1968 James Brown Day was declared in Los Angeles to honor his sellout concert at the Great Western Forum. Unfortunately, Brown wasn't there to accept the award. He had already left the proceedings because Mayor Sam Yorty showed up late. Moral: don't keep "the Godfather of Soul" waiting.

1977 Donna Summer's "I Feel Love" reached #1 in England and would soon be #3 pop in America. "The Queen of Disco" started out in the German productions of *Hair* and *Godspell* before being discovered by producer Giorgio Moroder at a Blood, Sweat & Tears demo session.

1983 Rick James charted with "Cold Blooded," reaching #1 R&B for six weeks and earning him his biggest R&B hit of twenty-seven singles through 1989. The song, reportedly written about his then-girlfriend, actress Linda Blair, only made it to #40 pop as MTV was ignoring Rick's and most black artists' videos.

1983 "All Night Long" by the Mary Jane Girls charted, eventually reaching #11 R&B. It was a busy and productive period for Rick James, who wrote and produced the record.

1988 After a twenty-year hiatus, the original Danleers of "One Summer Night" fame regrouped at the Westbury Music Fair on Long Island.

July

24

#1 R&B Song 1971: "Mr. Big Stuff," Jean Knight

Born: Barbara Love (the Friends of Distinction), 1941

1948 Louis Jordan & His Tympany 5 charted with "All for the Love of Lil," reaching #13 R&B. Jordan and his band appeared in several movies of the period, including *Follow the Boys*, *Swing Parade of 1946*, and *Meet Miss Bobby Sox*.

1954 The Orioles' "In the Chapel in the Moonlight" and the Vibranaires' rarer-than-rare "Doll Face" ($2,500) were issued.

1995 Boyz II Men and New Kids on the Block played a benefit basketball game at the Clark Athletic Center of the University of Massachusetts, Boston.

1998 Stevie Wonder performed at Kingsmead Stadium in Durban, South Africa, to celebrate Nelson Mandela's eightieth birthday. Thirteen years earlier, Wonder's records had been banned by South African radio due to a dedication Wonder made to Mandela after receiving an Oscar.

Boyz II Men

207

July 25

#1 R&B Song 1981: "Double Dutch Bus," Frankie Smith

Born: Rudy West (the Five Keys), 1932; Verdine White (Earth, Wind & Fire), 1951

1936 Ella Fitzgerald bounced onto the singles survey with "Sing Me a Swing Song" (#18). It became the first of fifty-three pop hits through 1963 for the all-time jazz great, who was discovered after a winning performance on the *Harlem Amateur Hour* in 1934.

1964 Stevie Wonder peaked at #29 pop with "Hey Harmonica Man," his first single without the "Little" Stevie Wonder moniker. Around this time he performed in the Annette Funicello and Frankie Avalon teen flicks *Muscle Beach Party* and *Bikini Beach*.

1970 The Spinners charted with "It's a Shame," written & produced by Stevie Wonder, reaching #4 R&B and #14 pop. The group, originally called the Domingos, renamed themselves after the large chrome hubcaps on cars. During their tenure with Motown (which was mostly hitless), the group did double duty as chauffeurs for the Jackson 5 and the Temptations, clerks in the shipping department, and chaperones for the label's female artists. (Try that with today's generation of would-be Snoops, Puffs, and Eminems.)

1970 Dawn's "Candida" charted, eventually reaching #3 pop. The group consisted of two African- American women, Telma Hopkins and Joyce Vincent, with Greek/Puerto Rican Tony Orlando singing lead. On "Candida," however, the background vocals were by two other studio singers, Toni Wine and Ellie Greenwich.

1992 Prince's single "Sexy M. F." did little in America (#66 pop, #76 R&B), but it reached #4 in England, despite being banned by all radio stations there. Maybe it should have been banned in the U.S. as well.

July

#1 R&B Song 1975: "Fight the Power Part 1," the Isley Brothers

Born: Erskine Hawkins, 1914; Al Banks (the Turbans), 1937; Darlene Love (Darlene Wright, the Blossoms), 1938; Bobby Hebb, 1941; Dobie Gray (Leonard Victor Ainsworth), 1942

1914 Erskine Hawkins, known as the "Twentieth-Century Gabriel" due to his trumpeting prowess, was born today. His orchestra, formed in 1934, was actually forged from the Alabama State Collegians Band. The Erskine Hawkins Orchestra became known for hits like "Tuxedo Junction," "Don't Cry Baby," and "Caledonia" in the late '30s and '40s.

1969 Dionne Warwick charted two albums ("Odds and Ends" #43 in 1969 and "No Night So Long," #23 in 1980) on the same day, eleven years apart.

1969 Billy Davis Jr. and Marilyn McCoo of the Fifth Dimension married, a week after their tenth pop hit, "Workin' on a Groovy Thing" charted (#20 pop, #15 R&B). McCoo had originally been in a group called the Hi-Fis, two of whose members later formed the Friends of Distinction. Davis was originally with a St. Louis doo-wop group called the Versatiles.

1970 Jimi Hendrix was given an honorary diploma by his alma mater, Garfield High School in Seattle, even though he never graduated.

1975 Jazz stylist Nancy Wilson hit the Top 200 with her LP "Come Get to Thee" (#119). It was the thirty-first of thirty-four chart albums for the veteran vocalist between 1962 and 1984.

1992 The Whispers and the O'Jays performed at two sold-out shows at the Valley Forge Music Fair in Devon, PA.

Erskine Hawkins

#1 R&B Song 1959: "There Goes My Baby," the Drifters

Born: Harvey Fuqua (the Moonglows), 1929

1946 Ella Fitzgerald and Louis Jordan entered the R&B hit list with "Petootie Pie," reaching #3—pretty good for a B-side. The A-side was the huge #1 hit "Stone Cold Dead in the Market."

1974 Dionne Warwick teamed with the Spinners on "Then Came You," which charted today. It became her first #1 after forty hits in twelve years.

1984 Prince's film *Purple Rain* premiered across America. The motion picture was loosely based on the artist's life, with emphasis on his romantic involvements.

1985 Whitney Houston's solo single debut "You Give Good Love" peaked at #3. A year earlier, the then-unknown singer recorded a duet with Teddy Pendergrass, "Hold Me," which only reached #46.

1991 When Natalie Cole brought the idea of singing a duet album with her late father Nat King Cole's old recordings to her label, EMI refused. She signed with Electra records, recorded the album, titled *Unforgettable...With Love*, and today it topped the album charts.

1995 Eddie Floyd's "Knock on Wood" was finally certified gold twenty-eight years after its release. More than sixty versions of the song had been recorded through 1995, and Floyd, an avid collector of his own hit, has a copy of every one of them.

1996 "Elevators (Me & You)" by Outkast jumped on the R&B Top 100, reaching #5 and #12 pop. The Atlanta rap duo would continue to have hits into the twenty-first century, including the mega-hit "Hey Ya!," which spent nine weeks at #1 pop in 2003.

July

28

1956 The Avons' "Our Love Will Never End" ($200), the Drifters' "Soldier of Fortune" ($30), the Moonglows' "See Saw" (#25 Pop, #6 R&B), and the Coasters' "Brazil" ($60) were released.

1956 Frankie Lymon & the Teenagers charted with "I Promise to Remember," reaching #10 R&B and #57 pop. The song was a cover of a Jimmy Castor & the Juniors recording. Castor, who sounded amazingly like Lymon, replaced Frankie in the group in 1957.

1958 The Quintones' doo-wop classic, "Down the Aisle of Love" was issued. It reached #18 pop and #5 R&B.

1958 Jerry Butler & the Impressions' "For Your Precious Love" charted, reaching #3 R&B (#11 pop). The group was originally known as the Roosters. Butler started out with the Northern Jubilee Gospel singers and then joined a doo-wop group called the Quails. "Precious Love" had been released on three different labels (Vee Jay, Falcon, and Abner) before finally succeeding and is considered one of the earliest examples of R&B music developing into soul.

1973 Barry White's sultry single, "I've Got So Much to Give" charted, reaching #5 R&B and #32 pop. White started out as a bass singer (not surprising) with three Los Angeles area vocal groups, the Upfronts, the Atlantics, and the Majestics. Unlike many aspiring acts of the time, each of White's groups had at least one single released.

1979 The Crusaders, a much-heralded jazz, blues, and R&B band, had their biggest success with the single "Street Life" (#17 R&B, #36 pop). The vocals by Randy Crawford helped to initiate her career. The band of tightly-honed musicians became tremendously active behind the scenes, contributing their expertise to more than 200 gold albums.

1994 Patti LaBelle, Ruth Pointer, and Bette Midler performed "Over the Rainbow" at the Harbor Lights Pavilion in Boston during LaBelle's current tour.

July

29

#1 R&B Song 1957: "Short Fat Fannie," Larry Williams

Born: Jazz musician Charlie Christian, 1916

1959 The Drifters recorded the samba-styled "Dance with Me" (#15 pop, #2 R&B), heralding the Latin influence on Jay & the Americans, Tony Orlando & Dawn, and future Drifters hits.

1959 The Isley Brothers recorded the immortal "Shout." The song was an adaptation of Jackie Wilson's perpetual classic, "Lonely Teardrops."

1965 The Supremes performed at the world famous Copacabana in New York at the start of a three-week stay, portions of which would be recorded for a future album.

1978 Prince's debut chart single, "Soft and Wet," reached #12 R&B and #92 pop. He was named after the Prince Rogers Trio, a jazz ensemble, and was inspired to become a performer after seeing a James Brown concert in 1968, when he was ten. He went on to learn to play more than twenty instruments.

1978 Earth, Wind & Fire charted with the Beatles' "Got to Get You into My Life" from the movie *Sgt. Pepper's Lonely Hearts Club Band*, reaching #1 R&B and #9 pop. The (often) ten-member group was considered one of the most exciting live performance acts of the '70s and '80s. The band also managed to have forty-eight R&B chart singles through 2004.

1987 Four Tops Day was declared by Michigan Governor James Blanchard to honor the quartet's contributions to music. The group performed at the governor's meeting with guest sax player, Arkansas governor and future president Bill Clinton, backing the act on-stage.

July

30

1936 One of the best blues guitarists of the '50s, Buddy Guy, was born today. He was so infatuated with the guitar that at age thirteen he made his own and taught himself to play. Moving to Chicago in 1957, he beat out Otis Rush, Magic Sam, and Junior Wells at a battle of the blues at the Blue Flame Club. Influenced by Lightnin' Slim, Lightnin' Hopkins, and T-Bone Walker, he was known more for performing than recording, and had his only R&B hit in 1962 with "Stone Crazy" (#12).

1949 Lucky Millinder & His Orchestra charted with "Little Girl, Don't Cry," peaking at #15 R&B. Big John Greer did the vocals on what is now a $50 collectible.

1955 Chuck Berry's classic first single "Maybellene" was released.

1955 Muddy Waters charted with "Mannish Boy," reaching #5 R&B. The tune was actually the same as Bo Diddley's "I'm a Man."

1989 John Lee Hooker performed at the Newport Folk Festival's Thirtieth Anniversary Show with Leon Redbone, Pete Seeger, and Theodore Bikel, among others.

1991 Arsenio Hall's entire TV program was devoted to Patti LaBelle.

John Lee Hooker

July

31

#1 R&B Song 1976: "You'll Never Find Another Love Like Mine," Lou Rawls

Born: Roy Milton, 1907

1948 The only time in music history that two brothers charted on the same day with separate singles on separate labels happened when Joe Liggins jumped on the R&B hit parade with "Dripper's Blues," reaching #9, while Jimmy Liggins entered the charts with "Teardrop Blues," rising to #7.

1954 The Castelles' "Over a Cup of Coffee" ($1,000) was released.

1961 The group that sang backup for most of Chubby Checker's hits finally hit with one of their own when the Dreamlovers' "When We Get Married" charted (#10 pop).

1965 Motown Records was in such a rush to get a new Four Tops single in the marketplace after the tremendous success of "I Can't Help Myself" that they recorded the group on a Thursday singing "It's the Same Old Song" and had the 45 in stores by the next Monday.

1967 Janis Joplin played a benefit for the Free Clinic with Blue Cheer and the Charlatans (with Bill Cosby on drums).

1976 George Benson's *Breezin'* album reached #1, selling more than a million copies for the jazz-soul artist.

1976 Natalie Cole secretly married her producer, Marvin Yancey Jr., but they did not announce it until seven months later (on Valentine's Day) when she also announced she was pregnant.

1986 With apparently no limits to his talent, Stevie Wonder was nominated for an Emmy for his performance on Bill Cosby's *The Cosby Show*.

August 1

#1 R&B Song 1960: "A Woman, a Lover, a Friend," Jackie Wilson

Born: Robert Cray, 1953

1953 Joe Bihari of Los Angeles's Flair Records signed a teen quintet from LA's Jefferson High School and named them the Flairs. They included Cornelius Gunter (later of the Coasters) and Richard Berry (later of "Louie, Louie" fame).

1953 The Royals charted with their first single, "Get It," an eventual #6 R&B hit. Within a year they would be known as Hank Ballard & the Midnighters.

1960 Aretha Franklin recorded her first secular songs upon signing with Columbia Records. The songs included "Over the Rainbow," "Today I Sing the Blues," Right Now," and "Love Is the Answer." She was eighteen, but had begun recording gospel music at fourteen for Checker Records of Chicago.

1960 When the originally-scheduled vocalist didn't show, producer Ike Turner took his twenty-two-year-old wife, Tina, and recorded her on "A Fool in Love," which was released today. It rose to #27 and became the first of twenty Hot 100 hits for the volatile couple.

1969 B.B. King performed in front of more than 110,000 fans at the Atlantic City Pop Festival in Atlantic City, NJ, along with Jefferson Airplane, the Byrds, and Creedence Clearwater Revival.

1987 The rap trio Salt-n-Pepa's debut album, *Hot, Cool and Vicious*, charted, reaching #26. It lingered on the Top 200 for more than a year, finally going platinum in 1988.

1997 Wyclef Jean, Aaliyah, Salt-n-Pepa, Ginuwine, and Blackstreet, among others, performed at the Summer Jam concert in George, Washington. (Yes, there really is such a place.)

2000 William Rosko Mercer, the legendary disc jockey known as Rosko, died today at age seventy-three. He was the first black deejay in Los Angeles (KBLA), and the first black news announcer on WINS in New York.

August

2

#1 R&B Song 1980: "One in a Million You," Larry Graham

Born: Edward Patten (Gladys Knight & the Pips), 1939; Doris Kenner (the Shirelles), 1941; Apollonia (Patricia Kotero), 1961

1962 *American Bandstand* welcomed newcomer Aretha Franklin, who was making her national TV debut singing "Try a Little Tenderness" and "Don't Cry Baby." She was still four years away from the soul style she would become famous for.

1963 Freddie Scott appeared on *American Bandstand* singing what would become his biggest hit, "Hey Girl."

1964 Ray Charles performed at the Star Club in Hamburg, Germany. Only a few years earlier, the venue had been the launching pad for the career of the Beatles.

1968 Junior Walker & the All-Stars started a European tour in Britain that would take them through Germany, Holland, Belgium, and France. Their kick-off gig was at the California Ballroom in Dunstable. Walker began as a construction worker and was influenced by sax man supreme Earl Bostic.

1969 The Whispers made their R&B chart debut with "The Time Will Come," reaching #17. They would go on to have forty-nine hits through 1997, including "Lady" and "Rock Steady." The group continues to record and perform more than forty years after forming in Los Angeles.

1991 Rick James and his girlfriend, Tanya, were arrested at his Hollywood Hills home on charges ranging from false imprisonment to assault with a deadly weapon. The alleged victim was a woman who was staying at James's house in July. James was granted bail of $1 million and released.

1997 Notorious B.I.G. (Christopher Wallace) charted R&B with "Mo' Money, Mo Problems," reaching #2, his fifteenth hit. The Brooklyn rapper, who was shot to death outside a car museum in Los Angeles five months earlier, has had more chart singles after his death (eighteen through 2004) than before.

2001 Ron Townson of the Grammy-winning pop group the Fifth Dimension died at his home in Las Vegas. Townson and his childhood friend LaMonte McLemore formed a doo-wop singing group in 1965 that they called the Versatiles. They soon renamed themselves the Fifth Dimension at the suggestion of Townson's wife.

August

#1 R&B Song 1959: "What'd I Say,"
Ray Charles

Born: Bluesman Mercy Dee Walton, 1915;
Beverley Lee (the Shirelles), 1941

1946 Big Joe Turner jumped on the R&B hit list with "My Girl's a Jockey," reaching #6. Turner appeared in the film *Shake, Rattle & Roll* having recorded (and taken to #1 R&B) the title song months before Bill Haley's rock version.

1956 The nutty novelty "Rubber Biscuit" by the Chips was recorded at New York's Beltone Studios. Twenty-three years later, the Blues Brothers had a Top 40 hit with it.

1959 The Shirelles charted pop with "Dedicated to the One I Love," only reaching #83 with the "5" Royales original. The group first heard the song while performing on a bill at Washington's Howard Theater, where the "5" Royales sang it. It would go on to be reissued in 1961, reaching #3 pop and #2 R&B for the Shirelles.

1969 Little Richard sung a duet with Janis Joplin at the Atlantic City Pop Festival.

1974 Barry White charted with "Can't Get Enough of Your Love Babe," reaching #1 pop and R&B and #8 in Britain. It was the sixth R&B Top 10 hit in a row for the singer/keyboardist, who had played piano on hits such as the Bobby Fuller Four's "I Fought the Law" and on Jesse Belvin's classic, "Goodnight My Love" (when he was eleven). Not bad for a guy who, at age sixteen, spent three months in jail for stealing 300 tires.

1974 B.T. Express entered the R&B hit list with "Do It (Til You're Satisfied)," topping off at #1 (#2 pop). The band's keyboard player, Michael Jones, went on to solo success under the name Kashif.

1991 Jasmine Guy, Heavy D, Salt-n-Pepa, Tara Kemp, and Monie Love performed at the Shoreline Amphitheater, Mountain View, CA, in the KMEL Summer Jam '91.

Barry White

August

#1 Song 1956: "My Prayer," the Platters

Born: Louis Armstrong, 1901; Big Dee Irwin (Defosco Erwin, the Pastels), 1939

1937 The legendary Golden Gate Quartet recorded an amazing fourteen songs in two hours at the Charlotte Hotel in Charlotte, NC.

1951 The Swallows, an excellent doo-wop group from Baltimore, charted with "Will You Be Mine," reaching #9 R&B. The real gem, however, was the flip side, the incomparable ballad "Dearest," which is a $1,500 collectible.

1956 The Ravens' powerful "Kneel & Pray" and the single "Tonight" came out from the original Supremes—a male group recording on Old Town.

1958 Gene Mumford, lead singer of the Ink Spots, the Larks and the Dominoes, signed as a solo act with Columbia.

1958 Bobby Day charted with "Rockin' Robin," an eventual #1 R&B and #2 pop hit that is considered a rock 'n' roll classic today.

1968 The Chambers Brothers performed at the Newport Pop Festival in Costa Mesa, CA, with Jefferson Airplane, the Byrds, and Steppenwolf, among others. Three years earlier, the band had played the Newport Folk Festival, one of the few black acts ever to appear at both festivals.

1986 Michael Jackson began work on his follow-up album to *Thriller* with Quincy Jones at Los Angeles' Westlake Studios. Also in attendance were his constant companions, Bubbles the chimpanzee and Crusher, his 300-pound snake.

1990 While performing at a concert in St. Louis, Janet Jackson collapsed from an ear infection and was hospitalized. She had only gotten through three songs.

1996 Al Green and Stevie Wonder performed at the closing ceremonies of the Olympic Games in Atlanta. The Pointer Sisters also performed, singing "I'm So Excited."

August

#1 R&B Song 1972: "Where Is the Love,"
Roberta Flack & Donny Hathaway

Born: Damita Jo (Damita Jo DuBlanc), 1940

1944 The Mills Brothers entered the charts with "You Always Hurt the One You Love," reaching #5 R&B and #1 pop for five weeks. Clarence "Frog Man" Henry would ride the song to #12 pop (#11 R&B) in 1961.

1952 The "5" Royales recorded "You Know, I Know," their second of a career fifty-one singles. They also recorded two songs at another studio as the gospel group the Royal Sons Quartet on the same day.

1957 Lee Andrews & the Hearts charted with their classic ballad "Long Lonely Nights," reaching #11 R&B and #45 pop. They were one of the smoothest doo-wop groups of the '50s, and the latter-day Hearts—Lee, with his wife and son—are still performing in the twenty-first century.

1957 The Paragons' "Let's Start All Over Again" ($60) and the Ravens' "Dear One" ($25) were released.

1957 The Bobbettes roared onto the Top 100 with "Mr. Lee," a song about their public school teacher that reached #6, making them the first female group in the rock era (black or otherwise) to have a Top 10 hit (and a #1 R&B record).

1960 The Regal Theater in Chicago hosted a great show with the Sheppards, the Isley Brothers, Dee Clark, Big Maybelle, Bill Doggett, Buster Brown, and Little Jimmy Scott performing.

1972 Bo Diddley, Little Richard, Bill Haley, and Jerry Lee Lewis, among others, performed at the first of its kind London Rock 'n' Roll Revival Festival at Wembley Stadium in London, England.

Bo Diddley

August

#1 R&B Song 1955: "A Fool for You," Ray Charles & His Band

Born: Jimmy Ricks (the Ravens), 1924; Judy Craig (the Chiffons), 1946; Randy DeBarge (DeBarge), 1958

1956 Filming began on Alan Freed's classic flick *Rock, Rock, Rock*, featuring LaVern Baker along with Frankie Lymon & the Teenagers, the Flamingos, the Moonglows, and Chuck Berry.

1960 Chubby Checker debuted "The Twist" on national TV when he performed it on *American Bandstand*. Dick Clark had originally asked Danny & the Juniors of "At the Hop" fame to record the song, but they turned it down. The recording, with vocal backing by Philadelphia doo-wop group the Dreamlovers was recorded in less than thirty-five minutes.

1966 The Supremes' "You Can't Hurry Love" was issued and raced to #1.

1972 Michael Jackson's "Ben" charted en-route to #1 pop (#5 R&B). Written for the movie Ben, the song was originally considered for Donny Osmond. It became the first of Jackson's lucky thirteen pop #1s through 2001.

1973 Stevie Wonder was seriously injured in a car accident on the road to Durham, NC, when his car crashed into a logging truck. Though he fully recovered, the accident robbed him of his sense of smell.

1998 Ray Charles performed at Radio City Music Hall in New York. He was sixty-eight at the time.

2004 The King of Punk Funk Rick James died today in his sleep of a heart attack in his Los Angeles home. His twelve pop hits and twenty-seven R&B charters tell only part of his story, as Rick was an icon and an influence to a generation of young rappers and pop and hip-hop artists, including Jamie Foxx, LL Cool J, Mary J. Blige, Mariah Carey, Eric Sermon, Redman, Erykah Badu, MC Hammer, Silk the Shocker, Kanye West, and many others.

1954 New York Giant Baseball Hall of Famer Willie Mays's recording with the Treniers, "Say Hey," was released. "Say Hey" was Willie's nickname (as in "the Say Hey Kid") because when he came up to the majors he didn't know anybody's name, so he used to just say, "Say, Hey."

1954 Ruth Brown charted with "Oh What a Dream," reaching #1 for eight weeks.

1956 The Harptones recorded two of their classics for Rama Records, "Three Wishes" and "That's the Way It Goes."

1961 Gary "U.S." Bonds charted with "School Is Out," eventually peaking at #12 R&B and #5 pop, his third pop Top 10 single in less than a year. Despite his educated lineage—he was the son of a music teacher and a college professor—Bonds managed to succeed by singing mindless party records.

1965 Martha & the Vandellas' "You've Been in Love Too Long" was released. It was their ninth hit (#36) in just two years.

1991 LL Cool J was sued for palimony in New York family court by his girlfriend. She asked for half of his income; he conceded to pay $1,650 a month.

1993 Cypress Hill's album *Black Sunday* reached #1 pop in its first week on the charts. The album also reached #13 in England.

1997 Twenty-seven years after reaching #1, the Jackson 5's "I Want You Back" was certified platinum by the RIAA.

August

8

#1 R&B Song 1970: "Signed, Sealed, Delivered I'm Yours," Stevie Wonder

Born: Jazz musician Benny Carter, 1907; bandleader Lucius "Lucky" Millinder, 1908; Jimmy Witherspoon, 1923; Joe Tex (Joseph Arrington), 1933; Airrion Love (the Stylistics), 1949

1908 More of a showman than a musician, Lucius "Lucky" Millinder was born today. Starting as a ballroom M.C., he had several orchestras before his '40s group took off featuring vocalists like Wynonie Harris, Annisteen Allen, Bullmoose Jackson, and Sister Rosetta Tharpe and musicians such as Bill Doggett, Charlie Shavers, Dizzy Gillespie, and Tab Smith. His biggest hit was "Who Threw the Whiskey in the Well," with Harris singing, in 1945. He later became a disc jockey and worked in public relations.

1960 One week after it charted pop, Chubby Checker's "The Twist" charted R&B on its way to #2 (#1 pop). The dance classic would be credited with being the first modern record to bring both teens and their parents on to the dance floor.

1968 Little Richard performed in New York's Central Park for the Shaefer Music Festival.

1987 Michael Jackson's duet with Siedah Garrett, "I Just Can't Stop Loving You," charted, reaching #1 pop and R&B and #1 in Britain. The ballad had been turned down by Whitney Houston and Barbra Streisand.

1998 Prince performed at the Plaza de Toros in Malaga, Spain, as part of his newest European tour.

August

#1 R&B Song 1969: "Mother Popcorn, Part 1," James Brown

Born: Billy Henderson (the Spinners), 1939; Kurtis Blow (Kurtis Walker), 1959; Whitney Houston, 1963; Barbara Mason, 1963

1947 "True Blues" by Roy Milton & His Solid Senders charted, reaching #4 R&B.

1953 The Drifters recorded their first hit, "Money Honey" (#1 R&B).

1986 Janet Jackson hit the charts with "When I Think of You," the first of ten eventual pop #1s through 2001 for the youngest member of the Jackson family.

1990 Aretha Franklin performed at New York City's Radio City Music Hall.

1990 LL Cool J began a twenty-one-show tour in Bloomington, MN.

1991 The Shirelles performed at the Apollo R&B Reunion to help raise funds for the financially strapped New York theater.

LL Cool J

August

#1 R&B Song 1946: "Stone Cold Dead in the Market (He Had It Coming)," Ella Fitzgerald & Louis Jordan & His Tympany 5

Born: Patti Austin, 1948; Michael Bivens (New Edition), 1968

1956 Almost two years after their original hit, the Penguins' re-recorded version of "Earth Angel" was released when the group signed with Mercury Records.

1959 The Platters' four male members were arrested in a Cincinnati, OH, hotel room for soliciting prostitutes. That three of the women were white probably had more to do with the incident becoming a scandal than anything else. Though the group was let off with a warning, radio stations began deleting Platters platters from their play lists.

1959 Lloyd Price charted with "I'm Gonna Get Married," reaching #1 R&B and #3 pop. It was his second #1 in a row and his tenth straight R&B Top 10 single in seven years.

1963 Stevie Wonder's "Fingertips, Part 2" reached #1 pop for three weeks and #1 R&B for six weeks. It was the first live recording to top either chart.

1967 The Temptations performed at the Copacabana in New York, starting a two-week engagement.

1968 The Chambers Brothers (four brothers and drummer Brian Keenan) debuted on the pop charts with "Time Has Come Today." The mixture of psychedelic soul and their fusion of folk, gospel, pop, and blues made for an exciting style. Though the single eventually reached #11 (their album reached #4), the group's recording career lasted only three years, during which they had six chart albums. Truly, their "time had come today."

1991 The Fifth Dimension received a star on the Hollywood Walk of Fame. The original quintet then began a reunion tour after having been two separate entities (The Fifth Dimension, Marilyn McCoo & Billy Davis) for sixteen years.

August

11

#1 R&B Song 1956: "Rip It Up,"
Little Richard

Born: Blues slide guitarist Crying Sam
Collins, 1887

1956 Shirley & Lee charted with their soon-to-be rock 'n' roll classic, "Let the Good Times Roll" (#20 pop and #1 R&B).

1956 Billy Ward & the Dominoes charted pop for the first time (after five years and eleven R&B chart singles) with "St. Theresa of the Roses," reaching #13. The lead singer of the venerable group was superstar-to-be Jackie Wilson.

1958 The Spaniels' classic version of "Stormy Weather" ($60) was issued.

1962 Formerly known as the Primettes, the newly named Supremes hit the Hot 100 with, "Your Heart Belongs to Me" (#95), their first of forty-seven pop hits through 1976.

1962 Booker T. & the M.G.'s charted with the tight, percussive instrumental "Green Onions." It went on to #3 pop and #1 R&B. M.G. stood for Memphis Group, as they were all session musicians at Stax Records in Memphis. Booker T. Jones had originally played in a band with Maurice White, later of Earth, Wind & Fire.

1969 Diana Ross invited 350 guests to the Daisy Club in Beverly Hills to unveil her new discovery, the Jackson 5.

Jackson 5

August 12

1957 Billy Ward & the Dominoes' "One Moment with You" and the Five Keys' "Face of an Angel" were released.

1966 Junior Walker & the All-Stars performed at the Beach Club in Myrtle Beach, SC.

1967 Aretha Franklin headlined the first New York Jazz Festival at Downing Stadium.

1978 Donna Summer's "Last Dance" reached #3 pop and #5 R&B. It would go on to earn an Academy Award for Best Song (from the film *Thank God It's Friday*) in 1979.

1984 Lionel Richie performed "All Night Long" as the last song of the closing ceremony of the XXIII Olympic Games in Los Angeles. The spectacle included 200 dancers and was seen by more than 2.5 billion people around the world.

1986 Prince performed in England for the first time in five years at London's Wembley Arena. Unlike his last, poorly-attended performance in Britain, all three of his dates were sold out.

1994 Dionne Warwick guested on the *Geraldo* (Rivera) TV show, but drew criticism when she supported and sympathized with O.J. Simpson regarding the murder of his wife.

#1 R&B Song 1977: "Float On," the Floaters

Born: Blues vocalist Jimmy McCracklin, 1921

1938 Robert Johnson and Sonny Boy Williamson performed at the Three Forks Roadhouse outside of Greenwood, MS. Known as a womanizer, Johnson took a swig from a bottle of moonshine whiskey which was poisoned (presumably by the husband of one of Johnson's conquests) and fell deathly ill.

1957 The "5" Royales recorded the original version of "Dedicated to the One I Love," which was covered two years later by the Shirelles.

1973 Johnny Moore rejoined the Drifters when the American group made the unprecedented move of signing directly with a British label while having no U.S. company. Moore had been with the original Drifters eighteen years earlier, in 1955.

1990 Curtis Mayfield was paralyzed during an outdoor concert on Wingate High School's football field in Brooklyn, NY, when a lighting stand fell on him during a storm.

1994 Twenty-five years after the one and only Woodstock, Richie Havens returned to Bethel, NY, to perform at Woodstock '94.

1994 The Isley Brothers and Bobby Womack performed at the Greek Theater in Los Angeles.

Richie Havens

August

#1 R&B Song 1971: "Mercy Mercy Me (The Ecology)," Marvin Gaye

Born: Jackie Brenston, 1927; Larry Graham, 1946

1961 The Marvelettes' first single, "Please Mr. Postman," was released. It delivered to the tune of #1, their only #1 of a twenty-three hit career.

1961 Chubby Checker's "Let's Twist Again" spent its second week at its peak of #8 pop, adding fuel to the worldwide "Twist" fire.

1961 The Mar-Keys performed their instrumental hit "Last Night" on *American Bandstand*.

1965 The most soulful white duo on the music scene, the Righteous Brothers charted with "Unchained Melody," climbing almost as high on the R&B charts (#6) as they did on the pop charts (#4).

The Marvelettes

1985 Michael Jackson drove a wedge into his relationship with Paul McCartney when he outbid the ex-Beatle for theATV Music Publishing catalog, which contained more than 250 Lennon/McCartney songs. The price was $47.5 million. Jackson had no trouble paying for the catalog, as he had received a royalty check three months earlier from Epic Records for more than $58 million.

1992 Tony Williams, lead of the world-famous Platters, died of emphysema at his New York home. His last live performance was with his wife, Helen, and son, Ricky, as Tony Williams & the Platters on New Year's Eve, 1991, in Thailand. He was sixty-four.

August 15

1953 The Prisonaires, five inmates from the Tennessee State Penitentiary, had their debut disc, "Just Walkin' in the Rain," issued on Sun records. Lead singer Johnny Bragg had been helped with his diction during their June recording session by a young would-be vocalist who was hanging around the studio. The teen's name was Elvis Presley.

1964 The Four Tops debuted on the charts with "Baby, I Need Your Loving," which reached #11. They would go on to have forty-five hit 45s through 1988. The quartet originally signed with Motown for a $400 advance.

1981 After a man was shot and killed returning from Stevie Wonder's concert at the Great Western Forum in Inglewood, CA, Stevie gave his gold album for *Hotter Than July* to the young man's girlfriend.

1992 Boyz II Men's "End of the Road" reached #1 pop today and stayed there for a precedent-setting thirteen weeks. Whitney Houston broke the record when her "I Will Always Love You" topped the charts for fourteen weeks in 1993.

1992 Mary J. Blige's first single, "You Remind Me" peaked at #29 on the pop charts while going on to #1 R&B. Blige, who sang in a Pentecostal church choir while living in Savannah, GA, started her pursuit of a music career with a demo she did of Anita Baker's "Caught Up in the Rapture" on a Yonkers, NY, shopping mall karaoke machine.

1998 Obviously a good day for Mary J. Blige, her fifth album, *The Tour*, topped off at #7 R&B. Three of Mary's five albums (*What's the 411?*, *My Life*, and *Share My World*) had reached the top spot between 1992 and 1997.

1998 Richie Havens, who performed at both 1969's Woodstock concerts and the twenty-fifth anniversary Woodstock '94, returned yet again to a Day in the Garden, a festival to commemorate the original achievement on its thirtieth anniversary.

August

16

#1 R&B Song 1990: "Upside Down," Diana Ross

Born: Al Hibbler, 1915; Richard Blandon (the Dubs), 1934; Ketty Lester, 1934

1938 Blues icon Robert Johnson died in Greenwood, MS, after being poisoned by a vengeful husband four days earlier. His music and guitar style became an influence for future generations of stars such as the Rolling Stones, Muddy Waters, Eric Clapton, Elmore James, and Taj Mahal. Johnson, who often performed with the likes of Memphis Slim, Howlin' Wolf, Sonny Boy Williamson, and Elmore James was only twenty-seven when he died.

1962 Little Stevie Wonder's first single, "I Call It Pretty Music (But the Old People Call It the Blues)," was released. It never charted but an original 45 today is an $80 collectible.

1969 The Dells' re-recording of their hit "Oh, What a Night" (#10 R&B) charted thirteen years after the original.

1969 Appearing at one of music history's most legendary concerts, Richie Havens performed his song "Freedom" at the Woodstock Music and Arts Festival in Bethel, NY. The song became an anthem of the times and his performance was included in the movie *Woodstock*. Another anthem literally was Jimi Hendrix's interpretation of "The Star-Spangled Banner," which became a classic moment of the three-day concert. Hendrix, who was paid more than any other performer in attendance ($125,000), was not even listed on the handbills given out for ticket sales.

1969 The Supremes performed at the Great Western Forum in Inglewood, CA, with the Jackson 5, who were making their performance debut as a Motown group. Though the press releases touted Diana Ross as the discoverer of the group, it was actually Gladys Knight who first saw them perform and alerted Motown's Berry Gordy Jr.

1986 Anita Baker, former lead singer of Chapter 8, swept onto the bestseller's list with "Sweet Love." After leaving Chapter 8 in 1980, she had taken an office job in Detroit until her chance to record solo came in 1983. "Sweet Love" was her first pop hit.

1986 Run-D.M.C.'s *Raising Hell* became the first rap album to reach #1 on the R&B chart.

1997 Mary J. Blige, Chaka Khan, Seal, Toni Braxton, Rod Stewart, and Jon Bon Jovi, among others, performed at London's Wembley Stadium for the Songs & Visions: The Carlsberg Concert '97 show.

#1 R&B Song 1963: "Fingertips, Pt. 2,"
Little Stevie Wonder

Born: Luther Allison, 1939

1959 Ray Charles's "What'd I Say" became his first million-seller when it reached #6 pop and #1 R&B. The song, written by Charles, would go on to become a rock 'n' roll standard and would be recorded in the '60s by Elvis Presley, Jerry Lee Lewis, and Bobby Darin.

1963 The Crystals charted with "Then He Kissed Me" (#6 pop).

1969 The Woodstock Festival's closing night included performances by Richie Havens, Sly & the Family Stone, and Jimi Hendrix. Also appearing during the three-day festival were Joan Baez; Jefferson Airplane; Crosby, Stills & Nash; Santana; Creedence Clearwater Revival; Iron Butterfly; Blood, Sweat & Tears; Joe Cocker; Sha Na Na; and John Sebastian. More than half a million people attended, and there were three deaths, two births, and six miscarriages. All that for $7.00.

1971 Five months after they performed together in San Francisco's Fillmore West, Aretha Franklin was singing at the funeral of King Curtis, who had been murdered on a street corner four days earlier. Joining Franklin in prayer and song were Cissy Houston and Stevie Wonder.

1973 Temptations member Paul Williams, deep in tax hell and with health and family problems overwhelming him, shot himself to death. He was found in his car a few streets from the Motown offices in Detroit.

1986 Run-D.M.C. performed at a concert in Long Beach, CA, and more than forty people were injured during a riot between rival gangs. It was the group's sixth concert with audience clashes and contributed to the association of rap with violence.

1990 Miles Davis, George Benson, and B.B. King, among others, performed at the JVC Jazz Festival in Newport, RI.

1993 The King of Pop was accused of child molestation as a police investigation started today based on charges brought by a thirteen-year-old's father. The allegations revolved around activities at Michael Jackson's home.

1996 Bobby Brown had another bad day behind the wheel (see April 22) when he crashed his wife, Whitney Houston's, Porsche into a street sign in Hollywood, FL. Having only minor neck and leg injuries, he was treated at a local hospital and released.

August

#1 R&B Song 1962: "You'll Lose a Good Thing," Barbara Lynn

Born: Sonny Til (Erlington Tilghman, the Orioles), 1928; Sarah Dash (LaBelle), 1945; Nona Hendryx (LaBelle), 1945; Barbara Harris (the Toys), 1945

1945 The Legendary Delta Rhythm Boys teamed up with "the first lady of jazz," Ella Fitzgerald, on "It's Only a Paper Moon," which entered the R&B hit parade and eventually reached #4 and #9 pop. The song was originally titled "If You Believe in Me," which was a line in the chorus.

1951 The Five Keys had their chart debut with "The Glory of Love," which reached #1 for four weeks. One of the best of the '50s vocal groups, the Keys charted seven times through 1956. "Glory" was their biggest hit. Though it reportedly sold at least half a million copies, a mint condition original label 45 today is worth more than $1,000.

1968 The Drifters and Bill Haley & the Comets performed at San Francisco's Avalon Ballroom.

1973 The Pointer Sisters charted with "Yes You Can Can," reaching #12 R&B and #11 pop with their debut Top 100 disc. The four sisters began as studio singers for the likes of San Francisco stars Dave Mason, Elvin Bishop, and Boz Scaggs.

1990 Michael Jackson, well known for his love of children, invited 130 from the YMCA to visit his Neverland Ranch, spending the day at his video arcade, theater, and zoo.

1992 El Debarge and Chaka Khan performed at New York's Beacon Theater. Two months earlier Chaka had become a grandmother at age thirty-nine.

Chaka Khan

August

#1 R&B Song 1944: "Till Then,"
the Mills Brothers

Born: Johnny Nash, 1940

1954 The Platters, B.B. King, and Johnny Otis performed at the Savoy Ballroom in Hollywood.

1957 The Chantels' debut 45, the harmony standard "He's Gone," was released.

1957 Bobby "Blue" Bland charted on his way to #1 R&B with his first chart single, "Farther Up the Road." The blues tune would also reach #43 pop. Bland started out as B.B. King's valet in 1949 and went on to have an astounding sixty-three R&B charters through 1985.

1972 Curtis Mayfield's "Freddie's Dead" from the film *Superfly* charted on its way to #4 pop and #2 R&B, his biggest of his thirty-two R&B singles between 1970 and 1997.

1972 Michael Jackson had his third Top 10 single in a row in England with a song never released in America, a cover of the Bill Withers hit "Ain't No Sunshine" (#8).

1976 Marvin Gaye faced two five-day jail terms for non-payment of child support and alimony and for contempt of court.

1978 George Clinton and Funkadelic (originally Parliament) charted with "One Nation Under a Groove, Part 1," which would become Clinton and company's third #1 R&B hit. By now the demonstrative performer was touring with an entourage in the neighborhood of forty musicians. His live stage shows included the use of an enormous flying saucer.

August

20

#1 Song 1977: "Best of My Love," the Emotions

Born: Paul Robi (the Platters), 1931; Isaac Hayes, 1942; KRS-One (Laurence Krisna Parker), 1965

1949 Dinah Washington entered the R&B hit list with "Long John Blues," peaking at #3.

1954 The Orioles began a weeklong engagement at Weekes Café in Atlantic City.

1955 Chuck Berry's debut disc, "Maybellene," charted on its way to #5 pop and #1 R&B. The classic would stay at #1 for eleven weeks and would be the first of twenty-seven pop and twenty-three R&B hits he would have through 1972. Not bad for a onetime hairdresser who began adulthood on the wrong side of the law. In 1944, at the age of eighteen, Berry began a three-year stint in a reform school following a conviction for armed robbery.

1988 Rick James, with guest rapper Roxanne Shante, topped the R&B chart with "Loosey's Rap." It was James's fourth and last #1.

1988 Karyn White, a former studio singer, stormed the R&B Top 100 with "The Way You Love Me," making it the first of three #1s in a row. The hits to follow were "Superwoman" and "Love Saw It."

1996 The Emotions, Billy Preston, the Brothers Johnson, and Isaac Hayes performed at the Universal Amphitheater in Universal City, CA. It was an especially enjoyable time for Hayes, as he was celebrating his fifty-fourth birthday.

Isaac Hayes

August 21

#1 R&B Song 1976: "Who'd She Coo?," the Ohio Players

Born: William "Count" Basie, 1904; Savannah Churchill (the Four Tunes), 1920; Clara Ward, 1924

1904 One of the best-loved and most legendary bandleaders of all time, William "Count" Basie was born today. He and his orchestra appeared in a dozen films and had eight R&B charters between 1943 and 1968. His vocalists ranged from Billie Holiday to Joe Williams, and his band recorded countless albums with such stars as Ella Fitzgerald, Jackie Wilson, the Mills Brothers, Sammy Davis Jr., and Frank Sinatra.

1920 A terrific singer who began her career out of necessity, not desire, Savannah Churchill was born today. When her husband died in a car accident in 1941, she began performing to support her two children. Recording mostly with the vocal group the Four Tunes, she scored her biggest hits with "I Want to Be Loved," which was #1 R&B for eight weeks, and "Daddy Daddy" (R&B #3). She also played a mean violin.

1954 The Harptones' "I'll Never Tell," with Bunny Paul singing lead, and the Singing Wanderers' "Say Hey Willie Mays" were released.

1965 The Ramsey Lewis Trio charted with their signature single, "The 'In' Crowd," reaching #2 R&B and #5 pop. A year later, two-thirds of the group, Eldee Young and Red Holt, would form their own trio, the Young Holt Trio, and have the hit ""Wack, Wack."

1971 Howlin' Wolf charted with his album *The London Howlin' Wolf Sessions*, reaching #79 pop and #28 R&B. The album included superstar support from Ringo Starr (the Beatles), Eric Clapton (Cream), Steve Winwood (Traffic), Charlie Watts, and Bill Wyman (the Rolling Stones). It would be his only pop chart album.

1971 Diana Ross reached #1 in England with "I'm Still Waiting." The single wasn't well-received in America, reaching only #40 R&B and #63 pop.

1983 Andre Crouch, Shirley Caesar, and Barry White performed in Jerusalem, Israel, at the First Annual Gospel Festival.

1996 Rick James was freed from Fulsom Prison after serving two years and thirty-four days of a five-year sentence. While there he had written more than 200 songs, though many turned out to be rough or unfinished. Others would become the nucleus of James's 1997 *Urban Rhapsody* album.

August

22

#1 Song 1964: "Where Did Our Love Go," the Supremes

Born: John Lee Hooker, 1917

1953 "Dragnet Blues," by Johnny Moore's Three Blazers, charted R&B, reaching #8. The song was inspired by the TV show *Dragnet*.

1960 Jackie Wilson reached #1 R&B for four weeks (#15 pop) with "A Woman, a Lover, a Friend." The song was based on the Royals' 1953 recording "I Feel So Blue," written by old friend Hank Ballard, then a new member of the Royals/Midnighters. As if that weren't enough for the red-hot Wilson, the B-side, "(You Were Made For) All My Love," reached #12 pop.

1964 Martha & the Vandellas' "Dancing in the Streets" charted, eventually reaching #2.

1988 *Aretha Franklin: The Queen of Soul*, a one-hour public television documentary, was aired. Appearing on the program with Franklin were Whitney Houston, Ray Charles, Smokey Robinson, and Eric Clapton.

1989 John Lee Hooker performed with Albert Collins, Carlos Santana, and Robert Cray, among others, at his seventy-second birthday party in the San Francisco-area Sweetwater Club.

Jackie WIlson

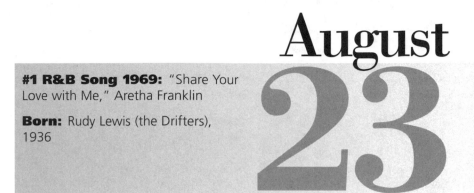

August 23

#1 R&B Song 1969: "Share Your Love with Me," Aretha Franklin

Born: Rudy Lewis (the Drifters), 1936

1963 Lou Rawls performed at Detroit's Twenty Grand Club.

1969 Ray Goodman & Brown's cover of the Platters' "My Prayer" (#47 pop, #31 R&B) charted, becoming the last of their fourteen Top 100 entries (including eleven as the Moments).

1975 Drummer Buddy Miles had his last of five R&B hits when "Rockin' and Rollin' on the Streets of Hollywood" charted, reaching #33.

1986 New Edition's "Earth Angel," from the film *Karate Kid II*, reached #3 R&B and #21 pop. The song had originally been a hit and subsequent standard for the Penguins in 1954-55.

1997 Two of the most raucous rock 'n' rollers you'd ever want to see, Little Richard and James Brown, performed at the New York State Fair. Brown once stated, "When I do my music I include a lot of people, but nobody's really involved except myself—just God and me. I guess I'm like Einstein—let 'em worry about my theory after I'm dead."

1997 Usher (Usher Raymond) jumped on the R&B hit list with "You Make Me Wanna," reaching #1 and #2 pop. It was the biggest of his twenty chart entries between 1993 and 2004.

1998 The O'Jays, the Isley Brothers, and Earth, Wind & Fire performed at the Chastain Park Amphitheater in Atlanta, GA.

August

24

#1 R&B Song 1968: "Stay in My Corner," the Dells

Born: Arthur "Big Boy" Crudup, 1905; Wynonie Harris, 1915; Willie Winfield (the Harptones), 1929; Ernest Wright Jr. (the Imperials), 1941; Jeffrey Daniels (Shalamar), 1957

1956 The Five Satins, the Channels, the Clovers, the Valentines, and the Schoolboys appeared at Dr. Jive's Rock 'n' Roll Show at the Apollo Theater.

1962 Bob B. Soxx & the Blue Jeans recorded the Phil Spector–produced, "Zip-A-Dee-Doo-Dah" (#8 pop). The group was really the Blossoms, with Darlene Love and studio singer Bobby Sheen on lead.

1989 Patti LaBelle appeared in the Who's *Tommy*, with an all-star cast including Phil Collins and Elton John, at the Universal Amphitheater in Los Angeles. She played the part of the Acid Queen.

1991 Boyz II Men's debut album, *Cooleyhighharmony*, reached #3 pop. The quartet was discovered by New Edition/Bell Biv DeVoe member Michael Bivins, who was performing at Philadelphia's Civic Center. They began singing to him as he left the stage, and two months later he signed them to Motown through his production company.

1991 Lenny Kravitz's "It Ain't Over 'Til It's Over" reached #2 pop, becoming his biggest hit.

1992 Wilson Pickett was arrested for driving with open bottles of vodka and beer cans in his car. This might have resulted in a lesser charge, but the discovery was made by police after Pickett hit the car of an eighty-six-year-old man, sending the driver to the hospital.

1996 Brandy, with help from Gladys Knight, Chaka Khan, and Tamia charted with "Missing You" (#25).

1997 As Michael Jackson was about to start a concert in the Olympic Stadium in Helsinki, Finland, an escaped mental patient attempted to set fire to the stage and was subsequently carted away by police.

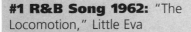

#1 R&B Song 1962: "The Locomotion," Little Eva

Born: Jazz man Wayne Shorter, 1933; Walter Williams (the O'Jays), 1942

1956 The Five Keys' "Out of Sight, Out of Mind" (#23 pop, #12 R&B), the Channels' "The Closer You Are," and the Duponts' "Must Be Falling in Love" were released. The Duponts featured sixteen-year-old lead Little Anthony two years before he recorded with the Imperials.

1958 "Come Back, My Love" (#29 R&B, $20), Jerry Butler & the Impressions' follow-up to their first hit, "For Your Precious Love," was issued.

1962 The Crystals' "He's a Rebel" was released, eventually climbing to #1 pop and #2 R&B. Unbeknown to the group at the time, producer Phil Spector had lifted their vocals and replaced them with Darlene Love & the Blossoms, even though the Crystals got the credit.

1962 Gary "U.S." Bonds's "Copy Cat" charted (#92 pop), becoming his last Top 100 for almost twenty years. His career in the '60s would likely have been extended had he not turned down the opportunity to record "If You Wanna Be Happy," a song his labelmate Jimmy Soul took to #1.

1990 Public Enemy performed at the Shoreline Amphitheater in Mountain View, CA, but they they didn't get to complete their set because a massive fight broke out in the audience.

1993 Snoop Doggy Dog was arrested as an accessory to the murder of a gang member who was shot from Snoop's Jeep by his bodyguard. The rapper paid $1 million bail for his freedom.

1995 Stevie Wonder received a Braille-inscribed brass plaque from former Motown backup singer Elisheva Bat-Israel in the town of Dimona, Israel, along with a humanitarian award from the African community of Hebrew Israelites.

2001 Aaliyah (born Aaliyah Haughton) died when the plane she was in crashed in the Caribbean. The young singer/actress had already had sixteen pop chart singles including her #1, "Try Again," in 2000. She was only twenty-two.

August

26

#1 R&B Song 1989: "It's No Crime," Babyface

Born: Valerie Simpson, 1946

1957 The Shells' "Baby Oh Baby" (#20 pop) and the Schoolboys' "Carol" (#91 pop) were issued.

1960 The Drifters reunited with former lead Clyde McPhatter (for a show) at the Apollo in New York. Also on the bill were the Bobbettes.

1961 The Temptations' first single, "Oh Mother of Mine," was released on the Motown-affiliated Miracle label but did not chart. They were signed to Berry Gordy Jr.'s company under the name the Elgins but were renamed by member Otis Williams.

1964 The Supremes' "Where Did Our Love Go" was #1 on this day. Before Diana Ross left in 1969, the trio would have eleven more chart-toppers.

1967 Jackie Wilson charted with one of his best records, "(Your Love Keeps Lifting Me) Higher and Higher," reaching #1 R&B and #6 pop. The record was so popular in England that it charted three times (1969 #11, 1975 #25, and 1987 #15). Backing Wilson on the hotter-than-hot recording were the Angels on vocals and the Motown musicians known as the Funk Brothers.

1967 The Jimi Hendrix Experience charted with their debut album *Are You Experienced?*, which rose to #5 on the pop album charts. Hendrix would go on to have twenty-eight chart albums through 1995, twenty-two of which charted after his death in 1970. *Experienced* would stay on the charts for 106 weeks.

1978 Singing and songwriting duo Ashford & Simpson entered the R&B hit list with "It Seems to Hang On," peaking at #2. Though the duo had thirty-five R&B chart singles through 1997, they're best-known for the songs they've written for others, including "Let's Go Get Stoned" (Ray Charles), "Ain't No Mountain High Enough" (Marvin Gaye), and "Ain't Nothing Like the Real Thing" (Marvin Gaye and Tammi Terrell).

1995 Newark, NJ, rapper Redman (Reggie Noble) charted R&B with "How High," reaching #10 and #13 pop.

27

#1 R&B Song 1955: "Maybellene,"
Chuck Berry

Born: Lester Young, 1909; Harold
Lucas (the Clovers), 1932

1909 Lester Young, one of the early jazz tenor saxophonists, was born today. He's best known for the hits "Just You, Just Me" and "Sometimes I'm Happy."

1949 The Orioles charted with their classic version of "A Kiss and a Rose," reaching #12 R&B.

1949 Lionel Hampton & His Orchestra charted with the macabrely-titled "Lavender Coffin," eventually reaching lucky #13 R&B.

1960 Lloyd Price appeared on Dick Clark's *American Bandstand*, performing "Personality."

1963 Sam Cooke performed on Johnny Carson's *Tonight Show*.

1966 Eddie Floyd hit the R&B charts with his single, "Knock on Wood," a 45 that would reach #1 and #28 pop. Over the next eleven years the soul singer would chart R&B eighteen times, but "Knock" would always be his biggest hit.

Lionel Hampton

1968 The Staple Singers performed at San Francisco's Fillmore West with Santana and Steppenwolf.

1994 "I'll Make Love to You" by Boyz II Men began an incredible run of fourteen weeks at #1, surpassing the group's record-breaking streak of thirteen weeks in the top spot in 1992 with "End of the Road." Written by Babyface, the song marked his first writing success without former partner L.A. Reid.

August

28

#1 R&B Song 1971: "Spanish Harlem," Aretha Franklin

1954 The Midnighters' "Annie Had a Baby" (#1, $30) was released.

1956 Alan Freed's second anniversary Rock 'n' roll Show at the Brooklyn Paramount featured the Harptones, the Penguins, the Cleftones, and Frankie Lymon & the Teenagers.

1958 The Chantels and the Quintones performed at the Apollo Theater in New York along with the Spaniels, the Coasters, and the Olympics.

1986 Tina Turner was honored with a star on the Hollywood Walk of Fame in front of Capitol Records, the company she recorded for.

1991 PBS-TV aired *Going Home to Gospel with Patti LaBelle* from Chicago's Quinn Chapel.

1993 Jodeci reached #4 pop and #1 R&B with the single "Lately," a remake of Stevie Wonder's 1981 ballad. It was their fourth R&B #1 in two years.

Jodeci

August

#1 R&B Song 1953: "Crying in the Chapel," the Orioles

Born: Dinah Washington (Ruth Lee Jones), 1924; Marion Williams, 1927; Michael Jackson, 1958; Pebbles (Perri McKissack), 1965; Carl Martin (Shai), 1970

1954 Capitol Records signed the Five Keys. The group went on to have four Top 100 hits, including the standard, "Out of Sight, Out of Mind." These hits were in more of a pop style than they had when recording R&B for Aladdin Records.

1958 Alan Freed's Brooklyn Fox show featured the Cleftones, the Danleers, and the Olympics, among others. The show ran for ten days.

1964 Six years after his first Top 5 hit, Bobby Freeman was back, peaking at #5 with "C'mon and Swim." The record was produced by a San Francisco–area disc jockey named Sylvester Stewart, who would later form his own band, Sly & the Family Stone.

1966 In a tribute to one of the artists who most influenced them, the Beatles performed Little Richard's "Long Tall Sally" as the last tune of their final concert at San Francisco's Candlestick Park.

1981 The Pointer Sisters' "Slow Hand" reached #2 pop and #7 R&B, becoming their biggest pop hit. The song that kept it from #1 was Lionel Richie and Diana Ross's "Endless Love."

1998 Mary J. Blige, Mariah Carey, Missy Elliot, Maze, and others performed in the KMEL-FM All-Star Jam at the Shoreline Amphitheater in Mountain View, CA.

1998 Janet Jackson was honored with the International Female Artist of the Year award in Oslo, Norway, at their first annual *HitAwards*.

August

30

#1 R&B Song 1986: "Love Zone," Billy Ocean

Born: Luther "Georgia Boy" Johnson, 1934

1963 New York disc jockey Murray the K held his annual Labor Day spectacular at the Brooklyn Fox Theater, featuring the Miracles, the Chiffons, the Shirelles, the Tymes, the Drifters, Ben E. King, Little Stevie Wonder, Jay & the Americans, Randy & the Rainbows, and many others.

1963 After six years of weekday shows, Dick Clark's *American Bandstand* held its last weekday shindig and became a Saturday-only affair. The show had been in the forefront of promoting black artists and their music since its 1957 inception.

1970 Jimi Hendrix performed at what would be his last British concert when he appeared on-stage at 3:00 a.m. at the Isle of Wight Festival.

1972 Stevie Wonder performed at a benefit for Willowbank Hospital at Madison Square Garden in New York with John Lennon and Yoko Ono.

1975 Natalie Cole bounced onto the Hot 100 with "This Will Be" (#6 pop), her first of eighteen hits through 1997.

1990 The Neville Brothers performed as guests of their longtime fan Linda Ronstadt at her concert at Jones Beach Theater in Long Island, New York.

1994 Gangsta rapper, former member of N.W.A. (Niggaz with Attitude), and all-around bad influence Dr. Dre (born Andre Young), was sentenced to five months in a Los Angeles jail for violating his probation in a 1992 assault on a TV show host during a brawl.

1997 James Brown performed in Beirut, Lebanon, at the Hotel Albustan. Soon after he would leave for Moscow to perform at the Kremlin Palace.

The Neville Brothers

August

#1 R&B Song 1968: "You're All I Need to Get By," Marvin Gaye and Tammi Terrell

Born: Wilton Felder (the Crusaders), 1940

1955 Chuck Berry's "Maybellene" reached #5 pop while spending eleven weeks at #1 on the R&B hit list. Chuck began his musical career as a member of the Johnny Johnson Trio in St. Louis in 1952.

1959 The Coasters' "Poison Ivy" charted, eventually becoming the group's fourth and final R&B #1.

1962 The Shirelles, Ben E. King, Little Eva, Chuck Jackson, Dee Dee Sharp, the Marvelettes, the Ronettes, the Del-Satins, the Majors, and Tony Orlando (years before Dawn) performed at Murray the K's annual New York Labor Day Rock 'n' Roll Show at the Brooklyn Fox Theater.

1963 The Miracles' "Mickey's Monkey" charted en route to #3 R&B and #8 pop.

1969 Richie Havens performed at England's Isle of Wight Festival with the Moody Blues, the Who, Joe Cocker, Bob Dylan, and others.

1976 George Harrison was found guilty of "subconscious plagiarism" of the Chiffons hit "He's So Fine" for similarities to his million-seller "My Sweet Lord." In a case of sweet retribution, the Chiffons then recorded their own version of "My Sweet Lord."

1987 *Michael Jackson: The Magic Returns* aired on CBS-TV, featuring his seventeen-minute video for "Bad."

1994 R. Kelly married new chart sensation Aaliyah in Rosemont, IL. The marriage was later annulled as Aaliyah was only fifteen years old at the time and the state law required people to be sixteen to marry.

September

#1 R&B Song 1951: "Don't You Know I Love You," the Clovers

Born: Tommy Evans (the Drifters), 1927; Archie Bell (the Drells), 1944

1956 The Keynotes' "Now I Know" ($100) was released. Its melody turned up a year later in Dion & the Belmonts' hit "I Wonder Why."

1956 Johnnie Ray's "Just Walkin' in the Rain" debuted, eventually reaching #2. The original version was done three years earlier by the Prisonaires, an R&B quintet who were all inmates of the Tennessee State Penitentiary.

1958 Two doo-wop classics, "I'm So Young" by the Students (#26 R&B) and the Moonglows' "Ten Commandments of Love" (#22 pop, #9 R&B), were issued.

1958 The Clara Ward Singers broke up, forming two gospel groups, the Gay Charmers and the Stars of Faith.

1961 The Marcels (formerly a mixed-race group) had their first session as an all-black group recording "Heartaches" (#7 Pop, #19 R&B).

1980 Smokey Robinson charted with his lucky thirteenth solo outing as "Cruisin' " became his first Top 5 hit sans the Miracles (#4 pop and R&B).

1984 Tina Turner's "What's Love Got to Do with It" reached #1 pop (#2 R&B) on the same day she was offered a part in the third of the *Mad Max* film series.

Smokey Robinson

September

2

#1 R&B Song 1967: "Baby I Love You," Aretha Franklin

Born: Sam Gooden (the Impressions), 1939; Joe Simon, 1943; Rosalind Ashford (Martha & the Vandellas), 1943

1955 Alan Freed held his historic Labor Day Rock 'n' Roll Show at the Brooklyn Paramount featuring the Moonglows, the Cadillacs, Chuck Berry, the Harptones, and the Nutmegs.

1957 The Channels' legendary version of "That's My Desire" was released.

1967 The Parliaments' "I Wanna Testify" peaked at #20 pop (#3 R&B) for the future funk group's first of forty-seven R&B chart records through 1996.

1968 Muddy Waters performed at Sultan, Washington's Sky River Rock Festival and Lighter-Than-Air Fair with bands including the Youngbloods, Santana, and the Grateful Dead.

1976 Grandmaster Flash & the Furious Five performed at the Audubon Ballroom in Harlem. It was their first major performance. Grandmaster (Joseph Sadler) earned a degree in electronics before he became a pioneering rapper.

1978 Balladeer and heartthrob Teddy Pendergrass performed at Avery Fisher Hall in New York in the first of numerous concerts for women only. The concept was the brainchild of Pendergrass's manager, Shep Gordon (who arranged for the ladies to receive teddy bear-shaped lollipops at the concert), and there was no known reaction from the ACLU as to the ethics of such gender exclusivity.

1988 A worldwide charity tour to raise money for Amnesty International began with a concert at London's Wembley Stadium featuring Tracy Chapman, Bruce Springsteen, and Sting.

1995 Michael Jackson's "You Are Not Alone," produced and written by R. Kelly, hit #1, thus becoming the first single ever to debut in the top spot.

September

3

#1 R&B Song 1983: "Cold Blooded," Rick James

Born: Memphis Slim (John "Peter" Chatman), 1915; Walter & Wallace Scott (the Whispers), 1943; Freddie King, 1934

1955 Overton Amos Lemons, apparently not happy with his name, became Smiley Lewis and charted with "I Hear You Knocking," reaching #2 R&B. His piano player on the session was Huey (Piano) Smith, who would have his own hit two years later with "Rocking Pneumonia and the Boogie Woogie Flu" (#5 R&B).

1960 The Platters performed "Smoke Gets in Your Eyes" and "Red Sails in the Sunset" on *American Bandstand*'s nighttime edition in New York. Meanwhile, across the country in Portland, OR, seventeen people were arrested when a riot broke out after the audience was notified that their Ray Charles show had been canceled. Charles was stuck in Seattle due to bad weather.

1962 The Pirates' "Mind Over Matter," a cover of the Diablos recent single, was released but failed to chart. The Pirates were actually the Temptations moonlighting under a different name in the hopes of having better luck than the two singles that failed while they were on the Motown subsidiary Miracle Records.

1962 Chubby Checker, in the midst of the twist mania, began his first of many concert tours of England, starting at Bristol's Colston Hall.

1983 Tony Award winner Jennifer Holliday (*Dreamgirls*) charted R&B with "I Am Love" (#2 pop).

1991 Ike Turner was released from prison after serving eighteen months of a four-year sentence for driving under the influence of cocaine. Turner had been arrested eleven times before and claimed in a *Variety* interview that he had indulged in cocaine to the tune of $11 million before becoming rehabilitated.

September

#1 R&B Song 1954: "Oh What a Dream,"
Ruth Brown & Her Rhythmakers

Born: Merald "Bubba" Knight (Gladys Knight
& the Pips), 1942

4

1948 Sonny Til & the Orioles' debut disc, "It's Too Soon to Know" was released. It reached #15 pop and #1 R&B. Never before had a black group singing black (not pop) music hit the pop Top 15.

1952 Gladys and Brenda Knight, along with their brother Merald and cousins William and Eleanor Guest, performed at Merald's tenth birthday party and decided they should become a group. They named themselves after the nickname of another cousin, James "Pips" Woods. It would be ten years before they became known as Gladys Knight and the Pips.

1954 Decca Records signed the Hollywood Flames.

1965 Otis Redding charted with "Respect," a song he cowrote with Premiers member Speedo Simms. The 45 reached #35 pop and #4 R&B, but would be better known two years later as the defining hit of Aretha Franklin's career.

1976 The Spinners hit the Hot 100 with "The Rubberband Man" (#2 pop), which would become their sixth and final #1 R&B hit.

1996 The Fugees' "Killing Me Softly" won the award for best R&B video at the MTV Video Music Awards in New York.

The Fugees

September

5

#1 R&B Song 1946: "Choo Choo Ch' Boogie," Louis Jordan & His Tympany 5

Born: George "Buddy" Miles (Electric Flag), 1946; Terry Ellis (En Vogue), 1966

1946 Buddy Miles, one of the top session drummers of the '60s and '70s, was born. A versatile musician, Buddy provided every kind of pop and rock 'n' roll rhythm for Dick Clark's Caravan of Stars tours. In the mid-'60s, he did his "soul thing" with Wilson Pickett's band. By the late '60s he had moved into hard rock with Electric Flag and was eventually in Jimi Hendrix's Band of Gypsies.

1953 Ella Fitzgerald and the Ray Charles Singers charted with a cover of the Orioles classic, "Crying in the Chapel." Fitzgerald and company raced up the charts to #15, but the Orioles won the competition, having reached #11.

1953 The Spaniels entered the R&B hit list for the first time with "Baby It's You," reaching #10. An original deejay copy on red plastic Vee-Jay will set you back $4,500 if you can find it.

1953 The pioneering rhythm & blues vocal group Billy Ward & the Dominoes landed on the R&B hit parade with "You Can't Keep a Good Man Down," reaching #8. It was Jackie Wilson's first chart hit as lead singer of the famous group after replacing Clyde McPhatter, who left to form the Drifters. An original copy of the fifty-three-year-old hit will cost you $100.

1963 King Curtis and his band performed at New York's Birdland.

1978 Frankie Lymon & the Teenagers member Joe Negroni died at thirty-seven. He was the third member of the group to die before the age of thirty-eight.

1991 Mariah Carey sang her hit "Emotions" (#1) at the eighth annual MTV Video Music Awards ceremony at the Universal Amphitheater in Universal City, CA.

1997 Erykah Badu received four awards at the third annual Soul Train Lady of Soul Awards, including Best Album, Best New Artist, Best Single, and Best Song. The visibly pregnant performer cohosted the show with one of her idols, Chaka Khan. Also honored was Janet Jackson, who received the Lena Horne Award for Outstanding Career Achievement.

September

6

#1 R&B Song 1952: "Ting-A-Ling," the Clovers

Born: Buddy "King" Bolden, 1877; Mathis James "Jimmy" Reed, 1925; Ce Ce Penniston, 1969

1877 Known as King Bolden, and considered to be the first jazz musician, cornet player Buddy Bolden was born today. The performer was a fixture in the dance halls and clubs of early twentieth-century New Orleans, and he had an improvisational style that became legendary. In 1906, according to reports, he had a complete mental breakdown whil performing in a parade and never played again. Sadly, he never recorded.

1952 With a blues singer and harmonica player supreme for a frontman, Little Walter & His Jukes jumped on the R&B hit list with "Juke," reaching #1 for a solid eight weeks, their biggest of fifteen hits through 1959.

1952 Smiley Lewis charted with his first of four hits, "The Bells Are Ringing," reaching #10 R&B.

1957 Frankie Lymon & the Teenagers, Chuck Berry, the Drifters, Clyde McPhatter, Buddy Holly & the Crickets, Paul Anka, the Everly Brothers, and others kicked off the Biggest Show of Stars for 1957 package tour at the Syria Mosque, Pittsburgh, PA. As an ironic result of the anti-black prejudice of the times, the white artists were forbidden from playing certain dates because of segregation laws that prohibited black and white artists from performing on the same stage.

1958 The Quintones performed their hit "Down the Aisle of Love" (#18 pop, #5 R&B) on *American Bandstand*.

1969 Isaac Hayes charted for the first time with "Walk on By," reaching #13 R&B and #30 pop. The song was originally a hit in 1964 for Dionne Warwick. Hayes started out playing with amateur bands like Sir Isaac & the Do-Dads. He graduated to become a member of the Stax Records house band, often playing behind Otis Redding while holding a day gig in a Memphis meatpacking plant.

1986 Actress and singer Melba Moore, along with Freddie Jackson, entered the R&B charts with "A Little Bit More," reaching #1 for her career best of thirty-two R&B hits from 1975 to 1990.

1997 Brian McKnight with Jacksonville, FL, rapper Mase (born Mason Betha), charted R&B with "You Should Be Mine (Don't Waste Your Time)," reaching #4 and #17 pop.

251

September

7

#1 R&B Song 1985: "Saving All My Love for You," Whitney Houston

Born: Little Milton (Milton Campbell), 1934; Benjamin Latimore, 1939; Gloria Gaynor, 1949

1956 Showing their international clout, the Platters charted in England with two hit A-sides back-to-back as "The Great Pretender"/"Only You" went on to #5.

1961 Chuck Jackson, the Shirelles, Chubby Checker, and Bobby Lewis performed at Palisades Amusement Park in Fort Lee, NJ.

1968 Fats Domino's cover of the Beatles' "Lady Madonna" charted, though it only reached #100 pop. It would be the last of sixty-six Top 100 singles in his career.

1984 Janet Jackson announced she had secretly married DeBarge's James DeBarge. It lasted all of seven months.

1990 MC Hammer's "U Can't Touch This" won for Best Dance Video and Best Rap Video at the seventh annual MTV Video Music Awards. New Edition reunited for the event and performed.

Fats Domino

1990 B.B. King was given a star on the Hollywood Walk of Fame.

2000 Legendary lead singer of gospel superstars, the Soul Stirrers, R.H. Harris died at his home in Chicago. He helped shape gospel music into what is today called the "quartet" style of singing with his high voice and performance gymnastics. He influenced many later R&B stars including Sam Cooke and Al Green. He was eighty-six and about to be inducted into the Vocal Group Hall of Fame.

September

#1 R&B Song 1956: "Let the Good Times Roll," Shirley & Lee

Born: Bluesman Harmonica Fats (Harvey Blackston), 1927

1956 More than five months and two labels after being initially released, the Five Satins' "In the Still of the Night" charted on its way to #24 pop, #3 R&B, and immortality. The single would go on to chart in 1960 and 1961 while becoming one of the all-time rock 'n' roll standards. The song was written by lead singer Fred Parris on guard duty while serving in the army. At about 3:00 A.M. he put down his rifle, picked up his pen, and wrote one of the greatest ballads of all time, which the group recorded live in a church basement in New Haven, CT, in December 1955.

1957 Jackie Wilson's solo debut, "Reet Petite" (cowritten by Berry Gordy Jr. in the pre-Motown days), was released.

1958 The Selah Gospel Singers, one of the oldest groups in the country, signed with Savoy Records.

1962 Thirteen days after its release, the Crystals' "He's a Rebel" charted, on its way to #1 for two weeks. The Gene Pitney song was rush-released to beat out a competing version by Vikki Carr.

1962 Switching from twisting to limboing, Chubby Checker charted with "Limbo Rock," which became a #3 hit and his fifth Top 10 pop single in two years.

1972 Bobby Bland, Howlin' Wolf, Junior Walker & the All-Stars, Otis Spann, and Muddy Waters performed at the Ann Arbor Jazz & Blues Festival in Ann Arbor MI.

1984 Chaka Khan reached the Hot 100 with "I Feel for You," her biggest hit (#3).

2000 Lead singer of the veteran Detroit soul group, the Fantastic Four, Sweet James Epps died today. The group's biggest hit was "The Whole World Is a Stage" (#6 R&B, 1967), released by Motown's biggest local rival, Ric Tic Records.

September

9

#1 R&B Song 1972: "Back Stabbers," the O'Jays

Born: Jacob Carey (the Flamingos), 1923; Joe Negroni (the Teenagers), 1940; Otis Redding, 1941; Luther Simmons (the Main Ingredient), 1942; Inez Foxx, 1942; Dee Dee Sharp, 1945; Billy Preston, 1946; Macy Gray, 1970

1957 Former Dominoes lead Jackie Wilson signed with Brunswick Records as a solo artist. His first single would be "Reet Petite," recorded the day before.

1967 Sam & Dave charted with "Soul Man," reaching #1 R&B for seven weeks and #2 pop. The record became a defining moment in classic soul music for decades to come.

1982 Patti LaBelle opened on Broadway, co-starring with Al Green in the gospel musical, *Your Arm's Too Short to Box with God*. The Alvin Theater schedule called for thirty shows, but due to rave reviews the show ran for eighty performances.

1995 B.B. King held his seventieth birthday party while performing at Nashville's Riverfront Stadium. The concert was hosted by the Gibson Guitar Company, the organization that made B.B.'s guitar, Lucille.

1995 Talk about a slow crawl: fifteen months after its debut, Seal's self-titled album peaked at #15 in England.

1998 Toni Braxton took over the role of Belle in the Broadway musical *Beauty and the Beast* at the Palace Theater in New York.

Toni Braxton

Daniela Federici

September

#1 Song 1966: "You Can't Hurry Love," the Supremes

Born: Roy Brown, 1925; Roy Ayers, 1948; Debra Laws, 1956; Big Daddy Kane (Antonio Hardy), 1968

1925 Roy Brown, an early New Orleans R&B influence, was born today. Starting as an amateur boxer, Brown began singing pop ballads before discovering the blues and writing songs like "Good Rockin' Tonight." Though many believe "Rocket 88" in 1951 was the first rock 'n' roll record, many feel it was Brown's "Good Rockin' " or Wynonie Harris's 1948 version. It has since taken on even greater appeal thanks to Elvis Presley's recording in 1954.

1949 Rhythm and blues great Ivory Joe Hunter entered the R&B charts not once but twice today, with recordings on two different labels. "Waiting in Vain" on King and "Blues at Midnight" on 4 Star both charted, pitting Ivory Joe in a battle with himself. "Waiting" won, reaching #5, while "Blues" stopped at #10.

1960 Dick Clark's *American Bandstand*'s Saturday night run ended. Though Clark had been a racial pioneer, bringing countless black acts to a national audience, his last night show included eight white artists and no black acts.

1963 Marvin Gaye, the Drifters, James Brown, Martha & the Vandellas, Ruby & the Romantics, the Crystals, Jimmy Reed, Doris Troy, Inez Foxx, and Major Lance began the Biggest Show of Stars for '63 package tour.

1977 Jeffrey Osborne and L.T.D. charted with "(Every Time I Turn Around) Back in Love Again," reaching #1 R&B and #4 pop. It became the group's biggest hit of fourteen charters.

1993 Luther Vandross performed at the Mobile Civic Center in Mobile, AL, at the beginning of a national tour.

September

11

#1 R&B Song 1965: "Papa's Got a Brand New Bag, Part 1," James Brown

Born: Bluesman Barbecue Bob (Robert Hicks), 1902; Ludacris (Christopher Bridges), 1977

1951 Ray Charles, having recently signed to Atlantic Records, attended his first recording session with producer Jesse Stone at the helm.

1956 The Harptones recorded the legendary "Shrine of St. Cecilia ($80) and "On Sunday Afternoon" ($80).

1961 Aretha Franklin's "Rock-A-Bye Your Baby" was released. It became her only Top 40 single of nine pop charters (#37) while on Columbia and in the misguided hands of Mitch Miller, who never saw her soul potential.

1965 New York trio the Toys hit the big time with "A Lover's Concerto" (#2 pop). The song's melody was based on a Bach's minuet from the Anna Magdalena Notebook.

1968 Sly & the Family Stone arrived in London to begin a tour, but customs officials ended that plan when they found drugs in the members' baggage. The group spent a week in London but didn't do a single performance.

1987 Paula Abdul won the Best Choreography award at MTV's fourth annual Video Music Awards for Janet Jackson's "Nasty." Abdul would go on to choreograph videos for such diverse talents as Dolly Parton, ZZ Top, Duran Duran, and Debbie Gibson.

1993 Janet Jackson made her film debut when the motion picture Poetic Justice hit theaters today.

1996 B.B. King and the Neville Brothers performed at New York's Radio City Music Hall in the Blues Music Festival '96.

1996 Isaac Hayes's publisher slapped a cease and desist demand on the Dole Presidential Campaign for using Hayes's song "Soul Man" as "Dole Man" without the publisher's permission. The embarrassed Republican promptly stopped using the song after the story hit the press.

September

#1 R&B Song 1960: "Kiddio,"
Brook Benton

Born: Warren Corbin (the Cleftones),
1938; Barry White, 1944

1954 The Drifters, the Spaniels, and the Counts performed at the Brooklyn Paramount.

1960 The Chiffons, locked in a cover battle with the Shirelles, charted today with "Tonight's the Night." Though New Jersey's Shirelles out-paced the Bronx, NY, quartet (#39 to #76 pop), the recording is notable for being the Chiffons' first Hot 100 offing of a career twelve hits through 1966.

1964 The Temptations' "Girl (Why You Wanna Make Me Blue)" charted on its way to #26 pop, the group's first Top 30 hit.

1970 The Miracles' "Tears of a Clown" reached #1 in England. The three-year-old recording was a forgotten gem until a British Motown executive decided to release it as a single. Based on its British success, it was released in America, where it also reached the top spot.

1981 Morris Day & the Time charted with their debut album *The Time*, reaching #50 pop. The album was written and produced by Jamie Starr, a pseudonym for a soon-to-be-star named Prince. Two of the group's musicians were a future songwriting/producing success story in their own right, Jimmy "Jam" Harris and Terry Lewis.

1987 Michael Jackson began his *Bad* world tour in Korakuen Stadium, Tokyo, Japan. The tour would take more than a year to complete, covering Australia, North America, and Europe. Keeping Michael company were his manager, his personal chef, his hairdresser, and a retinue of about 250.

1994 Lenny Kravitz performed at Chicago's Soldier Field as opening act for the Rolling Stones.

September

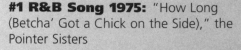

13

#1 R&B Song 1975: "How Long (Betcha' Got a Chick on the Side)," the Pointer Sisters

Born: Tenor sax man Leon "Chu" Berry, 1910; Charles Brown, 1922, Nell Carter, 1948

1964 Martha & the Vandellas, the Supremes, the Temptations, the Miracles, Marvin Gaye, the Ronettes, and the Shangri-Las, among others, performed in Murray the K's ten-day Rock 'n' Roll Spectacular at the Brooklyn Fox Theater.

1969 Chuck Berry, Little Richard, Jerry Lee Lewis, Bo Diddley, John Lennon, Alice Cooper, Gene Vincent, and the Doors appeared at the Toronto Rock 'n' roll Revival Concert.

1985 Tina Turner won the Best Female Video trophy at the second annual MTV Video Music Awards, held at New York's Radio City Music Hall, for "What's Love Got to Do with It?" The famine-relief recording "We Are the World" by USA for Africa won Best Group Video and Viewers' Choice awards.

1986 Lavert's "(Pop, Pop, Pop, Pop) Goes My Mind" reached #1 R&B. It would be the first of five R&B #1s for the trio, which contained two sons (Gerald and Sean) of O'Jays lead singer Eddie O'Jay. They would not come close to beating their dad's record of ten #1s with his group.

Lavert

1992 Michael Jackson performed at the famous Hippodrome in Paris, France.

1992 James Ingram and Patti Austin performed on PBS-TV's *Evening at the Pops* with John Williams and the Boston Pops Orchestra.

1997 Prince was the featured artist on *The Muppets Tonight* season opener on the Disney Channel.

1998 Lenny Kravitz performed on tour with Sean Lennon, son of Beatle John Lennon, at the Paramount Theater in Seattle, WA.

September

#1 R&B Song 1974: "Can't Get Enough of Your Love, Babe," Barry White

Born: Paul Kossoff (British blues artist), 1950

14

1955 Little Richard finished his first recording session for Specialty Records, cutting "Tutti Frutti" (#17 pop, #2 R&B).

1963 The O'Jays made their chart debut with a classic doo-wop single, "Lonely Drifter" (#93 pop). They named themselves after their mentor, Cleveland deejay Eddie O'Jay, but recorded some terrific harmony sides as the Mascots (King Records), such as "Lonely Rain" in 1961. Before King, they auditioned for Decca and were turned down.

1963 Patti LaBelle & the Bluebelles charted pop with "Down the Aisle (Wedding Song)," reaching #37 and becoming their first of eleven R&B charters (#14) as both the Bluebelles and, later, LaBelle. The group formed in 1961 from two school groups, the Del Capris and the Ordettes.

1970 Stevie Wonder married Syreeta Wright. Wright, previously a secretary at Motown Records, would have the hit "With You I'm Born Again" in 1980 (#4) with Billy Preston.

1974 Eric Clapton reached #1 pop with the Bob Marley song "I Shot the Sheriff."

1988 Prince began a tour at the Met Center in Bloomington, MN. The twenty performances were his first tour in four years.

1989 Shirley Alston Reeves of the Shirelles joined with members of the Five Satins, the Silhouettes, the Jive Five, and the Falcons in a doo-wop performance outside Boston's Berklee Performance Center to promote the formation of the doo-wop Hall of Fame of America.

1990 Disney chairman Michael Eisner presented Michael Jackson with the Michael Jackson Good Scout Humanitarian Award on behalf of the Los Angeles Area Council of the Boy Scouts of America.

1992 British songstress Joan Armatrading appeared on NBC-TV's *The Tonight Show with Jay Leno*.

September

15

#1 R&B Song 1979: "Don't Stop 'Til You Get Enough," Michael Jackson

Born: Blues singer James "Snooky" Pryor, 1921; Bobby Short, 1924; Julian "Cannonball" Adderly, 1928

1956 The Dells' standard "Oh, What a Nite" (Vee Jay, #4 R&B, $120) was released.

1956 The Cadets, who were on the charts with their hit "Stranded in the Jungle," sang backup in Los Angeles on the ballad "I Confess." The lead singer and writer was a white Canadian teenager named Paul Anka.

1968 Martha & the Vandellas performed on the debut episode of NBC-TV's music show *Soul* with Lou Rawls.

1989 Natalie Cole hosted a forerunner of *American Idol* with her weekly show *Big Break*.

1991 Whitney Houston spoke at London's Hyde Park at the Reach Out and Touch People with HIV and AIDS Rally.

1991 The mayor of San Francisco presented B.B. King with the keys to the city on his sixty-sixth birthday (actually a day early) at the annual San Francisco Blues Festival. Members of King's band on that joyous occasion included Bobby McFerrin, Robert Cray, and Boz Scaggs.

1995 James Brown performed "I Got You (I Feel Good)" and "It's a Man's, Man's, Man's World" at the Rock and Roll Hall of Fame in Cleveland.

The Dells

September 16

1957 Norman Fox & the Rob Roys' "Tell Me Why" was issued.

1964 Sam Cooke performed on the debut of the rock 'n' roll TV show *Shindig* with the Righteous Brothers and the Everly Brothers.

1972 The Spinners "I'll Be Around," the group's Atlantic Records debut, charted, reaching #1 R&B for five weeks and #3 pop. The song was originally the B-side, but radio play forced the label to flip it.

1990 Janet Jackson performed at New York's Madison Square Garden. After the show she presented the United Negro College Fund with a check for $450,000.

1992 Dionne Warwick appeared at a fund-raiser for presidential hopeful Bill Clinton at millionaire Ted Field's Beverly Hills mansion and sang "Amazing Grace."

1994 Whitney Houston began the first of seven performances at Radio City Music Hall in New York. All of the shows were sell-outs, grossing more than $2,500,000.

1995 Seal charted with "Kiss from a Rose." Though reaching only #52 R&B, it became #1 pop and would go on to win Record of the Year honors at the Grammys.

2003 The Vocal Group Hall of Fame held its sixth annual induction ceremonies in Sharon, PA. Co-hosts Mary Wilson of the Supremes and publisher/author Jay Warner anchored the proceedings, which saw the Whispers, Martha & the Vandellas, the Five Satins, the Charioteers, the Isley Brothers, the Impressions, Earth, Wind & Fire, and the Commodores inducted.

September

17

#1 R&B Song 1949: "All She Wants to Do Is Rock," Wynonie Harris

Born: Bill Black, 1926; Lamont McLemore (the Fifth Dimension), 1940; Doug E. Fresh (Doug Davis), 1966

1955 Ella Fitzgerald and Peggy Lee's album, *Songs from Pete Kelly's Blues*, ascended the album hit list, leveling off at #7. It became Fitzgerald's biggest of eleven charters through 1969.

1977 The *Diana Ross & the Supremes 20 Golden Greats* compilation reached #1 in England and stayed there for seven weeks.

1983 Lionel Richie's "All Night Long" charted. It would eventually be #1 pop for four weeks and #1 R&B for seven weeks, making it Motown's biggest hit worldwide up to that time.

1990 Natalie Cole married record producer Andre Fischer, the former drummer for Rufus.

1994 Boyz II Men's *II* album debuted at #1 pop, becoming the first Motown album since Stevie Wonder's 1976 *Songs in the Key of Life* album to reach the top spot in its first week on the charts. By year's end the Boyz album had sold six million copies.

1994 Mariah Carey and Luther Vandross's remake of the Diana Ross/Lionel Richie hit "Endless Love" reached #3 in its chart debut in England. Stateside, it would reach #2 pop and #7 R&B.

September

#1 R&B Song 1971: "Stick-Up,"
Honey Cone

Born: Ricky Bell (New Edition), 1967

1948 Muddy Waters's debut 78 and his first R&B hit, "I Feel Like Going Home," reached #11. Waters (McKinley Morganfield) got his name as a child while playing in a muddy creek near the Mississippi River. The Delta blues innovator was influenced by early pioneers Son House and Robert Johnson.

1954 The Diablos' R&B standard "The Wind" was released.

1970 Jimi Hendrix, who in 1965 had confided to his writing partner, Curtis Knight, that he would die in five years, fulfilled his own prophesy when he died on the way to a London hospital after being found at his girlfriend's house. His last known words were left on his manager's answering machine: "I need help bad, man."

1976 Diana Ross and Alice Cooper (now that's an interesting pairing.) cohosted *Don Kirshner's Rock Awards*.

1984 Michael Jackson won three awards at the inaugural MTV Video Music Awards, Best Choreography, Best Overall Performance Video, and Viewer's Choice, for *Thriller*. The ceremonies were held at New York's Radio City Music Hall and were hosted by Bette Midler and Dan Akroyd. Tina Turner also performed at the awards.

1985 Gladys Knight debuted in the sitcom *Charlie & Co.* with Flip Wilson. The show ran for one season.

September

19

#1 Song 1960: "The Twist," Chubby Checker & the Dreamlovers

Born: Pianist Cora "Lovie" Austin, 1887; Billy Ward (the Dominoes), 1921; Brook Benton (Benjamin Franklin Peay), 1931; Freda Payne, 1945; Nile Rodgers (Chic), 1952

1953 Big Joe Turner charted R&B with "Honey Hush," reaching #1 for eight straight weeks. Turner's big chance came when he performed at Carnegie Hall's Spirituals to Swing concert in 1938.

1960 Hank Ballard & the Midnighters became the first group with three hit singles on the Top 100 at the same time when "Let's Go, Let's Go, Let's Go" joined "Finger Poppin' Time" and "The Twist."

1960 Seventeen-year-old Mary Wells played a song for producer Berry Gordy Jr., and on the basis of "Bye Bye Baby" she was signed to his newly-formed Motown label. The song (which she originally wrote for Jackie Wilson) was released today, reaching #45 pop and #8 R&B.

1970 Diana Ross's "Ain't No Mountain High Enough" reached #1, becoming her first chart topper minus the Supremes. Produced by its writers, Valerie Simpson and Nick Ashford, it was originally a hit (#19) in 1967 for Tammi Terrell and Marvin Gaye.

1991 *Ray Charles: 50 Years in Music* was filmed to be aired on October 6. The show was filmed in Pasadena, CA, and a highlight was Ray's duet with Stevie Wonder on "Living for the City."

1992 Michael Jackson performed in Bucharest, Romania, while on his *Dangerous* tour.

1992 Patti LaBelle's NBC-TV *Out All Night* sitcom debuted with the diva playing a singer in her own Los Angeles nightclub.

1996 George Benson was honored with a star on Hollywood's Walk of Fame.

September

20

1952 The Ravens, one of two founding fathers of rhythm and blues (with the Orioles), charted with "Rock Me All Night Long," reaching #4 R&B. It was the last of eleven hits for the New York quartet of R&B legends.

1959 The first oldies compilation album, *Oldies but Goodies* (Original Sound Records), was issued. Of the twelve recordings, eleven were by black acts, and the twelfth, the Mello-Kings classic "Tonite, Tonite," was thought at the time to have been by a black group.

1973 Sly, Slick & Wicked's single "Sho Nuff" was issued on James Brown's People label. The Cleveland trio were performance specialists, having worked with the likes of the Dells, the O'Jays, B.B. King, the Ohio Players, Peabo Bryson, Con Funk Shun, and, of course, James Brown. When records with Paramount, Motown, and Epic failed, lead singer John Wilson went on to produce for the Jacksons.

1978 Marvin Gaye re-inked with Motown Records for $600,000 each for the first two albums $1 million per album thereafter in a seven-year deal.

1980 The Commodores and Bob Marley performed at Madison Square Garden in New York.

1990 B.B. King and Ray Charles performed in Taiwan during a world tour that would not end for another two months.

Bob Marley

September

21

#1 R&B Song 1959: "I Want to Walk You Home," Fats Domino

Born: Jazz musician Leroy "Slam" Stewart, 1914

1959 The Isley Brothers charted pop with "Shout" (#47), their first of forty-six Top 100 hits over a forty-two-year period. The record would soon sell more than a million copies. It never made the R&B charts, however, as it was considered to be more of a rock 'n' roll standard.

1963 Martha & the Vandellas' "Heat Wave" peaked at #4 pop while reaching #1 R&B for four weeks and selling more than a million copies. Martha started out earning $35 a week as a secretary at Motown for Smokey Robinson and the writers of "Heat Wave," Holland, Dozier, and Holland.

1969 The Fifth Dimension performed on *The Woody Allen TV Special* on CBS.

1980 Bob Marley collapsed while jogging in Manhattan's Central Park and was later told he had cancer.

1984 James Brown married Modell Rodriquez.

1991 Diana Ross performed the last of three sellout shows at New York's Radio City Music Hall, grossing more than $650,000 (not a bad weekend's work).

1996 A remixed hip-hop version of Roberta Flack's 1973 hit, "Killing Me Softly with His Song," hit #1 on the Hot Dance Music chart. The remix release was motivated by the success of the Fugees' cover of "Killing Me" from earlier in the year.

1996 The Harlem Boys Choir, Babyface, Vanessa Williams, Seal, and Elton John, among others, entertained at the MGM Grand in Las Vegas at the Agassi Slam for Children, a benefit concert held by tennis star Andre Agassi.

September 22

#1 R&B Song 1973: "Let's Get It On," Marvin Gaye

1956 Frankie Lymon & the Teenagers' "ABC's of Love" (#77 pop) was released.

1958 The Solitaires' classic "Please Remember My Heart" was issued. If you've got a copy on the original Old Town label (first pressing), it's worth about $2,000.

1958 The Quintones, one of the best of the one-hit wonder doo-wop groups, charted with their classic "Down the Aisle of Love," stopping at #5 R&B and #18 pop.

1960 Hank Ballard & the Midnighters, the Bobbettes, Bo Diddley, Sam Cooke, the Olympics, Marv Johnson, and Dion & the Belmonts performed at the Veterans Memorial Auditorium in Columbus, OH, as part of the ongoing Biggest Show of Stars '60 tour.

1995 Michael Jackson performed "You Are Not Alone" with the Union Temple Baptist Choir prior to being inducted into the Black Entertainment Television (BET) Walk of Fame in Washington, DC.

1998 The Isley Brothers, the O'Jays, and Earth, Wind & Fire finished their summer tour at the Virginia Beach Amphitheater in Virginia Beach, VA.

Frankie Lymon & the Teenagers

September

23

#1 R&B Song 1978: "Got to Get You into My Life," Earth, Wind & Fire

Born: Tiny Bradshaw, 1905. Albert Ammans, 1907; Ray Charles (Ray Charles Robinson), 1930; Claude Feaster (the Chords), 1933; Ben E. King (Benjamin Earl Nelson), 1938

1957 The Rays' "Silhouettes" (#3 pop and R&B) was issued.

1961 The Cleftones, the Drifters, the Platters, Dee Clark, the Jarmels, Brook Benton, Gary "U.S." Bonds, Gene McDaniels, Curtis Lee, and Phil Upchurch performed at the Opera House in Chicago.

1966 The Temptations, Gladys Knight & the Pips, Martha & the Vandellas, Jimmy Ruffin, Stevie Wonder, and a host of lesser acts started a weeklong engagement at Detroit's Fox Theater in what is historically known as the Motortown Revue.

1966 Ike & Tina Turner kicked off a tour of England with the Rolling Stones and the Yardbirds at the Royal Albert Hall in London.

1967 Aretha Franklin's "A Natural Woman" was released, eventually reaching #8 pop and #2 R&B.

1978 Solomon Burke charted with his thirty-first and last 45 when "Please Don't You Say Goodbye to Me" hit the R&B list at #91. The soul vocalist was originally discovered at a Liberty Baptist Church talent show in 1955 by Viola Williams, the wife of deejay Kae Williams. By the '90s, Solomon had a dual career, as both a respected soul singer and the owner of a chain of mortuaries throughout the West Coast.

1987 Dionne Warwick was praised for her philanthropic work when the city of New York honored her for raising more than a million dollars for AIDS research.

1990 Little Richard (born Richard Wayne Penniman) performed in his hometown of Macon, GA, for the first time in thirty-five years when he appeared at the City Auditorium. A street was also named for him as Penniman Boulevard.

1998 Prince, Larry Graham, and Chaka Khan played the MCI Center in Washington, DC.

September

#1 R&B Song 1966: "Beauty Is Only Skin Deep," the Temptations

Born: Herb Jeffries, 1911; Allen Bunn (Larks & Wheels), 1924; Wayne Henderson (the Crusaders), 1939; Rosa Lee Hawkins (the Dixie Cups), 1944; Cedric Dent (Take 6), 1962

1955 The Eldorados' doo-wop classic "At My Front Door" (#17 pop, #1 R&B) was released.

1956 The Five Satins, the Channels, the Clovers, and the Valentines headlined Dr. Jive's weeklong party at the Apollo.

1966 The Jimi Hendrix Experience was formed in London and included drummer Mitch Mitchell and bassist Noel Redding. Hendrix, who was influenced by B.B. King, Muddy Waters, Chuck Berry, Elmore James, and Eddie Cochran, started performing when he bought a guitar from his father's friend for $5.

1992 Luther Vandross entertained at an AIDS Research benefit in Los Angeles called the Jean Paul Gaultier in L.A. fashion benefit.

1998 Aretha Franklin, Natalie Cole, and Boyz II Men performed at the Mentoring Big Night at the Garden benefit at New York's Madison Square Garden.

1999 The Vocal Group Hall of Fame in Sharon, PA, held its second annual induction ceremonies with hosts Mary Wilson of the Supremes and publisher/author Jay Warner overseeing the proceedings. Among the fourteen acts enshrined were the Coasters, the Delta Rhythm Boys, the Four Tops, Hank Ballard & the Midnighters, the Jackson 5, Little Anthony & the Imperials, the Moonglows, the Spinners, the Temptations, and the Ink Spots.

Mary Wilson

September

25

#1 R&B Song 1954: "Annie had a Baby," the Midnighters

Born: Joseph Russell (the Persuasions), 1939; Wade Flemons, 1940; Will Smith (the Fresh Prince), 1968

1948 Dizzy Gillespie entered the R&B singles chart for the first and last time with "Manteca," reaching #13. Gillespie, who received a Grammy Lifetime Achievement Award in 1989, was known as the father of modern jazz.

1954 The Charms' "Hearts of Stone" (#15 pop, #1 R&B) was released.

1954 Jubilee Records issued a special Four Tunes *Harmonizing Quartet* LP. The album was marked with bass, tenor, alto, and baritone so would-be vocalists could sing along to its collection of standards.

1960 The Upfronts, a Los Angeles R&B group, recorded their second single, "Too Far to Turn Around," for the local Lummtone label. The group would have six singles through 1964, and their best-known 45, "Most of the Pretty Young Girls," was their last. With no chart success, the group soon broke up. Their bass singer, however, would stay in the business, and by the '70s he was a household name in contemporary soul. He was Barry White.

1973 Stevie Wonder performed with Elton John at the Boston Garden singing the Rolling Stones' "Honky Tonk Woman."

1981 After escaping a brutal relationship with husband Ike Turner with 36 cents and a Mobil gas credit card to her name, Tina Turner began her come-back as the supporting act for the Rolling Stones' tenth American tour, which kicked off at JFK Stadium in Philadelphia. Prior to the performance, Tina was $500,000 in debt and working anywhere she could, including less-than-exotic venues in Bahrain, Yugoslavia, and Poland.

1982 Jennifer Holliday climbed the R&B charts with "I Am Changing" (#29), the song she sang in the Broadway play *Dreamgirls*.

1992 Roberta Flack and Dionne Warwick, known for their numerous ben-efit performances, once again helped out at the *Caring in Concert AIDS Benefit* TV special broadcast from the Mann Music Center in Philadelphia.

September

#1 R&B Song 1981: "Endless Love," Diana Ross and Lionel Richie

Born: George Chambers (the Chambers Brothers), 1931; Cindy Herron (En Vogue), 1965

1937 "Empress of the Blues" Bessie Smith died today. Influenced by Ma Rainey, Smith was simply the best of the classic blues singers. Her first recording in 1923, "Down Hearted Blues," sold more than 750,000 copies in a few months. She was known to have influenced many stars, including Billie Holiday, Mahalia Jackson, Ella Fitzgerald, and Janis Joplin. Though there were more than 7,000 people at her funeral, her grave remained without a marker until the '60s when Joplin paid for one.

1953 Seven of the R&B chart's Top 10 positions were occupied by vocal groups, including the Orioles, the Clovers, the "5" Royales, the Royals, the Spaniels, the Dominoes, and the Coronets.

1957 The Monotones' immortal "Book of Love" (#5 pop, #3 R&B) was recorded.

1960 Maurice Williams & the Zodiacs charted R&B with "Stay," reaching #3 and #1 pop. The Zodiacs were actually the Gladiolas, who in 1957 had the R&B hit "Little Darlin,' " (#11) which the Diamonds made into a monster hit on the pop charts. "Stay," by the way, was the shortest #1 record ever at 1:50 in length. Williams said that it would have been shorter but the group really got carried away in the fade.

1963 Baby Washington, Sam Cooke, Freddie Scott, the Tymes, Little Willie John, and Bobby "Blue" Bland performed in New Orleans.

1981 Patti Austin's Quincy Jones-produced *Every Home Should Have One* album charted on its way to #36, becoming Patti's biggest of five Top 200 albums through 1990. Austin was more well-known behind the scenes, having provided backing vocals on albums by such stars as Michael Jackson (*Off the Wall*), Paul Simon, Billy Joel, and George Benson, among many others.

1992 Bobby Brown appeared as the performing guest on the season opener of NBC-TV's *Saturday Night Live*.

September

27

#1 R&B Song 1969: "Oh, What a Night," the Dells

Born: Mark Calderon (Color Me Badd), 1970

1952 The son of a former Memphis preacher, Johnny Ace (actually John Alexander Jr.) hit #1 today on the R&B charts with his first single, "My Song." His "song" would stay there for nine weeks. Sixteen years later (1968), Aretha Franklin would reenergize "My Song" to the tune of #10 R&B (#31 pop).

1968 The Jackson 5, Gladys Knight & the Pips, Bobby Taylor & the Vancouvers, and Shorty Long performed at a benefit for the Mayor of Gary, IN, at the Gilroy Stadium in Gary. The Jacksons were originally called the Ripples & Waves Plus Michael.

1969 The Originals' "Baby I'm for Real" (#14 pop, #1 R&B) was released. Freddie Gorman of the quartet had penned the Marvelettes hit "Please Mr. Postman" eight years earlier.

1987 Marvin Gaye received a star on the Hollywood Walk of Fame.

1992 The Neville Brothers performed in Luciano Pavarotti's horse stable in Modena, Italy (now there's an interesting venue), as a fund-raiser to benefit leukemia research.

1994 George Benson sang a duet with the Muppets for the *Kermit Unpigged* album, which was issued today.

September

#1 R&B Song 1963: "Heat Wave," Martha & the Vandellas

Born: Koko Taylor, 1935

1946 The Ink Spots charted with "To Each His Own," reaching #3 R&B and #1 pop. The song was written for the film of the same name but never used in it.

1956 Hollywood's Shrine Auditorium hosted a rock 'n' roll show featuring West Coast groups the Coasters, the Six Teens, the Turks, the Gassers, and the Dots.

1963 San Francisco's Cow Palace hosted a Surf Party featuring the Coasters, Bobby Freeman, Dionne Warwick, the Drifters, Dee Dee Sharp, the Righteous Brothers, and the Beach Boys.

1987 Smokey Robinson and Gladys Knight guested for a week on the TV show *$10,000 Pyramid*.

1988 Anita Baker and Luther Vandross performed in Washington, DC, at the start of their The Heat tour.

1996 Gladys Knight, Chaka Khan, Brandy, and Tamia sang together on the hit "Missing You" from the film *Set It Off*. The record reached #25 pop and #10 R&B today.

Anita Baker

Buckmaster

September

29

#1 R&B Song 1945: "The Honeydripper (Parts 1 & 2)," Joe Liggins & His Honeydrippers

Born: Shirley Gunter (the Queens), 1934

1956 The Marigolds' "Juke Box Rock & Roll" ($350) was released. Lead singer Johnny Bragg and the rest of the quintet were all residents at the Tennessee State Prison, as was Bragg's previous group, the Prisonaires. Also issued that day were the Heartbeats' "A Thousand Miles Away" (#53 pop, #5 R&B) and Paul Anka (singing lead for the Cadets) with "I Confess" (Modern).

1959 Little Anthony and the Imperials recorded "Shimmy, Shimmy, Ko Ko Bop" (#14 pop, #24 R&B), a song that would become their last hit for five years and a record Anthony was quoted calling "stupid."

1973 Former New York City model Millie Jackson nudged her way onto the Top 200 album list with "It Hurts So Good" (#175), her second of fourteen hit LPs.

1975 Jackie Wilson suffered a heart attack on-stage during Dick Clark's Good Ol' Rock ' n' Roll Revue at Cherry Hill, NJ's, Latin Casino. The Spinners and Barry White were among several acts that held benefits to raise money for his medical expenses. He was singing "Lonely Teardrops" at the time.

1990 Ray Charles and B.B. King began a world tour in Taiwan capital, Taipei.

1990 The Braxtons, a trio of teen sisters from Maryland, charted with their soul debut, "Good Life," reaching #79 R&B. One of the siblings would soon go on to solo success: Toni Braxton signed with Arista Records in 1991.

1990 Take 6, an a cappella gospel group, did the near-impossible in the rap era when they charted R&B with "I L-O-V-E U," reaching #19.

1992 *USA Today* called Shabba Ranks the new Bob Marley. Meanwhile, the new Marley was accused of rape by a woman appearing in his video "Loada Girls." It was the fourth time Shabba had been accused of rape.

1995 Kool & the Gang, the Isley Brothers, Gladys Knight, and Aretha Franklin performed at New York's Madison Square Garden at the KISS-FM Classic Soul concert.

September

#1 R&B Song 1957: "Mr. Lee," the Bobbettes

Born: Cissy Houston, 1933; Johnny Mathis, 1935; Arzel "Z.Z." Hill, 1935; Frankie Lymon (the Teenagers), 1942; Marilyn McCoo, 1943; Sylvia Peterson (the Chiffons), 1946; Patrice Rushen, 1954

1957 The legendary girl group the Chantels' first single, "He's Gone," written by lead singer Arlene Smith, debuted on the charts, peaking at #71 pop.

1957 Little Richard's "Keep a Knockin' " charted on its way to #2 R&B and #8 pop.

1957 The Val Chords' "Candy Store Love" and the Sh-Booms' "I Don't Want to Set the World on Fire" were released. The Sh-Booms were actually the Chords of "Sh-Boom" fame.

1967 The Precisions entered the R&B hit list with one of the great but overlooked soul singles of the late '60s, "If This Is Love (I'd Rather Be Lonely)," reaching #26 and #60 pop.

1972 Chuck Berry's single "My Ding-A-Ling" charted R&B, reaching #42. it went on to reach #1 pop. It was the last of Berry's twenty-three hit R&B singles and the only pop #1 he ever had. The song had previously been recorded by New Orleans musician Dave Bartholomew in 1952 and by the Bees in 1954 under the name "Toy Bell." The risqué tune was also cut by Berry in 1966 under the name "My Tambourine." His hit version was backed by the Average White Band.

1991 Diana Ross, spokeswoman for the National Children's Day Foundation, spoke before a House Select Committee on Children, Youth, and Families in Washington, DC.

1993 Whitney Houston and husband Bobby Brown had their limousine pulled over at New York's Kennedy International Airport by nine police officers with guns drawn, looking for drugs.

1995 Mary J. Blige reached #17 in England with her recording of "Mary Jane (All Night Long)," based on "All Night Long," the hit by the Mary Jane Girls that was written and produced by Rick James. The record made it to #37 R&B without selling any singles; it earned its chart status strictly from airplay, and the label decided (unwisely) not to issue a single for the public.

1998 Luther Vandross performed at the Johannesburg Stadium in Johannesburg, South Africa.

October

1

#1 R&B Song 1949: "Baby Get Lost," Dinah Washington

Born: Barbara Parritt (the Toys), 1944; Herbert "Tubo" Rhoad (the Persuasions), 1944; Donny Hathaway, 1945; Howard Hewett (Shalamar), 1957

1955 The Platters' "Only You" charted on its way to #5, starting a streak of forty Top 100 hits over a twelve-year span (1955–1967). The group originally recorded the song in 1954, but that version was weakly produced and did little upon its release on the Federal label. When they signed to Mercury, manager and producer Buck Ram, who wrote the song, redid it, creating the version that became the standard.

1958 Little Anthony & the Imperials recorded Neil Sedaka's "The Diary," which was slated to be their next single. When producer George Goldner went out of town, he left instructions with his associate, Richard Barrett, to release the record but Barrett instead issued a song titled "So Much" (which he just happened to have written). When Sedaka heard that the Imperials single was not coming out, he recorded "The Diary" himself and had the hit.

1991 Anita Baker paid $100,000 for *The Autobiography of Malcolm X* by Alex Haley at an auction of Haley's works on his Knoxville, TN, farm.

1993 Wilson Pickett received a one-year jail term and five years probation for his 1992 drinking, driving and collision escapade. The sentence also included 200 hours of community service, treatment for alcoholism, and a $5,000 fine. He would begin serving the term on January 3, 1994.

1994 Actress/singer Brandy charted with "I Wanna Be Down" (#6), her first of eighteen R&B hits through 2004.

October

#1 R&B Song 1982: "Love Come Down,"
Evelyn King

Born: Freddie Jackson, 1956; Claude
McKnight (Take 6), 1962

2

1948 Nellie Lutcher charted with "Alexander's Ragtime Band," reaching #13 R&B. The song was originally a #1 pop hit in 1911 for Arthur Collins and Byron Harlan.

1948 The Cecil Gant Trio of Nashville jumped on the R&B hit parade with "Another Day—Another Dollar," stopping at #6.

1961 The Crystals' debut, "There's No Other," was released. Produced by Phil Spector, it was the first successful single on the now legendary Philles label. The B-side ballad in a Chantels-style went on to #20 pop and #5 R&B.

1991 B.B. King began a world tour in Istanbul, Turkey.

B.B. King

October

3

#1 R&B Song 1970: "Ain't No Mountain High Enough," Diana Ross

Born: Monk Higgins (Milton Bland), 1930; Chubby Checker (Ernest Evans), 1941; Ronnie Laws, 1950

1958 The Coasters began touring on the Biggest Show of Stars for 1958 tour with Buddy Holly & the Crickets, Clyde McPhatter, Bobby Darin, Bobby Freeman, and Dion. The nineteen performances were done in sixteen days.

1977 Michael Jackson began rehearsing for his part in the film *The Wiz*, based on *The Wizard of Oz*, in New York. The frenzy Michael created had become legendary, such as when he had to escape across the rooftop of a Woolco store in Memphis a few months earlier as more than 10,000 fans clamored for autographs.

1990 Whitney Houston celebrated National Children's Day by performing at the White House.

1990 Bobby Womack played the Town & Country Club in London.

1994 Whitney Houston returned to the White House, this time for a performance in the Rose Garden celebrating the visit of Nelson Mandela.

1997 John Lee Hooker's club, the Boom Boom Room, opened in Redwood City, CA.

October

#1 R&B Song 1975: "This Will Be," Natalie Cole

Born: Duke Robillard, 1948

4

1958 George Goldner, owner of End Records, signed the Flamingos. They would have their most productive period at End with hits like "I Only Have Eyes for You," "Lovers Never Say Goodbye," and "Mio Amore."

1969 "You've Lost That Lovin' Feelin'," a remake of the Righteous Brothers hit by Dionne Warwick, charted, reaching #13 R&B and #16 pop.

1975 Quincy Jones, featuring the Brothers Johnson, entered the R&B Top 100 with "Is It Love That We're Missin'," peaking at #18.

1986 The Commodores charted with "Goin' to the Bank," which they cashed in at #2 R&B. It was the last of sixteen Top 10 hits for the band between 1974 and 1988, when they last made it onto the charts.

1996 Gladys Knight and the O'Jays performed at the Universal Amphitheater in Universal City, CA.

Quincy Jones

October

5

#1 R&B Song 1959: "Poison Ivy," the Coasters

Born: Arlene Smith (the Chantels), 1941

1959 The Miracles charted for the first time with "Bad Girl," reaching #93 pop. The new group out of Detroit was originally called the Matadors.

1963 The Impressions charted on their way to their biggest hit when "It's All Right" reached #1 R&B and #4 pop. The group created the song backstage at a Nashville concert.

1963 Little Richard performed on a British tour with the Everly Brothers.

1974 The Pointer Sisters single "Fairytale" charted, reaching #13 pop and #37 country. The group was on tour at the time and by no small coincidence wound up playing at Nashville's Grand Ole Opry.

1985 Comedian Eddie Murphy charted with "Party All the Time," the dance/novelty classic written and produced by Rick James, reaching #2 pop and #8 R&B.

1995 Wu-Tang Clan, Mary J. Blige, Jodeci, Brandy, Salt-N-Pepa, Run-D.M.C., and the Notorious B.I.G., among others, performed in an all-star show at Madison Square Garden in New York.

Eddie Murphy

October

#1 R&B Song 1951: "Glory of Love," the Five Keys

Born: Millie Small, 1946; Thomas McClary (the Commodores), 1949

1956 The Flamingos' "The Vow" ($80), the Valentines' "Nature's Creation" ($100), and the El Venos' "Now We're Together" ($80) were released.

1958 B.B. King, known for his cutting-edge blues recordings, sang lead with a doo-wop group, the Vocal Chords, on the relatively sedate yet still hip single, "Please Accept My Love," which was released today. The single reached #9 on the R&B charts.

1961 The Apollo Theater in New York billed tonight's show as an all-girl revue featuring the Chantels, Big Maybelle, the Bobbettes, Tiny Topsy, and Gladys Knight (with the Pips, who we guess they didn't count).

1981 Rick James peaked at #16 pop with the single "Super Freak (Part 1)" (#3 R&B). The song would become part of rap history when the bass line was lifted for MC Hammer's multimillion seller, "U Can't Touch This" in 1990.

1991 *Ray Charles: 50 Years in Music* aired on Fox-TV. The musical tribute to the icon included duets with Michael Bolton ("Georgia on My Mind"), Willie Nelson ("Busted"), and Stevie Wonder ("Living for the City"), along with performances by James Ingram ("I Can't Stop Loving You"), Michael McDonald ("I Got a Woman"), and Randy Travis ("Your Cheatin' Heart").

1994 Patti LaBelle debuted her own hometown night club, Chez LaBelle, in Philadelphia.

2000 Pops Staples of the Staples Singers was honored at the White House with the National Heritage Fellowship presented by First Lady Hillary Rodham Clinton.

October

7

#1 R&B Song 1967: "(Your Love Keeps Lifting Me) Higher and Higher," Jackie Wilson

Born: Tony Sylvester (the Main Ingredient), 1941; Toni Braxton, 1968

1957 The Crests' first single, "My Juanita," was released. The record reached #86 pop, earning each of the five group members $17.50.

1957 The Penguins signed with Dootone after stints at Mercury and Atlantic failed. Meanwhile, the Harptones recorded "Cry Like I Cried" ($60) and the Universals' incredible "Again" ($200) and the Flamingos' "My Faith in You" ($30) were released.

1962 Little Richard performed on England's *Thank Your Lucky Stars* TV show in his British singing debut.

1967 The Staples Singers charted with a cover of Buffalo Springfield's "For What It's Worth," reaching #66 pop.

1978 It was reported by *Billboard* magazine that Marvin Gaye had filed for bankruptcy twice during the year, having been more than $7 million in the hole.

1979 Chaka Khan's "I'm Every Woman" charted, rising to become her first of four R&B #1s. Chaka (Yvette Stevens) assumed her new first name, which means "fire," while working for the Black Panthers' breakfast program in Chicago and her second name after marrying musician Hassan Khan at age seventeen.

1995 A one-time-only reunion of LaBelle on record resulted in the #1 dance chart hit "Turn It Out" from the film *To Wong Foo, Thanks for Everything, Julie Newmar*.

The Penguins

October

8

#1 R&B Song 1977: "It's Ecstasy When You Lay Down Next to Me," Barry White

Born: Doc Green (the Drifters), 1934; Fred Cash (the Impressions), 1940; Robert Bell (Kool & the Gang), 1950

1962 Sam Cooke and Little Richard toured England. Cooke would soon return to tour the U.S. with Jackie Wilson.

1977 Patti LaBelle had her first R&B solo chart single with "Joy to Have Your Love " (#31). She would have thirty-five more solo R&B hits through 1998.

1977 The Emotions (the Hutchinson Sisters Wanda, Sheila, and Jeanette) charted with "Don't Ask My Neighbors" (#44 pop, #7 R&B), the follow-up to their huge hit "Best of My Love" (#1 pop and R&B). It was the seventeenth of thirty R&B hits they would have between 1969 and 1984.

1988 Ziggy Marley & the Melody Makers tumbled onto the R&B hit list with "Tumblin' Down," reaching #1. Ziggy and the three members of the group were all children of the late Bob Marley and achieved something with their first chart single that he had not accomplished in his whole life, reaching the top of the charts.

1989 Chuck Berry received a star on the Hollywood Walk of Fame on the same day the legend's movie/biography *Hail! Hail! Rock and Roll* premiered.

1994 Fats Domino and Michael Bolton sang "Jailhouse Rock" at the Elvis Aaron Presley: The Tribute concert at the Pyramid Arena in Memphis, TN.

1995 Boyz II Men performed at Camden Yards in Baltimore, MD, home of the Baltimore Orioles baseball team, as part of the welcoming ceremonies for Pope John Paul II, who was there to celebrate Mass with more than 50,000 Catholics.

1996 Michael Jackson was denied a permit to hold a concert in Kuala Lumpur by the local government, which refused because of "the effect it would have on the young."

October

9

#1 Song 1961: "Hit the Road Jack," Ray Charles

Born: Overton Vertis "O.V." Wright, 1939

1952 The Five Keys recorded one of their most beautiful ballads, "Someday, Sweetheart" ($800), but their label, Aladdin Records showed little interest, waiting a year and a half before releasing it in March 1954.

1954 The Drifters' "Someday You"ll Want Me to Want You" (Atlantic $40) was issued, as was the Orioles' "If You Believe" (Jubilee $50).

1954 Shirley Gunter & the Queens, a Los Angeles female quartet, hit the R&B singles survey with "Oop Shoop" (#8). By the time "Oop Shoop" was released, Shirley (sister of Coasters member Cornel Gunter) was legally blind.

1964 The Supremes made their first visit to England and performed on the British TV show *Ready, Steady, Go!*

1976 Warm-voiced West Indian vocalist Joan Armatrading hit the album Top 200 for the first time with her self-titled LP, eventually reaching #67. She would go on to have eleven more albums chart in America through 1990.

1982 Diana Ross charted with "Muscles," reaching #10 pop (#4 R&B). The song was written and produced by Michael Jackson, and it's no coincidence that Muscles was the name of Michael's pet snake.

October

#1 R&B Song 1953: "Shake a Hand," Faye Adams

Born: Ivory Joe Hunter, 1914; Cyril Neville (the Neville Brothers), 1948; Mya (Mya Harrison), 1979

1914 Rhythm & blues pioneer Ivory Joe Hunter was born today. He started his career doing gospel music and ended it as a country performer, but his success was in R&B, where he had twenty-one chart hits between 1945 and 1958, including "I Almost Lost My Mind" and the classic "Since I Met You Baby," two of his four #1s.

1958 The Dells opened a weeklong engagement headlining at New York's Apollo Theater.

1962 Little Richard and Sam Cooke performed at the Granada Theater in Mansfield during their tour of England.

1972 The O'Jays' "Backstabbers" reached its pop peak in America at #3 while becoming their first (#14) of nine hits in England.

1992 HBO was reported to have paid $20 million for the rights to air Michael Jackson's recent performance in Bucharest, Romania. The show was called *From Bucharest: The Dangerous Tour*.

1991 Thanks to their 1977 hit "Brick House," the Commodores were inducted into the National Association of Brick Distributors Brick Hall of Fame in New York.

1992 Shabba Ranks charted with "Slow and Sexy," reaching #10 R&B. Obviously unconcerned about alienating a portion of his fan base, he would later be quoted in a British publication saying that "gays deserve crucifixion."

October

11

1952 Lloyd Price's second single became a two-sided hit when "Oooh, Oooh, Oooh" reached #4 R&B and its flip, "Restless Heart," reached #5.

1960 Aretha Franklin performed at a folk club, the Village Vanguard, in New York's Greenwich Village, doing standards. She was still thirteen days away from her first R&B chart single, "Today I Sing the Blues."

1969 Muddy Waters was critically injured in a car crash in Illinois but would recover to record and perform again.

1975 Stevie Wonder and Bob Marley & the Wailers performed at the National Arena in Kingston, Jamaica. A highlight was the bands' version of "I Shot the Sheriff" with Stevie on keyboards.

1986 When Janet Jackson's "When I Think of You" reached #1, she and her brother Michael became the first siblings to have solo #1s in the rock era. Michael's first #1 was "Ben" in 1972.

1991 B.B. King performed on Johnny Carson's *Tonight Show*.

1994 John Lee Hooker performed for the benefit of Willie Dixon's Blues Heaven Foundation at the House of Blues in Los Angeles.

Thelonious Monk

October

#1 R&B Song 1959: "Sea of Love,"
Phil Phillips with the Twilights

Born: Nappy Brown (Napoleon Brown
Goodson Culp), 1929; Sam Moore (Sam &
Dave), 1935; Melvin Franklin (the Temptations),
1942

1931 The Mills Brothers recorded "Tiger Rag," their debut single and the first of five #1 hits.

1956 An incredible all-group show featuring the Flamingos, the Channels, the Velours, the Solitaires, the Dells, and the Pearls was held at the Apollo Theater.

1957 While on a tour of Australia, Little Richard renounced rock 'n' roll and is said to have embraced God. He later revealed that when an engine on a plane he was flying on caught fire, he vowed that if he landed safely he would change his ways.

1962 The Soul Stirrers were the featured act at an all-gospel show at New York's Apollo Theater.

1966 The Jimi Hendrix Experience was formed in London.

1974 Gladys Knight & the Pips charted with "I Feel a Song in My Heart," written and produced by Tony Camillo. The song reached #21 pop and #1 R&B, earning another gold disc for the Atlanta quartet.

1994 Seal performed at Toad's Place in New Haven, Connecticut.

1996 Rapper/songwriter/producer Puff Daddy (Sean "Puffy" Combs) made his R&B chart debut with "No Time," reaching #9 and #18 pop. (The recording was billed "Lil' Kim featuring Puff Daddy"). Combs would later form the successful Bad Boy record label and go on to have forty-two R&B hits through 2004.

October

13

#1 R&B Song 1958: "It's All in the Game," Tommy Edwards

Born: Shirley Caesar, 1938; Dorothy Moore, 1947

1951 John Lee Hooker scored on the R&B charts with his 78 "I'm in the Mood," his sixth hit. In the next few years, it would sell more than one million copies, as would his first single, "Boogie Chillen.' "

1956 The Heartbeats' standard, "A Thousand Miles Away" (#53 pop, #5 R&B), was released. The group's lead singer, James Sheppard, wrote the standard while lounging in his bathtub.

1956 The Chips' "Rubber Biscuit" ($100), the Cleftones' "String Around My Heart" ($40), and the Cadillacs' "The Girl I Love" ($100) were issued.

1957 Specialty Records, upon hearing of Little Richard's plans to leave rock 'n' roll, scheduled a quick eight-song recording session before the rocker could enter a theological seminary.

1963 Brook Benton followed the Beatles on *Sunday Night at the London Palladium*, his British TV debut. In essence, the Beatles opened for him.

1977 Orlons member Shirley Brickley was shot to death. The Orlons were one of the hottest dance music groups of the early '60s, and Brickley was a member through all nine of their Top 100 hits. She was only thirty-two.

1979 Michael Jackson's "Don't Stop Till You Get Enough" reached #1 pop and R&B. It was his first solo #1 in seven years and reached #3 in England and #2 in Germany.

1979 The Sugar Hill Gang charted R&B with "Rapper's Delight," reaching #4 and #36 pop. They became the first pop success on the rap scene with what turned out to be their biggest hit.

1990 Fifty-two years after his death, Robert Johnson finally made the charts. A meticulously and lovingly compiled collection of Johnson's recordings titled *The Complete Recordings* started a thirty-one-week run and earned platinum status despite only reaching #80 pop.

October

#1 R&B Song 1967: "Soul Man," Sam & Dave

Born: Karyn White, 1965; Usher (Usher Raymond), 1978

1957 The Rays' timeless tune "Silhouettes" charted en route to #3 in the nation.

1960 The Vibrations, B.B. King, Joe Hinton, and Harvey Fuqua (of the Moonglows) performed at Chicago's Regal Theater.

1967 Gladys Knight & the Pips' "I Heard It Through the Grapevine" was released and quickly rose to #2.

1967 The Jimi Hendrix Experience peaked at #65 pop with "Purple Haze," their debut American release. Though Hendrix would have seven pop chart singles in his career, the psychedelic blues guitarist would never chart R&B. In fact he had more hits in England (eleven) than the U.S.

1967 Sam & Dave, Eddie Floyd, Otis Redding, Carla Thomas, Percy Sledge, Arthur Conley, and Booker T. & the M.G.'s brought the Soul Explosion Tour to England, performing at Finsbury Park in Astoria, London.

1972 Harold Melvin & the Blue Notes charted with their first Top Five hit, "If You Don't Know Me by Now," reaching #1 R&B and #3 pop.

1990 John Lee Hooker won Contemporary Blues Album of the Year for *The Healer*, Best Contemporary Male Blues Artist, and Blues Vocalist of the Year at the W.C. Handy Blues Awards at the National Blues Awards in Memphis.

1992 Seventy-five-year-old John Lee Hooker, still performing and touring, appeared on NBC-TV's The Tonight Show.

Usher

October

#1 R&B Song 1983: "Ain't Nobody," Rufus and Chaka Khan

Born: Victoria Spivey, 1906; Nellie Lutcher, 1915; Mickey "Guitar" Baker (Mickey & Sylvia), 1925; Marv Johnson, 1938; Tito Jackson, 1953; Ginuwine (Elgin Baylor Lumpkin), 1975

1906 Singer/pianist Victoria Spivey, one of the great '20s blues interpreters, was born. Best known for her "Black Snake Blues" in 1926, Victoria performed up until her death in 1976.

1954 The Five Keys began a week of performances at the Apollo Theater. They were followed by the Clovers.

1955 Johnny "Guitar" Watson made his R&B chart debut with "Those Lonely, Lonely Nights," reaching #10. He would go on to have twenty charters through 1995, including 1977's "A Real Mother for You," his biggest solo hit (#5 R&B and #41 pop). His biggest pop hit was as a member of the Shields, a doo-wop group from Los Angeles who reached #12 with the immortal "You Cheated" in 1958.

1976 More than three months after Tina Turner escaped the years of abuse from husband/producer Ike, Ike & Tina Turner announced that their nineteen-year professional association was over.

1983 Michael Jackson and Paul McCartney's second hit duet, "Say, Say, Say," charted, reaching #1 pop for six weeks.

1991 B.B. King performed in Seville, Spain, at Guitar Legends, a concert series that was part of Spain's forthcoming Expo 92.

1994 James Ingram performed in Washington, DC, at the Celebrity Tribute to Medicine, honoring twenty-eight extraordinary African-Americans in the fields of medicine and science. In his early days, Ingram worked for ATV Music Publishing, earning $50 for each demo he sang. Ingram, who started his performance career as a member of a band called Revelation Funk, ironically became one of the great balladeers of the '80s.

October

#1 R&B Song 1971: "Thin Line Between Love & Hate," the Persuaders

Born: Big Joe Williams, 1899; Mahalia Jackson, 1911; Sugar Pie De Santo (Umpeylia Marsema Balinton), 1935

1951 Little Richard made his first recordings for RCA Camden in Atlanta. The songs from this and a 1952 session, "Get Rich Quick" and "Every Hour," weren't released until 1956.

1957 The Chantels recorded their now legendary hit "Maybe" (#15 pop, #2 R&B) in a New York studio that was actually a refurbished church.

1962 Mary Wells and the Supremes began a two-month tour in Washington, DC, along with a slew of other Motown acts, including the Miracles, Little Stevie Wonder, and Marvin Gaye.

1986 Chuck Berry celebrated his sixtieth birthday (two days early) by participating in an all-star concert in St. Louis that was filmed as part of the film *Hail! Hail! Rock 'n' Roll*. Performers included Keith Richards, Julian Lennon, Robert Cray, Linda Ronstadt, and Eric Clapton.

1988 A benefit concert featuring Joan Armatrading called Smile Jamaica was held in London at the Dominion Theater for the victims of a hurricane in the Caribbean.

1990 Bo Diddley appeared on opening night of Guitar Legends, a concert series that was part of Expo '92 in Seville, Spain. Diddley was originally with a band called the Langley Avenue Jive Cats in Chicago and learned to play violin before he mastered the guitar.

1993 Aretha Franklin sang America's national anthem at the Skydome in Toronto before the first game of the World Series between the Philadelphia Phillies and the Toronto Blue Jays.

The Chantels

October

#1 Song 1960: "Save the Last Dance for Me," the Drifters

Born: William Randolph "Cozy" Cole, 1909; Ziggy Marley, 1968; Wyclef Jean, 1972

1909 William Randolph "Cozy" Cole, one of the premier jazz drummers of the '30s and '40s, was born today. Though he performed with the bands of Jonah Jones, Louis Armstrong, Cab Calloway, Benny Carter, and Benny Goodman, Cole is best remembered not for jazz but for his rock 'n' roll instrumental hit "Topsy Part 2," which reached #3 pop and #1 R&B for six weeks. He performed in the film *Make Mine Music* with Benny Goodman, and, in fact, "Topsy" had been a hit for Goodman in 1938 (#14 pop).

1953 The Orioles charted with "In the Mission of St. Augustine," reaching #7 R&B while becoming the last of their eleven hits.

1964 Martha & the Vandellas' scintillating "Dancing in the Streets" hit #2 pop. The song was written by producer Mickey Stevenson and Marvin Gaye and was originally turned down by Motown artist Mary Wells.

1970 The Jackson 5 reached #1 pop (five weeks) and R&B (six weeks) with "I'll Be There." It was their fourth chart topper in a row.

1992 Ike Turner; Lou Rawls; Chaka Khan; Bobby Womack; Earth, Wind & Fire; Al Green; and Bill Withers performed at two concerts in Redondo Beach, CA, as benefits for the family of deceased former Temptations member Eddie Kendricks.

Wyclef Jean

October

#1 Song 1969: "1 Can't Get Next to You," the Temptations

Born: Charles Edward Anderson "Chuck" Berry, 1926

1963 Muddy Waters, Sonny Boy Williamson, Memphis Slim, and Willie Dixon all performed at the American Negro Blues Festival at Fairfield Halls in Surrey, England.

1966 The Jimi Hendrix Experience made their performance debut in Paris at the Paris Olympia as the opening act for French superstar, Johnny Hallyday.

1967 Chuck Berry, the Platters, the Five Satins, and many others performed at Richard Nader's First Rock 'n' Roll Revival Concert at New York's Madison Square Garden. The concert ushered in the oldies revival still going on to this day.

1969 Ella Fitzgerald's album *Ella* scratched the Top 200 (#196), becoming her last of eleven chart LPs. She went on to become the most honored jazz vocalist in history.

1969 The Jackson 5 performed on ABC-TV's *Hollywood Palace*. It was their national TV debut. The Jacksons' father/manager, Joe Jackson, was a former guitar player for the Falcons of "You're So Fine" fame.

1986 For the first time in rock history, three females held the top three positions on the Hot 100 singles charts. They were Janet Jackson ("When I Think of You"), Tina Turner ("Typical Male"), and Cyndi Lauper ("True Colors").

1998 Stop the presses! B.B. King's famous guitar "Lucille" disappeared as the tour bus it was riding in got lost on its way to a performance in Kingston, New York. The mayor ordered police to comb the city until the bus, seen leaving town, was headed off and given a full escort to the theater.

October

#1 R&B Song 1959: "You Better Know It," Jackie Wilson

Born: Piano Red (William Lee Perryman), 1911; George McCrae, 1944; Wilbert Hart (the Delfonics), 1947; Jennifer Holliday, 1960

1954 The Penguins' classic "Earth Angel" (#8 pop, #1 R&B) was released.

1956 The world premiere of the rhythm and blues film *Rockin' the Blues* was held at New York's Apollo Theater. The cast included the Harptones, the Wanderers, the Hurricanes, and the Miller Sisters. The flick was followed by a stage show featuring the Wheels of "My Heart's Desire" fame.

1960 The Shirelles appeared on *American Bandstand* performing what had become their first R&B charter nine days earlier, "Tonight's the Night."

1963 Brook Benton began the British tour billed as The Greatest Record Show of 1963 along with Dion, Trini Lopez, Timi Yuro, and Lesley Gore. The tour's first stop was the Finsbury Park Astoria in London.

1964 Sonny Boy Williamson, Willie Dixon, Howlin' Wolf, and Lightnin' Hopkins began a five-day concert series at the second American Negro Blues Festival at Fairfield Halls in Surrey, England.

1991 Aaron Neville peaked at #8 pop with a cover of the Main Ingredient's 1972 hit "Everybody Plays the Fool." The original reached #3.

1991 The Temptations performed at the Alabama State Fair in Birmingham.

1992 Donna Summer performed at the Palais Omnisports in Paris, France.

Donna Summer

October

1885 Jelly Roll Morton, a pioneering and inventive jazz and blues pianist, was born today. He started playing in houses of prostitution in New Orleans and became one of the first jazz artists to use written arrangements. He's best known for songs like "King Porter Stomp" and his 1927 pop chart hits "Black Bottom Stomp" (#13) and "Original Jelly Blues" (#17).

1958 The Dubs recorded "Chapel of Dreams" (#74), their third and last pop hit. Surprisingly, none of their twenty-three superb singles ever charted R&B.

1958 Ivory Joe Hunter charted with "Yes I Want You," his twenty-first and final R&B hit, reaching #13.

1961 LaVern Baker, Johnnie & Joe, the Halos, Little Caesar & the Romans, the Mar-Keys, the Starlets, and Wade Flemons performed at the Regal Theater in Chicago.

1990 James Ingram's "I Don't Have the Heart" hit #1 pop. The single was his first credited solo Top 40 hit: his previous seven Top 40 entries were all either duets or were uncredited.

1991 Because Ray Charles was on a United Nations blacklist for performing in South Africa more than a decade earlier, a Swedish concert promoter canceled Ray's scheduled concert there.

1991 Seal performed at Sunderland Empire in England at the beginning of a European tour, during which his touring truck was blown over in Sweden. A kindly butcher loaned the performer a van, and Seal continued on to his scheduled show in Denmark.

October

21

#1 R&B Song 1944: "Gee, Baby, Ain't I Good to You," the King Cole Trio

Born: John Birks "Dizzy" Gillespie, 1917; Norman Wright (the Dell-Vikings), 1937; Garfield Bright (Shai), 1969

1917 Dizzy Gillespie, known as the father of modern jazz, was born. While performing with Cab Calloway's band, he joined Thelonius Monk and Charlie Parker, among others, in jam sessions that would result in the founding of bebop in 1941. He performed with such stalwarts as Duke Ellington, Earl "Fatha" Hines, Ella Fitzgerald, Benny Carter, Lucky Millinder, Sonny Rollins, and Stan Getz, to name a few. In 1953 someone fell on Dizzy's trumpet. When he realized it sounded better with the horn bent upwards, he left it that way as an enduring but unintentional trademark.

1950 Lionel Hampton, the King of the Vibraphone charted with "Everybody's Somebody's Fool," his fourteenth and final hit, reaching #6 R&B. The song would be a doo-wop pop charter for the Heartbeats seven years later.

1957 Bobby Day & the Hollywood Flames (sometimes known as the Satellites) recorded their soon-to-be hit "Buzz, Buzz, Buzz" (#11 pop, #5 R&B). Also in the revolving door group at the time was the Penguins' Curtis Williams.

1957 Sam Cooke, a former gospel singer (lead of the Soul Stirrers), debuted in the secular world with "You Send Me," an eventual #1 pop for three weeks and #1 R&B for six weeks.

1972 Curtis Mayfield's soundtrack album *Superfly*, from the blaxploitation film of the same name, reached #1 pop for four weeks.

1972 Johnny Nash bounced onto the R&B hit list with "I Can See Clearly Now," reaching only #38 but crossing over to #1 pop for four weeks. The heavy reggae influence on the record was provided by backing musicians the Wailers, Bob Marley's band.

1990 Janet Jackson performed at Wembley Arena in London during her European tour.

October

22

1960 Ike & Tina Turner's chart debut, "A Fool in Love," reached #2 R&B and #27 pop. Tina only got her break to sing on the record because Ike's scheduled singer failed to show up at the session.

1961 Though "The Twist" had been off the charts for ten months, Chubby Checker's appearance on Ed Sullivan's TV show re-ignited interest in the recording as the dance was already sweeping the world. Within a month it would chart again for another historic ride to #1.

1966 Muddy Waters performed at Jazz Expo '66 at the Hammersmith Odeon Theater in London. Asked how he felt about Mick Jagger and the Rolling Stones, who covered Muddy's songs, he said, "He took my music, but he gave me my name."

1970 Bo Diddley and Lightnin' Hopkins played at San Francisco's famed Fillmore West.

1974 James Brown, B.B. King, Lloyd Price, and the Spinners spent some time in Zaire to perform and to celebrate the world heavyweight title bout between George Foreman and Muhammad Ali.

Muddy Waters

1988 Prince performed in Worcester, Massachusetts, ending a twenty-city tour that included a benefit performance to establish a scholarship in the name of seventeen-year-old Frederick Weber, who was killed by a car while waiting on line for Prince tickets outside a record store in Boston.

1992 The man who never stopped touring, B.B. King began a concert series through South America starting in Caracas, Venezuela.

October

#1 R&B Song 1976: "The Rubberband Man," the Spinners

Born: Charlie Foxx, 1939; Barbara Anne Hawkins (the Dixie Cups), 1943; Perry Lee Tavares (Tavares), 1954; David Thomas (Take 6), 1966

1954 Black radio giant WDIA in Memphis began banning all records with what they considered suggestive lyrics, including the Drifters' "Honey Love," the Bees' "Toy Bell," and the entire "Annie" series of singles by the Midnighters.

1954 The Castelles' "Marcella" ($1,200) was issued. The Philadelphia group, with high tenor George Grant singing lead, was a forerunner of the falsetto rock 'n' roll groups to come.

1966 The Supremes became the first female vocal group to top the album charts when their *Supremes a Go Go* LP hit #1 today.

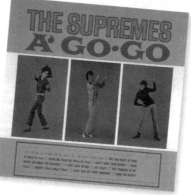

1966 The Jimi Hendrix Experience recorded for the first time, doing tracks on "Hey Joe" and "Stonefree" at London's De Lane Lea Studios.

1971 The Chi-Lites charted with the heavily narrated ballad "Have You Seen Her," which reached #3 pop and #1 R&B. The group was originally called the Hi-Lites before changing to avoid confusion with another act claiming the name. They added the "C" in homage to their hometown, Chicago.

1988 Michael Jackson visited the original Motown Records home in Detroit, where Berry Gordy Jr. started the label in 1959. While there, Michael donated $125,000 toward the Motown Museum.

1993 Toni Braxton had her first of two R&B #1 singles when "Seven Whole Days" reached the top. She had previously had three singles peak at #2 before reaching the milestone. They were "Give U My Heart," "Love Shoulda Brought You Home," and " Another Sad Love Song."

1996 The Fugees performed in Dublin, Ireland, at the Point, where their encouragement of the audience resulted in a near riot, with more than 100 people treated for a variety of injuries.

October 24

#1 Song 1970: "I'll Be There," the Jackson 5

Born: Sonny Terry, 1911; Willie Mabon, 1925; Big Bopper (J.P. Richardson), 1930; Bettye Swann (Betty Jean Champion), 1944; Monica (Monica Arnold), 1980

1942 Louis Jordan ushered in a new era in music when he entered the charts with his innovative and irreverent debut disc, "I'm Gonna Leave You on the Outskirts of Town," reaching #3 R&B. He would go on to have fifty-six more hits in only nine years.

1942 Billie Holiday hit the R&B hit parade with "Trav'lin' Light" as band vocalist with the Paul Whitman Orchestra. The record spent three weeks at #1.

1954 Clyde McPhatter recorded with the Drifters for the last time. The only single released from the session was "Everyone's Laughing."

1957 Chuck Willis, known as the Sheik of the Blues because he wore a turban, entered the R&B hit list with "C. C. Rider," reaching #1 and #12 pop. The recording kicked off "The Stroll" dance craze and was originally called "See See Rider Blues" like the 1925 recording by Ma Rainey.

1960 Jerry Butler's "He Will Break Your Heart" charted en route to #1 R&B for seven weeks (#7 pop), making it Butler's biggest solo hit of fifty-nine R&B chart entries between 1958 and 1983.

1960 Aretha Franklin charted with her first single release for Columbia Records, "Today I Sing the Blues," which reached #10 R&B. The Queen of Soul decided on a career in singing after hearing her mentor, Clara Ward, sing "Peace in the Valley" at a funeral. She would go on to have an astounding ninety-eight R&B chart singles through 2003.

1962 James Brown appeared at the Apollo Theater in Harlem, New York. The electrifying performance was taped for a live album, a rarity for a black artist at the time.

1987 Michael Jackson's "Bad" reached #1 pop and R&B, becoming his second of five #1s in a row.

1991 Fats Domino Day was proclaimed in New Orleans by Mayor Sidney Barthelemy.

October

25

1969 Gladys Knight & the Pips' "Friendship Train" (#17 pop, #2 R&B) became their lucky thirteenth of sixty-six pop charters between 1961 and 1994.

1970 Ray Charles appeared at Hammersmith Odeon in London while on a British tour.

1972 Hank Ballard and his latest group, the Midnight Lighters, charted with "From the Love Side," reaching #43 R&B. It would become the last of Ballard's twenty-two R&B hits since starting with the Royals in 1953. When the Midnighters split up in 1962, Ballard went solo. He toured with James Brown before recording with the Dapps and, lastly, the Midnight Lighters.

1974 Soul singer Al Green was burned while taking a shower when his girl-friend threw a pan of hot grits over him before shooting herself. Soon after, Green returned to gospel music, bought a church, and became its minister.

1980 Diana Ross had her twenty-sixth solo turn on the charts when "It's My Turn" sashayed onto the Hot 100 (#9).

1997 Rick James, Zapp, the Gap Band, and Cameo, among others, performed at Funk Fest at the Coca-Cola Starplex Amphitheater in Dallas, TX. It was James's comeback tour after spending two years in jail.

Al Green

October

#1 R&B Song 1985: "Part Time Lover," Stevie Wonder

Born: Charlie Barnet, 1913; William "Bootsy" Collins, 1951

1962 The first Motortown Revue began in Washington, DC, at the Howard Theater. Previous rock 'n' roll and R&B package tours had consisted of acts from various labels; this was the first time that only acts from one label, Motown, were on the bill. The acts included the Supremes, the Temptations, Mary Wells, the Marvelettes, Little Stevie Wonder, the Contours, Martha & the Vandellas, and Marvin Gaye.

1974 Dionne Warwick teamed with the Spinners and struck gold when their recording of "Then Came You" reached #1 today. After the recording session, Dionne indicated she didn't think much of the song. It was the first #1 single for both acts, even though Dionne had had thirty-nine previous pop charters over twelve years and the Spinners had reached the Top 100 thirteen times since 1961.

1974 B.B. King hooked up with his old chauffeur Bobby "Blue" Bland for *Together for the First Time...Live*. The album reached #43 pop and hung around the hit list for twenty weeks.

1989 Chubby Checker performed on a British tour starting at Swansea Leisure Center in Swansea, Wales. Earlier, Checker had met up with Hank Ballard, who wrote "The Twist," and had the original recording. Though never friends, the two worked together on a documentary about the twist craze in Kitchener, Ontario, Canada.

1992 Cissy Houston, Odetta, Judy Collins, Carly Simon, Lucy Simon (Carly's sister), Lesley Gore, Maureen McGovern, and the Roaches recorded "America the Beautiful" and "Michael Row the Boat Ashore" as the Clintones for torchlight parades across America to promote the Women Light the Way for Change cause.

1996 Former member of the all-sisters group the Braxtons, Toni Braxton reached the Hot 100 with "Un-Break My Heart" (#1), her eleventh hit since 1992.

1996 Curtis Mayfield, still partially paralyzed from a 1990 accident, charted with the album *New World Order*, his first album in five years, which he recorded flat on his back.

October

27

1958 The Flamingos' first single for End Records, "That Love Is You," was released, but its flip side, "Lovers Never Say Goodbye," became the classic hit (#52 pop, #25 R&B). "Lovers" was originally released under the title "Please Wait for Me."

1960 Ben E. King began his solo career after leaving the Drifters when he recorded four songs including "Spanish Harlem" and "Stand by Me."

1962 Dionne Warwick's debut disc "Don't Make Me Over," was released, rising to #5 R&B and #21 pop. It began a streak of thirty-three chart hits sung by Warwick and written and produced by Burt Bacharach and Hal David and was the start of one of the most successful long-term careers for a female artist in music history.

1966 Ike & Tina Turner's "A Love Like Yours" charted in England reaching #16. The song, produced by Phil Spector, was originally a B-side for Martha & the Vandellas.

1973 Gladys Knight & the Pips reached #1 pop (two weeks) and #1 R&B (four weeks) with "Midnight Train to Georgia." The song, written by country writer Jim Weatherly, was originally recorded by him as "Midnight Plane to Houston."

1988 Aaron Neville sang "Amazing Grace" at the New Orleans wedding of actor John Goodman.

Ike & Tina Turner

October

28

#1 R&B Song 1972: "I'll Be Around," the Spinners

Born: Cleo Laine, 1927; Telma Hopkins (Dawn), 1948

1964 The Supremes performed in the T.A.M.I. (Teenage Music International) show, a stage extravaganza that included James Brown, Chuck Berry, Marvin Gaye, Smokey Robinson & the Miracles, Lesley Gore, the Beach Boys, Jan & Dean, and the Rolling Stones, among others. The performance at the Civic Auditorium in Santa Monica, CA, was videotaped for British movie release and American TV broadcast.

1978 Chic's "Le Freak" charted on its way to #1 pop for five weeks and #1 R&B for six weeks. The disco hit of the age would go on to be one of the best-selling singles of the '70s.

1978 Turning everything she could get her hands on into a disco recording, Donna Summer reached #5 in Britain with the 1968 Richard Harris epic, "MacArthur Park." It would also make #1 pop and #8 R&B in the U.S.

1989 The Gap Band charted with "All of My Love," an eventual #1 R&B hit and the last of their four chart toppers, starting with "Burn Rubber" in 1980.

1993 George Benson and Patti Austin performed at London's Wembley Arena, kicking off a five-date British tour.

1994 Seal performed as the opening act for the Rolling Stones at the Oakland-Alameda County Stadium in Oakland, CA.

October

29

#1 R&B Song 1983: "All Night Long (All Night)," Lionel Richie

Born: Hadda Brooks, 1916; Eugene Daughtry (the Intruders), 1939; Randy Jackson, 1961

1902 The Dinwiddie Colored Quartet recorded for the first time, consequently becoming the first black voices on record. They sang a pop song and five spirituals for the Victor Talking Machine Company's Monarch Records in Camden, NJ.

1952 R&B group the Diamonds (Atlantic) recorded their initial four sides, including the exquisite debut disc "A Beggar for Your Kisses" ($1,500).

1955 The first R&B show held at Carnegie Hall in New York included Etta James & the Peaches, the Five Keys, Gene & Eunice, the Clovers, and Big Joe Turner.

1977 The disco group Chic charted for the first time with "Dance, Dance, Dance (Yowsah, Yowsah, Yowsah)" on their way to #6 pop and R&B. The group, helmed by producers Bernard Edwards and Nile Rodgers, were originally a '60s rock band called New World Rising and then a rock-fusion aggregation, the Big Apple Band, before freaking out altogether as Allah & the Knife-Wielding Punks (no kidding!) for a short time. A return to sanity soon followed with the much more acceptable Chic.

1979 Michael Jackson's album *Off the Wall* reached #3 and would go on to sell more than 10 million copies around the world.

1983 Lionel Richie Day was proclaimed by the mayor of Richie's hometown, Tuskegee, AL.

1991 Interstate highway 55 in Jackson, MS, was renamed the B.B. King Freeway.

1997 The O'Jays filed a copyright infringement suit for $1.5 million against rapper Master P for his use of their 1978 hit "Brandy" in his "I Miss My Homies."

#1 R&B Song 1965: "Rescue Me," Fontella Bass

Born: Eddie Holland, 1939

1952 The "5" Royales recorded their biggest hit, "Baby, Don't Do It" (#1 R&B, $400), and the legendary "Laundromat Blues" ($120).

1954 The Midnighters "Annie's Aunt Fannie" (#10 R&B, $60) and the Rivileers' "Eternal Love" ($120) were released. In addition, the Charms, with Otis Williams on lead (not the Temptations' Otis Williams), charted with "Hearts of Stone," reaching #1 for an astounding nine weeks R&B while rising to #15 pop. It was a tremendous feat considering that the pasteurized pop version by the Fontane Sisters reached #1 pop.

1971 Michael Jackson charted with his solo debut, "Got to Be There," reaching #4 on both the pop and R&B hit lists. Jackson was influenced from childhood by the recordings of Jackie Wilson and James Brown. The single would be the first of forty-six pop hits for the King of Pop through 2001.

1971 "You Are Everything" by the Stylistics hit the R&B charts, rising to #10 (#9 pop). It was the third of twelve straight Top 10 R&B hits.

1994 Little Richard performed at Washington, DC's Ford Theater at the Gala for the President with a beaming President Clinton looking on.

1998 The Vocal Group Hall of Fame and Museum in Sharon, PA, held its inaugural induction, hosted by legendary deejays Jack "The Rapper" Gibson, Martha Jean "The Queen" Steinberg (the first black female deejay), and publisher/author Jay Warner. Among the fourteen groups enshrined were the Platters, the Drifters (with Clyde McPhatter), the Supremes, the Five Blind Boys of Mississippi, the Ravens, the Mills Brothers, the Golden Gate Quartet, and Sonny Til & the Orioles.

October

#1 Song 1964: "Baby Love," the Supremes

Born: Ethel Waters, 1896; Illinois Jacquet, 1922; Julia Lee, 1902; Otis Williams (the Temptations), 1941; Bernard Edwards (Chic), 1952

1953 Perhaps the most perfect R&B vocal group single ever issued, the Flamingos' third 45, "Golden Teardrops" ($1,200), was released.

1959 Bo Diddley had his biggest pop hit when "Say Man" reached #20 (#3 R&B) today. Diddley (actually Otha Ellas Bates) was nicknamed after a one stringed African guitar called a "Bo Diddley." He decided to be a blues musician after hearing "Boogie Chillen' " by John Lee Hooker.

1960 Gary "U.S." Bonds charted with his debut 45, "New Orleans," which went on to #5 R&B and #6 pop. Bond's producer decided to change his name from Gary Anderson to "U.S." Bonds because of the government's successful and highly publicized campaign for people to "Buy U.S. Bonds." Gary himself did not find out about the name change until he heard his recording on the radio. Why should anyone tell him? He was only the artist!

1960 The Blue Notes, a doo-wop group from Philadelphia, charted with "My Hero," reaching #19 R&B and #78 pop. The group would go on to become Harold Melvin & the Blue Notes, featuring Teddy Pendergrass.

1964 Ray Charles was arrested by customs agents after arriving at Logan Airport in Boston for a show at the Back Bay Theatre. He was charged with possession of narcotics after a hypodermic needle, a small amount of marijuana, heroin, and a spoon were found in his possession.

1992 Thirty years after it charted in America, John Lee Hooker's "Boom Boom" peaked at #16 in Britain, his highest of four chart singles there. Patience must be a virtue: he was seventy-five at the time.

November

#1 R&B Song 1952: "My Song,"
Johnny Ace & the Beale Streeters

Born: Beula "Sippie" Wallace, 1898;
Phil Terry (the Intruders), 1943

1962 John Lee Hooker performed at San Francisco's Sugar Hill Club.

1976 Britain's Hot Chocolate charted, reaching #3 pop and #6 R&B with "You Sexy Thing."

1984 LL Cool J, Kurtis Blow, the Fat Boys, the Beastie Boys, and others appeared in the early rap movie *Krush Groove*.

1986 Anita Baker's "Sweet Love" peaked at #8 on the pop charts today. Baker started her career as lead singer of the Detroit group Chapter 8, which had five R&B chart singles starting in 1979. An international bestseller, "Sweet Love" even reached #13 in England.

1992 Nancy Wilson hosted a benefit at UCLA for the National Council of Negro Women. Among the guests was Dionne Warwick.

1993 Public Enemy's Flavor Flav was arrested in the Bronx for the attempted murder of his neighbor. Claiming that the man had slept with his girlfriend, the rapper said he had to protect her honor by shooting at the man. Two years later he would be sentenced to only ninety days in jail for attempted murder.

1996 Bob Marley's *Legend* was certified as having sold 9 million copies, the best-selling reggae album ever.

1997 Rick James charted R&B with his twelfth album, *Urban Rhapsody*, on the Private I Records label. It reached #31 and #170 pop. Many of the songs were written during James's time incarcerated at Fulsom Prison between 1994 and 1996.

November

#1 R&B Song 1985: "Part Time Lover," Stevie Wonder

Born: Earl Carroll (the Cadillacs), 1937; Maxine Nightingale, 1952; Alvin Chea (Take 6), 1967

1956 The Platters continued their international popularity with "My Prayer," reaching #4 in England.

1959 The Ben E. King lineup of the Drifters charted with a two-sided hit, "True Love, True Love" (#33 pop, #5 R&B) and "Dance with Me" (#15 pop, #2 R&B). Though King sang lead on "Dance," Johnny Lee Williams was featured on "True Love."

1962 Little Richard performed the second of fourteen days at the Star Club in Hamburg, West Germany. Also on the bill with Richard was a young unknown group called the Beatles, whose bass player, Paul McCartney, had reportedly asked Richard if he could teach him his vocal style.

1985 Stevie Wonder hit #1 on the pop, adult contemporary, R&B, and dance/disco charts with "Part Time Lover." It was the first time in music history that a single had topped all four charts.

1990 The O'Jays and Regina Belle performed at the Topworld Casino in Atlantic City, NJ.

1997 Whitney Houston starred in *Cinderella* as fairy godmother to Brandy. The ABC-TV movie cost more than $10 million to make, a record for the time.

The Platters

November

1948 John Lee Hooker recorded "Boogie Chillen' " in Detroit, his first session ever.

1951 Arthur "Big Boy" Crudup charted with "I'm Gonna Dig Myself a Hole" (#9), the last of his six R&B titles. With Crudup it was all or nothing, as each of his six chart singles out of numerous releases all made the Top 10.

1955 The Platters' single "The Great Pretender" was issued. The group's manager, Buck Ram, in a euphoric state after their debut 45, "Only You," reached #1 (#5 pop), informed the record label that he already had the band's next hit, entitled "The Great Pretender." Ram was obviously a confident individual, as he had not yet *written* "The Great Pretender" (the song title perfectly described him). His prophecy, however, was correct as the "new" single did reach #1 both pop and R&B.

1956 The Cadillacs' "Rudolph the Red-Nosed Reindeer" (#11) was released. It began the official holiday season but didn't chart until ten days after Christmas.

1962 The Crystals' smash, "He's a Rebel" hit #1 for the first of two weeks. Unfortunately for the New York–based Crystals, it wasn't their voices on the hit. Producer Phil Spector used the Blossoms, a West Coast back-up group featuring Darlene Wright (later Darlene Love) when he needed to rush-release the 45 so as to beat Vickie Carr's rival version to the marketplace.

1984 Billy Ocean's "Caribbean Queen" reached #1 pop and #1 on the dance charts. The song was originally released as "European Queen," and after it became a hit was redone for certain markets as "African Queen."

1988 Most legendary singers get a day in their honor, but Michael Jackson got a month when Los Angeles Mayor Tom Bradley proclaimed it Michael Jackson Month.

1989 The Coasters, Chuck Berry, Bo Diddley, the Five Satins, Jay & the Americans, and the Skyliners, among others, performed in a twentieth anniversary Rock 'n' Roll Revival concert.

November

4

#1 Song 1972: "I Can See Clearly Now," Johnny Nash

Born: Harry Elston (the Friends of Distinction), 1938; Puff Daddy (Sean Combs), 1969

1948 The Ravens' recording of "White Christmas" (the forerunner of the Drifters' version) was issued.

1957 Jackie Wilson's "Reet Petite," his first single under his own name peaked at #62 in the U.S. while having a much bigger impact in England, where it rose to #6. Wilson originally sang under the name Sonny Wilson for Dizzy Gillespie's Dee Gee Records, recording "Rainy Day Blues" in 1951.

1964 Martha & the Vandellas visited Britain and performed on the popular TV show *Top of the Pops*.

1967 The Supremes' "In and Out of Love" (#9 pop) was released today.

1987 Bo Diddley and Ron Wood (of the Faces and the Rolling Stones), performing as the Gunslingers, began a North American tour in Columbus, OH, at the Newport Music Hall.

1990 Tina Turner's Foreign Affair Tour ended in Rotterdam, the Netherlands. By the time it was over, more than three million people had seen Tina strut her stuff.

1991 Ben E. King, the Four Tops, the Stylistics, Jimmy Ruffin, Edwin Starr, and Junior Walker & the All-Stars performed in Bognor Regis, West Sussex, England.

1996 A news report stated that Michael Jackson's girlfriend, Debbie Rowe, was pregnant by artificial insemination and was allegedly to receive $528,000 to have the baby. Jackson would later say, "I am thrilled that I will soon be a father and am looking forward, with great anticipation to having this child." The loving couple would be married ten days later in Australia. Upon hearing the news, Elton John said of Australia that it's where "all the loonies get married."

November

#1 R&B Song 1955: "Only You," the Platters

Born: Jack McVea, 1914; Ike Turner, 1931

1955 The Heartbeats' "Crazy for You" ($600) was released. Though never charting nationally, it became a New York–area standard.

1958 After only three singles together, including the legendary "For Your Precious Love," Jerry Butler & the Impressions split up.

1966 Muddy Waters performed at the Fillmore West in San Francisco along with rock band Quicksilver Messenger Service.

1989 Chaka Khan began a European tour in Hamburg, West Germany.

1994 Brandy's debut single, "I Wanna Be Down," went gold while still rising up the charts on its way to #6 pop. The fifteen-year-old beauty was already an accomplished actress, having appeared on the TV shows *Thea* and *Moesha*.

1998 Fats Domino was honored with the National Medal of the Arts, which was presented to him by President Clinton at the White House.

Fats Domino

November

6

#1 R&B Song 1943: "Don't Cry, Baby," Erskine Hawkins & His Orchestra

Born: Eloise Laws, 1943

1954 B.B. King charted R&B with "You Upset Me Baby," becoming his fourth #1 in four years out of only eight chart entries. Though King would register seventy-five R&B charters through 1992, he would never have another #1.

1961 The Chantels' only up-tempo hit, "Well, I Told You" (#29 pop), was issued today.

1962 A European tour called the American Folk Blues Festival began at the Kongress Halle in Frankfurt, West Germany, and included T-Bone Walker, John Lee Hooker, Sonny Terry & Brownie McGee, and Memphis Slim.

1971 Isaac Hayes's soundtrack album from the movie *Shaft* hit #1 pop (#2 R&B). The album was performed and composed by Hayes and would be his only #1.

1982 Marvin Gaye's "Sexual Healing" reached #1 R&B (#33 pop), and stayed there for an astounding ten weeks. The last record to top the R&B charts for that long had been Ray Charles's "I Can't Stop Loving You," twenty years earlier. It was Marvin's fifty-sixth of a career fifty-seven pop chart hits between 1962 and 2001 and his thirteenth #1 R&B smash of sixty-three chart hits through 1990.

1982 Grandmaster Flash & the Furious Five's "The Message" reached #62 pop and #4 R&B while attaining gold status in less than a month.

1982 Donna Summer led an all-star backup group of Dionne Warwick, Stevie Wonder, Michael Jackson, James Ingram, Lionel Richie, and Kenny Loggins in the "State of Independence" single, but it wasn't enough, as it only reached #41 pop and #31 R&B today.

1997 Janet Jackson was honored as the Best Female Artist at MTV's European awards in Rotterdam, the Netherlands.

1998 While performing at Denver's Mile High Stadium, Rick James suffered the popping of a blood vessel. After leaving the stage to regroup for a few minutes, the "Superfreak" came back and finished his set, after which he went to the hospital.

November

#1 Song 1960: "Save the Last Dance for Me," the Drifters

Born: John Jordan (the Four Vagabonds), 1913; Delecta "Dee" Clark, 1938

1942 Pioneering pianist/composer Fats Waller jumped on the R&B charts for the first and last time with "The Jitterbug Waltz," rising to #6. Waller's distinctive vocals and popular stride piano style earned him sixty-three pop hits between 1929 and 1943. His first of those sixty-three hits was the immortal "Ain't Misbehavin' " (#17), which was the name of the '70s Broadway musical honoring his songs.

1953 Blues pianist and singer Memphis Slim & His House Rockers entered the R&B hit list with "The Come Back," reaching #3.

1960 The Heartbeats' perennial "A Thousand Miles Away" charted for the second time (#96 pop) in four years.

1969 Ike & Tina Turner were the opening act on a Rolling Stones U.S. tour that started in Denver.

1981 The Four Tops, who had just signed with Casablanca Records, hit #11 pop and #1 R&B with their debut on the label, "When She Was My Girl."

1995 Michael Jackson reportedly merged his ATV Music Catalog with Sony for a sum in the neighborhood of $90 to $100 million.

1996 John Lee Hooker was given the Blues Foundation's Lifetime Achievement Award at B.B. King's Blues Club in Los Angeles.

Fats Waller

November

#1 R&B Song 1975: "Low Rider," War

Born: Laura Webb (the Bobbettes), 1941;
Gerald Alston (the Manhattans), 1942;
Minnie Riperton, 1947

1952 B.B. King and his legendary guitar, Lucille, had their second #1 R&B in a row with "You Know I Love You," also his second chart single. At the time, King had his own radio show in Memphis called *The Sepia Swing Show*. Lucille was named when a fight broke out at a show and a fire started. King, realizing he had left his guitar inside during the confusion, ran back in for it. He later found out the fight was over a girl named Lucille.

1969 The Supremes' swan song as an entity including Diana Ross, "Someday We'll Be Together," was the last of the group's twelve #1s, but, technically, it was not the Supremes at all. Ross wound up recording the song with vocal backing studio pros the Waters, along with Johnny Bristol on bass.

1970 The Four Tops performed on *The Ed Sullivan Show* on CBS-TV.

1991 Barry White was a guest on *The Arsenio Hall Show*.

1997 The O'Jays' "Baby You Know" charted, reaching #34 R&B and #76 pop, giving them a total of fifty-nine R&B hits and thirty pop winners over a thirty-four year chart life.

1999 Gwen Gordy Fuqua, who had convinced her family to stake brother Berry Gordy Jr. the $800 he needed to start Motown Records, died in San Diego. Fuqua, former wife of Moonglows leader Harvey Fuqua, started Motown's artist development department, guiding the careers of acts like the Supremes and the Temptations. She was seventy-one.

November

9

#1 R&B Song 1963: "It's All Right," the Impressions

Born: Leroy Fann (Ruby & the Romantics), 1936

1959 Johnny Mathis charted with one of the great recordings of the fifties, "Misty," reaching #10 R&B and #12 pop. Mathis was a track star in college who was invited to the Olympic tryouts; lucky for music lovers, he chose a singing career instead. He started as a jazz singer and had more than seventy pop chart albums and forty-five pop hits through 1984.

1963 The Shirelles began their first British tour at the Regal Cinema in Edmonton, London, along with Little Richard and Duane Eddy.

1965 Wilson Pickett made his performance debut in London at the Scotch Saint James Club backed by members of the Animals.

1968 Eivets Rednow peaked at #66 pop with the title song from the film Alfie. After sixteen pop hits in a row it seems that Eivets wanted to test his audience's loyalty to his sound, if not to his name. Eivets Rednow is Stevie Wonder spelled backwards.

1985 The Winans gospel group crossed over to secular music with the chart debut of "Let My People Go" (#42 R&B).

1996 En Vogue charted en route to #1 R&B (#2 pop) with "Don't Let Go (Love)" from the film *Set It Off*, starring Queen Latifah. It was the last of their six #1s of sixteen charters through 1998 and eighteen pop hits through 2001.

En Vogue

November

10

#1 R&B Song 1962: "Do You Love Me," the Contours

Born: Hubert Laws, 1939; Eve (Eve Jihan Jeffers), 1978

1956 The Dells' classic "Oh What a Nite" charted on its way to #4 R&B. It would be the first of forty-seven R&B hits through 1992.

1958 LaVern Baker's "I Cried a Tear" was released. It became her biggest hit (#6) of twenty Top 100 singles between 1955 and 1966.

1958 Two future standards, "Smoke Gets in Your Eyes" by the Platters (#1 pop, #3 R&B) and "Sixteen Candles" by the Crests (#20 pop, #4 R&B), were released.

1958 B.B. King charted with "Please Accept My Love," reaching #9 R&B. The blues giant was singing a doo-wop song as lead singer for the group the Vocal Chords.

1958 James Brown & the Famous Flames hit the R&B charts with their eventual #1, "Try Me." Brown would go on to have seventeen R&B #1s through 1998. It was also his first Top 100 entry at #48. Pretty good for a kid raised by his aunt in an Augusta, GA, bordello.

1991 Roberta Flack performed at a benefit at Symphony Hall in Boston to help families of ill children at the Cohen Hillel Academy in Marblehead, MA.

1999 The Staple Singers performed at a rainforest benefit at the Hammerstein Ballroom in New York.

1996 Tina Turner was interviewed on *60 Minutes*, the acclaimed newsmagazine on CBS-TV.

Roberta Flack

316

November

#1 R&B Song 1978: "I'm Every Woman," Chaka Khan

Born: Annisteen Allen, 1920; LaVern Baker (Delores Williams), 1929

1957 The Valiants' "This Is the Night" (#69 pop) and Lee Andrews & the Hearts' "Teardrops" (#20 pop, #4 R&B) were released.

1958 Hank Ballard & the Midnighters recorded the original version of "The Twist," which would later become one of the most important records in rock 'n' roll history as sung by Ballard sound-alike, Chubby Checker. Ballard's version was based on the Drifters' 1953 recording, "Whatcha Gonna Do."

1960 Savannah Churchill, Sonny Boy Williamson, Little Willie John, the Sheppards, and the Upsetters played the Regal Theater in Chicago.

1967 Wilson Pickett's version of his early influence Lloyd Price's "Stagger Lee" charted on its way to #13 R&B, #22 pop. The song was based on legendary folk blues artist Mississippi John Hurt's '30s recording, "Stack-O-Lee."

1978 Donna Summer's disco version of the 1968 Richard Harris hit "MacArthur Park" climbed to #1 and stayed there for three weeks.

1978 The Pointer Sisters' "Fire" charted, reaching #2 pop and #14 R&B.

1991 In a very funny episode, Aretha Franklin appeared on CBS-TV's Murphy Brown, playing herself opposite a worshipping but totally out-of-tune Candice Bergen (as Murphy Brown). Their show closing "You Make Me Feel Like a Natural Woman" was the highlight of the season.

1991 Isaac Hayes, Natalie Cole, Stevie Wonder, and Dionne Warwick, among others, performed at the Celebrity Theater in Los Angeles to raise money for cancer patient and former Motown star Mary Wells. Sadly, Wells would die within nine months at age forty-nine.

November

#1 R&B Song 1966: "Love Is a Hurtin' Thing," Lou Rawls

Born: Ruby Nash (the Romantics), 1939; Jimmy Hayes (the Persuasions), 1943; Booker T. Jones (Booker T. & the M.G.'s), 1944

1953 The Drifters recorded their eventual #2 R&B hit, "Such a Night."

1955 *Billboard* magazine named Fats Domino the nation's favorite R&B artist.

1957 *Jamboree*, one of the early rock 'n' roll movies, premiered in Hollywood with a cast of current hit acts including Fats Domino, Louis Lymon & the Teenchords (Frankie Lymon's brother), Count Basie & His Orchestra, Jerry Lee Lewis, and Carl Perkins, among others. In England the film was called *Disc Jockey Jamboree*.

1983 Cincinnati-based sextet the Deele made their R&B chart debut today with "Body Talk," eventually rising to #3 (#77 pop). They would have eight charters in all through 1988 while birthing the superstar writing/production team of L.A. and Babyface. Antonio "L.A." Reid Rooney was nicknamed for the hat he doggedly wore and was the son of the '60s hit makers Brenda Reid and Herb Rooney of the Exciters.

1983 James Ingram charted with his first album, *It's Your Night*, which reached only #46 pop despite selling more than 500,000 copies. Ingram's early days included a two-year stint recording and touring with Ray Charles.

1994 Babyface made his solo performance debut at a fund-raiser for the Boarder Baby Project in Washington, DC. Also performing were El Debarge and the group After Seven, which included Babyface's two brothers, Melvin and Kevon.

1998 Ex-Fugee member Lauryn Hill gave birth to a daughter, Seluh Marley, in New York. The father was her fiancé, Rohan Marley, son of reggae star Bob Marley.

November

13

#1 R&B Song 1971: "Inner City Blues,"
Marvin Gaye

Born: Louisa "Blue Lu" Barker, 1913;
Jeanette "Baby" Washington, 1940

1954 The Moonglows' first hit, "Sincerely" (#20 pop, #1 R&B), and "Shoo Doo Be Doo" by their alter ego, the Moonlighters, were released the same day. Also released were the Flamingos' "Blues in a Letter" ($600), the Orioles' "Runaround" ($50), and the Platters "Shake It Up Mambo" ($200), all collectors' rarities.

1961 Gene McDaniels charted with "Tower of Strength," reaching #5 both R&B and pop. McDaniels started out singing in a gospel-turned-R&B group in Nebraska. They recorded as the Sultans in 1954 and later became the Admirals. As a writer, McDaniels is best known for creating Roberta Flack's smash "Feel Like Makin' Love."

1963 Picking up on Motown's Motortown Revue idea, Atlantic Records began its own Atlantic Caravan of Stars and pulled into the Apollo Theater with an all-Atlantic roster including the Drifters, Ben E. King, Rufus Thomas, Otis Redding, the Falcons, Doris Troy, and King Curtis and his crew.

1965 The Crystals embarked on their second Dick Clark Caravan of Stars tour, starting in New Haven, CT, along with the Supremes, Dee Dee Sharp, the Drifters, Bobby Freeman, Brian Hyland, and Lou Christie.

1975 British songstress Joan Armatrading began a thirty-city tour of the United Kingdom, along with labelmates Supertramp, at Colston Hall, Bristol, Avon, England. Armatrading was a self-taught musician on piano and guitar and was influenced by the first album she bought at nineteen, Van Morrison's *Astral Weeks*.

November

14

#1 R&B Song 1942: "Stormy Monday Blues," Earl Hines

Born: Clarence Carter, 1936; Cornel Gunter (the Coasters), 1938

1942 The Royal Harmony Quartet charted with "Praise the Lord and Pass the Ammunition," reaching #10 R&B. The song was motivated by the speech of a Navy chaplain after the attack on Pearl Harbor. The group would later record as the Jubalaires.

1950 Billy Ward & the Dominoes made their recording debut with four sides including "Do Something for Me" (#6 R&B, $800). Before recording, the group called themselves the Ques.

1960 The Shirelles (formerly known as the Poquellos), with writer Carole King playing drums, had their soon-to-be standard "Will You Love Me Tomorrow" released today.

1960 Ray Charles's "Georgia on My Mind" became his first pop #1 and second million-seller. After hearing his chauffeur repeatedly sing the standard, Ray decided to record it.

1961 Ray Charles was arrested in his Indianapolis hotel room after a performance and charged with heroin possession. The secret he had kept about his addiction since he was sixteen had now become public. A judge would later determine that the search was illegal, violating Charles's constitutional rights, and throw the case out.

1967 The Jimi Hendrix Experience began a British tour at the Royal Albert Hall, playing twice a night for fifteen days along with Pink Floyd and others.

1970 Gladys Knight & the Pips' "If I Were Your Woman" (#9 pop, #1 R&B) was released on this day.

1970 The Spinners charted in Britain with "It's a Shame," reaching #20. Because there was a folk group by the same name, they changed their name, first to the Motown Spinners and later the Detroit Spinners, becoming the only American act to be known by two different names in different countries.

November

15

1969 The Jackson 5's debut disc, "I Want You Back," charted en route to #1. It was their first of thirty-one Top 100 hits over twenty years.

1975 Jackie Wilson, who in 1951 started his chart career with a group (the Dominoes), ended it with a group after a seventeen-year Hall of Fame career as a solo artist. He charted today singing lead for the Chi-Lites in a one-off recording, "Don't Burn No Bridges," which reached #91 R&B. It was his forty-seventh R&B entry. His last pop hit was "You Got Me Walking," which was his fifty-fourth single on the Top 100.

1975 Harold Melvin & the Blue Notes charted with "Wake Up Everybody," reaching #1 R&B and #12 pop. It was the group's fourth #1 in three years and would be revitalized in 2005 by Babyface and many other stars on a compilation album of the same name produced for the Democratic National Committee to motivate young people to vote.

1989 James Ingram and Patti LaBelle began a five-month U.S. tour at the Orpheum Theater in Minneapolis.

1990 Stevie Wonder received the Honorary Global Founders "Don't Drive Drunk" Award from the Recording Artists Against Drunk Driving. This may not be as ironic as it sounds. Though Wonder had been blind since birth, rumors persisted that he liked to go out to uninhabited areas with his friends and drive by himself at top speeds to his heart's content while they followed (presumably at a safe distance) in a second car.

1991 Diana Ross performed at London's Wembley Arena.

1994 Gladys Knight and Stevie Wonder sang "For Once in My Life" with Frank Sinatra on his *Duets II* album, released today.

Frank Sinatra's Duets II

November

16

1873 "W.C." Handy, "the Father of the Blues," was born in Florence, AL. The first to put jazz and blues on paper, Handy was a brilliant composer who created classics like "St. Louis Blues" (1914), reportedly the most recorded song of all time, and "Memphis Blues" (1912). The bandleader, cornet player, and music teacher first charted pop with "Livery Stable Blues" (#7) in 1918. He died in 1958, the year Nat King Cole portrayed him in a film about his life.

1946 Erskine Hawkins & His Orchestra charted with "Hawk's Boogie," reaching #3 R&B.

1963 The Coasters recorded "Tain't Nothin' to Me" (#64). It was their last chart single of the '60s and the B-side of "Speedo's Back in Town" featuring Cadillacs lead Earl "Speedo" Carroll.

1968 Jimi Hendrix's *Electric Ladyland* album topped the American charts, becoming his biggest seller of twenty-eight career albums.

1986 Robert Cray won six W.C. Handy Awards at the seventh annual National Blues Awards Show, hosted by B.B. King.

1991 R. Kelly charted with "She's Got the Vibe," his debut single, reaching #7 R&B. It would take the disc four more months to reach the pop charts, leveling off at #59. Kelly's popularity is reflected by the fact that he had amassed thirty pop hits by 2002 and sixty-seven R&B winners by 2004. The Donny Hathaway–inspired singer/keyboardist's first name is Robert.

November

17

1956 The Heartbeats' "A Thousand Miles Away" charted (#53 pop, #5 R&B), and the Continentals' inspiring "Dear Lord" ($200) was released.

1958 Jackie Wilson's supreme classic, "Lonely Teardrops," charted R&B reaching #1 for seven weeks and #7 pop.

1958 The Chanters' "Over the Rainbow" was issued.

1964 Marvin Gaye, who was in England for TV performances, left to visit Dionne Warwick after hearing she had had a car accident.

1996 Patti LaBelle, Stevie Wonder, and Luther Vandross performed at Celebrate the Dream: 50 Years of *Ebony* Magazine at Los Angeles' Shrine Auditorium.

1998 Janet Jackson, while on a South African Tour, met President Nelson Mandela, and all twenty-nine of his grandchildren, at his home.

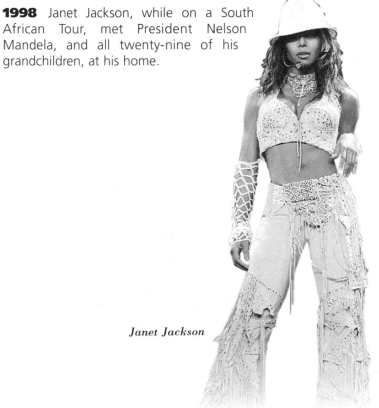

Janet Jackson

November

#1 R&B Song 1972: "If You Don't Know Me by Now," Harold Melvin & the Blue Notes

Born: Hank Ballard (the Midnighters), 1936; Fabolous (John Jackson), 1979

1956 Chuck Berry performed at the Forum in Wichita, KS, on a bill with the Platters, Frankie Lymon & the Teenagers, the Clovers, Clyde McPhatter, and Bill Haley & the Comets, among others.

1956 Fats Domino performed "Blueberry Hill" on Ed Sullivan's CBS-TV show.

1957 Bobby Day & the Satellites charted with "Little Bitty Pretty One," reaching #57 pop. The single was beaten out in a cover battle by Thurston Harris & the Sharps, whose version reached #6. It seems many vocal groups of the day were using aliases: the Satellites were actually the Hollywood Flames, and the Sharps would later become the Rivingtons.

1972 Stevie Wonder charted with "Superstition," reaching #1 pop and R&B, his first pop #1 since "Fingertips, Pt. 2" in 1963. Wonder originally wrote the song for rocker Jeff Beck.

1995 The James Bond film *Goldeneye* premiered with the Tina Turner theme song. The single reached its #10 peak in England in its first week of release, but it would only make it to #89 R&B and #102 pop in America.

1996 Lionel Richie received a Lifetime Achievement Award in London at the first Music of Black Origin (MOBO) ceremonies.

Lionel Richie

November

#1 R&B Song 1966: "Knock on Wood," Eddie Floyd

Born: Warren "Pete" Moore (the Miracles), 1939

1955 The Cues, known mostly as a studio backup group for the likes of Atlantic stars Ruth Brown and LaVern Baker, had their first chart single with "Burn That Candle" (#86 pop).

1962 Influential '50s blues star Savannah Churchill made a comeback performance at the Room at the Bottom in New York's Greenwich Village. She had been badly injured several years earlier when a fan fell on top of her.

1964 The Supremes became the first all-girl group to reach #1 in Britain when "Baby Love" hit the coveted top spot.

1968 The Supremes performed at the Royal Variety Show in London before Queen Elizabeth.

1971 B.B. King began a European tour in London on his twenty-fifth anniversary in the music business.

1979 Chuck Berry left prison after a stay for tax evasion.

1992 Janet Jackson's *Rhythm Nation 1814* album was certified six times platinum (six million copies) by the RIAA.

1995 Little Milton, Bobby "Blue" Bland, Johnny "Guitar" Watson, and Clarence Carter appeared at the Grand Olympic Auditorium in Los Angeles on the last night of their Heavyweights of Blues caravan tour.

1998 Natalie Cole sang "They Can't Take That Away from Me" at Frank Sinatra's eightieth birthday party at the Shrine Auditorium in Los Angeles. If that didn't do it for Ol' Blue Eyes, Little Richard's rendition of "Old Black Magic" surely did.

November

20

#1 R&B Song 1971: "Have You Seen Her," the Chi-Lites

Born: Gospel singing pioneer Sallie Martin, 1896

1954 Known as "Little Miss Share Cropper," LaVern Baker (Delores Williams) had her debut disc, "Tweedlee Dee," released today. It reached #4 R&B and #14 pop, beginning her string of twenty-one hits through 1966.

1954 The Drifters' quintessential R&B version of "White Christmas" was released, rising to #2 R&B.

1955 Bo Diddley performed on *The Ed Sullivan Show*, playing "Bo Diddley" even though he was scheduled to play "16 Tons."

LaVern Baker

1961 Solomon Burke reached #24 pop today with "Just Out of Reach," which eventually rose to #7 R&B. Interestingly, he did it singing a country song. It was one of the first country/R&B crossbreeds, a style that would soon find its place in soul music. As a youth, Burke was known as "the Wonder Boy Preacher" at his own Solomon's Temple, which was started for him by his grandmother.

1961 The Crystals' debut single, "There's No Other," charted (#20 pop, #5 R&B), becoming the first of their eight hits.

1991 Michael Jackson's *Dangerous* was released. It was apparently so popular that 30,000 copies of the album, worth more than $400,000, were stolen by shotgun-wielding thugs from a terminal at Los Angeles International Airport.

1993 Anita Baker's "Witchcraft" duet with Frank Sinatra, from his *Duets* album, reached its peak at #2 pop in its first week on the charts.

1993 Augusta, GA, honored one of their own when a portion of Ninth Street was officially renamed James Brown Boulevard.

November

#1 Song 1960: "Stay," Maurice Williams & the Zodiacs

Born: Saxophone legend Coleman Hawkins, 1904; Big John Greer, 1923; Alphonse Mouzon, 1948

1942 The King Cole Trio debuted on the R&B charts with "That Ain't Right," which soared to #1. They would have four #1s out of their first five chart singles and instantly become one of the most popular pop-jazz aggregations in the nation.

1953 Clyde McPhatter & the Drifters reached #1 R&B with "Money Honey" and stayed there for an amazing eleven weeks. Though the group (with a variety of lineups) name would go on to have thirty-seven R&B hits, "Money Honey," their first release, would remain their biggest. On the strength of that one hit, the group secured a ten-year contract to appear twice a year at the Apollo Theater in New York.

1961 The Impressions performed their hit "Gypsy Woman" on *American Bandstand*.

1974 Wilson Pickett was arrested for brandishing a gun during an argument in Andes, NY. Performing with passion was apparently not confined to his stage show.

1990 En Vogue performed at the Summit in Houston while touring as a supporting act for MC Hammer.

1991 Jimi Hendrix received a star on the Hollywood Walk of Fame. Though only five of his albums came out during his lifetime and only eight were authorized by him, it's reported that his name appears on more than 300 albums, most of which are bootlegs.

1991 B.B. King ended a world tour in Washington, DC. The tour had begun seven weeks earlier in Istanbul, Turkey.

1992 Sade performed on *Saturday Night Live*.

1996 The reclusive Prince gave a rare interview to Oprah Winfrey on her TV show.

November

#1 R&B Song 1969: "Baby I'm for Real," the Originals

Born: Steven Caldwell (the Orlons), 1942

1963 Mary Wells and Sam Cooke performed their first of two concerts today at New York's Apollo Theater. Between shows, word came that President Kennedy had been assassinated. Cooke immediately canceled his performance and flew back to Los Angeles.

1967 The Chambers Brothers began a weeklong engagement with Blood, Sweat & Tears at New York's the Scene.

1969 Jazz diva Nina Simone charted with "To Be Young, Gifted, and Black." The song obviously had a more receptive audience among R&B chart listeners as it reached #8 while only making it to #76 pop. Simone's first chart single ten years earlier had been the passionate, "I Loves You, Porgy," from George Gershwin's *Porgy & Bess*, which reached #2 R&B.

1975 Natalie Cole peaked at #6 pop while reaching #1 R&B with her dazzling recording of "This Will Be." Daughter of legendary pop-jazz vocalist Nat King Cole, Natalie started out in a jazz group called, of all things, the Malibu Music Men, which included keyboard player Daryl Dragon (later of Captain & Tennille).

1980 Parliament charted with "Agony of DeFeet," reaching #7 R&B. It would be the last of twenty-three hits for Parliament before they became Funkadelic and went on to twenty-four more hits under their new name.

1980 Yarbrough & Peoples had their chart debut and biggest hit all in one when "Don't Stop the Music" flew onto the R&B hit register, stopping at #1 for five weeks.

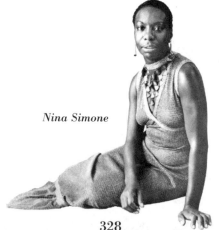

Nina Simone

November

#1 R&B Song 1968: "Who's Making Love," Johnnie Taylor

Born: Ruth Etting, 1907; Gloria Lynn, 1931; Betty Everett, 1939

1936 Legendary blues artist Robert Johnson recorded his first session at the Gunter Hotel in San Antonio, TX, for American Record Corporation's Vocalion label. Some of the eight classics recorded included "I Believe I'll Dust My Broom," "Kind Hearted Woman Blues," "Sweet Home Chicago," "Travelin' Riverside Blues," "Cross Road Blues," and "Terraplane Blues." His first and most successful 78 RPM single would soon be "Terraplane Blues" backed with "Kind Hearted Woman Blues."

1967 Aretha Franklin appeared in New York's Thanksgiving Day Parade on the Lady in the Show Float.

1968 Marvin Gaye's "I Heard It Through the Grapevine" charted on its way to #1 both pop and R&B for seven weeks, becoming his biggest pop hit. Gaye started out in 1957, with a vocal group called the Marquees, on a single titled "Wyatt Earp." The group, discovered by Bo Diddley, became the new Moonglows when they auditioned for Moonglows leader Harvey Fuqua outside a performance of the original Moonglows at a Washington, DC, theater. After hearing the Marquees, Fuqua fired his old vocalists and replaced them with Gaye's group.

1973 Harold Melvin & the Blue Notes, the O'Jays, and the Stylistics performed at San Francisco's famed Cow Palace.

1985 Rapper LL Cool J (James Todd Smith, whose stage name stands for "Ladies Love Cool James") charted with "I Can't Live Without My Radio," reaching R&B #15.

1991 Patti LaBelle sang her favorite song, "Over the Rainbow," on CBS-TV's *Party for Richard Pryor*. She recorded the standard twice as a single, once with the Bluebelles and once solo; neither of the stirring renditions charted. Also performing were the Pointer Sisters and Bobby Womack.

1991 Seal reached #8 in Britain with the "Killer" EP, featuring Jimi Hendrix's "Hey Joe." The promo clip featured the first ever 3D video.

1995 Junior Walker (born Autry DeWalt Walker), the master sax player who charted twenty-six times with and without his soul group the All-Stars, died today of cancer in Battle Creek, MI. His group was named when an enthusiastically inebriated man jumped up at a show and proclaimed, "These guys are all stars." Junior was sixty-four.

November

#1 R&B Song 1956: "Blueberry Hill," Fats Domino

Born: Ragtime legend Scott Joplin, 1868

1956 The Dell-Vikings recorded nine a cappella songs, including "Come Go with Me." After instrumentation was added, "Come" went on to be the first Top 10 pop hit by a racially mixed rock 'n' roll vocal group.

1956 Frankie Lymon & the Teenagers' "Baby Baby/I'm Not a Juvenile Delinquent," from the film *Rock, Rock, Rock*, was released. A hit in England (#12), it bombed in America.

1956 LaVern Baker's "Jim Dandy" was released. It soared to #1 R&B and #17 pop.

1958 The soul era began with the release of the Fiestas' "So Fine" (#11 pop, #3 R&B), a cover of the Sheiks' 1955 single.

1958 Ruth Brown's "Mama, He Treats Your Daughter Mean" was released for the second of three times. The first time, in 1953, the fiery tune reached #1 R&B, while a third remake in 1962 scratched the bottom of the pop charts at #99. The 1958 issue went nowhere.

1972 *Don Kirshner's Rock Concert* TV show, debuted featuring Chuck Berry.

1979 Donna Summer reached #1 pop (#20 R&B) with her Barbra Streisand duet "Enough Is Enough." The Bruce Roberts/Paul Jabara tune spent two weeks in the top spot.

1991 Little Richard officiated at the New York wedding of Cyndi Lauper to actor David Thornton while Patti LaBelle sang "A Whiter Shade of Pale."

1993 Michael Jackson entered into an administration deal with EMI for the ATV music catalog he had bought (which contained more than 250 Beatles songs) for a princely sum reported to be $70 million for five years of representation.

November

#1 R&B Song 1957: "You Send Me," Sam Cooke

Born: Stride pianist Willie Smith, 1897; Etta Jones, 1928; Percy Sledge, 1940; Stacy Lattisaw, 1966; Eric Sermon, 1968

1953 The Flamingos signed with Associated Booking Agency and began touring with Duke Ellington.

1954 The Moonglows appeared at East Chicago's Masonic Temple.

1960 Ike & Tina Turner, the Clovers, Larry Williams, Sugar Pie DeSanto, and Bill Black's Combo appeared at Chicago's Regal Theater for the Thanksgiving holidays.

1968 The Fifth Dimension performed on the TV special *Francis Albert Sinatra Does His Thing*.

1976 Muddy Waters performed at the Band's farewell concert, the Last Waltz, in San Francisco.

1990 Gladys Knight & the Pips reunited for the *Motown 30: What's Goin' On!* CBS-TV special. Also performing were Patti LaBelle and Stevie Wonder.

1992 Whitney Houston's film debut, *The Bodyguard*, opened nationally. The film, which co-starred Kevin Costner, was written twenty years earlier and was originally cast with Diana Ross and Ryan O'Neal.

1996 Bo Diddley was the opening act for the Rolling Stones in front of an audience of more than 55,000 at Joe Robbie Stadium in Miami.

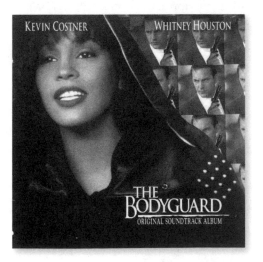

November

#1 Song 1966: "You Keep Me Hangin' On," the Supremes

Born: Tina Turner (Anna Mae Bullock), 1938

1955 The Turbans appeared on the R&B charts with their rock 'n' roll classic "When You Dance," reaching #3 and #33 pop. The group's gimmick was to actually wear turbans on-stage.

1965 Muddy Waters, John Lee Hooker, and Otis Spann performed at the Café Au Go Go in Greenwich Village, NY.

1970 Pearl Bailey, Dionne Warwick, and the Supremes appeared on an Andy Williams NBC-TV special.

1982 Rick James, Gladys Knight and Aretha Franklin performed at the Jamaica World Music Festival in Montego Bay, Jamaica, before more than 45,000 fans.

1983 Michael Jackson's single "Thriller" reached #10 on the British charts a full six months before the record's release in America.

1991 ABC-TV aired the *Gladys Knight Holiday Family Reunion*, which had been taped in September on the campus of UCLA.

1994 James Ingram, Roberta Flack, and Peabo Bryson began the Colors of Christmas tour at the Palace of Auburn Hills in Auburn Hills, MI.

1994 R. Kelly's album *12 Play* charted in England, reaching #39. Interestingly, it charted five times in a year before finally reaching #39. All told, it sold more than 300,000 copies. (If at first you don't succeed...)

November

#1 R&B Song 1948: "It's Too Soon to Know," the Orioles

Born: Jimi Hendrix, 1942

1954 Sarah Vaughn reached the hit list with "Make Yourself Comfortable" (#6), her biggest single of thirty-three hits.

1961 Ray Charles had his eighteenth of a career seventy-six chart singles when "Unchain My Heart" reached the Top 100.

1965 The Royalettes, a Baltimore vocal group in the image of the Chantels and the Shirelles, charted with "I Want to Meet Him," peaking at #26 R&B. The group is better known for its scintillating recording of "It's Gonna Take a Miracle" from earlier in the year.

1969 Tina Turner and Janis Joplin sang together at the Rolling Stones concert in Madison Square Garden.

1982 The Pointer Sisters' contagious dance track "I'm So Excited" reached #30 pop. A slightly different version of the song, with a more pulsating mix, would be released two years later and would reach #9.

1982 Marvin Gaye's album *Midnight Love* reached #10 in England and eventually #7 in America. The album was recorded in Belgium with old Moonglows mate Harvey Fuqua co-producing with Marvin. Despite its success, Gaye was so heavily in debt to the IRS that he soon had to sell his million-dollar home to pay the taxes.

November

28

#1 R&B Song 1953: "Money Honey," the Drifters

Born: Berry Gordy Jr., 1929; R.B. Greaves, 1944; Dawn Robinson (En Vogue), 1968

1929 Berry Gordy Jr., founder of Motown Records, was born. Though he is best known as a pioneering executive who built a record, publishing and touring empire, Gordy's start was as a songwriter. He wrote several songs for a young Jackie Wilson, who had just left the Dominoes and was signed to Brunswick Records, including "Reet Petite," "I'd Be Satisfied," "That's Why (I Love You So)," and "To Be Loved." He also wrote and produced Marv Johnson & the Miracles. These achievements gave Gordy the confidence to build a successful company, and with an $800 loan from his family he did just that…and more.

1953 Billy Ward & the Dominoes charted R&B with "Rags to Riches," peaking at #2. Their lead singer at the time was Jackie Wilson, as Billy Ward never sang lead. In fact, he rarely sang at all: he was the group's founder and musical director, and the original members were mostly students from his music class in New York City.

1960 Hank Ballard & the Midnighters' "Hoochie Coochie Coo" was released, reaching #23 pop and #3 R&B.

1964 Dionne Warwick and the Isley Brothers performed on Britain's *Thank Your Lucky Stars* TV show.

1992 Thirty-six years after the Five Satins original legendary hit, Boyz II Men's remake of "In the Still of the Night" charted, soaring to #3 pop, #4 R&B. The feat was all the more impressive in the rap era as the Boyz sang the recording a cappella.

1992 Whitney Houston's "I Will Always Love You" reached #1 R&B for eleven weeks and #1 pop for fourteen weeks. The original version of the song was by Dolly Parton in 1982. Kevin Costner, Houston's costar in *The Bodyguard*, suggested she record it. It would become her biggest hit.

November

1915 Big band composer/arranger supreme Billy Strayhorn was born. Strayhorn was the behind-the-scenes glue to many a Duke Ellington hit, collaborating on such classics as "Take the A Train," Johnny Come Lately," and "Rain Check." He was with Ellington for twenty-eight years.

1969 Jackie Wilson, Gary "U.S." Bonds, and a slew of other rock 'n' roll stars from the '50s and '60s performed at Richard Nader's second Rock 'n 'Roll Revival concert at Madison Square Garden in New York.

1969 B.B. King performed at the Boston Garden in Boston, MA, as the opening act for the Rolling Stones on their current U.S. tour.

1975 The Sylvers charted with "Boogie Fever," reaching #1 pop and R&B. It would become their biggest of thirteen R&B Top 100 singles in their thirteen-year career.

1996 James Ingram, Roberta Flack, Aaron Neville, and Peabo Bryson began their Colors of Christmas tour at the Ruth Eckerd Hall in Clearwater, FL.

1997 When Whitney Houston was belatedly informed that the Washington, DC, concert she was to appear at was actually a mass wedding for 25,000 couples of "Moonies," she apparently came down with flu-like symptoms that prevented her from performing. The show would have earned her a cool million.

Billy Strayhorn

November

#1 R&B Song 1974: "I Feel a Song (In My Heart)," Gladys Knight & the Pips

Born: Walter "Brownie" McGhee, 1915; Johnny "Shuggie" Otis, 1953; June Pointer (the Pointer Sisters), 1954

1956 The Jive Bombers recorded their immortal "Bad Boy" (#36 pop, #7 R&B). For their lead vocalist, thirty-nine year old Clarence Palmer, who had been performing since the '20s, the hit ended a thirty-year drought.

1959 The Five Satins' "Shadows" charted, becoming their third of seven Top 100 singles. Their classic "In the Still of the Night" charted three of those seven times.

1960 Jackie Wilson's "Talk That Talk" charted, reaching #3 R&B and #34 pop.

1963 The Supremes charted with "When the Lovelight Starts Shining Through His Eyes," reaching #23 and becoming their first pop hit record.

1968 Sly & the Family Stone's "Every Day People" hit the Top 100, eventually reaching #1 pop and R&B.

1988 LL Cool J performed at the first rap concert in Côte D'Ivoire, Africa. The Ivory Coast was apparently not ready for rap, as fights broke out, the stage was attacked, people fainted, and the police ended the performance halfway through the show.

1994 En Vogue performed at Wembley Arena in England. They quit the tour, ostensibly because of member Cindy Herron's pregnancy, though rumors indicated their departure was due to stress related to working with Luther Vandross.

LL Cool J

December

#1 R&B Song 1973: "The Love I Lost,"
Harold Melvin & the Blue Notes

Born: Billy Paul (the Blue Notes), 1934;
Lou Rawls (the Pilgrim Travelers), 1935

1954 Johnny Ace was named Most Programmed Artist of 1954 by Cash Box magazine while on tour with Willie Mae "Big Mama" Thornton of "Hound Dog" fame.

1957 Sam Cooke performed "You Send Me" on *The Ed Sullivan Show* on CBS-TV.

1962 Marvin Gaye's solo artist debut, "Stubborn Kind of Fellow," reached #8 R&B (#46 pop). The backup vocals on "Stubborn" were done by Martha & the Vandellas. Before his vocal success, Gaye was a studio drummer for acts like Stevie Wonder and the Miracles.

1973 The Love Unlimited Orchestra charted with an eight-minute instrumental, "Love's Theme," which reached #1 R&B and #10 pop. The forty-piece pseudo symphony was formed and led by Barry White as backing for his girl group, Love Unlimited, and, in fact, the recording was on the Love Unlimited album as an introduction to their song "I'm Under the Influence of Love." When disco deejays proved fond of playing only the instrumental track, White had it released as a single.

1982 Michael Jackson's unprecedented album *Thriller* was issued. It would go on to be the best-selling album of all time with more than 40 million sales worldwide and more than one million in Los Angeles alone. Seven hit singles would be released off of *Thriller*, setting a record. It would garner twelve Grammy nominations, also a record.

1984 Diana Ross moved onto the Hot 100 with "Missing You," a #10 hit that was written and produced by Lionel Richie as a dedication to slain singer Marvin Gaye.

1989 For driving under the influence of drugs (cocaine in this case), Sly Stone received a sentence of fifty-five days in jail. Thirteen days later he pled guilty to additional counts of drug possession and was sentenced to up to fourteen months in a drug rehab.

December

2

#1 R&B Song 1950: "Please Send Me Someone to Love," Percy Mayfield

Born: Roebuck "Pop" Staples (the Staple Singers), 1915

1952 Joe Davis produced four sides for Dean Barlow & the Crickets. On the strength of that session he not only secured a recording contract for the act with MGM, but he obtained an A&R position with the label as well. The debut 45 from that session, "You're Mine," became a #10 R&B hit in 1953.

1957 Due to a last-minute cancellation by Little Anthony & the Imperials, newcomers Danny & the Juniors performed their new single "At the Hop" on Dick Clark's *American Bandstand*. A month later the record was #1.

1957 The Chantels' "Maybe" (#15 pop, #2 R&B) and the Pastels' "Been So Long" (#24 pop, #4 R&B) were released.

1971 Martha & the Vandellas played their farewell concert at Cobo Hall in Detroit. Martha Reeves went on to a solo career while her sister Lois joined the soul group Quiet Elegance.

1972 The era-defining soul classic, "Papa Was a Rolling Stone" by the Temptations, reached #1 pop (#5 R&B). The recording was more than eleven minutes long, yet many stations were playing the full version despite the availability of a radio edit.

1972 Al Greene & the Soul Mates charted reaching #5 R&B (#41 pop) with "Back Up Train." Greene, who had sung with the gospel group the Greene Brothers and then with the Creations, would soon change the spelling of his name to Green and go solo on his way to thirty-two R&B hits through 1995.

1979 Stevie Wonder's album *Journey Through the Secret Life of Plants* reached #4 pop and R&B. He performed some of the recordings with the National Afro-American Philharmonic Orchestra.

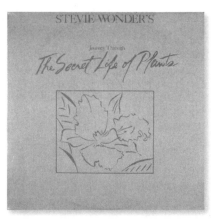

1995 Mariah Carey, singing lead for Boyz II Men, reached the best-seller's list with "One Sweet Day," a recording that spent an incredible sixteen weeks at #1, making it the #1 hit of the rock era.

December

1949 John Lee Hooker charted with "Crawlin' King Snake," an eventual #6 R&B hit and a staple of white electric blues bands of the '60s.

1955 The Robins charted with "Smokey Joe's Café" (#10 R&B), their last single before half the act separated to form the Coasters. The single also managed to reach #79 pop, but while the Coasters became rock 'n' roll legends, the Robins never had another chart 45.

1966 Ray Charles was given a five-year suspended sentence, a $10,000 fine and four years' probation for possession of heroin. Charles would eventually go cold turkey during a ninety-two-hour stay in a California hospital.

1976 Seven gunman charged into Bob Marley's house in Kingston, Jamaica. Though he was wounded, he survived the ordeal and promptly moved to Miami.

1977 Twenty-nine year old Patti Austin's debut album, *Havana Candy*, charted reaching #116. Goddaughter of jazz great Dinah Washington, Austin had been performing since she took the stage at the Apollo Theater at the age of four.

1988 Choreographer-turned-singer Paula Abdul charted with "Straight Up," a dance tune that zoomed to the top spot, becoming the first of her six #1s in less than three years.

1992 Stevie Wonder received a Lifetime Achievement Award from the National Academy of Songwriters at their seventh annual Salute to the American Songwriter in Los Angeles.

1995 B.B. King was honored at the annual Kennedy Center Honors in Washington, DC.

1998 Performing a benefit on the aircraft carrier USS Intrepid, B.B. King raised more than $450,000 for American troops overseas.

December

#1 Song 1971: "Family Affair," Sly & the Family Stone

Born: Lee Dorsey, 1924; rapper Jay-Z (Shawn Carter), 1970

1961 The Shirelles' B-side "Baby It's You" was issued, soon becoming one of their biggest hits (#8 pop, #3 R&B).

1961 Bobby "Blue" Bland charted R&B with "Turn on Your Love Light," reaching #2. the song became one of his signature hits, crossing pop to the tune of #28. His energetic blues style had earned him the nickname "Blue." On the same day, blues singer/drummer/guitarist Albert King had the first and biggest of his nineteen hits when he debuted on the R&B charts with "Don't Throw Your Love on Me So Strong," reaching #14.

1965 Gene Chandler charted with "Rainbow '65 Part 1" (#2 R&B), his biggest hit after "Duke of Earl." Chandler, who often performed under the name "The Duke of Earl," would appear on stage wearing a cape, a top hat, and a monocle.

1972 Al Green's "Let's Stay Together" reached the charts, rising to #1 R&B for nine weeks and #1 pop. He would go on to have six #1 R&B smashes, including "I'm Still in Love with You" and "Living for You."

1993 Snoop Doggy Dogg charted with his debut solo single, "What's My Name," reaching #8 pop and R&B. He hit #4 in England the same day he charted in America.

1996 LL Cool J was given the Rap Artist of the Year award at Billboard magazine's seventh annual showcase at the Aladdin Hotel in Las Vegas, NV.

1997 Salt-n-Pepa, LL Cool J, Ginuwine, and Shaggy, among others, performed at Super Jam 97 at the Fleet Center in Boston.

December

#1 R&B Song 1960: "He Will Break Your Heart," Jerry Butler

Born: Reverend James Cleveland, 1931; Little Richard (Richard Wayne Penniman), 1932

1953 The Harptones' standard, "A Sunday Kind of Love" ($1,500), was released. It was their first of twenty-nine singles between 1953 and 1982.

1979 One of rap's earliest singles, "Christmas Rappin' " by Kurtis Blow, made its debut. Though it failed to chart (despite reportedly selling nearly 400,000 copies), it would be recognized by the British public, who sent it to #30. The single would eventually chart three times in the '90s, strictly based on airplay. Blow had the distinction of being the first rapper signed to a major label (Mercury).

1990 Aretha Franklin was honored by the National Academy of Recording Arts and Science (NARAS) with a Living Legend award.

1992 Lloyd Price, Little Richard, Little Eva, Bobby Vee, Duane Eddy, and Johnny Preston, among others, hit England on the Giants of Rock 'n' Roll concert at Wembley Arena in London.

1998 Brandy charted with "Have You Ever," which would soon become her second #1 pop in less than seven months. Not bad for a teen heartthrob who decided she wanted to be an entertainer after watching Whitney Houston's "How Will I Know" video. She was also influenced by a Little Richard concert she attended at age eleven.

1998 Lauryn Hill performed on NBC-TV's *Saturday Night Live*.

Lauryn Hill

December

#1 R&B Song 1975: "I Love Music (Part 1)," the O'Jays

Born: Helen Cornelius, 1941

1975 Donna Summer's sex-saturated single "Love to Love You Baby" (#2 pop) became her first of thirty-four charters today, spanning twenty-five years through 2000. The seventeen-minute version done in Germany was originally released to discos before a radio edit was shipped. It also reached #3 R&B and #4 in England.

1995 The King of Pop, while in rehearsal for his TV special *Michael Jackson: One Night Only*, collapsed onstage at the Beacon Theater in New York. Jackson was diagnosed with a viral infection, which he had been apparently walking around with for a week.

1995 Mary J. Blige's *My Life* was honored as the Top R&B Album at the sixth annual *Billboard* Music Awards at New York's Coliseum.

1997 Erykah Badu's album *Live* peaked at #4 on the Top 200 chart in its debut week. It would soon reach #1 for three weeks on the R&B chart. The album included covers of Heatwave's "Boogie Nights," Chaka Khan's "Stay," and the Mary Jane Girls' "All Night Long." Badu started out as a rapper, appearing on Dallas radio station KNON-FM when she was fourteen.

2003 Luther Vandross hit the R&B charts for the fifty-sixth time with "Think About You," reaching #29. His first chart single, in 1976, was "It's Good for the Soul," as a member of the group Luther.

December

#1 Song 1968: "Love Child," the Supremes

Born: Barbara Weathers (Atlantic Starr), 1963

1963 Dionne Warwick charted with the haunting "Anyone Who Had a Heart," reaching #8. It was her first pop Top 10 hit.

1967 Otis Redding and co-writer Steve Cropper recorded their new song, "(Sitting on) The Dock of the Bay," in Memphis, but Redding would never live to see his biggest hit released (see December 10).

1985 With her mother, Cissy, singing backup vocals, Whitney Houston jumped onto the hit list with "How Will I Know," an eventual #1.

1992 On this Pearl Harbor Day, B.B. King began the Japanese portion of his Asian tour in Osaka, Japan.

1992 The Temptations performed at Walt Disney World in Florida.

1995 Super Jam 95 at Boston's Fleet Center featured Shai, Brian McKnight, Montell Jordan, Coolio, Salt-n-Pepa, After Seven, and Silk, among others. On the day before, Salt-N-Pepa had received a commendation from the governor of Massachusetts for portraying positive images for women.

1996 Toni Braxton's "Un-Break My Heart" hit #1 on the pop charts and stayed there for eleven weeks. It would become her fourth #2 hit on the R&B charts. The song featured backing vocals by Shanice Wilson.

December

#1 R&B Song 1958: "A Lover's Question," Clyde McPhatter

Born: Jimmy Smith, 1925; Jerry Butler (the Impressions), 1939

1951 Howlin' Wolf (Chester Arthur Burnett) charted R&B for the first time with "How Many More Years," reaching #4. The flip side, "Moanin' At Midnight," reached #10. Wolf earned his nickname from his "blues yodeling" singing style, reminiscent of Jimmie Rodgers, and learned blues guitar from early pioneers Willie Brown and Charlie Patton.

1956 The Schoolboys' two-sided classic, "Please Say You Want Me"/ "Shirley" (#13 pop, #15 R&B), was released as were the Flamingos' "Would I Be Crying" ($80), the Jaguars' "The Way You Look Tonight" ($600), and the Moonglows' "I Knew From the Start" ($60).

1958 Lloyd Price entered the national hit list with "Stagger Lee," eventually reaching # 1. It also hit the top spot R&B, retaining its supremacy on both charts for four weeks. The record also reached #7 in Britain.

1962 The Miracles charted with "You've Really Got a Hold on Me," reaching #1 R&B and #8 pop.

1975 Roberta Flack performed at Madison Square Garden in New York during Bob Dylan's Rolling Thunder Revue tour. That night's concert was a benefit for boxer and convicted murderer Rubin "Hurricane" Carter, whom many believed had been wrongly imprisoned.

December

#1 R&B Song 1967: "I Heard It Through the Grapevine," Gladys Knight & the Pips

Born: Donald Byrd (Donaldson Toussaint L'Ouverture II), 1932; Sam Strain (the Imperials and the O'Jays), 1940; Joan Armatrading, 1950

1957 "Hey Little School Girl" by the Marquees was released. Though it failed to chart, the group would be picked by Harvey Fuqua to become the new Moonglows in 1959.

1966 Junior Walker & the All-Stars peaked at #24 pop and #38 R&B with a smooth version of the Supremes' hit, "Come See About Me."

1981 Legendary Orioles lead singer Sonny Til died of a heart attack at fifty-one.

1989 Exposé's "Tell Me Why" reached the Hot 100 on its way to #9. It was the Miami trio's seventh straight Top 10 hit between 1987 and 1989.

1992 Cypress Hill won the Hot Rap Singles Artist category at the Billboard Music Awards third annual ceremonies at the Universal Amphitheater.

1994 Seal performed at the Wiltern Theater in Los Angeles at the end of a successful North American tour.

Cypress Hill

December

10

#1 R&B Song 1983: "Time Will Reveal," DeBarge

Born: Guitar Slim (Eddie Jones), 1926; Jessica Cleaves (the Friends of Distinction), 1948; Ralph Tavares (Tavares), 1948

1949 Twenty-one-year-old Antoine "Fats" Domino recorded his first million-seller, "The Fat Man." The song, originally called "Junker's Blues" was rewritten by Domino and songwriter Dave Bartholomew. Fats went on to sell more than 65 million records in a six-decade career.

1966 Jackie Wilson's "Whispers (Getting Louder)" became the star's crossover to soul music as it reached #11 pop and #5 R&B. The song was written by the secretary of Carl Davis, Wilson's producer. She would later go on to have some hits of her own as Barbara Acklin, including "Love Makes a Woman" in 1968.

1967 During a flight to a performance in Madison, WI, Otis Redding's new plane crashed, killing the soul singer and all but one member of the band the Bar-Kays. A who's who of Southern soul singers, including Sam Moore (of Sam & Dave), Percy Sledge, Joe Simon, Joe Tex, Don Covay, and Solomon Burke, served as his pallbearers.

1983 Rick James and Smokey Robinson's duet "Ebony Eyes" charted, reaching #43 pop and #22 R&B. The original release listed the artists as Rick James and Friend.

1988 Natalie Cole won the best female artist category at NAACP's twenty-first Image Awards.

Otis Redding

1995 Michael Jackson received word from his wife, Lisa Marie Presley Jackson, that their marriage of eighteen months was over (huge surprise.). As with their wedding, the public didn't find out for a month.

1997 Wyclef Jean of the Fugees performed at the Beacon Theater in New York at the Gift of Song concert in honor of UNICEF's fiftieth anniversary.

December

1954 The Harptones' beautiful ballad "Since I Fell for You" ($100) was issued.

1958 The Coasters recorded "Charlie Brown" (#2 pop and R&B) in New York.

1964 Sam Cooke was killed in a seedy Los Angeles motel by manager Bertha Franklin after Cooke was reportedly attempting to rape a young woman there.

1971 Brenda Lee Eager and Jerry Butler's duet "Ain't Understanding Mellow" charted, reaching #3 R&B (#21 pop). It was Eager's first and biggest hit of six charters (four of them with Butler) and his fortieth visit to the R&B hit list. Eager, who was discovered in a Chicago choir run by the Reverend Jesse Jackson, would go on to become a member of Butler's backing group, the Peaches.

1971 Michael Jackson reached #4 pop and R&B with his debut solo single, "Got to Be There."

1972 After a concert in Knoxville, TN, James Brown was arrested while talking to fans about drug abuse when someone told police that he was trying to incite a riot. He was charged with disorderly conduct but was quickly released after threatening the city with a million-dollar lawsuit.

1990 LL Cool J appeared at the Martin Luther King Jr. Middle School in Dorchester, MA, to promote his Cool School video program. The program encouraged kids to stay in school by getting involved in a make-your-own-video contest.

1996 Donna Summer, Chaka Khan, and Gloria Estefan performed as the Three Divas on Broadway at the Lunt Fontanne Theater in New York.

December

#1 R&B Song 1970: "The Tears of a Clown," Smokey Robinson & the Miracles

Born: Joe Williams, 1918; Dionne Warwick; 1940, Grover Washington Jr., 1943; Sheila E. (Sheila Escovedo), 1959

1918 Jazz and blues vocalist Joe Williams was born. Starting with a gospel group called the Jubilee Boys, Williams went on to perform with some of the nation's best big bands, including Coleman Hawkins, Lionel Hampton, Red Saunders, Albert Ammons, Andy Kirk, and Count Basie. In 1952, his "Every Day I Have the Blues" reached #8 R&B, and over the years he became a staple of TV variety shows, even landing in two films, *The Moonshine War* and *Cinderfella*.

1954 The Platters played the Riverside Rancho in California.

1960 The Miracles charted R&B for the first time with "Shop Around," reaching #1 for eight weeks while hitting #2 pop. The R&B classic, the first million-seller for the group and for their label, Motown, would become a symbol of the Motown machine's power to manufacture hits.

1967 Ray Charles performed as the headline act at New York's first Jazz Festival, held at Downing Stadium.

1993 Patti LaBelle performed at the twelfth annual Christmas in Washington benefit.

Joe Williams

December

#1 R&B Song 1969: "Someday We'll Be Together," Diana Ross & the Supremes

Born: Jazz drummer William "Sonny" Greer, 1895

1947 The Ravens' first release, "Write Me a Letter," became the first R&B record to hit the pop Top 25, reaching #25. It also peaked at #5 R&B.

1956 The Moonglows recorded their exquisite version of the standard "Blue Velvet," but Chess Records didn't get around to issuing it as a single for five years.

1957 The Paragons, the Chantels, and the Clovers performed at the Apollo Theater.

1968 Sam & Dave performed at the legendary rock 'n' roll venue the Fillmore East in New York.

1987 Lionel Richie's "Ballerina Girl" charted, reaching #5 R&B and #7 pop. Interestingly, the B-side, "Deep River Woman," reached #10…on the country charts! The wily performer probably suspected the song's potential crossover appeal since the background vocals were provided by Alabama. As to the A-side, it was his thirteenth Top 10 pop and R&B solo hit in a row.

1991 Mavis Staples of the Staple Singers performed at UCLA's Royce Hall at the annual Stellar Awards for Gospel Music.

December

14

#1 R&B Song 1968: "I Heard It Through the Grapevine," Marvin Gaye

Born: Joyce Vincent Wilson (Dawn), 1946

1952 "Stormy Weather" by the Five Sharps (Jubilee #5104) was issued today. Considered the rarest R&B record of all time, only two or three 78 RPM copies are known to exist, and the estimated value, if auctioned, would be more than $15,000. A 45 RPM copy has never been seen, but if it existed, the value would be astronomical.

1963 Dinah Washington, known to many as "the Queen of the Blues" died of an overdose of sleeping pills. At the time, she was married to Detroit Lion Dick "Night Train" Lane, her seventh husband. She was only thirty-nine.

1963 The Sam Cooke recording of the Willie Dixon blues tune "Little Red Rooster" peaked at #11 pop and #7 R&B. The piano player at Cooke's session was Ray Charles.

1969 The Jackson 5 appeared on *The Ed Sullivan Show*.

1985 Artists United Against Apartheid peaked at #38 in the U.S. and #21 in England with the single "Sun City." The artist collective consisted of forty-nine acts (most of whom were black), including Curtis Blow and Afrika Bambaataa.

1991 Michael Jackson's *Dangerous* album reached #1, making him the first artist since Elton John (1975) to have consecutive chart-topping albums.

1992 Rick James and his girlfriend, Tanya, turned themselves in to police on charges of assaulting a woman at the Saint James Club on Sunset Boulevard in Hollywood.

1993 Jeffrey Osborne, Roberta Flack, Peabo Bryson, and Patti Austin brought their Colors of Christmas tour to New York's Beacon Theater.

December

#1 R&B Song 1958: "Lonely Teardrops,"
Jackie Wilson

Born: Jesse Belvin, 1933; Alan Freed, 1922;
Cindy Birdsong (the Bluebelles), 1939; Harry
Ray (Ray; Goodman & Brown), 1946; Stevie D.
Lundy (Force M.D.'s), 1965

15

1956 The Nutmegs' "Comin' Home" ($40) and the Cufflinks' "Guided Missiles" ($80) were released.

1973 While Isaac Hayes's single "Joy" charted, reaching #7 R&B, the singer was suing his record label over a $270,000 check they paid to him that promptly bounced.

1979 Sax player Jackie Brenston, whose 1951 hit "Rocket 88" is considered by many to be the first rock 'n' roll record, died of a heart attack at age forty-nine. The recording was #1 R&B for five weeks. Brenston was actually a vocalist and sax player in the uncredited band on the single, Ike Turner & His Kings of Rhythm.

1988 James Brown was sentenced to six years in jail for various criminal activities over the previous year, most notably the events of May 18, when he took police on a high-speed chase through two states.

1996 Luther Vandross sang "Have Yourself a Merry Little Christmas" at the fifteenth annual Christmas in Washington concert at the National Building Museum.

James Brown

December

16

#1 R&B Song 1972: "Me & Mrs. Jones," Billy Paul

Born: Michael McCary (Boyz II Men), 1972

1931 The Mills Brothers recorded their second #1 pop hit, "Dinah," and this time the lead singer was Bing Crosby.

1960 Maurice Williams & the Zodiacs performed their chart-topper "Stay" on *American Bandstand*.

1966 The Jimi Hendrix Experience recording "Hey Joe" was issued in England on Polydor Records. Decca Records had previously passed on the group.

1967 Gladys Knight & the Pips reached #2 pop and #1 R&B (for six weeks) with "I Heard It Through the Grapevine," which would later become Marvin Gaye's signature song. "Grapevine" also became the biggest of Knight's sixty-eight R&B hits between 1961 and 1996.

1978 Originally a member of the Soul Satisfiers (1971), Gloria Gaynor attacked the singles survey with "I Will Survive," a #1 anthem for women and the sixth of her seven hits between 1974 and 1979.

1994 Stevie Wonder performed in Accra, Ghana, at the PanaFest concert. Trooper that he is, he did his show on a badly out-of-tune piano.

Gloria Gaynor

December

17

#1 R&B Song 1983: "Time Will Reveal," DeBarge

Born: Arthur Neville (the Neville Brothers), 1937; Eddie Kendricks (the Temptations), 1939; Wanda Hutchinson (the Emotions), 1951

1941 The Four Vagabonds recorded "The Duke of Dubuque," their first of sixteen singles, just ten days after the Japanese bombing of Pearl Harbor.

1967 The Temptations sang on *The Smothers Brothers Comedy Hour* TV show.

1977 Manchild hit the R&B charts with their single "Especially for You," which only reached #70 but was the debut chart performance of one of their members, Kenneth Edmonds, later known as Babyface.

1977 Showing the developing power of TV related to music in the '70s, Gladys Knight & the Pips' K-tel double-album collection of *30 Greatest Hits* reached #3 in England.

1984 Rap group Run-D.M.C.'s self-titled album reached only #53 pop but became the first rap collection to be certified gold by the RIAA—largely on its R&B sales, as it peaked at #14 R&B.

1988 Anita Baker hit #3 on the pop charts with "Giving You the Best That I Got." A week later (perhaps in celebration of the hit) she married her long-time boyfriend, Walter Bridgeforth.

1999 Jazz great Grover Washington Jr. died. The Saxophonist passed away after taping a performance for CBS's The Saturday Early Show. President Clinton, who had played sax with Washington in 1993 after a White House jazz concert, said of him, "Grover Washington was as versatile as any jazz musician in America, moving with ease and fluency from vintage jazz to funk and from gospel to blues and pop. I will miss both the man and his music."

December

#1 R&B Song 1954: "Hearts of Stone," the Charms

Born: Connie C. "Pee Wee" Crayton, 1914

1948 Charlie Parker, a pioneer in progressive jazz, entered the R&B hit parade with "Barbados," reaching #15. It was Parker's first and only singles chart appearance.

1962 The Shirelles charted with "Baby It's You," one of their best recordings, reaching #8 pop and #3 R&B. The song was originally titled "I'll Cherish You."

1964 Bobby "Blue" Bland performed at Sam Cooke's funeral in Chicago, IL. Legend has it that almost 200,000 of Cooke's faithful came to pay their respects. James Brown attempted to attend but an onslaught of fans forced his limousine to leave the scene as he did not want to cause any further chaos.

1965 James Brown's "I Got You (I Feel Good)" peaked at pop #3, becoming his biggest hit. It spent six weeks at #1 R&B. The song, initially known as "I Found You," was produced by Brown for Yvonne Fair in 1962.

1976 LaBelle's sixth and final R&B Top 100 entry, "Isn't It a Shame," charted, reaching #18 less than two months after the group had broken up. Lead singer Patti LaBelle would go on to stunning success as one of rock and R&B's legendary divas.

1981 Tina Turner, promoting her comeback without husband Ike, was the opening act for Rod Stewart at Los Angeles's Great Western Forum.

1982 Janet Jackson's "Young Love" reached the hit list today (#64), becoming her first of forty-two charters through 2002.

1996 Dionne Warwick appeared at the Vatican—but not to perform. She had a special audience with Pope John Paul II. (One can only wonder if her friends at the Psychic Friends Network had foretold of the meeting.)

1999 Joe Higgs, known as "the Father of Reggae Music" and the vocal coach mentor of Bob Marley, died in Los Angeles. He was fifty-nine.

December

#1 Song 1964: "Come See About Me," the Supremes

Born: Saxman Clarence Ford, 1929; Maurice White (Earth, Wind & Fire), 1941

1955 One of the first singles on George Goldner's Gee label, "You Baby You" by the Cleftones ($30), was issued. It was the vocal group's debut disc.

1964 Patti LaBelle & the Bluebelles charted with the old standard "Danny Boy" (based on the 1855 Irish tune "Londonderry Air"). It was their third of six Hot 100 singles (#75) before they became LaBelle in 1975.

1981 Diana Ross' first RCA single after two decades with Motown, "Why Do Fools Fall in Love," a remake of the Frankie Lymon & the Teenagers' classic, peaked at #7 pop, #6 R&B, and #4 in England.

1992 Regina Belle, featured female vocalist with the Manhattans in the mid-'80s, made a case for her solo success when "A Whole New World" hit the Hot 100 on the way to #1.

1992 Whitney Houston's single "I Will Always Love You" sold a record 399,000 copies in one week, breaking the record set by the Bryan Adams single, "(Everything I Do) I Do for You" a year earlier.

1997 Chaka Khan and B.B. King performed in Vatican City for the annual Vatican Christmas Concert.

Reesig & Taylor

Regina Belle

December

20

1947 Charles Brown had one of the most successful Christmas records ever when his "Merry Christmas Baby" charted, reaching #3 R&B. It also went on to chart Top 10 in 1948 and 1949 and is considered a blues classic today.

1954 The Penguins headlined the Christmas show at the Embassy Auditorium in Los Angeles.

1980 Jackie English, a white songwriter known for only having songs recorded by black artists, including George Benson, Patrice Rushen, Ronnie Laws, and Eloise Laws finally had a hit by a white artist when she herself charted with "Once a Night" (from the movie *Hopscotch*).

1981 The musical *Dreamgirls* opened on Broadway. It was reportedly based on the history of the Supremes.

1986 Rebbie Jackson paired with rocker Robin Zander of Cheap Trick to chart with "You Send the Rain Away," reaching #50 pop. The song had been intended for Barbra Streisand and Neil Diamond, but an A&R exec at Columbia sent the song to Jackson by mistake.

1986 Ben E. King's standard, "Stand by Me," reached #9 pop twenty-five years after it was originally a hit (#4, 1961), due in large part to the use of the song in the film of the same name.

1986 Bobby Brown, formerly of New Edition, made his single solo debut on the pop charts with "Girlfriend." Though it only reached #57, it was a portent of things to come, as his next nine singles all made the Top 10. The seventeen-year-old had made his first stage appearance as an unwitting accomplice to his mother's aspirations when she pushed him on-stage at the age of three during the intermission at a James Brown concert in Boston.

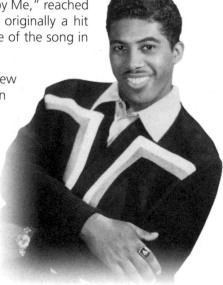

Ben E. King

December

#1 R&B Song 1974: "She's Gone,"
Tavares

Born: Earl Forest, 1926; Carla
Thomas, 1942; Gwen McCrea, 1943;
Betty Wright, 1953

1956 In the midst of their success with "A Thousand Miles Away," the Heartbeats were signed to Rama Records. The company acquired the "Thousand Miles" master from the original label, Hull Records.

1961 The Marcels recorded "My Melancholy Baby" (#58 pop), their last chart single.

1962 The Dells, Patti LaBelle & the Bluebelles, Lloyd Price, Little Esther Phillips, Etta James, the Radiants, and Erma Franklin performed at Chicago's Regal Theater for the start of their annual Christmas shows.

1968 Wilson Pickett charted pop with the Beatles' "Hey Jude" (#23, #13 R&B) despite the fact that the Fab Four were still on the hit list with their own version, which charted three months ahead of him. Even more impressive, he scored in the Beatles' own backyard, reaching #16 in Britain. Pickett recorded the song at the insistence of Allman Brothers guitarist Duane Allman, who played on Pickett's session.

1969 Diana Ross & the Supremes made their final TV appearance together when they performed "Someday We'll Be Together" on *The Ed Sullivan Show*.

1985 Lionel Richie's "Say You, Say Me" reached #1 R&B and pop, giving him his tenth #1 R&B, six of which were with the Commodores.

1989 Martha & the Vandellas reunited for the first time in eighteen years, playing a British tour starting with a performance at the Talk of the Town in Manchester. When not working with Martha, Rosalind Ashford worked for the phone company and Annette Sterling was working in a hospital.

1991 Queen Latifah (born Dana Owens) hit the R&B charts with "Latifah's Had It Up to Here," reaching #13. Considering that her name means sensitive and delicate, the brash and bellicose Queen must enjoy the irony. Nevertheless, the bawdy broad sure can sing!

December

#1 R&B Song 1973: "If You're Ready (Come Go with Me)," the Staple Singers

Born: Lilian "Lil" Green, 1919

1956 Mickey & Sylvia charted with their rock 'n' roll classic "Love Is Strange," reaching #1 R&B and #11 pop. Mickey "Guitar" Baker went on to become a highly sought-after session musician while Sylvia Vanderpool had a dozen hits in the '70s and '80s, including the #1 "Pillow Talk."

1961 New York disc jockey Murray the K Kaufman hosted the Brooklyn Paramount's Christmas show featuring Johnny Mathis, the Isley Brothers, the Crystals, the Chantels, the Vibrations, Bobby Lewis, Gary "U.S." Bonds, and the most soulful white girl of the times, Timi Yuro.

1961 The teen film *Twist Around the Clock*, featuring Chubby Checker & the Marcels, opened nationally.

1963 Scheduled for an earlier release but held up due to the assassination of President Kennedy, Darlene Love's epic Christmas classic "Christmas (Baby Please Come Home)" was finally issued. Background vocals on rock's greatest holiday recording were by the Ronettes, the Crystals, and Cher.

1966 Otis Redding performed at San Francisco's Fillmore Auditorium.

Mickey & Silvia

December

#1 R&B Song 1978: "Le Freak," Chic

Born: Little Esther Phillips (Esther May Jones), 1935; Eugene Record (the Chi-Lites), 1940

1955 The Five Keys and the Turbans tore the house down at Dr. Jive's Brooklyn Paramount Christmas show.

1957 Sam Cooke charted with "I'll Come Running Back to You," his second #1 R&B hit in two tries. Cooke was the father of Linda Womack of the duo Womack & Womack. Cooke originally recorded under the name Dale Cooke so as not to offend the spiritual audience he sang to as a member of the gospel group the Soul Stirrers.

1959 Chuck Berry was arrested and charged with violating the Mann Act after he took a fourteen-year-old Apache Indian to work as a hat-check girl in the nightclub he owned in St. Louis. The arrest was predicated on the police position that he had transported a minor across a state line for immoral purposes. When Berry fired her, believing she was working as a prostitute, she reported him to the police. He was initially convicted and sentenced to the maximum of five years in jail, and fined $2,000. Due to racist comments by a judge, however, Berry was freed before he could be retried.

1960 The Brooklyn Paramount kicked off its annual Christmas rock 'n' roll shows, which ran through January 3. Among the sixteen acts appearing were Chubby Checker, the Drifters, Bo Diddley, Ray Charles, Little Anthony & the Imperials, the Shirelles, the Coasters, and the Blue Notes.

1976 Adding his name to the long list of performers who couldn't keep a handle on their finances, Isaac Hayes filed for bankruptcy, with debts ranging from $6 million to $9 million.

1978 Chic's *C'est Chic* album, one of the albums that defined the disco age, reached #4.

1991 British TV's BBC2 aired *Christmas in Vienna*, a special featuring Diana Ross and Placido Domingo, from the Vienna City Hall.

1998 Cissy Houston, Roberta Flack, and Phoebe Snow backed Darlene Love as she did her yearly rendition of the immortal Phil Spector record "Christmas (Baby Please Come Home)" on David Letterman's CBS-TV show.

December

24

#1 R&B Song 1966: "(I Know) I'm Losing You," the Temptations

Born: Dave Bartholomew, 1920; Lee Dorsey, 1924

1954 R&B balladeer Johnny Ace shot himself while playing Russian roulette backstage at the Negro Christmas Dance at Houston's City Auditorium. His weapon of choice was a 22-caliber H&R revolver, which he used after consuming a large quantity of vodka. He was only twenty-five. Many consider his demise the first rock 'n' roll casualty.

1954 The Clovers began a ten-day stint at Los Angeles' 5-4 Ballroom.

1961 The holiday revue at Chicago's Regal Theater included the Spaniels, the Dukays, Lloyd Price, Erma Franklin, Mittie Collier, and the Sheppards.

1984 Stevie Wonder, a longtime native of Detroit, was given the keys to the city. Buoyed by this experience, he would later state his intention to run for mayor.

1990 Stevie Wonder performed at the Dome in Tokyo, Japan.

1993 Aaron Neville performed at Harry Connick Jr.'s Christmas concert, singing "The Christmas Song."

1999 Zeke Carey, leader of the Flamingos (of "I Only Have Eyes for You" and "I'll Be Home" fame), died today. The Flamingos were considered by many fans and music historians as the greatest vocal group of all time. Carey, born January 24, 1933, was sixty-six.

Aaron Neville

December

#1 R&B Song 1965: "I Got You (I Feel Good)," James Brown

Born: Cabell "Cab" Calloway III, 1907; Chris Kenner, 1929; O'Kelly Isley (Isley Brothers), 1937

1948 The Ravens' incredible version of "White Christmas" entered the R&B hit registry, reaching #9. It was the standard by which all future R&B versions would be judged, even the legendary Drifters version, which was almost a note-for-note copy. The 78's B-side, a haunting version of "Silent Night," reached #8.

1948 "The Christmas Song," one of the season's most enduring standards, charted, reaching #8 R&B. Though it has long since been credited to Nat King Cole, the original recording was attributed to the King Cole Trio.

1954 The Penguins' classic "Earth Angel" charted en route to #8 pop. It is considered to be the most popular R&B oldie of all time.

1958 Alan Freed's Christmas Rock 'n' Roll Spectacular at the Loews State Theater in New York City included performances by Jackie Wilson, Bo Diddley, Chuck Berry, Dion, the Everly Brothers, and Eddie Cochran.

1961 Gladys Knight & the Pips charted R&B with their doo-wop classic, "Letter Full of Tears," reaching #3 R&B and #19 pop. The group began in the '50s, performing on tours with the likes of Jackie Wilson, Sam Cooke, and B.B. King. Their first single, in 1959, was a cover of the Moonglows' rocker "Whistle My Love."

1971 In an unusual recording move, LaBelle did all the backup vocals on Laura Nyro's *It's Gonna Take a Miracle*, a collection of doo-wop and rock 'n' roll standards including "Desiree," "The Wind," "I Met Him on a Sunday," "You've Really Got a Hold on Me," and the title song. The album reached #46 pop and #41 R&B.

1971 The Staples Singers reached #12 pop and #2 R&B with "Respect Yourself," their breakthrough hit 45.

1976 The Supremes' "You're My Driving Wheel" reached #85 pop, becoming their last of forty-seven singles to hit the Top 100. The last original member, Mary Wilson, then left the group to form Mary Wilson & the Supremes.

1981 A Christmas Day phone greeting from Michael Jackson to Beatle Paul McCartney led to their decision to write and record together. The result of their eventual collaboration was "The Girl Is Mine," which they recorded the following year.

December

#1 R&B Song 1987: "The Way You Make Me Feel," Michael Jackson

Born: Abdul "Duke" Fakir (the Four Tops), 1935

1960 The Shirelles, the Drifters, the Coasters, Chubby Checker, Little Anthony & the Imperials, Bo Diddley, and the Blue Notes, among others, appeared at the Paramount Theater in Brooklyn for an all-star Christmas Show.

1960 Charles Brown's Christmas classic "Please Come Home for Christmas" charted R&B, reaching #21.

1968 Sly & the Family Stone played the Fillmore West.

1981 Bobby Womack charted with his classic soul album *The Poet*, reaching #29 pop and #1 R&B for five weeks. He had offered the publishing on the album to K-tel publishing president Jay Warner for $15,000. Warner enthusiastically said yes, but the K-tel board wouldn't give him the money, as they were preoccupied with their newest venture, drilling holes in Louisiana looking for oil. (They never found any oil, but Womack's album went gold!)

1986 Ray Charles was honored at the Kennedy Center Honors ninth annual ceremony in Washington, DC.

1992 Lou Rawls hosted his annual Lou Rawls Parade of Stars telethon in Los Angeles to raise money for the United Negro College Fund. Stars like Dionne Warwick participated, and they raised more than $11 million.

1999 Curtis Mayfield, hit R&B artist/writer (*Superfly*) and former original member of the Impressions, died today.

December

#1 R&B Song 1952: "I Don't Know," Willie Mabon & His Combo

Born: John "Buddy" Bailey (the Clovers), 1931

1964 The Supremes made their TV debut on *The Ed Sullivan Show*.

1966 Ike & Tina Turner performed at the Galaxy in Los Angeles as part of a weeklong engagement.

1969 B.B. King charted with "The Thrill Is Gone," his biggest pop hit, reaching #15 (#3 R&B). The song was originally done in 1951 by Roy Hawkins. In answering a question about the similarity of many '50s blues songs, King said, "I don't think anybody steals anything; all of us borrow."

1975 The Staple Singers reached #1 pop and R&B with Let's Do It Again," having just signed to former Impression Curtis Mayfield's Curtom label.

1986 Jackie Wilson's debut hit of 1958, "Reet Petite," reentered England's charts twenty-nine years after first appearing and two years after Wilson's death. Today it reached #1 for four weeks, selling more than 700,000 singles.

1994 Babyface made his concert tour debut when he began a five-week tour with Boyz II Men at the Target Center in Minneapolis, MN.

Babyface

Reisig & Taylor

December

#1 R&B Song 1974: "Boogie on Reggae Woman," Stevie Wonder

Born: Billy Williams, 1910; Johnny Otis (John Veliotes), 1921; Leonard "Chick" Carbo (the Spiders), 1927

1956 Alan Freed's Christmas show at the Brooklyn Paramount set a one-day attendance record of $27,200. The show was part of his eight-day Christmas extravaganza featuring the Moonglows, Shirley & Lee, the Dells, the Heartbeats, Screamin' Jay Hawkins, Jesse Belvin, and the G-Clefs.

1957 Jackie Wilson, the Five Satins, the Ravens, and the Hollywood Flames performed at Chicago's Regal Theater.

1966 Jimmy Ruffin, Gladys Knight & the Pips, the Temptations, Stevie Wonder, and Martha & the Vandellas performed at the Fox Theater in Detroit in what became known worldwide as the Motortown Revue.

1968 The top two singles on the pop charts were both by Motown acts with Marvin Gaye at #1 with "I Heard It Through the Grapevine" and Stevie Wonder at #2 with "For Once in My Life."

1968 Richie Havens, Chuck Berry, Marvin Gaye, Junior Walker & the All-Stars, and others performed at the Miami Pop Festival in front of more than 100,000 fans at Gulfstream Racing Park in Hallandale, FL.

1994 At the seventeenth annual Kennedy Center Honors, shown on CBS-TV this night, honoree Aretha Franklin was fêted with performances by Patti LaBelle, the Four Tops, and Detroit's New Bethel Baptist Church choir.

Alan Freed

December

#1 R&B Song 1962: "You Are My Sunshine," Ray Charles

Born: Patti Drew, 1944; Yvonne Elliman, 1951

1954 The Nutmegs' "A Story Untold" (#2 R&B) was released. It took six months to hit the national charts.

1956 The Orioles' "For All We Know" ($30) and the Ravens' spiritual yet secular ballad "A Simple Prayer" ($80) were released.

1962 Ray Charles reached #7 pop with "You Are My Sunshine." Ironically, the R&B icon was putting cash in the pocket of a segregationist with every record sold, as the tune was written by former Louisiana governor Jimmie Davis.

1962 The Crystals charted with "He's Sure the Boy I Love" (#11 pop). Unfortunately, as with their previous hit, "He's a Rebel," it wasn't the Crystals singing on the record but Darlene Love & the Blossoms, thanks to the decision-making shenanigans of producer Phil Spector.

1962 The Supremes charted R&B with "Let Me Go the Right Way," reaching #26 (#90 pop). It was their first of forty-three R&B hits through 1977.

1966 The Jimi Hendrix Experience appeared on London's *Top of the Pops* show, performing their first single, "Hey Joe," a cover of the Leaves' hit.

1982 To honor the recently departed Bob Marley, a commemorative stamp was issued by the Jamaican government.

1990 Lou Rawls hosted the *Lou Rawls Parade of Stars Telethon* to raise money for the United Negro College Fund. Also performing was Patti LaBelle.

1992 B.B. King performed for 300 inmates at the Gainseville Drug Treatment Center in Gainseville, FL. Among the prisoners was his daughter Patty, incarcerated for three years for drug trafficking. Forty-one years earlier to the day, B.B. had charted with his first R&B hit, "3 O'Clock Blues." Amazingly, despite a career that's still going in the twenty-first century, and with more than seventy R&B hits, that first one was his biggest, reaching #1 for five weeks.

December

30

#1 Song 2000: "Independent Women, Part I," Destiny's Child

Born: Bo Diddley (Ellas Otha Bates McDaniel), 1928

1950 Billy Ward & the Dominoes (with bass Bill Brown on lead) recorded their monster hit, "60 Minute Man," which spent three and a half months at #1 R&B in 1951 (#17 pop).

1957 Alan Freed's Brooklyn Paramount Christmas Show extravaganza featured the Moonglows, the Heartbeats, the Dells, the G-Clefs, and the Three Friends.

1972 The Spinners' "Could It Be I'm Falling in Love" hit the Pop Top 100, leveling off at #2 while going to #1 R&B.

1972 Jermaine Jackson charted with "Daddy's Home," reaching #2 R&B and #9 pop. The song was originally a hit for Shep & the Limelites in 1961, reaching #2 pop. Jackson once said of his famous sibling, "A lot of Michael's success is due to timing and luck. It could have just as easily been me."

1995 LL Cool J and Boyz II Men's single, "Hey Lover," reached #3 pop and R&B.

1995 The Neville Brothers played at Warfield Theater in San Francisco.

Rod Spicer

Destiny's Child

December

#1 R&B 1955: "Adorable,"
the Drifters

Born: Odetta (Odetta Gordon), 1930;
Donna Summer, 1948

1949 The Orioles charted R&B with their seasonal classic "(It's Gonna Be a) Lonely Christmas," reaching #5. Its B-side, the appropriately titled "What Are You Doing New Year's Eve," would reach #9 after only two weeks on the charts.

1960 The future standard "Will You Love Me Tomorrow" by the Shirelles entered the charts on this last day of the year, rising to #2 R&B and #1 pop.

1960 A former gospel vocalist in the Manhattans and the Royaltones, Maxine Brown reached the hit list with "All in Your Mind," her first of fifteen charters through 1969.

1962 Advertised as an all-night gospel sing, the Dixie Hummingbirds, the Caravan Singers, the Swanee Quartet, Sam Cooke, and Cooke's previous group the Soul Stirrers performed at the Armory in Newark, NJ.

1986 Freddie Jackson, Gladys Knight, and Melba Moore performed on CBS-TV's *Happy New Year America* show.

1990 The O'Jays performed on *Dick Clark's New Year's Rockin' Eve* ABC-TV show.

1991 Bell Biv DeVoe appeared on *Dick Clark's New Year's Rockin' Eve* ABC-TV show.

1993 The Isley Brothers performed at Atlanta, GA's Fox Theater for their New Year's Eve show.

1993 Donna Summer performed at the Resorts Casino Hotel in Atlantic City, NJ, for Merv Griffin's third annual New Year's Eve special, which was shown on Fox-TV. It was also Summer's forty-fifth birthday.

1993 Grandmaster Flash, Kool Moe Dee, Kurtis Blow, Whodini, Melle Mel, and Biz Markie performed at the Apollo Theater's New Year's Eve show.

1994 Babyface and Boyz II Men performed to a sellout audience of more than 16,000 fans at Madison Square Garden in New York.

1994 Stevie Wonder performed at Detroit's Fox Theater to a sell-out crowd.

1995 Chaka Khan performed at a New Year's Eve show at the Beacon Theater in New York.

Index

About the Author

Jay Warner is a six-time Grammy-winning music publisher, recipient of the Heroes and Legends Foundation "Pioneer" Award, and first publisher to be entered into The Congressional Record for his contributions to the music industry. He has turned his meticulous passion for information into a distinct and separate career as an author and music historian with a series of best-selling books and his definitive series of Music-Cals™, the mini book in a day-by-day format.

As a music publisher Warner has represented writer-artists as diverse as Bruce Springsteen, Barry Manilow, and Rick James, and has published more than 100 Top 40 hits, including "Blinded By the Light" (Manfred Mann), "Born to Run" (Bruce Springsteen), "Up, Up and Away" (The 5th Dimension), "By the Time I Get to Phoenix" (Glen Campbell), "Midnight Train to Georgia" (Gladys Knight & the Pips), "Groovin'" (The Rascals), "Party All the Time" (Eddie Murphy), "In My House" (Mary Jane Girls), "Love Is All We Need" (Mary J. Blige), and many more.

In 1978 Jay wrote the first in-depth text on publishing, songwriting, and copyright law in layman's terms, *How to Have Your Hit Song Published* (Hal Leonard). Twenty-five years later, it is in its fifth printing, is still the definitive text on the subject, and has never been out of print.

In 1993 Warner's encyclopedic work *The Billboard Book of American Singing Groups, A History 1940–1990* was published to rave reviews as the ultimate resource on the subject.

In 1997 Warner's *Billboard's American Rock-n-Roll in Review* continued his streak of entertaining references. His *Just Walkin' in the Rain* (the true story of a convict quintet, a liberal governor, and how they changed Southern history through rhythm and blues) shook up the establishment in 2001 with a mind-boggling best-seller that is now an acclaimed documentary and a soon-to-be motion picture.

Jay lives in Los Angeles with his wife, Jackie, and favorite four-legged friends, Napoleon and Sunny.

Acknowledgements

To my biggest believers: my father, Bob, and my mother, Ray; my uncle Archie "Willie" Friedberg; my aunt Sydelle and uncle Hymie Sherman; Sam Shatzman; my cousins Michael, Jerry, and Deanna; and my loving and loyal wife, Jackie. May your spirit, faith, and love forever guide me, and may God always bless you.

I'd also like to thank a few long-standing supporters who have given of themselves truly out of friendship: Dennis Wolfe, Sam Atchley, John Wilson, Barry Peterman, Phil Kozma, Chas Peate, Peter Foldy, Stu Nadel, Ellis Rich, Felix Cavalleiri, and my wonderful assistant, Debra Veres. I feel rich indeed to know you and wish you everything I wish for those I hold most dear.

Lastly I want to thank the entire Hal Leonard organization, whom I have been privileged to know and work with for more than twenty years, especially Keith Mardak, Jeff Schroedl, John Cerullo, Belinda Yong, Jenna Young, and Larry Morton. I appreciate your belief in my work. You're a class act.